A HISTORY OF ADULT EDUCATION
IN GREAT BRITAIN

A History of Adult Education in Great Britain

By THOMAS KELLY

M.A., Ph.D., F.R.Hist.S.

Professor of Adult Education and
Director of Extra-Mural Studies in the University of Liverpool

LIVERPOOL UNIVERSITY PRESS

1970

Published by
LIVERPOOL UNIVERSITY PRESS
123 Grove Street Liverpool 7
Copyright © 1962, 1970 by Thomas Kelly

Printed in England by
Hazell Watson & Viney Ltd
Aylesbury, Bucks.

First published 1962
Second edition (revised and enlarged) 1970

PREFACE

In 1851 J. W. Hudson published his *History of Adult Education*, which was concerned mainly with adult schools and mechanics' institutes. Since then no one has attempted a full-scale study of the subject, though there have been many works on specialised aspects and a number of valuable short surveys, e.g. in the *Final Report* of the Adult Education Committee of the Ministry of Reconstruction (1919), and in the opening chapters of Professor Robert Peers's recent volume, *Adult Education: a Comparative Study* (1958). The present work makes no pretence to be a final and definitive account: it is merely an attempt to bring together, from my own researches and those of others, an outline narrative of what appears to me a significant and neglected aspect of English social and educational history. I hope that it will be of interest to the general reader, and that it will also serve as a framework of reference within which further research may be carried on.

The scope and title of the book call for a word of explanation. The term 'adult education', though variously defined, in current usage nearly always implies a measure of formal instruction, a relationship of teacher and taught. Such instruction, however, is only one of the means by which adults are educated. Other agencies, involving little or no formal teaching, have always played a significant part. In earlier times the most important instruments of adult education were the pulpit and the press; and even to-day the public library, the cinema, the radio, and television are more potent influences than the class-room. I have tried, therefore, perhaps rather rashly, to sketch the complete picture: to describe the development of formal adult education in all its variety, and at the same time to trace the influence of other and less formal modes of instruction. Indeed, had it not been for the clumsiness of the title, I would have preferred to call the book not 'A History of Adult Education', but 'A History of the Education of Adults'.

I have drawn on a wide range of original and secondary sources, but even so I am conscious that many gaps remain—particularly, perhaps, in relation to Scotland and Wales. Each of these countries really needs its own independent history, and I hope that the material I have been able to gather will be helpful when the time comes for these to be written. For England the material, though scattered, is much more complete, but I have necessarily had to deal in broad generalisations which may not always do full justice to regional peculiarities. This is a field, however, in which a great deal of research has still to be done: we badly need more regional studies in which the development of local institutions is related to the national pattern.

I have given in the footnotes full references to the sources used. The place of publication of the works cited is London unless otherwise stated, and where the dates of two editions are given the later edition is the one used. I have not thought it necessary to include a complete bibliography, since this need will shortly be met by a revised edition of the *Select Bibliography of Adult Education in Great Britain*, originally published by the Universities Council for Adult Education and the National Institute of Adult Education in 1952.

In the writing of the book I have been indebted for assistance to a great many people—friends and colleagues in this and other universities, librarians in many parts of the country, and secretaries of numerous voluntary organisations. I wish I could thank them all by name, but space forbids. I must, however, express my special obligation to Mr Kenneth Povey, formerly Librarian of the University of Liverpool, and his staff; to Mr Edward Hutchinson and the staff of the National Institute of Adult Education; to Mr B. W. Pashley, of the Liverpool Extra-Mural Department, who has assisted in the preparation of statistical material for Chapters 16 and 19; to Dr John Lowe and Mr J. J. Bagley, also of the Extra-Mural Department, who have given me the benefit of their advice at the manuscript and the proof stage respectively; to my wife, who has assisted me in many ways and especially by reading the final proofs; and lastly to the Liverpool University Press for undertaking the responsibility of publication.

T.K.

PREFACE
TO THE SECOND EDITION

In this second edition I have made minor amendments throughout, and in place of the former Epilogue I have added three new chapters dealing with the period from 1939 to the present. These thirty years correspond almost exactly with my own full-time work in adult education, and in dealing with them I cannot hope to have avoided errors of omission or misrepresentation, but I have done my best to be both comprehensive and impartial.   I am again indebted to many friends and colleagues for assistance on particular points, and especially to Mr J. Burr and Mr P. B. Rowley of the Liverpool University Extra-Mural Department; Professor A. J. Allaway and Professor H. A. Jones of the University of Leicester; Mr Norman Dees of the University of Glasgow; Mr Donald Garside of the University of Manchester; and Mr E. M. Hutchinson of the National Institute of Adult Education. My wife too has shared with me the considerable task of revising the index. None of these, however, bears any responsibility for the final result.

T.K.

CONTENTS

I

The Middle Ages

EDUCATION FOR SALVATION

Anglo-Saxon Origins

HISTORICALLY the earliest motive for adult education was religious, and if we begin our story with the Anglo-Saxon settlement of Britain we may say that the first recorded adult educators were the missionaries who came from Ireland or the Continent to convert the heathen inhabitants of this island to Christianity. We think, for example, of St. Columba labouring among the Picts of the Scottish Highlands, of St. Augustine in Kent, of St. Paulinus in Northumbria. Their advent meant the introduction not merely of a new system of belief but also of an organised Church which became, and for many centuries remained, the greatest educational force in the country.

The duty of teaching was laid upon the clergy from the beginning. It was emphasised, for example, in the treatise on *Pastoral Care*, written by Pope Gregory, who sent Augustine to England, and it was clearly stated in the decrees of the early English Church Councils. The Council of Clofesho (746) decreed that every bishop should every year make a visitation of his diocese 'and that he should call to him at convenient places the people of every condition and sex, and plainly teach them who rarely hear the word of God . . .' The priests in the districts assigned to them were also to be active in teaching. 'And then let them who know it not, learn to construe and explain in their own tongue, the Creed and Lord's Prayer, and the sacred words which are solemnly pronounced at the celebration of the Mass, and in the office of Baptism.'[1]

It was not easy to maintain an efficient clergy in those turbulent times; and the Norse and Danish invasions of the ninth century rendered the difficulty almost insuperable. Alfred, King of Wessex, in an oft-quoted letter addressed to Werferth, Bishop of Worcester, lamented that by the time he came to the throne (in 871) learning

---

[1] H. Gee and W. J. Hardy (eds.), *Documents Illustrative of English Church History* (1914), pp. 17–18, 20; cf. p. 33.

had so fallen away among the clergy 'that there were very few on this side Humber who could understand their mass-books in English, or translate a letter from Latin into English; and I ween that there were not many beyond the Humber'.[1]

Alfred the Great himself must be accounted one of the great religious adult educators. Though his own education had been very belated (at twelve years of age he was still unable to read English and he was 38 before he began to learn Latin) he determinedly embarked on an ambitious plan for the re-education of his people. With the help of a small band of learned clergy recruited from England and abroad—Plegmund, Archbishop of Canterbury, Werferth of Worcester, Asser, Bishop of Sherborne, and others—Alfred produced English renderings of a number of key works, 'most needful for all men to know', for the instruction of the clergy and the people. The first was Pope Gregory's *Pastoral Care*, a manual for the clergy: a copy of this was sent to every cathedral church in the kingdom. Of the others the chief were Bede's *Ecclesiastical History*, Orosius's *Seven Books of Histories against the Pagans* (a history of the ancient world with additions dealing with the peoples of central and northern Europe), and Boethius's *On the Consolation of Philosophy*. The renderings were very free, and often embellished with additional reflections and examples drawn from the contemporary scene.

Alfred evidently had in mind a widespread provision of education for the children of the upper classes, and he himself set the example by establishing a boys' school in the royal household in which the pupils learned to read and write and studied Saxon and Latin authors. He did not, however, confine himself to the education of the young. His biographer Asser tells us that when he found his ealdormen or reeves deficient in their judgments, he bade them either yield up their office or apply themselves to study.

Wherefore in a marvellous way almost all the ealdormen, reeves and officers, who had been illiterate from infancy, studied the art of letters, preferring to learn an unwonted discipline with great toil than to lose the exercise of power.[2]

The reforms attempted by Alfred were followed in the tenth

[1] H. Sweet (ed.), *King Alfred's West Saxon Version of Gregory's Pastoral Care* (Early English Text Society, 1871), p. 3.
[2] W. H. Stevenson, *Asser's Life of King Alfred* (Oxford 1904), pp. 94–5. For a general account of Alfred's educational work see R. H. Hodgkin, *A History of the Anglo-Saxons* (Oxford 1935, 2nd edn. 1939), Vol. II, Ch. xviii; and F. M. Stenton, *Anglo-Saxon England* (Oxford 1943), pp. 267–72. It would be unwise to rely too closely on the details of Asser's narrative, but in spite of many criticisms, e.g. by J. W. Adamson in '*The Illiterate Anglo-Saxon*' (Cambridge 1946), and by V. H. Galbraith in *An Introduction to the Study of History* (1964), it is still generally accepted as authentic.

century by a great revival of learning and religion in the English Church, which from this time until the close of the Middle Ages maintained its unique position as the repository of scholarship and the principal agent in the education of the people.

The Extent of Medieval Literacy

The notion that these centuries were a time of widespread ignorance and illiteracy needs to be modified when we reflect on the vast mass of written material—statutes, charters, deeds, wills, indentures, account-books, letters, chronicles, poems, devotional works, and the like—which the Middle Ages have transmitted to us. It is true that the majority of the people throughout the period received no literary education: their education was of that practical kind which is acquired at the plough-tail, at the bench, or in the kitchen. But there is an impressive body of evidence to suggest that even the early medieval period was more literate than has often been supposed, and that the later Middle Ages saw a rapid rise in the general level of literacy.

The clergy, educated in schools attached to monasteries, churches, and other ecclesiastical establishments, sometimes also in the universities when these came into existence, formed the main core of the educated population. They included not only the ecclesiastical hierarchy proper but also the considerable array of domestic chaplains, secretaries, physicians, lawyers, stewards, and civil servants needed for the conduct of public and private business. Some were great scholars—men such as the theologian John of Salisbury, the great jurist Henry de Bracton, or Robert Grosseteste, Bishop of Lincoln. At the other end of the scale were monks and priests who had scarce Latin enough to read their mass-books; and there was every gradation between.

The number of the clergy was never very great: for the late thirteenth century it is estimated for England as about one per cent of the population.[1] It is, however, important to remember that this world of learning was not a closed one: it was open, not certainly on equal terms, but still open, to the poor as well as the rich, and there are examples enough to show that even the peasant's son might climb to a position of eminence in church or state. Indeed a distinguished historian of education has claimed that the schools 'served an intellectual rather than a social class'.[2]

[1] Sir Maurice Powicke, *The Thirteenth Century* (Oxford 1953), p. 445. Cf. H. Maynard Smith, *Pre-Reformation England* (1938), p. 38, for rather similar estimates for the fifteenth century.
[2] J. W. Adamson, *A Short History of Education* (Cambridge 1919), p. 76.

Up to about the twelfth century very few people outside the clergy had any substantial education, though it seems that the nobles and the well-to-do merchants commonly had at least the rudiments of learning: they might not be literate in the sense of knowing Latin, but they could read and often write in English, or perhaps in French. In the later Middle Ages, however, and especially in the fifteenth century, the rapid growth of commerce and industry, and the development of town life, made a fairly widespread measure of literacy essential.

This was made possible partly by an increase in the number of grammar schools, partly by the development, either within or outside the grammar school framework, of provision for elementary education—in reading, writing, and casting accounts—in the vernacular. A well-known instance, which shows the way the wind was blowing, is to be found in the establishment in 1483 of Jesus College, Rotherham. Here it was provided that in addition to the usual masters for grammar and song there should be a third master, skilled in the art of writing and keeping accounts, to train those who did not wish to attain the high dignity of the priesthood for 'the mechanical arts and other worldly concerns'.[1]

Sir Thomas More, in his *Apology* of 1533, remarks apropos of the translation of the Bible into English that 'farre more than fowre partes of the whole [people] divided into tenne could never read englishe yet', which would imply that more than half the population *could* read. Few scholars are prepared to accept this statement at its face value, but all would agree with Dr. Eileen Power that 'in the fifteenth century most men and women of the upper and middle classes could read and write',[2] and there is evidence that literacy was also spreading downwards into the ranks of the yeomen and craftsmen.[3]

In these circumstances it is surprising to find no trace, even in the fifteenth century, of adult education applied to secular purposes. We might expect to find, at least in London, schools of the type

---

[1] A. F. Leach, *Educational Charters* (Cambridge 1911), p. 424.

[2] E. Power, *Medieval People* (1924), p. 116. She admits that 'their spelling was sometimes marvellous to behold, and St. Olave's Church is apt to become Sent Tolowys Scryssche beneath their labouring goosequills, and punctuation is almost entirely to seek'.

[3] On medieval education generally see especially A. F. Leach, *Schools of Medieval England* (1915), and A. W. Parry, *Education in England in the Middle Ages* (1920). For the specific question of literacy see M. Deanesly, *The Lollard Bible* (Cambridge 1920), Ch. viii; V. H. Galbraith, *The Literacy of the Medieval English Kings* (reprinted from *Proceedings of the British Academy*, Vol. XXI, 1935); J. W. Thompson, *The Literacy of the Laity in the Middle Ages* (University of California Publications in Education, Vol. 9, 1939), Chs. v and vii; Adamson, '*The Illiterate Anglo-Saxon*', Chs. i and iii; Smith, *Pre-Reformation England*, pp. 102–4; and R. Irwin, *The Origins of the English Library* (1958), pp. 150–5. Mr. Irwin suggests that More's statement may have been true of the London he knew.

recorded a little later at Basel, where in 1516 there were school-masters offering to teach reading and writing to all comers—citizens, journeymen craftsmen, ladies, boys and girls.[1] In England, however, the records have so far revealed no similar example, and throughout the Middle Ages the only recognisable provision of adult education is the religious instruction provided by the Church, or in the closing phase by its Lollard rivals.

The Teaching Work of the Church

The main instrument of this education was the parish priest, and it formed part of the general duty constantly enjoined upon him by the canons of Church Councils, the decrees of provincial synods, and the constitutions of bishops, to instruct his parishioners, old and young, in the faith of the Church. We have already had an example of this from the eighth century, and if we look forward to the central period of the Middle Ages we find similar injunctions in which the priest's teaching duties are set out in more detail.[2]

Robert Grosseteste, in the thirteenth century, instructed his clergy in the diocese of Lincoln to teach the boys of their parishes the Lord's Prayer, the Creed, and the Hail Mary, and how to make the sign of the cross, and continued:

And since, as we have heard, even some adults are ignorant of these matters, we ordain that when the lay people come to confession, they be diligently examined whether they know the aforesaid matters, and that they be instructed therein by the priests according as it may seem expedient.[3]

It will be noted that this instruction was to be given in association with the confessional, for at this period the preaching of sermons was not regarded as a normal part of the priest's duties. A little later, however, in 1281, a Council held at Lambeth by the reforming Archbishop John Peckham decreed that every priest having the care of souls must, once every three months, either himself or through another, expound to the people in the popular tongue and without any fantastical subtleties the fourteen articles of faith, the ten commandments, the two precepts of the Gospel, the seven works of mercy, the seven mortal sins, the seven principal virtues, and the seven sacraments. This decree became known as *Ignorantia Sacerdotum*, from

---

[1] Adamson, *Short History of Education*, p. 79.
[2] For a general account of this subject see E. L. Cutts, *Parish Priests and their People in the Middle Ages in England* (1888), Ch. xiv; and F. A. Gasquet, *Parish Life in Medieval England* (1906), pp. 211–22; and for a sceptical view G. G. Coulton, *Ten Medieval Studies* (Cambridge 1930), Ch. viii.
[3] *Epistolae Roberti Grosseteste*, ed. H. R. Luard (Rolls Series, 1861) p. 155.

its opening words: 'The ignorance of priests plunges the people into the pit of error.'[1]

In the fourteenth century John Thoresby, Archbishop of York, was able to go further. In 1357 he prescribed that his clergy should expound these matters to their parishioners, men and women, and teach them to the children, 'at least on Sundays', and that at least during Lent they should examine their parishioners to ascertain whether they knew these things and had taught them to their children.

It was easy to lay down rules of this kind: it was more difficult to secure their observance, for the education of the priesthood was often lamentably inadequate for the tasks imposed upon it. Only a minority of the parish clergy were graduates, and the number trained in theology was smaller still.[2]

The Church did its best to help. From the twelfth century onwards many of the great cathedrals made provision for the teaching of theology, some also for the teaching of the arts.[3] There were also various manuals of instruction setting out the principal points of Christian faith and practice, the standard work in the later Middle Ages being a brief manual in Latin prepared by Archbishop Peckham and appended to the decree *Ignorantia Sacerdotum*.[4]

The fact that Thoresby expected his clergy to preach every Sunday, whereas Peckham less than eighty years earlier stipulated only a minimum of four times a year, may be a reflection of the increasing importance of the sermon in the later medieval period. Undoubtedly this change was in part due to the advent of the Dominican and Franciscan friars in the third decade of the thirteenth century. Both became learned orders, though the Franciscans were not originally intended as such; both attached great importance to

---

[1] D. Wilkins (ed.), *Concilia Magnae Britanniae et Hiberniae* (1737), Vol. II, p. 54. A translation is given by Cutts, *op. cit.*, pp. 216–17.

[2] The illiteracy of the parish clergy was one of G. G. Coulton's favourite themes: see, for example, his *Medieval Garner* (1910), pp. 270–3, on clerical examinations in the diocese of Salisbury, 1222.

[3] See especially W. A. Pantin, *The English Church in the Fourteenth Century* (Cambridge 1955), pp. 110–19. For the secular cathedrals see also K. Edwards, *English Secular Cathedrals in the Middle Ages* (Manchester 1949), pp. 187–208, which supersedes earlier accounts by Leach and others. For the education of the clergy generally, see J. R. H. Moorman, *Church Life in England in the Thirteenth Century* (Cambridge 1945), Ch. viii; Maynard Smith, *Pre-Reformation England*, pp. 38–45; and especially Deanesly, *The Lollard Bible*, Chs. vi–vii (the best general introduction to the subject).

[4] Translated by Cutts, *Parish Priests*, pp. 217–22. For contemporary English versions see T. F. Simmons and H. E. Nolloth (eds.), *The Lay Folks' Catechism* (Early English Text Society, 1901). Another popular manual, also indebted in part to Peckham, was John Myrc's *Instructions for Parish Priests*, written *c.* 1400 (ed. E. Peacock, E.E.T.S. 1868, rev. edn. 1902). Pantin, *op. cit.*, Ch. ix, gives an interesting account of fourteenth-century manuals.

popular preaching, and trained their members specially for the task. The friars' sermons, delivered in simple language and spiced with homely examples and humorous anecdotes, always attracted eager audiences, often to the dismay and discomfiture of the parish priest, who found himself obliged, however ignorant and unpractised he might be, to enter the lists against them.

It has been well said that 'the history of the pulpit as we know it begins with the Preaching Friars. They met, and stimulated, a growing popular demand for sermons. They revolutionised the technique. They magnified the office'.[1] In the closing period of the Middle Ages the friars fell into disrepute, but the sermon maintained its new popularity, and played as time went on an increasingly significant part in the Church's teaching work. The coming of the preaching orders also increased the facilities available for the education of the priesthood, for the schools which they established for the training of their own members were often open also to the secular clergy.

In preaching, as in general pastoral work, there was no lack of manuals of instruction, for the fourteenth and fifteenth centuries saw a tremendous outpouring of preachers' aids of all kinds, amongst others handbooks of sermon outlines—sometimes known as 'sleep-wells' (*dormi secure*) because they enabled the parson to sleep in peace without having to worry about his next sermon.

A really complete and fully developed medieval sermon, as it might be delivered by one of the famous preachers at Paul's Cross, was an awe-inspiring affair, constructed according to an elaborate formal pattern and luxuriantly illustrated with historical, allegorical, topological and anagogical meanings, citations from authority, and analogies from nature, the Bible and the lives of the saints.

The ordinary sermon to the laity, however, was much simpler and more straightforward, and the advice given by the handbooks on methods of delivery has often a curiously modern ring. Speak slowly and distinctly, the preacher is told: vary the pitch of your voice, but do not shout one minute and whisper the next. Be sure to make clear the division of your sermon and to emphasise the principal links of your argument. Do not try to crowd in too much, or make your sermon too long, for 'excessive prolixity induces sleep'. Let your gestures be natural: do not stand still like a statue, nor on the other hand indulge in exaggerated movements. Dress soberly, avoiding outrageous garments. If you are a beginner, practise in some place apart where there is nobody to laugh at you.

[1] C. Smyth, *The Art of Preaching, 747–1939* (1940), p. 13.

These are hints which are just as topical and valuable today as they were five or six hundred years ago.[1]

This brief account of the religious education of adults must be taken as referring to England only. In medieval Scotland and Wales life was more lawless and primitive; the general standard of education was much lower; and the Church was hindered in its teaching work, even more than in England, by the inadequacy of the human instruments at its disposal.

In Scotland the Church had a constant struggle to secure a minimum standard of decency in personal behaviour and in the performance of the Church ceremonies, and in the surviving medieval statutes there is in fact only one brief reference to the educational duties of the priesthood. It occurs in a compendious statute copied from the table of contents of the diocesan constitutions of Robert Grosseteste: 'that they teach their people the Lord's Prayer and the Creed'.[2] Not until 1549, on the eve of the Reformation, was any serious attempt made to provide for systematic preaching and teaching by the clergy, and then it was too late: the statutes were never put into force.[3]

In Wales it was only in the late thirteenth century, when the English military conquest had been completed, that the Archbishops of Canterbury were able to wield effective authority. 'Such illiterate priests and clergy we never remember to have seen', declared Archbishop Peckham on a visitation of the diocese of St. Asaph in 1284; and later in the year he wrote to Edward I from Newport recommending that the Welsh youths should be sent to England to learn letters and manners, 'for the clergy of the country hardly know more of letters than the laity'.[4] No doubt he exaggerated, but compared with England, Wales was and remained educationally backward.

The Lollards as Teachers

In the activities of John Wycliffe and the Lollards in the late fourteenth century we discern the first faint beginnings of nonconformity in religious adult education. The revolutionary feature of

[1] The standard work on medieval preaching is G. R. Owst, *Preaching in Medieval England* (Cambridge 1926), which draws on a wealth of manuscript material. An older but still valuable survey, on a European scale, is E. C. Dargan, *History of Preaching* (1905), which extends to 1572. On sermon construction see also Canon Smyth's *Art of Preaching* (cited above), Ch. ii, and H. G. Pfander, *The Popular Sermon of the Medieval Friar in England* (New York 1937), pp. 15–19.
[2] D. Patrick, *Statutes of the Scottish Church, 1225–1559* (Scottish History Society, Edinburgh 1907), p. 55.
[3] The statutes are printed in Patrick, *op. cit.*, pp. 98 sqq.
[4] A. W. Haddan and W. Stubbs, *Councils and Ecclesiastical Documents relating to Great Britain and Ireland*, Vol. I (Oxford 1869), pp. 566, 570.

Wycliffe's teaching was his insistence on the overriding authority of the Bible in matters of faith, and on the supreme importance of Bible-reading not only by the clergy but also by the laity. The New Testament, he declared, was 'open to the understanding of simple men in the points that be most needful for salvation', and 'no man was so rude a scholar, but that he might learn from the words of the Gospel according to his simplicity'.[1] Here was an idea which was to have a most potent effect on adult education, for the desire to read the words of Holy Scripture became for centuries one of the greatest incentives to literacy among humble people.

From about 1377 Wycliffe's itinerant 'Poor Preachers' began to spread the new gospel throughout the country, and in 1380 he and his helpers embarked on the stupendous task of providing an English version of the Bible as a basis for their teaching. In Wycliffe's lifetime the Lollard preachers were usually clerks, but later the function was often assumed by laymen—sometimes self-taught laymen. Their sermons had a puritanical severity very different from the racy humour of the friars, but they did not lack converts, particularly among the artisan classes in the towns. By the middle of the fifteenth century persecution by Church and State had driven the movement underground, but it persisted in secret in many parts of England and Scotland until the coming of the Reformation.

In the records of the late fourteenth and early fifteenth centuries there are frequent references to Lollard 'schools'. For example in the notorious act of 1401 for the burning of heretics (*de haeretico comburendo*) it is recited that the Lollards 'make unlawful Conventicles and Confederacies, they hold and exercise Schools, they make and write Books, and they do wickedly instruct and inform People, and as much as they may excite and stir them to Sedition and Insurrection'.[2] The schools here referred to were adult schools, for the instruction of converts and for mutual improvement and edification among the faithful. They probably resembled, in their general nature and purpose, the Methodist class-meetings and reading circles of the eighteenth century. One of the earliest groups had its headquarters in 1382 at the chapel of St. John the Baptist, outside the town of Leicester, and we are told that

there was in that place an inn and lodging-house for all such who might come, and there they had a school of their wicked doctrines and opinions, and communicated their errors and heresies [*ibi habuerunt gignasium*

---

[1] B. A. Workman, *John Wyclif* (Oxford 1926), Vol. II, p. 151.
[2] 2 Hy. IV c. 15, *Statutes of the Realm*, Vol. II (1816), p. 126. For other such references see J. Gairdner, *Lollardy and the Reformation in England*, Vol. I (1908), Chs. i–ii *passim*.

malignorum dogmatum et opinionum, et errorum haereticorumque communicationem].[1]

This group included among others William Swynderby, priest, Richard Waytestathe, chaplain, and William Smith, a blacksmith who, after taking to religion and learning to read and write, was for eight years engaged in the copying of the Wycliffite gospels and other Lollard works.[2]

In 1409 Nicholas Bubbewyth, Bishop of Bath and Wells, was commissioned to take action against secret Lollard schools in Bristol.[3] In 1424 it was alleged that Richard Belward, of Earsham, in Norfolk, 'Keepeth schooles of Lollardy in the English tongue' in the neighbouring town of Ditchingham, and that John Goddesel of Ditchingham, parchment-maker, 'bringeth him all the bookes concerning that doctrine from London'.[4] Five years later a Norfolk Lollard named William Wright, having turned informer, declared that

Nicholas Belward, son of John Belward, dwelling in the parish of Southelam [South Elmham], is one of the same sect, and hath a new Testament which he bought at London for foure marks and forty pence, and taught the said William Wright and Margery his wife, and wrought with them continually by the space of one year, and studied diligently upon the said New Testament.[5]

A remarkable feature of this and other records of Lollardy is the large number of quite humble people—tailors, turners, servants and the like, both men and women—who are revealed as able to read, and it seems at least possible that some of the schools actually taught people to read, using their precious copies of the English Bible as texts.[6]

After 1424 we hear no more of Lollard 'schools' under that name, but in bishops' registers from various parts of England during the late fifteenth and early sixteenth centuries there are several cases in which groups of people are accused of meeting together in secret for the reading and exposition of the Gospel and other works in English.[7] From Scotland, too, we have the interesting story of

---

[1] J. R. Lumby (ed.), *Chronicon Henrici Knighton* (Rolls Series, 1889–95), Vol. II, p. 182.
[2] *Op. cit.*, pp. 180 sqq., 313.
[3] *Calendar of Patent Rolls, Henry IV, 1408–1413* (1909), p. 109.
[4] J. Foxe, *Acts and Monuments*, ed. S. R. Cattley (London 1837–41), Vol. III, pp. 585–6.
[5] *Op. cit.*, pp. 596–7.
[6] *Victoria County History, Norfolk*, Vol. II, ed. W. Page (1906), p. 248, says Nicholas Belward taught Wright and others to read, but this goes beyond the evidence given by Foxe, who is cited as authority.
[7] E.g. in the diocese of Hereford, 1472 (*Registrum Johannis Stanbury*, ed. A. H. Bannister, Canterbury and York Society, 1919, pp. 123–30); and in the diocese of Lincoln, 1521 (Foxe, *Acts and Monuments*, Vol. IV, pp. 221–40). The best general account of Lollard activities is in Deanesly, *The Lollard Bible*, Chs. ix and xiv.

Murdoch Nisbet of Hardhill in Ayrshire, who, having left the country early in the reign of James V, made for himself a copy of the Wycliffite New Testament in the Scots dialect. He returned about 1539, but when two of his companions had been taken and burnt as heretics, he 'digged and built a vault in the bottom of his own house, to which he retired himself, serving God and reading his new book. Thus he continued, instructing some few that had access to him', until the death of James V in 1542 gave him the opportunity to come forth from his retirement and take a hand in the work of reformation.[1]

Books and Libraries

Although this chapter has been restricted to the organised teaching work of the Church, and of its Lollard rivals, no one will suppose that this was the only educational influence brought to bear upon the English adult in the Middle Ages. If one were to attempt a complete catalogue of such influences one would have to include the frescoes and carvings of the churches; the miracle and morality plays; the traditional lore of wandering bards and minstrels; the civic training provided by the guilds; and a score more of such intangible factors.[2] To examine the educational implications of all these activities would involve us in almost unlimited commitments, especially in describing the developments of later centuries, but we must find space for a brief comment on the educational influence of books.

It is a common belief that, before the advent of printing, books were exceedingly rare and costly. This is because the medieval manuscripts most people are familiar with are the beautifully written and elaborately illuminated examples which are the showpieces of the libraries. These, however, are the *éditions de luxe*, handed down from generation to generation by royalty, nobility, and the aristocracy of commerce. The parish priest's missal or sermon handbook, the Lollard's copy of the Gospels, the merchant's book of devotion or romance, was commonly a much inferior affair. All too often it was written in a cramped hand, perhaps even in a variety of hands; there

---

[1] K. A. Tweedie (ed.), *Select Biographies* (Wodrow Society, Edinburgh 1845–7), p. 378. Nisbet's Scots Testament has survived, and has been edited by T. G. Law for the Scottish Text Society (3 v. Edinburgh 1901–5—see Introduction pp. x–xiv).

[2] The influence of the bards as popular teachers was particularly important in Wales and Scotland, where, as in Ireland, the office of bard was held in high esteem. The bards had recognised ranks and degrees, the highest of which were attained only after a long and elaborate training; their poems not merely preserved the laws, history and legends of the people but also enshrined a secular native culture quite distinct from, and in some ways hostile to, the Latin culture of the Church. See for Wales Evans J. Jones, *Education in Wales during the Later Middle Ages* (Swansea University College 1947), pp. 31–8; and for Scotland J. Edgar, *History of Early Scottish Education* (Edinburgh 1893), Ch. iii.

was little or nothing in the way of ornament; and in the later Middle Ages it might well be on paper instead of parchment.

The fact is that by the mid-fifteenth century books, though still scarce and expensive by our standards, were much more plentiful than in any previous age: London, indeed had begun to develop *scriptoria* employing a staff of scribes for the reproduction of manuscripts on a commercial scale. It was no uncommon thing for a middle-class merchant to possess ten or a dozen books, besides, perhaps, a common-place book written in his own hand. Chaucer does not tell us whether the Clerk of Oxford's 'twenty bokes clad in blak or reed, of Aristotle and his philosophye' were an actual possession or just a golden dream, but fifty years after Chaucer's death they might well have been a reality: one fifteenth-century parson bequeathed no fewer than 93 books to the Common Library at Cambridge. A few wealthy people, of course, had much larger collections: the outstanding figure in the fifteenth century was the humanist Humphrey, Duke of Gloucester, whose magnificent gifts formed the basis of the Bodleian Library at Oxford.[1]

This period saw also the first faint foreshadowings of the public library system. Hitherto the only substantial libraries, apart from private collections, had been those in the universities, in the cathedrals and collegiate churches, and in the monasteries. These were not, of course, public libraries, though they were probably freely accessible to visiting scholars, including the occasional scholarly layman. In the fifteenth century it became increasingly common for parish churches to possess a few books, other than service books, which were available to the clergy and others who could profit by them,[2] and we also have two examples of libraries which, while not public in the modern sense, pointed the way towards public library provision.

In 1425 the executors of Richard Whittington and William Bury established at the Guildhall a library for the City of London. This library, which was under the care of a chaplain attached to the Guildhall College, was intended primarily for clergy and theological students. As a later description put it (1549): 'The saied library is a house appointed by the saied Maior and cominaltie for . . . resorte of

---

[1] On books in the fifteenth century see C. L. Kingsford, *Prejudice and Promise in XVth Century England* (Oxford 1925), pp. 39–43; and H. S. Bennett, 'The Production and Dissemination of Vernacular MSS. in the Fifteenth Century', in *The Library*, 5th Ser., Vol. I (1947), pp. 167–78. G. S. Joy has an interesting chapter on the commercial book trade in an unpublished thesis on *The Make up of Middle English Verse Manuscripts* (Ph.D., London 1953). For commonplace books kept by private citizens see R. H. Robbins (ed.), *Secular Lyrics of the XIVth and XVth Centuries* (Oxford 1952), pp. xxviii–xxx; and for early private libraries Irwin, *Origins of the English Library*, Ch. x.

[2] Central Council for the Care of Churches, *The Parochial Libraries of the Church of England* (1959), p. 14.

all students for their education in Divine Scriptures.'[1] In 1458 or earlier John Carpenter, Bishop of Worcester, established a library open to all in the chantry chapel connected with his cathedral charnel-house; and in 1464 he founded a similar library at Bristol in the house of the Gild of Kalendaries—an ancient religious fraternity of clergy and laity which was accommodated over the north aisle of the church of All Saints, and was attached to the monastery of St. Augustine. The regulations decreed that the keeper of the library, who was to be the chantry chaplain at Worcester and the Prior of the Gild at Bristol, must be a bachelor of divinity, or at least a graduate, sufficiently instructed in Holy Scriptures and a ready preacher. It was also laid down that

on every weekday, for two hours before None and two hours after None, all who wish to enter that library for the purpose of study shall be free to come and go; and the aforesaid Master and Keeper shall, when duly required, expound doubtful and obscure passages of Holy Scripture to the best of his knowledge.

The keeper was also to give a public lecture in the library once a week.[2]

None of these libraries, it should be said, was a lending library; all three were chained libraries of reference.[3] None of them survived the Reformation.

It is clear that already before the invention of printing there was a growing reading public. But of course it remains true that the introduction of printing into England by William Caxton in 1476, and into Scotland by Walter Chapman and Andrew Myllar in 1507, was a major landmark in adult educational history. By multiplying the production of relatively cheap copies of books it not merely led to a great and immediate extension of reading among the educated classes but also provided the basic tools by means of which, ultimately, the art of reading was to be spread throughout all classes of society.

---

[1] J. E. Price, *A Descriptive Account of the Guildhall of London* (1886), p. 139. For the history of this library see R. Smith, 'The Library at Guildhall in the 15th and 16th Centuries,' Parts I and II, in *Guildhall Miscellany*, Vol. I, Nos. 1 and 6 (1952–56); and T. Kelly *Early Public Libraries* (1966), pp. 29–31.

[2] For further details and references concerning the Worcester and Bristol libraries see Kelly, *op. cit.*, pp. 31–5.

[3] I can find no evidence to substantiate the remarkable statement in A. R. Powys, *The English Parish Church* (1930), p. 155, that in 1402 the churchwardens of St. Michael's, Bath, were lending books from the parish library at 2d. per volume.

2

The Sixteenth Century

REFORMATION AND RENAISSANCE

THE traditional elements in religious adult education were not changed by the Reformation of the early sixteenth century. The reformed Church of England regarded itself as the true heir of the Catholic Church, and the canons of 1604, which gathered together and consolidated the ecclesiastical legislation of the reforming period, set out the teaching duties of the clergy—regular preaching, instruction of the 'youth and ignorant persons' of the parish in the elements of the faith—in terms almost precisely similar to those in use in the later Middle Ages.[1] Yet one cannot read the ecclesiastical records of this period without becoming conscious of two distinctive features. In the first place, the translation of the Bible, the prayer-book, and other religious works, into English, and their multiplication through the printing-press, opens the way to a much wider dissemination of religious knowledge. In the second place the key position occupied by the Bible in Protestant theology leads to a new concern for the study of the Bible and a new emphasis on preaching as the exposition of God's word.

The Printed English Bible

The story of the printed English Bible, which was an event of, immense significance in the history of adult education, goes back before the Reformation, but we may begin with the injunction issued by Thomas Cromwell, as Vicar-General to Henry VIII, in 1536:

that every parson, or proprietary of any parish church within the realm, shall on this side the feast of S. *Peter ad Vincula* next coming, provide a book of the whole Bible, both in Latin, and also in English, and lay the same in the choir, for every man that will to look and read thereon, and shall discourage no man from the reading of any part of the Bible, either in Latin or in English; but rather comfort, exhort, and admonish every man

[1] E. Cardwell, *Synodalia* (Oxford 1842), Vol. I, pp. 273–5, 280; cf. M. E. C. Walcott (ed.), *Constitutions and Canons Ecclesiastical of the Church of England* (Oxford 1874), pp. 68–70, 83–4.

to read the same as the very word of God, and the spiritual food of man's soul . . .[1]

The English Bible here referred to was the first complete English Bible to be printed. It was produced by Miles Coverdale in 1535, and embodied translations of the New Testament and parts of the Old Testament made by William Tyndale during the preceding decade. Coverdale's version provided the basis for the so-called 'Great Bible' of 1539, which was long the officially authorised version: it was, in fact, authorised before publication in an injunction of 1538. This injunction was in similar terms to the one of 1536, but it omitted the reference to the Latin Bible, and specified instead 'one book of the whole Bible of the largest volume, in English'.[2]

John Strype, in his *Memorials of Thomas Cranmer* (1694), gives an enthusiastic description of the joy with which the Book of God was received throughout England, not only by the learned, but by the common people:

Everybody who could bought the book, or busily read it, or got others to read it to them, if they could not themselves; and divers more elderly persons learned to read on purpose.

To this we may add the story related by William Maldon, in the reign of Elizabeth, to John Foxe:

When the King had allowed the Bible to be set forth to be read in all churches, immediately several poor men in the town of Chelmsford in Essex, where his father lived and he was born, bought the New Testament and on Sundays sat reading of it in the lower end of the church: many would flock about them to hear their reading: and he among the rest, being then but fifteen years old, came every Sunday to hear the glad and sweet tidings of the Gospel.[3]

The popular enthusiasm was such, especially in London and the south-eastern counties, where Protestant influences were strongest, that the King and many of the bishops became alarmed. Cranmer, Archbishop of Canterbury, complained to Cromwell in 1539 that divine service was being hindered by the crowds of people gathering

---

[1] W. H. Frere and W. M. Kennedy, *Visitation Articles and Injunctions of the Period of the Reformation* (1910), Vol. II, p. 9. On the authenticity of this injunction, concerning which there has frequently been confusion, see *ibid.*, pp. 1–2.

[2] Frere and Kennedy, *op. cit.*, Vol. II, pp. 35–6. This order was reinforced by a royal proclamation in 1541. The Great Bible was a substantial volume, and cost the then substantial sum of ten or twelve shillings.

[3] Both these passages are to be found in Strype, *Cranmer*, Vol. I, p. 91. H. Maynard Smith, who quotes them in *Henry VIII and the Reformation* (1948), pp. 342–4, thinks both derive from Foxe's manuscripts.

for the reading of the Bible, which was carried on 'as in a common school, expounding and interpreting Scriptures'.[1] In 1543, accordingly, Parliament limited the reading of the Bible by laymen. Henceforth it might be read only in private, by noblemen, gentlemen, ladies and merchants: the lower orders were forbidden to read it at all. Under Edward VI, however, and again (after the Marian interlude) under Elizabeth, free access to the Bible was restored.[2]

In 1568 the Great Bible appeared in a revised form as the Bishop's Bible, which became in due course the starting-point for the Authorized Version of 1611. Another very popular version, especially among the Puritans, was the Geneva Bible, produced under Calvinist influence by a group of English exiles. It appeared in 1560, the year of the Scottish Reformation, and quickly established itself as the household Bible in that country. In Wales the first complete Welsh translation of the Bible, by William Morgan, Bishop of Llandaff, was produced in 1588; revised by Richard Parry, Bishop of St. Asaph, it became the Authorized Version of 1620.[3]

Preaching and Prophesying

The new concern for the study and preaching of the Bible was especially noticeable among the Calvinist groups in the reforming movement—the Presbyterians of the Church of Scotland, the Puritan wing within the Church of England, and the various English separatist sects which began to develop almost immediately after the Reformation. The official position of the Church of England was broadly Lutheran: looking upon itself as the true heir of Catholic Christendom, it was prepared in matters not clearly defined in the Bible to give due weight to the tradition of the Church. To the Calvinists, however, the Bible was all in all, the supreme rule of liturgy and of life: for them the primary function of the Church was the pure preaching of the word, and the sermon took the place formerly occupied by the mass as the central feature of the Church's Service.

In Scotland the First Book of Discipline (1560) made elaborate provision for the religious instruction of adults through sermons and

---

[1] R. W. Dixon, *History of the Church of England* (3rd edn. Oxford 1895), Vol. II, p. 167 note.

[2] Injunctions of Edward VI, 1547, and Elizabeth, 1559, in Frere and Kennedy, *Visitation Articles*, Vol. II, pp. 117–18; Vol. III, pp. 10–11.

[3] The best general account of the advent of the English Bible and its significance is in Maynard Smith's *Henry VIII and the Reformation*, pp. 276–350. For further details see Dixon's *History of the Church of England*, and on the bibliographical side C. S. Lewis, *English Literature in the Sixteenth Century* (Oxford 1944), pp. 204–15.

Scripture readings.[1] The Scots also introduced, following Continental examples, a religious practice known as the 'prophesying' or 'exercise'. This was based on a passage in St. Paul's *First Epistle to the Corinthians*:

Let the prophets speak two or three, and let the other judge . . .
For ye may all prophesy one by one, that all may learn, and all may be comforted.[2]

As developed in Scotland, the exercise was a meeting of the clergy and learned people of a district, in the presence of the local congregation, for the exposition and discussion of a Bible text. The Book of Discipline declared that 'this Exercise must be patent to such as list to heir and learne . . . and everie man shall have libertie to utter and declair his mynd and knowledge to the comfort and edification of the Churche'.[3]

The exercises became in due course the basis of the presbytery organisation of the Scottish Church, and long continued in association with the weekly presbytery meetings: as late as 1638 we find the presbytery at St. Andrews working its way verse by verse through the Scriptures. By this time, however, the exercise had become an occasion for preaching only, and the element of congregational discussion had disappeared.[4]

In England, in Elizabeth's reign, vigorous and on the whole successful attempts were made by the ecclesiastical authorities to improve the standard of the parish clergy. At the outset of the period, owing to the upheavals of the previous generation, there was a desperate shortage of clergy, and all kinds of unsuitable people had been presented to benefices. Matthew Parker, Archbishop of Canterbury, confessed as much in a letter to Edmund Grindal, Bishop of London, in 1560: 'occasioned by the great want of ministers, we and you both, for tolerable supply thereof, have heretofore admitted into the ministry sundry artificers and others, not traded [trained] and brought up in learning, and, as it happened in a multitude some that were of base occupations'.[5] Henceforth every

---

[1] The First Book of Discipline was compiled by John Knox and others, and is printed in Vol. II of Knox's *Works* (ed. D. Laing, Edinburgh 1848). Though never officially adopted it exerted a profound influence on the organisation of the early Scottish Reformed Church.

[2] 1 Corinthians xiv. 29, 31.

[3] Knox, *Works*, Vol. II, p. 243.

[4] See on this W. McMillan, *The Worship of the Scottish Reformed Church, 1550–1638* (1931), Appendix III.

[5] J. Bruce and T. T. Perowne (eds.), *Correspondence of Matthew Parker* (Parker Society 1853), p. 120, quoted A. T. Hart, *The Country Clergy in Elizabethan and Stuart Times* (1958), p. 24.

effort was made to secure ministers 'learned fit to teach the people', and a constant stream of royal and episcopal ordinances (enforced by visitations) enjoined the clergy to be diligent in the study of the Scriptures and in the performance of their parochial duties.

These measures undoubtedly brought about a substantial improvement, but even at the end of the reign more than half the clergy were still neither graduates nor licensed preachers, and in spite of widespread pluralism many small benefices were entirely without incumbents. In these circumstances the requirements regarding preaching could not be very stringent. A licensed preacher was expected to deliver a sermon once a month; a clergyman not licensed to preach was expected to provide for a sermon once a quarter. For other occasions the congregation had to be content with the reading of one of the official homilies. There is a good deal of evidence that even these modest duties were often not fulfilled, and that some parishes did not hear a sermon, sometimes not even a homily, from one year's end to the other.[1]

It is against this background that we must consider the attempt of the Puritan party within the Church to create a preaching ministry. As early as 1564 we hear of 'prophesyings' at Norwich.[2] In 1571 rules drawn up by the Puritans of Northampton provided for a sermon every Sunday and holy day in the principal church of the town, a service every Tuesday and Thursday for the reading and exposition of the Bible, and a 'prophesying' for the ministers of the town and neighbourhood every other Saturday morning.[3]

The prophesyings rapidly spread to many other parts of England, especially in the North and East, and for a few years they were very popular. A contemporary description is given by William Harrison, who says they were held 'in some places weekly, in others once in fourteen days, in divers monthly, and elsewhere twice a year'.[4] For our purposes, however, the most convenient account is that given by Strype[5]:

the Ministers of such a division, at a set time, met together in some church belonging to a market or other large town; and there each in

---

[1] For the Elizabethan clergy generally see Hart, *op. cit.*, Ch. ii; and for the position at the close of the reign R. G. Usher, *The Reconstruction of the English Church* (New York 1910), Vol. I, Ch. x.

[2] *Calendar of State Papers, Domestic, Addenda 1547–1565*, p. 552. In this case persons who knew no Latin, or were engaged in secular occupations, were excluded.

[3] J. Strype, *Annals of the Reformation* (1709–31, new edn. Oxford 1824), Vol. II, Pt. i, pp. 133–40.

[4] L. Withrington (ed.), *Elizabethan England: from 'A Description of England'*, by William Harrison (London, Camelot Series), p. 67.

[5] *Life and Acts of Edmund Grindal, Archbishop of Canterbury* (1710). The quotation here given is from the 1821 edition, p. 326.

their order explained, according to their ability, some particular portion of Scripture allotted to them before. And after all of them had done, a Moderator, who was one of the gravest and best learned among them, made his observations upon what the rest had said, and determined the true sense of the place. And all was to be despatched within such a space of time . . .

At these assemblies were great confluxes of people to hear and learn. And by this means the Ministers and Curates were forced to read authors, and consult expositors and commentators, and to follow their studies, that they might speak to some purpose when they were to appear in public: and hereby they considerably profited themselves in the knowledge of the Scripture. But the inconvenience was, that at these meetings happened at length confusions and disturbances: some affecting to shew their parts, and to confute others that spake not so appositely perhaps as themselves. They also sometimes would broach heterodox opinions. And some that had been silenced from their preaching for their incompliance with the established worship, would intrude themselves here, and vent themselves against the Liturgy and hierarchy; some would speak against states or particular persons. The people also fell to arguing and disputing much upon religion: sometimes a layman would take upon him to speak; so that the exercises degenerated into factions, divisions, and censorings.[1]

Elizabeth herself distrusted popular preaching as giving rise to dissension and sedition, and in 1577, by her command, the prophesyings were peremptorily forbidden.

This was not, however, quite the end of them. There was a limited revival, with official approval, in Lancashire a few years later, and similar practices are recorded, here and there, well on into the seventeenth century.[2] Virtually, however, 1577 marks the end of public prophesyings carried on with the sanction of the Church.

[1] For the full story of the prophesyings see also Strype, *Annals of the Reformation*, Vol. II, Pt. i, pp. 133–40, 472–81; Vol. II, Pt. ii, pp. 110–11, 113–15, 612–13. London, Rochester, Lincoln, Peterborough and Norwich are mentioned as dioceses in which prophesyings were organised with the approval of the bishop. J. Browne, *History of Congregationalism in Norfolk* (London 1877), pp. 16–20, gives an account of prophesying in the Norwich diocese, and prints the 'Order of the Prophesie' at Christ Church, Norwich, in 1575. Many of the relevant documents are printed in G. W. Prothero (ed.), *Select Statutes and other Constitutional Documents illustrative of the Reigns of Elizabeth and James I* (Oxford 1894, 4th edn. 1913), pp. 202–8.

[2] In the 1580s the Privy Council found it necessary, in order to combat Popery, to encourage a revival of the exercises in Lancashire, but it was made plain that the main object was the training of the clergy. The public were admitted to the principal sermon but entirely excluded from the discussions. Even with this limitation the monthly exercise was immensely popular. According to B. Brook, *Lives of the Puritans* (1813), Vol. III, pp. 341–3, the prophesyings were also revived in the diocese of York under the archbishopric of Tobias Matthew (1606–28), and this has recently been confirmed by R. A. Marchant, *The Puritans and the Church Courts in the Diocese of York, 1560–1642* (1960), pp. 30–1, 169.

For these later prophesyings see Strype, *op. cit.*, Vol. II, Pt. i, p. 481; Vol. II, Pt. ii, pp. 544–9; Vol. III, pp. 476–80; and R. Halley, *Lancashire: its Puritanism and Nonconformity*, Vol. I (Manchester 1859), pp. 130–2. See also next chapter.

Preaching Lectureships

Henceforward the public appetite for preaching had to be satisfied, in the main, in other ways, and the principal way in which it
was satisfied, in the latter years of Elizabeth's reign, was by the
development of a system of preaching lectureships, supplementary
to the normal services of the Church.

These lectureships were held by ordained clergymen appointed
for the special purpose of preaching sermons, and supported, not out
of Church revenues, but out of private endowments. Quite frequently,
in market towns, the town authorities maintained a preacher.
Lectureships were founded in increasing numbers as the century
drew to its close, and inevitably attracted to themselves many of the
ablest of the clergy, and particularly those of Puritan leanings, who
appreciated the greater freedom of a lecturer's pulpit. William Haller,
in his illuminating study of the rise of Puritanism, has indeed
demonstrated the emergence, during the late Elizabethan period,
of something like a school of Puritan preachers associated with the
University of Cambridge.

These Puritan preachers, whether lecturers or beneficed clergy,
were distinguished not only by their doctrine but also by their style
of preaching—a plain, homely style in which learning was subdued
to the necessity of making an impression on the mind of the ordinary
man and woman. Henry Smith, who became lecturer at St. Clement
Danes in 1587, said the aim should be 'to preach plainly and per-
spicuously, that the simplest man may understand what is taught, as
if he did hear his name'. This 'spiritual' preaching, as it was called,
was in strong contrast to the 'witty' preaching of the conservative
clergy, who delighted in learned allusions and intricate verbal con-
ceits. The parallel with the preaching of the medieval friars springs
at once to mind, and Haller does not hesitate to compare the
Puritan lecturers with the mendicant preachers.[1]

Bible Study

The Puritans were zealous in proclaiming the importance of
education, on religious grounds. Parents were urged to have their
children educated, at least in reading and writing. This, it was
pointed out, would be a great advantage to them throughout life,
but its principal end should be 'that they may read the word of God
to their comfort and instruction to salvation'. The need for study by

[1] On all this see W. Haller, *The Rise of Puritanism* (New York 1938), espec. Chs. i–ii.
A more recent and more detailed account of the Cambridge Puritans is given in H. C.
Porter, *Reformation and Reaction in Tudor Cambridge* (Cambridge 1958), Ch. x.

adults was also stressed. Some Puritan ministers undertook the instruction of adults in their spare time, and one minister is said to have
taught forty people over forty years of age to read.[1] This is the
earliest example known to me of formal adult education under
religious auspices.

We also have evidence of groups of lay people meeting on their
own initiative for the study and exposition of the Bible. From the
parishes of Balsham and Streethall, on the borders of Cambridge-
shire and Essex, for example, comes the story of a group of humble
people who, about the year 1574, resolved to give up the drinking,
cards, and other vain pastimes in which they had customarily spent
their holidays and leisure hours, in order 'to bestow the time in
soberly and godly Reading the Scriptures'.[2] These people, when
their meetings were suppressed, claimed to be loyal to the Church,
but most such groups belonged to one or other of the separatist sects,
precursors of the later Nonconformists. Concerning the activities of
these sects we are not particularly well-informed, but the character
of their secret conventicles is illustrated by the story of a group of
Barrowists (forerunners of the Independents) who for some years
prior to 1592 used to meet every Sunday on the outskirts of London:

In the summer time they meet together in the fields a mile or more
about London. There they sit down upon a bank and divers of them
expound out of the Bible . . . In the winter time they assemble themselves
by 5 of the clock in the morning to that house where they make their conventicle, for that Sabbath day men and women together there they
continue in their kind of prayer and exposition of Scriptures all that day.[3]

It is in activities of this kind, rather than in the official canons of
the Church, that we must look for the growing points of religious
adult education at this period. In the popular enthusiasm for the
English Bible, in the crowded audiences at the prophesyings, and in
the meetings for Bible study both inside and outside the Church, we
see the development of that movement towards a working-class
culture based on the Bible, which had its origins in the Bible-reading
of the Lollards, and was to remain until the nineteenth century a
characteristic feature of English life.

'The Free Libertye of the Mind'

It was not, however, only in the sphere of religious adult education
that new ideas were stirring. Out of the new questing spirit of the

[1] M. M. Knappen, *Tudor Puritanism* (Chicago 1939), pp. 468–9.
[2] J. Strype, *Life and Acts of Matthew Parker, Archbishop of Canterbury* (1711), p. 473.
[3] C. Burrage, *Early English Dissenters* (Cambridge 1912), Vol. II, p. 27. I have modern-
ised the spelling.

Renaissance there was born in this century a wider and more generous concept of adult education, a concept that was finely expressed, almost at the outset of the period, in Sir Thomas More's *Utopia*:

in the institution of that weale publique, this ende is onelye and chiefely pretended and mynded, that what time maye possibly be spared from the necessarye occupations and affayres of the commen wealth, all that the citizeins shoulde withdrawe from the bodely service to the free libertye of the minde, and garnisshinge of the same. For herein they suppose the felicitye of this liffe to consiste.

Only a few people in More's ideal commonwealth are brought up to the learned professions, but all receive instruction in their youth, and most people, 'bothe men and women, throughe oute all their whole lyffe doo bestowe in learninge those spare houres, which we sayde they have vacante from bodelye laboures'.

For it is a solempne custome there, to have lectures daylye early in the morning, where to be present they onely be constrained that be namelye chosen and appoynted to learninge. Howbeit a greate multitude of every sort of people, both men and women go to heare lectures, some one and some an other, as everye mans nature is inclined. Yet, this notwithstanding, if any man had rather bestowe this time upon his owne occupation, (as it chaunceth in manye, whose mindes rise not in the contemplation of any science liberall) he is not letted, nor prohibited, but is also praysed and commended, as profitable to the common wealthe.[1]

At the time of writing this must have seemed little more than an academic fancy, but before the century was out a beginning had been made in the task of translating it into reality.

Foster Watson has shown[2] that it was among the upper and upper middle classes, i.e., among the nobility, gentry, merchants and well-to-do tradesmen, that the impact of Renaissance ideals in education first made itself felt. This was because the education of these groups was not limited by the traditional curriculum of the grammar schools and universities (even where they attended these institutions). As a general rule people in these classes had the advantages of private tuition, in which there was much more scope for experiment; and the young men might also enjoy the broadening influence of foreign travel, and perhaps spend a year or two at the Inns of Court,

---

[1] The quotations are from the second English edition of 1556, ed. J. R. Lumby (Cambridge 1879), pp. 80, 85, 102. H. P. Smith, 'Adult Education in England—an Introductory Chapter', in *Rewley House Papers*, Vol. III, No. IV (1955–6), has some interesting reflections on More's concept of adult education.

[2] *The Beginning of the Teaching of Modern Subjects in England* (1909), Introduction.

where the study of the law and its associated subjects of history and government could be undertaken in more congenial company and in a more liberal atmosphere than at the universities.[1]

The old medieval ideal of training in chivalry, which had so long governed the education of the nobility and gentry, was giving place, by the middle of the sixteenth century, to the new humanist ideal of the virtuous and cultivated gentleman, skilled in the arts of government, in languages ancient and modern, in sciences such as geometry, astronomy and physic, and in music and physical exercises. Such was the ideal set forth in such works as Sir Thomas Elyot's *The Governor* (1531), Castiglione's *The Courtier* (the greatest of the Italian courtesy books, translated in 1561), and in the abortive scheme devised by the explorer Sir Humphrey Gilbert (*c.* 1570) for an Academy for the education of the sons of the nobility and gentry. It was an ideal that found its embodiment chiefly in the upper classes, in men such as Gilbert, Raleigh, Essex, and above all Sir Philip Sidney, but it was not without its reflections, also, in humbler spheres.

The Beginnings of Secular Adult Education

It was in the capital, and not in the university towns, that the centre of the new intellectual life was to be found, and here towards the close of the Tudor period there arose a demand for new forms of public education, especially in scientific subjects, in which the grammar schools and universities were slow to adapt themselves to new discoveries and new needs. Professor E. G. R. Taylor has demonstrated, for example, how developments in geographical discovery and in the art of warfare created, during the second half of the sixteenth century, a need for instruction in mathematics and astronomy, with particular reference to the practical applications of these subjects in the fields of navigation, surveying, horology, and gunnery; and how this need was met, first by the provision of new textbooks, and at a later date by the organisation of regular courses of instruction.[2]

Such instruction was usually given on a private basis by mathematical practitioners—instrument-makers and the like—but occasionally schoolmasters made provision for adults as well as children

---

[1] The Inns of Court in London, originating in the late thirteenth century as centres for the study of the law, were at this period often used as finishing schools for the sons of the gentry, even if they had no intention of entering the legal profession. In addition to the law, the students had the opportunity to learn 'singing and all kinds of music, dancing and such other accomplishments and diversions . . . as are suitable to their quality'.

[2] E. G. R. Taylor, *The Mathematical Practitioners of Tudor and Stuart England* (Cambridge 1954).

in their schools. Thus in 1562 a London arithmetic school teacher advertised:

Such as are desirous, eyther themselves to learn or to have theyr children or servants instructed in any of these Artes and Faculties heere under named: It may please them to repayre into the house of Humphrey Baker, dwelling on the North side of the Royall Exchange, next adjoyning to the signe of the shippe . . .[1]

In 1588 we have an interesting example of a course of public lectures in mathematics delivered in London by Dr. Thomas Hood, a Cambridge graduate, under the patronage of the City authorities. These lectures were a consequence of the alarm caused by the threat of the Spanish Armada, and they were intended in the first instance for the captains of the London train-bands, but in practice they appealed to a much wider audience—'eager artisans, soldiers, and seamen, who had had little scholarly training but were inflamed with a passionate desire for useful knowledge'.[2] The lectures continued for at least four years, and Hood's surviving textbooks show that they dealt with the fundamental principles of arithmetic, geometry, and astronomy and their practical applications.[3] In this experiment we see one of the first steps towards the association of scientific scholarship with the hitherto despised 'mechanic arts' of the practical craftsman—an association which, gathering strength during the seventeenth century, was to lead to notable advances both in pure science and in technical education.[4]

In medicine the study of anatomy and physiology was revolutionised by the researches of Vesalius and Servetus; and in 1582 we find Lord Lumley collaborating with Dr. Richard Caldwell, a former President of the Royal College of Physicians, in the establishment in the College of a twice-weekly public lecture on surgery, for which Dr. Richard Forster, in 1584, was the first lecturer.

These lectures were designed 'for the great commoditie of those which shall give and incline themselves to be diligent hearers for the

[1] Watson, *Teaching of Modern Subjects*, p. 321.
[2] F. R. Johnson, *Astronomical Thought in Renaissance England* (Baltimore 1937), p. 200.
[3] J. Stow, *Survey of London* (1598, 6th edn. ed. J. Strype, 1754), Vol. I, p. 129. A fuller and more correct account is given by Johnson in the work just cited, pp. 198–205, and in an article by the same author, 'Thomas Hood's Inaugural Address as Mathematical Lecturer to the City of London (1588)', in *Journal of the History of Ideas*, Vol. III (1942), pp. 94–106. See also D. W. Waters, *Art of Navigation in England in Elizabethan and Early Stuart Times* (1958), pp. 185–90, 243. The lead in arranging the course was taken by Thomas Smythe, afterwards first Governor of the East India Company, and it was in Smythe's house in Gracechurch Street that the fine opening lecture reprinted by Johnson was given.
[4] See Johnson's introduction to Hood's inaugural lecture, *loc. cit.*, and for the seventeenth-century movement below, Ch. 4.

obteining of knowledge in surgerie, as whether he be learned or unlearned that shall become an auditor or hearer of the lecture, he may find himself not to repent the time so imploied'. They were given in the mornings, for three-quarters of an hour in Latin and for the remaining quarter in English, and the original plan was for a six-year course, with a dissection each winter 'for five daies together, as well before as after dinner; if the bodies may so last without annoie'.[1]

Occasionally we find notices of adult instruction in other subjects. Michael Angelo Florio, who became pastor of the Italian Protestant Church in London in 1550, is said to have taught Italian; his son John Florio taught Italian and other modern languages while a student at Oxford in the 1580s; and Richard Hakluyt lectured on geography at Oxford about the same period.[2]

Instruction in such subjects as these clearly appealed to a variety of motives. There was the vocational motive, which was no doubt the dominant one in the craftsman or apprentice who attended Baker's arithmetic school; there was the motive of civic service, which must have been present at least at the outset of Hood's mathematics course; and there was the motive of sheer intellectual curiosity. This last motive should not be underestimated, even in such a subject as medicine, for the field of knowledge was still sufficiently manageable, and the tastes of the educated man sufficiently catholic, for people to interest themselves in fields now regarded as technical specialisms.

A good example is afforded by John, Lord Lumley, just mentioned. Prominent in the political life of the period (he was imprisoned for over a year for his pro-Catholic sympathies) Lumley was a man of wide intellectual interests. He was a member of the original Society of Antiquaries, was a painter and a patron of painters, formed a fine collection of portraits, and gathered a library of more than 3,000 volumes (including numerous works on scientific subjects) which was afterwards acquired by James I for Henry, Prince of Wales, and so ultimately found its way to the British Museum. Besides endowing the lectureship in surgery already referred to, he took a prominent part in the establishment of Hood's mathematical lectures.[3]

For another example we may cite Sir Henry Billingsley, Sheriff of London in 1584 and Lord Mayor in 1596. Billingsley studied at both

---

[1] R. Holinshed, *Chronicles of England* (1577, rev. edn. 1807–8, Vol. IV, pp. 496–9). The original plan proved too ambitious, and by the time William Harvey took over the Lumleian lectureship in 1615 the lectures had been reduced to three days in each year. It was at these lectures that Harvey announced his discovery of the circulation of the blood.
[2] Watson, *Teaching of Modern Subjects*, pp. 101–2, 447–8.
[3] See the account by G. Goodwin in *D.N.B.*, and Stow, *Survey, loc. cit.*

Oxford and Cambridge without taking a degree, and while at Oxford acquired a knowledge of mathematics from a former Augustinian friar named Whytehead. Later he was apprenticed to a London haberdasher and in course of time became a wealthy merchant, but he maintained his early love for mathematics, provided a home in his own house for Whytehead in the latter's declining years, and produced in 1570 the first English translation of Euclid.[1]

Gresham College

This catholic attitude towards knowledge is well illustrated by the foundation, near the close of the century, of Gresham College. Sir Thomas Gresham, one of the great merchant princes of Elizabeth's reign, was a wealthy London mercer who was knighted by the Queen for his services as her financial agent. He became famous during his lifetime as the founder of the Royal Exchange, and on his death in 1579 bequeathed funds to the Mercers' Company and the Corporation of London for the establishment of lectureships in divinity, law, physic, astronomy, geometry, rhetoric and music. This intention was carried into effect in 1597, after the death of Gresham's widow, when his former house in Bishopsgate Street was converted into a college with seven resident professors.

In spite of superficial resemblances, and in spite of the fact that the advice of Oxford and Cambridge was sought on the appointment of the original professors, this was not an attempt to establish a third university. According to the regulations drawn up in 1597, the College was intended 'for the common benefit of the people of this city', and it was anticipated that the auditors would be 'merchants and other citizens', 'such citizens and others, as have small knowledge of the Latin tongue'. The subject and methods of treatment were prescribed in some detail and were adapted to this type of audience.

The professors (who received the handsome stipend of £50 a year) lectured weekly during term time, each lecture being customarily delivered in Latin in the morning, for the benefit chiefly of foreign visitors, and then repeated in English in the afternoon. An exception was, however, made in favour of Dr. Bull, the first professor of music, who knew no Latin and was therefore permitted to lecture entirely in English.[2]

The purpose of the divinity lectures, we are told, was 'that the

---

[1] See the account by Sir Sidney Lee in *D.N.B.*, and the Introduction to *The Lumley Library: the Catalogue of 1609*, ed. S. Jayne and F. R. Johnson (British Museum 1958).
[2] This was John Bull, the famous organist and composer.

common people be well grounded in the chief points of the Christian religion'. They were accordingly to deal with 'the chief points of our Christian faith, especially those wherein the church of England differs from the common adversaries the papists, and other sectaries'.

The law lectures were to deal exclusively with civil law, and it was directed that they 'be not read after the manner of the university; but that the reader cull out such titles and heads of law, that may best serve to the good liking and capacity of the said auditory, and are more usual in common practice'.

In physic the wish was expressed that the reader should follow the method of the French physician Fernel, 'by reading first physiologie, then pathologie, and lastly therapeutice; whereby the body of the said art may be better imprinted by good method in the studious auditors, rather than be disjointed and delivered out of order by exposition of some part of Galen or Hippocrates' (the method still followed, at this time, in the English universities).

No specific directions were given concerning the lectures on rhetoric, but geometry was to include some treatment of arithmetic; astronomy was to be directed especially to the needs of mariners, and to include geography and the art of navigation; and in music the first part of each hour was to be devoted to theory, and the second to 'the practique by concent of voice or of instruments'.

The lectures were, we are told, 'both constantly read and well attended'. They quickly established themselves as a valued feature of the life of the capital, and we shall see that they played an important part in the developments of the seventeenth century.[1]

It will be seen that the mercers and city aldermen had clearly in mind the practical value of some of the courses to the merchants and craftsmen of London, and from this point of view Gresham College has its place in the early development of modern technical and professional education; but bearing in mind the range of subjects offered, and the type of audience aimed at, we must also regard it as the first major enterprise in the field which it is now customary to call adult education.

---

[1] The quotations in this account are from J. Ward, *The Lives of the Professors of Gresham College* (1740), which is prefaced by accounts of the history of the College and of Gresham's life. See also Stow, *Survey of London*, ed. Strype, Vol. I, pp. 129–42; J. W. Burgon, *Life and Times of Sir Thomas Gresham* (1839). The original college continued in existence till 1768, when on the ground of the expense involved the trustees secured permission to pull it down and dispose of the site. For many years the lectures were relegated to a room in the Royal Exchange, but a new college was built in 1843, and the present Gresham College, on the same site, in 1913. The lectures are still carried on, but are now limited to twelve per session.

The Society of Antiquaries

The Society of Antiquaries mentioned above is also worthy of passing comment, as providing our earliest precedent, at least in the secular sphere, for a type of activity which was to play an important role in English cultural development, the voluntary society for the pursuit of learning in a more or less defined sphere. The Society was founded about 1586 (the year of the publication of William Camden's *Britannia*) and was concerned less with antiquities, in the modern sense of material objects, than with the origins and history of families and institutions. John Spelman afterwards gave the following account of its inauguration:

About forty two Years since, divers Gentlemen in London, studious of Antiquities, fram'd themselves into a College or Society of Antiquaries, appointing to meet every Friday weekly in the Term, at a Place agreed of, and for Learning sake to confer upon some Questions in that Faculty, and to sup together. The Place, after a Meeting or two, became certain at Darby-house, where the Herald's Office is kept: and two Questions were propounded at every Meeting, to be handled at the next that followed; so that every Man had a Sennight's respite to advise upon them, and then to deliver his Opinion. That which seem'd most material, was by one of the Company (chosen for the purpose) to be enter'd in a Book; that so it might remain unto Posterity. The Society increased daily; many Persons of great Worth, as well noble as other learned, joining themselves unto it.

The Society lasted only until about 1608. A half-hearted attempt at revival in 1614 was frustrated by the opposition of James I, who feared lest the members should meddle with affairs of state, and the present Society dates only from 1707. The continuous history of such learned societies, and all their more popular offspring in the educational field, must thus be reckoned not from the Society of Antiquaries but from the Royal Society, whose origins will be recounted in the next chapter.[1]

Printed Texts

Public lectures of the type provided in London were not, as far as is known, available in any provincial centre—the examples recorded above from Oxford, limited in extent and no doubt for a limited clientèle, can hardly be regarded as an exception. It would, however, be a mistake to suppose that for this reason adult education

[1] The history of the Elizabethan Society of Antiquaries is conveniently summarised in J. Evans, *A History of the Society of Antiquaries* (Oxford 1956), Ch. i, from which the above quotation is taken. R. J. Schoeck, in *Notes and Queries*, N.S., Vol. I (Oct. 1954), pp. 417–21, points out that the members were predominantly lawyers.

was non-existent, for from the early sixteenth century onwards we have to take account of the powerful and pervasive influence of the printing-press.

It is an influence which can hardly be overrated. In the centuries that have passed since the invention of printing, books have constantly been the means by which the rich man has widened and deepened his knowledge, and the poor man has taken the first faltering steps towards self-improvement; they have facilitated the processes of learning, and rendered it more enduring by multiplying the opportunities for its exercise. This is still so to-day. But in the first century of the printed word, when other facilities for adult education were few, the supply of books was supremely important.

The output of printed works, a mere trickle at the close of the fifteenth century, increased rapidly in quantity and variety as the sixteenth century progressed, in spite of printing monopolies and other vexatious restrictions, and the literate Elizabethan could take his choice among chronicles and histories, travel-books, romances, jest-books, ballads, herbals, books on etiquette, popular guides to medicine, natural history, and astronomy, and devotional works of many kinds. Editions were commonly small, and the price of bound books was high, so that only the well-to-do could form substantial libraries, but an unbound Shakespeare play might be had for 6d., Spenser's *Shephearde's Calendar* for 1s., and Lyly's *Euphues* for 2s., so that even a person of quite modest means could hope to accumulate a few volumes.

A significant development of the late Tudor period is the appearance in increasing numbers of manuals and educational works in English, many of which were obviously intended for working-class readers. Edmund Coote's *Englische Scholemaister* (1596) was designed not only for the teacher, but also for 'the unskilfull, which desire to make use of it, for their owne private benefit', and must be reckoned as one of the earliest manuals for self-education. It continued to be reprinted for nearly a century, and ran through more than forty editions. There were also books on social improvement, such as Walter Darell's *Short Discourse of the Life of Servingmen* (1578); collections of model letters, such as William Fulwood's *Enimie of Idleness* (1568); and a variety of elementary technical treatises.

Robert Recorde published four elementary textbooks on mathematics between 1542 and 1557; Leonard Digges, about the same time, wrote works on geometry and astronomy for the craftsman; and his son Thomas followed in his footsteps. William Bourne, himself a man of humble origin, wrote a manual of seamanship for sailors

(1574) and a guide for the 'simple and unlearned' to the practical applications of geometry (1575). John Blagrave's *Mathematicall Jewell* (a description of an astrolabe, published in 1585) contains in its dedication to Lord Burghley a passage which anticipates in a remarkable fashion the kind of thing that was to be said about working-class education in the days of the mechanics' institutes, for he speaks of opening the arts mathematical 'unto everie ingenious practiser . . . whence many inventions yet unthought of may spring from the common sort of handicraftmen and workmen'.[1]

The importance of works of this kind as an instrument of popular education is commented on by an American scholar, who remarks: 'Thanks in part to convenient handbooks, information, of a sort, became common property. No longer was learning a monopoly of clerk and aristocrat.[2]

Literacy in the Elizabethan Age

How many Elizabethans were in fact literate is a question that admits of no precise answer. We can safely say that the proportion was much higher than used to be thought, but any generalisation as to the extent of literacy must be qualified by the recognition of social and regional differences. Literacy was greater among the upper classes than among the lower, among men than among women; London was more literate than the provinces, the towns than the countryside, the South of England than the North; and England as a whole was better educated than Wales or Scotland. In England, in spite of the temporary setback caused by the dissolution of the chantries, and the closure of many of the schools attached to them, under the acts of 1545 and 1547, facilities for education were fairly plentiful. The grammar schools, which offered a strictly classical education, numbered between three and four hundred by the end of the Tudor period, and were patronised especially by the middle classes. There were also numerous schools—A.B.C. schools, petty schools, writing schools, and the like—offering an elementary or non-classical education. Some of these were town or village schools, conducted by the parson, or the parish clerk, or a paid schoolmaster; many more, probably, were private venture schools, often conducted as a side-line by people engaged in some other occupation.

---

[1] Taylor, *Mathematical Practitioners*, pp. 41–2, where it is pointed out that this dedication shows the influence of the *Mathematicall Preface* written by John Dee for Billingsley's translation of Euclid (1570).

[2] L. B. Wright, *Middle-Class Culture in Elizabethan England* (N. Carolina Univ. P. 1953), p. 169. For handbooks of improvement generally see Ch. v of this work; for Recorde and Bourne see also Taylor, *op. cit.*, pp. 33, 167. W. H. G. Armytage, *Civic Universities* (1955), Ch. iv, surveys intellectual and educational developments during this period.

Thus Coote's *Englische Scholemaister*, referred to above, is stated in the preface to be intended for 'such men and women of trade as Taylors, Weavers, Shoppekeepers, Seamsters and such others as have undertaken the charge of teaching others'.[1] Such schools cannot have been very efficient, but at least they provided a chance for the children of the poor to acquire the rudiments of letters.

We can say with some confidence that the ability to read, write, and keep accounts was widespread down to the level of the tradesman and the craftsman in the towns and the yeoman farmer in the country. The dependants of the upper and middle classes—journeymen, apprentices, serving-men and the like, shared to a greater or lesser degree in these accomplishments, but beyond their circle we are in the realm of conjecture. A good many humble people may have been literate in the sense of being able to read, sufficiently at any rate to spell out a placard or a ballad—but Professor Altick is probably right in concluding, in a recent study of the subject, that reading cannot have had more than the most incidental place in the life of the masses.[2]

Concerning Wales and Scotland it is not possible to be so precise. In the towns there were grammar schools, and in one way or another provision was made for more elementary teaching. There were also some village schools, but the system of parish schools which had been adumbrated by Knox, and was one day to be the glory of rural Scotland, had not yet come into existence, and it is difficult to believe that either here or in rural Wales the people enjoyed, or indeed felt the need of, any substantial measure of literacy.

[1] J. W. Adamson, 'The Illiterate Anglo-Saxon' (Cambridge 1946), p. 56.
[2] R. D. Altick, The English Common Reader (Chicago Univ. P. 1957), p. 29. The novels of industrial life by Thomas Deloney, silk-weaver, in 1597–1600, provide some interesting sidelights on working-class literacy. In The Gentle Craft, which deals with shoemaking, we read of an apprentice whose love for his mistress plays havoc with his arithmetic. In Thomas of Reading, on the other hand, we have the story of the Earl of Shrewsbury's daughter who, fallen into distress, seeks employment as a maidservant. Meeting two other maids at Gloucester fair, she mentions that she is able to read and write. 'Good Lord (quoth they) are you bookish? we did never heare of a Maide before that could reade and write.' See Works of Thomas Deloney, ed. F. O. Mann (Oxford 1912), pp. 194, 257.

3

The Seventeenth Century

THE IMPACT OF PURITANISM

Religious Instruction before the Civil War

By the close of the Tudor period the strands that made up the emerging picture of adult education were becoming more numerous and more complex. First there was religious education, still dominantly medieval in character, but gradually assuming fresh forms under the impact of Protestantism. We have seen also the beginnings of secular adult education through public teaching and lecturing—an education aimed chiefly at the upper and middle classes, partly cultural, partly vocational, and closely linked with the growing interest in science. And alongside both these movements we have noted the powerful influence of the printing press, opening up new horizons of knowledge and ideas, both religious and secular, to the whole range of literate society.

In the sphere of religious adult education the outstanding feature of the early Stuart period is the continued development of preaching lectureships of the kind already described in the last chapter. This was essentially a Puritan activity, and a passage in the *Autobiography* of Samuel Clarke (noted as the biographer of the Puritan Saints) shows how closely the activities of these preachers were related, at times, to the forbidden prophesyings of Elizabeth's reign—with the difference that a more prominent part was taken by the laity. In his earlier years Clarke was a preacher in Cheshire, and he tells how the godly came to hear him from six or seven miles around, 'Young and Old, Men and Women, Wet and Dry, Summer and Winter, to their very great pains and labour'; and how every three weeks there was a general conference of the faithful at some rich man's house.

In the Morning when they first met, the Master of the Family began with Prayer, then was the question to be conferred of read, and the younger Christians first gave their answers, together with their proofs of Scripture for them; and then the more experienced Christians gathered up the other answers which were omitted by the former; and thus they continued until Dinner time, when having good provision made for them by the Master of the Family, they dined together with much cheerfulness; after Dinner, having sung a Psalm, they returned to their conference upon the other questions (which were three in all) till towards Evening; at which time, as the Master of the Family began, so he concluded with Prayer, and I gave them three new questions against their next Meeting.[1]

Haller has stressed the powerful effect of such teaching on the popular mind:

The people were brought together. They learned to read, to use a book, to exchange ideas and experiences, to confer intellectually after their own fashion upon common problems, to partake of the exhilaration of discussion and self-expression.[2]

A group of twelve London Puritans—four clergymen, four lawyers, and four merchants—formed themselves in 1625 into a body of trustees to buy up ecclesiastical properties which had fallen into lay hands, and use them 'for the maintenance and relief of godly, faithful, and painful ministers of the word of God'. William Laud, who became Bishop of London in 1628 and Archbishop of Canterbury in 1633, saw in these developments a dangerous attempt to subvert the Church from within, and brought his powerful influence to bear to suppress the lectureships or at least bring them under control. In 1629 steps were taken to ensure that only orthodox clergy should be appointed to such posts, and sermons on Sunday afternoons (a favourite time for the lectures) were forbidden in favour of catechising. In 1632–3 the operations of the London Puritan group were declared illegal, and the properties they had acquired were confiscated.[3]

In many parts of the country, however, the faithful evidently continued to meet, and as late as 1638 we find Richard Montagu, Bishop of Norwich, and William Piers, Bishop of Bath and Wells, still campaigning against Puritan lecturers. Montagu, in his visitation articles refers to the 'running' or itinerant lecturers,

perchance beneficed, but rotten at the roote, who appoint upon such a day to meet at such a Church, most an end in some County towne or village, and then after Sermon, and dinner at some house of their disciples, [the auditors] repeate, censure, and explaine the Sermon, discourse

---

[1] S. Clarke, *Lives of Sundry Eminent Persons* (1683), pp. 4–22, quoted by Haller, *Rise of Puritanism*, p. 63.
[2] Haller, *ibid.*
[3] On this episode see H. R. Trevor Roper, *Archbishop Laud* (1940), pp. 104–9; I. M. Calder, 'A Seventeenth Century Attempt to Purify the Anglican Church', in *American Historical Review*, Vol. LIII (1947–8), pp. 760–75; the Introduction to the same author's *Activities of the Puritan Faction of the Church of England, 1625–33* (1957); D. A. Williams, 'Puritanism in the City Government, 1610–1640', in *Guildhall Miscellany*, No. 4 (Feb. 1955), pp. 3–8; and C. Hill, *Economic Problems of the Church* (Oxford 1956), Ch. xi.

of points proposed at their last meeting, by the head of that Classe or Assembly, even to the promoting of their owne fancies, and derogation from the Doctrine and Discipline of the Church . . . and appoint to meet next, at such a Church in like sort, to like purpose: such I found in Sussex at my comming thither.[1]

Many of the Puritans were driven by the Laudian persecution out of the Church of England into the ranks of Nonconformity. Throughout the 'thirties the Presbyterians, Independents, Baptists, and other Nonconformist sects rapidly gathered strength, and the influence of the older generation of preachers was reinforced or supplanted by a new army of working-class preachers who all too often despised the worldly learning they did not themselves possess. These were the heroes of the conventicle and the tub, earnest and worthy men very often, but often also ignorant and fanatical. 'In stead of Orthodoxe Divines' complained Richard Carter in 1640, 'they set up all Kinde of Mechanicks, as Shooe-makers, Coblers, Taylers, and Botchers: Glovers, who preach of nothing but Mag-pies and Crows, Boxe-Makers, and Button-Makers, Coach-men, and Felt-makers, and Bottle-Ale-sellers'.[2]

'A Perpetual Sabbath'

With the opening of the Long Parliament in November 1640 the preachers came into their own again, and the sects began to emerge from their secret conventicles and organise themselves openly in defiance of the law. Religion now became intertwined with political issues as the Puritans joined hands with the Parliament party in a common opposition to King and bishops, and in August 1642 the struggle issued in civil war.

For a time, from 1643 onwards, political expediency led to an alliance with the Scottish Presbyterians, and an ineffectual attempt to impose on England a Presbyterian form of worship and church government. The Directory for Public Worship, adopted in 1645, was intended to replace alike the English Book of Common Prayer and the Scottish Book of Common Order. It made, as might be expected, generous provision for public preaching, and also ordained that

Besides public reading of the Scriptures, every person that can read is to be exhorted to read the Scriptures privately (and all others that cannot read, if not disabled by age, or otherwise, are likewise to be exhorted to learn to read), and to have a Bible.[3]

[1] *Articles of Enquiry and Direction for the Diocese of Norwich . . . 1638* (1638), Titulus 4.
[2] Quoted by Haller, *op. cit.*, p. 263, from *The Schismatick Stigmatized*.
[3] D. Neal, *History of the Puritans* (1732–8, ed. J. Toulmin, 1837), Vol. III, p. 527.

This passage is of interest, not because there was at this time anything uncommon in Bible-reading by lay people, but because it is, as far as I know, the first specific reference in a Church ordinance to the need for the instruction of adults in reading. There is a similar reference in connection with the singing of psalms.[1]

The period from 1641 to the Restoration of 1660 was the heyday of sectarianism. In the later years especially, when the power of the Church had been broken and no authoritative system had been put in its place, a score of new sects sprang up to dispute the allegiance of the people. For the preachers it was like a perpetual Sabbath, for the public appetite for sermons seemed insatiable. In London, at the outbreak of the Civil War, there were according to Neal 'lectures and sermons every day of the week in one church or another, which were well attended, and with great appearance of zeal and devotion'.[2] In the Parliamentary armies there was the same enthusiasm. Sir Charles Firth quotes from the narrative of one Nehemiah Wharton, a sergeant in Essex's army in 1642:

Friday morning worthy Obadiah Sedgwick gave us a worthy sermon . . . Saturday morning, John Sedgwick gave us a famous sermon . . . Sabbath morning, Mr Marshall, that worthy champion of Christ, preached to us; in the afternoon Mr. Ash . . .[3]

Among the Scots, with their natural taste for theological discourse, this zeal for the giving and receiving of religious instruction was carried at this time to extravagant lengths. During the later Cromwellian period a group known as the Protesters, or Remonstrants, made the communion service the occasion for a positive orgy of preaching, the services extending over three or four days, with some thirty or forty sermons delivered to two or three separate congregations.[4]

In dealing with the Scotland of this period, however, it is misleading to single out one element only in religious instruction. The Scottish ministers, in this high noon of the Presbyterian power, wielded a theocratic authority that made its influence felt in every aspect of life, civil and ecclesiastical, public and private. Preaching, important as it was, was only part of a whole complex of religious

[1] Op. cit., Vol. III, p. 545.
[2] Op. cit., Vol. II, p. 156.
[3] C. H. Firth, Cromwell's Army (1902, 2nd edn. 1912), p. 314.
[4] R. H. Story (ed.), The Church of Scotland, Past and Present (1890), Vol. II, p. 531. As a sequel to negotiations between the Scots and Charles I in 1647, the Scottish clergy divided into two hostile groups, called respectively the Protesters (or Remonstrants) and the Resolutioners.

instruction and discipline—sermons, lectures, services, school-teaching, home visiting and catechising, meetings of the kirk session, and so forth—that held in its iron grip child and adult alike. The same was true of some of the more Puritan parts of England, but to a much lesser extent, for here the very multiplication of the sects operated to mitigate the tyranny of any one of them.

The Development of Popular Education

Both during the Anglican period of the early seventeenth century, and under the Puritan régime, the association of religion with education remained very close. The canons of 1604 carried forward into the Church of England the medieval provision that every schoolmaster must be licensed by the bishop of the diocese, and although the machinery of control inevitably weakened when episcopacy was abolished, the frequent coupling of ministers and schoolmasters in acts and ordinances reveals that the government was just as determined to maintain orthodoxy in the schools as in the churches.

Throughout this period the provision for popular education continued to increase: the number of new schools endowed between 1601 and 1651 (186) exceeded by one the total of new foundations during the whole of the previous century, and although the great period of endowed elementary schools was still to come there are many instances of non-classical schools intended either to prepare for the grammar schools or to provide elementary instruction for boys and girls whose parents did not wish them to have a classical education. De Montmorency has traced, in the Report presented to Parliament by the Charity Commissioners in 1842, 72 non-classical endowed schools founded before 1660 which received additional endowments between 1660 and 1730, and there must have been many others which did not happen to figure in the records in this way.

The revolutionary period was, however, one of particular zeal in the cause of education, a zeal which is to be observed both among ordinary people and in the policy of the government. In general schoolmasters were dealt with by the government on the same footing as the clergy, and under the same legislation: 'scandalous and malignant clergy and schoolmasters', i.e. those who were disaffected to the régime, were ruthlessly removed, and 'godly and able ministers and schoolmasters' were appointed in their places. Ecclesiastical revenues were also used to found new schools, especially in Wales, where over 60 free schools (mostly grammar schools) were established under the Propagation Act of 1650.[1] The government also took advantage of certain acts of Elizabeth's reign, concerning the misuse of charities, to reorganise a number of old foundations (including Rugby), and to appropriate unattached charities for the establishment of new schools.[2]

In Scotland, too, some progress was being made. The burgh schools continued to flourish, and some burghs permitted or even encouraged private adventure schools. The system of elementary education envisaged in the First Book of Discipline was still far from achievement, but an act of the Scottish Privy Council in 1616, and acts of Parliament of 1633 and 1646, successively attempted to establish the principle of a school in every parish, supported by the parishioners, and in some parts of the country at least a considerable number of new schools were founded. In the Highlands, of course, with their scattered and poverty-stricken population, the difficulties in the way of establishing schools were enormous, and an order of the Protector in 1658 appropriating £1,200 from the Church revenues for educational development in the Highlands came too late to be effective.[3]

Thus in general, at this period, the picture is one of increasing facilities for school education and, as far as we can judge, an increasing measure of literacy among the population. There were, of course, still plenty of illiterates among the lower orders, especially in the countryside, but when we find Parliament, in 1651, agreeing to send to the soldiers of Cromwell's army in Ireland 'four thousand Bibles, or to every six men one . . . to reade in their tents or quarters',[4] and

---

[1] Of these schools only that at Cardigan survived the Restoration.

[2] The fullest account of educational developments during this period is in W. A. L. Vincent, *The State and School Education, 1640–1660* (1950). See also F. Watson 'The State and Education during the Commonwealth', in *English Historical Review*, Vol. XV (1900), pp. 58–72; J. E. G. de Montmorency, *State Intervention in English Education* (Cambridge 1902), pp. 90–104; J. W. Adamson, *Pioneers of Modern Education* (Cambridge 1921), pp. 85–93, 97–100; M. James, *Social Problems and Policy during the Puritan Revolution, 1640–1660* (1930), pp. 314–23; and for the Welsh schools T. Richards, *A History of the Puritan Movement in Wales* (1920), Ch. xv, and *Religious Development in Wales* (1923), Part I, Ch. iv. D. Mathew, *Social Structure in Caroline England* (Oxford 1948), pp. 61 sqq., has interesting information on educational opportunities for the poor in the earlier part of the century.

[3] J. Edgar, *History of Early Scottish Education* (Edinburgh 1893), pp. 326–7; A. Morgan, *Rise and Progress of Scottish Education* (Edinburgh 1927), Chs. iv–v; De Montmorency, *op. cit.*, pp. 117–21; James, *op. cit.*, p. 323; H. M. Knox, *Two Hundred and Fifty Years of Scottish Education* (Edinburgh 1953), pp. 3–5; and the note by J. M. Beale in G. Donaldson (ed.), *Common Errors in Scottish History* (Historical Association 1956), pp. 17–18. Although the present tendency is to think that more substantial progress was made in this century than was once believed, we may safely ignore the pious but over-enthusiastic claim of a contemporary Presbyterian witness, Rev. James Kirkton, that by 1660 'every paroch hade a minister, every village hade a school, every family almost hade a Bible; yea, in most of the country all the children of age could read the Scriptures'—quoted H. G. Graham, *The Social Life of Scotland in the Eighteenth Century* (1899, 3rd edn. 1901), p. 418 note.

[4] Firth, *Cromwell's Army*, p. 332.

when we learn that 'in several thousand petitions or receipts of Cromwell's army, usually signed by the men but sometimes by their wives, the vast majority, even of the non-commissioned officers and men, could sign their names; and, in the relatively few documents containing the signatures of all the officers and men of regiments in Cromwell's army, perhaps four-fifths of the men signed their names'[1]—in the face of such evidence it is difficult to persist in the belief that the mass of the people at this period were completely illiterate.[2]

It may, of course, be objected that mere ability to scrawl a signature is a very low measure of literacy, but at least it is something, and it seems reasonable to infer that those who could write, even a little, could also read a little, especially as opportunities for reading were now being multiplied on every hand.[3] The period of the Civil War, especially, saw a great spate of controversial literature, both religious and political. George Thomason, a London bookseller, who at the opening of the Long Parliament set himself to collect at least one copy of everything that appeared from the London press, collected in twenty years close on 15,000 books and pamphlets, and there were others published outside London which escaped his attention.[4]

Church and Chapel

As a result of the Restoration of 1660, and the Act of Uniformity of 1662, the distinction between the Establishment and Nonconformity, between Church and Chapel, became a permanent feature of English religious and social life. To be a Nonconformist was no longer illegal, but Nonconformist clergy were driven from the Church, and Nonconformist congregations were harried and persecuted under a whole series of hostile laws, until at last the Revolution of 1688, and the accession of William of Orange, brought some relief in the form of the Toleration Act of 1689.

Among the victims of persecution in the Restoration period was the Baptist tinker and preacher John Bunyan, whose *Pilgrim's Progress*, written, it is traditionally supposed, during his imprisonment

---

[1] G. Davies, *The Early Stuarts* (Oxford 1937), p. 356 note.

[2] George Fox the Quaker, addressing a field meeting at Leominster in 1657, was able when his views were challenged to call on the people to take out their Bibles and turn up the relevant passage—W. Armistead (ed.), *Journal of George Fox* (1852), Vol. I, p. 298.

[3] See D. Bush, *English Literature in the Earlier Seventeenth Century* (Oxford 1945), pp. 26–7, for figures regarding the increase in the number of books and printers.

[4] G. K. Fortescue (ed.), *Catalogue of the Pamphlets, Books, Newspapers and Manuscripts collected by George Thomason, 1640–1661* (1908), Vol. I, Preface, p. xxi. The collection is now in the British Museum.

at Bedford, and published in 1678, achieved an immediate and world-wide success, and remained for many generations the great classic of working-class religious literature.[1] Another Nonconformist victim, and an even more prolific writer, was Richard Baxter, who before the Restoration was pastor of the parish church at Kidderminster. In contrast to Bunyan, Baxter represents the more rational and intellectual side of Nonconformity, and his *Saint's Everlasting Rest*, which had been written in 1650, was widely known and treasured as a work of piety, though it never became so popular as the *Pilgrim's Progress*.

Both in the Church of England and in the sects the work of religious education, by preaching, lecturing, and catechising, continued as before, and indeed has continued to our own day. It was at first among the Nonconformist sects, which had suffered in the fires of persecution, that this work was taken most seriously. The main emphasis, as in the Civil War days, was on sermons and lectures, and it was not uncommon for people to take notes during the sermon, and afterwards assemble at a private house, with or without the preacher, to recapitulate and discuss the main points.[2]

In the Church of England the more serious element was represented by the Religious Societies, which began to be formed in London, under the inspiration of Dr. Anthony Horneck of the Savoy Chapel,[3] about 1678. They were mostly societies of young working men—master-craftsmen, journeymen, and apprentices—and their primary purpose was to promote strict religious observance. They bound themselves to regular attendance at church, met together regularly for religious reading and discussion, and co-operated in the relief of the poor, the promotion of charity schools and other good works. Many societies also organised weekly or monthly public lectures. There were about forty societies in and about London by the end of the century, besides many others in provincial centres, and although their subsequent history is obscure they evidently maintained their activity well into the eighteenth century.[4]

[1] H. P. Smith, 'Adult Education Emerges', in *Rewley House Papers*, Vol. III, No. V (1956–7), rightly stresses the importance of this working-class religious culture, which, firmly based on the Bible, was often hostile to humane learning.

[2] C. E. Whiting, *Studies in English Puritanism from the Restoration to the Revolution* (1931), pp. 448–9. Cf. the practice of the itinerant lecturers in the diocese of Norwich before the Civil War, above, pp. 33–4; and for meetings of this kind conducted by Baxter at Kidderminster during the Commonwealth period see *Reliquiae Baxterianae* (1696), Part I, p. 83, and F. J. Powicke, *Life of the Reverend Richard Baxter* (1924), pp. 92–3.

[3] A disciple of the German pietist leaders Spener and Francke, who were urging a more practical and devout form of Christianity.

[4] The prime authority is J. Woodward, *An Account of the Rise and Progress of the Religious Societies in the City of London* (1697, 4th edn. 1712). The most important parts are reprinted in D. E. Jenkins (ed.), *Religious Societies: Dr. Woodward's 'Account'* (Denbigh 1935). For

The love of sermons and religious lectures which Puritanism had
done so much to foster survived also in the restored Church of
England. 'Preaching is now thought to be the principal part of a
clergyman's duty'; complained one Anglican cleric, 'nay, so in-
fatuated are the people . . . that they seem to imagine that the main,
if not the whole of a parish minister's business is to preach, and that
the people have little else to do besides sit in great ease and state,
and to hear and judge how well the parson preaches'.[1] The practice
of catechising, on the other hand, was at a low ebb, and attempts to
revive it met with only modest success.

The last thirty years of the century saw a marked change in the
Anglican style of preaching. The elaborate and ornate manner which
had been inherited from the Middle Ages, and which is magnifi-
cently exemplified in the mid-seventeenth century in the sermons of
Jeremy Taylor, now was finally discarded in favour of a plain, easy,
commonsense style which owed much to the example of John Tillotson, a former Puritan who became after the Restoration successively
Dean of Canterbury, Dean of St. Paul's, and at length, albeit
reluctantly, Archbishop of Canterbury (1691-4). His sermons, in
their printed form, were long immensely popular, and established a
tradition which, in spite of the Evangelical revival, has persisted
into our own time.[2]

In Scotland as in England, the restoration of episcopacy led to a
period of harsh religious persecution, especially in the South-West,
where the Presbyterian Covenanters, assembling in the fields and on
the moors for their conventicles, had frequent and bloody clashes
with the authorities. With the Revolution of 1688 Presbyterianism
became once more the official religion, and though the Kirk never
again wielded quite the political influence of Commonwealth times,
the old religious discipline was now revived in all its tyrannical
rigour. The ministers of this period, many of them with bitter
memories of the Covenanting days, were an austere and often fanatical lot, preaching a narrow and bigoted Bible religion. Two

later accounts see J. H. Overton, *Life in the English Church (1660-1714)* (1885), pp. 207-13;
and J. W. Legg, *English Church from the Restoration to the Tractarian Movement* (1914), Ch. ix.
See also below, p. 70.

The Religious Societies tended to be confused at the time, and have often been confused
since, with the contemporary Societies for the Reformation of Manners, which, though
supported by many of the same people, were in reality distinct organisations, aimed at
the suppression of vice.

[1] Overton, *Life in the English Church*, pp. 231-2.
[2] See Overton, *op. cit.*, Ch. vi; W. F. Mitchell, *English Pulpit Oratory from Andrewes to
Tillotson* (1932), Ch. ix; C. Smyth, *The Art of Preaching* (1940), Ch. iv. Taylor, a royalist,
became after the Restoration Bishop of Down and Connor. His *Discourse of the Liberty of
Prophesying* (1646), was a notable contribution to the cause of toleration in religion.

sermons and a lecture on the Sabbath, and a sermon on market-day, were the usual custom, besides the periodical 'exercises' at the Presbytery meetings, and occasionally one of those monster communion meetings which we have referred to above, attended by hundreds of people from the surrounding countryside.

Few of the rank and file clergy at this period had any substantial education, and to many of them the preparation of so many sermons must have been a grievous burden. Preaching was commonly in the 'affectionate' or emotional style which was popular also among the English Puritans, and woe betide the minister who attempted to read his sermon. The themes, too, were conventionally restricted within a very narrow range, and to make things worse the minister was by almost universal custom expected to preach a whole series of sermons on the same text: it is on record that Rev. Thomas Boston, who became minister of Simprin in Berwickshire in 1699, preached a hundred sermons on a single verse of the *Song of Solomon*.[1]

Academies and Charity Schools

Two developments of the Restoration period contributed notably to raise the general educational level among the English people. One, a direct consequence of the open split between the Church and Nonconformity, was the establishment of the Dissenting academies, which provided an alternative form of higher education, not only for Nonconformist students, who were excluded from the English universities, but also as time went on for many Anglican students also. Nearly a score of academies, conducted for the most part by ministers ejected under the Act of Uniformity, maintained an illegal and often precarious existence before the Revolution. After the Act of Toleration the number increased, and many institutions were supported by denominational funds for the purpose of training young men for the ministry. Because of their relative freedom from tradition, these academies led the way in the development of a wider and more modern curriculum.[2]

More significant, from our present point of view, was a development at the other end of the educational scale, namely the growing sense among almost all parties that religious instruction could be effective only if those taught had at least sufficient education to be

[1] Graham, *Social Life of Scotland in the Eighteenth Century*, p. 295. Chs. viii and ix of this work contain a great store of interesting information on church life in Scotland from the Restoration to the close of the eighteenth century. For a more recent account see G. D. Henderson, *Religious Life in Seventeenth-Century Scotland* (Cambridge 1937), Ch. ix.

[2] For a list of the academies, see H. McLachlan, *English Education under the Test Acts* (Manchester 1931), pp. 6 sqq.

able to read the Bible for themselves. In Scotland, of course, this idea had long been familiar, and indeed had been from the time of the Reformation onwards the main inspiration of the attempt to found a national system of parish schools.

Richard Baxter emphasised the point in a striking passage in his last work, *The Poor Husbandman's Advocate* (1691), which was a plea to landlords on behalf of the small tenant-farmers. These people, he laments, are usually so poor that they cannot spare the time to read the Bible or instruct their families. Many of them are unable to read, and those that can have no money to buy books.

And reading much is of so great advantage for knowledge that, without it, the poore people are the lesse capable of profitting at the Church by hearing. How little successe have ministers usually with such, by their publike reading or preaching! And how can the Pastor teach all these to understand the catechisme and learne it? The eye taketh in Sentiments more effectually than the ears: especially when men can ofter Read than Heare, and can choose a subject and booke that is most suitable to them, and can then review what they had forgotten. They cannot so often heare againe and recall the same sermon which they had heard in publike.[1]

In another passage Baxter contrasts the lot of the husbandman with that of the craftsman who works in the house:

I have known many that weave in the Long Loome that can set their sermon-notes or a good book before them and read and discourse together for mutual edification while they worke. But so the poore husbandman can seldom do.[2]

This new perception of the need, on religious grounds, for a literate populace gave a powerful impetus to the movement for the foundation of charity schools to provide an elementary education for poor children, and by the end of the century no fewer than 460 such schools existed in England and Wales.[3] Particularly notable were the efforts of the Welsh Trust, which between 1672 and 1681 established over eighty elementary schools in various parts of Wales (especially the south). The prime mover in establishing the Trust was Thomas Gouge, ejected minister of St. Sepulchre's, Southwark, but it was supported by clergy of all denominations, including

---

[1] This treatise was first published by F. J. Powicke in 1926 ('Rev. Richard Baxter's Last Treatise', in *John Rylands Library Bulletin*, Vol. X, pp. 163 sqq.). The passage quoted is on p. 182.

[2] *Op. cit.*, p. 184. The reference is to the woollen weavers of Kidderminster—cf. *Reliquiae Baxterianae*, Part I, p. 88.

[3] On the development of the general concept see R. B. Schlatter, *Social Ideas of the Religious Leaders, 1660–1688* (1940), pp. 31–59.

Tillotson, who in 1681, as Dean of Canterbury, preached Gouge's funeral sermon.[1]

In 1699 there was founded the Society for Promoting Christian Knowledge, through whose efforts, in the century following, elementary education was to achieve a remarkable expansion.

In the meantime in Scotland the work of building a system of parish schools was going slowly forward, and in 1696 the legislation of 1633 and 1646 was renewed in the Act for Settling of Schools, which has long been regarded as the effective foundation deed of modern Scottish elementary education. Once more the parishioners in each parish were required to build a commodious schoolhouse and provide a salary for a schoolmaster, but whereas in previous enactments it had been provided that the cost should be borne by the heritors, i.e. the landholders, it was now stipulated that half the cost should be borne by the tenants. Even so there remained at the end of the century extensive areas of the country, not only in the Highlands but also in the Lowlands, in which there were few or no facilities for schooling, and in which the people, though possessed of much abstruse theological lore, had not even the rudiments of secular education.

The Development of Public Libraries

We have so far no record, either in England or in Scotland, of any attempt at this period to provide for the instruction of illiterate adults, but it would be strange if the attempt were not made, and indeed we have a hint of it in the title of a book published by Tobias Ellis, an ejected Commonwealth minister. This was *The English School: containing a catalogue of all the words in the Bible . . . being the readiest way for teaching children and elder persons, to spell, pronounce, read and write true English*.[2] In general, however, efforts for the education of the adult poor seem to have been limited to the distribution of free or cheap literature. Baxter attributed much of his success during his ministry in Kidderminster to his practice of giving copies of the Bible and other religious works to those who could not afford to purchase them, and he constantly urged the wealthy to imitate his example. One of those who did so was his friend Henry Ashhurst, who founded schools and distributed books in his native county of Lancashire.

[1] M. G. Jones, *The Charity School Movement* (Cambridge 1938), pp. 281–9, gives a useful short account of the work of the Trust. In the light of these facts I find it difficult to accept the suggestion of R. D. Altick, *The English Common Reader* (Chicago Univ. P. 1957), that literacy in England and Wales showed a sharp decline between 1660 and the end of the century.
[2] 5th edn. London 1680.

Gouge, both from his own resources and with the help of the funds raised by the Welsh Trust, organised the distribution of religious books in Wales on a large scale. Tillotson says of him that he had two excellent designs:

one, to have poor children brought up to read and write, and to be carefully instructed in the principles of religion; the other, to furnish persons of grown age, the poor especially, with the necessary helps and means of knowledge, as the Bible and other books of piety and devotion, in their own language . . .

For this purpose, Tillotson tells us, Gouge arranged for the Catechism and a variety of pious treatises, in Welsh, to be sent to Wales in great numbers, and distributed free or at cheap rates to the people.

But, which was the greatest work of all . . . he procured a new and very fair impression of the Bible and Liturgy of the church of England in the Welsh tongue . . . to the number of eight thousand; one thousand whereof were freely given to the poor, and the rest sent to the principal cities and towns in Wales to be sold to the rich at very reasonable and low rates, viz. at four shillings a-piece . . .[1]

In the meantime provision was increasingly being made for the supply of books through public libraries. We have seen that there were anticipations of this kind of provision, in connection with the churches, as early as the fifteenth century. Most of the collections formed at that time disappeared at the Reformation, but by the time of Queen Elizabeth quite a number of parish churches had acquired, by gift or bequest, small collections of books, mainly theological, for the use of the clergy and such of the laity as were able to read them. Similar libraries were established in connection with a number of grammar schools.

In the early seventeenth century we begin to hear also of town libraries, endowed by pious founders for the benefit of their fellow-townsmen. Some of the early parochial and school libraries, in fact, were partly under municipal control,[2] but the first independent municipal libraries were founded at Norwich in 1608, at Bristol in 1615, and at Colchester in 1631. In non-corporate towns libraries were often placed in the hands of trustees. Thus some time before 1634 Henry Bury, of Bury in Lancashire, gave

[1] J. Tillotson, *Works*, ed. T. Birch, Vol. II (1820), pp. 345–6.
[2] E.g. the parochial libraries at St. Giles's, Edinburgh (1580), St. Mary's, Dundee (by 1598), St. Wulfram's, Grantham (1598), and St. Mary Tower, Ipswich (1699), and the grammar school library at Coventry (1601).

to certain ffeffoes in trust for the use of Bury parish and the countrie therabouts, of ministers also at ther metinge, and of schole maisters and others that seek for learninge and knowledge, above six hundreth bookes and some other such things as I thought might helpe for ther delight, and refresh students, as globes, mappes, pictures and some other things not every wheare to be seene.

The famous Chetham's Library in Manchester was bequeathed to trustees by Humphrey Chetham, merchant, in 1653, 'for the use of schollars and others well affected to resort unto . . . the same books there to remaine as a publick library forever.'[1]

Towards the close of the seventeenth century there were, in addition to the town libraries, some seventy or more parochial libraries.[2] There was also the well-known library at St. Martin's in the Fields, founded in 1684 by the vicar Thomas Tenison, afterwards Archbishop of Canterbury, but this was intended specifically for the use of the clergy.[3] The next advance was due to the learned Dr. Thomas Bray, the principal architect of the S.P.C.K. and its offshoot the Society for Propagating the Gospel in Foreign Parts. Bray was Rector of Sheldon in Warwickshire from 1690 to 1729, and also Rector of St. Botolph's Aldgate from 1706 until his death in 1730. In 1695 he was selected by the Bishop of London as commissary to organise the Anglican Church in Maryland, and it was when he came to grapple with the problem of recruiting clergy for this distant colony that he realised the importance of providing in each parish an adequate supply of books.

Clearly however, it was not only abroad that such provision was needed: the need was almost as great in England, where one-third of the clergy, he estimated, were too poor to buy the books they needed. In 1697, therefore, Bray published *An Essay towards promoting all Necessary and Useful Knowledge, both Divine and Human, in all parts of his Majesty's Dominions, both at home and abroad*, in which *inter alia*, he propounded a plan for establishing a lending library in every deanery in England. These libraries were to be placed in the market towns, for the use of both clergy and gentry, and were to be paid for by local subscriptions. Initially each library would comprise books to the value of about £30, but a complete library would be sent on payment of a first instalment of £6. The books suggested

---

[1] For details of these early libraries, and full references, see T. Kelly, *Early Public Libraries* (1966), Ch. iv.

[2] For lists see Central Council for the Care of Churches, *The Parochial Libraries of the Church of England* (1959), pp. 63 sqq; and Kelly, *op. cit.*, App. II.

[3] E. Carpenter, *Thomas Tenison, Archbishop of Canterbury* (1948), pp. 33–5. Archbishop Tenison's Library was housed in a special building designed by Christopher Wren, and survived until sold by auction in the mid-nineteenth century.

included theology, history, geography and travel, Latin classics, a volume on anatomy, and *The Compleat Gardener*.[1]

There are two notable features about these proposals. The first is the suggested provision for the laity. Bray is not thinking here, it will be observed, of the poor, but of the middle classes—'Gentlemen, Physicians and Lawyers', who have had a university education but now, residing in the country, can no longer procure the books they need to maintain and improve their education.

The second interesting feature is the wide range of books suggested. The phrase 'useful knowledge', which was to become a catchword of adult education in the nineteenth century, here puts in an interesting early appearance. The inclusion of secular works was not intended solely for the benefit of the laity, however, for in an earlier work Bray had declared that it was 'not a little indecent' that the clergy should so often be outmatched by the ordinary laymen 'in *Philology, Philosophy, Mathematicks, Antiquity*, or any part of useful learning'.

Bray also developed plans for smaller libraries of catechetical works for the use of country clergy, and for laymen's libraries to be administered by the clergy for the benefit of their parishioners, all these schemes being linked in his mind with a revival of the pastoral duties of the Church. Between 1695 and 1699 he succeeded in raising, by public subscriptions, close on £2,500 to finance his various ventures. Most of this was spent on the colonies, but part went to the establishment of libraries at home: 36 'Lending Catechetical Libraries' in fifteen dioceses, and 38 'Parochial Catechetical Libraries', including 10 in the Carlisle diocese and 16 in the Isle of Man.[2]

A later chapter will have something to say regarding the development of Bray's pioneering work from 1699 onwards, in association with the S.P.C.K., and also about the closely related plan of a Scots minister, James Kirkwood, for parish libraries in Scotland. In the meantime it will be of interest to add that on his death Bray bequeathed his personal library, valued at £100, to any market town which was willing to contribute a further £50 and establish a lending library. The bequest ultimately went to Maidstone.[3]

[1] See H. P. Thompson, *Thomas Bray* (1954), espec. pp. 17–20, 22–4; Kelly, *op. cit.*, pp. 104–6.
[2] Thompson, *op. cit.*, pp. 27–30; Kelly, *loc. cit.*
[3] Thompson, *op. cit.*, p. 102.

4

The Seventeenth Century

THE IMPACT OF MODERN SCIENCE

I N the field of secular adult education the dominating factor throughout the seventeenth century was the development of science. Popular interest in scientific investigation received a powerful stimulus from the writings of Francis Bacon, who in the *Advancement of Learning* (1605) and the *Novum Organum* (1620), emphasised the need for a systematic and comprehensive survey of the whole field of knowledge, and for the use of inductive methods based on observation and experiment. A little later the influence of Bacon was reinforced by that of the great Moravian educationist Comenius, who visited England in 1641–2, and whose ideas were interpreted for English readers by Samuel Hartlib and John Dury.

The Royal Society

Hence arose a growing demand, especially during the creative period of the Civil War and the Commonwealth, for the introduction of science subjects into the schools, and for effective science teaching in the universities, where the old Aristotelian philosophy still held sway. There were also plans, harking back in some respects to a scheme propounded in Bacon's *New Atlantis*, for the establishment of some kind of central college or bureau for the collection and dissemination of scientific and, as we should now say, technological information. Samuel Hartlib, Sir William Petty the economist, Edward 2nd Marquis of Worcester, John Evelyn the diarist, and Abraham Cowley were amongst those who experimented with, or at least propounded, schemes of this kind. In some of them we find the germ of ideas later developed by mechanics' institutes and technical colleges.[1]

[1] The best account of this educational movement is that by J. W. Adamson, *Pioneers of Modern Education, 1600–1700* (Cambridge 1921), Chs. i–viii. For the significance of the new association between science and craftsmanship see W. E. Houghton, Jr., 'The History of Trades: its Relation to Seventeenth-Century Thought', in *Journal of the History of Ideas*, Vol. II (1941), pp. 33–60. Dr. Nicholas Hans has sought to establish a connection with the continental Rosicrucian movement, which aimed at universal brotherhood and the diffusion of scientific knowledge ('The Rosicrucians of the Seventeenth Century and John Theophilus Desaguliers', in *Adult Education*, Vol. VII, 1934–5, pp. 229 sqq.).

The practical outcome of these proposals was negligible, but in 1660 the new interest in science found expression in the foundation of the Royal Society. This was not, in its origins, the learned society we know to-day, but rather a kind of mutual improvement society—'a gentlemen's club for the discussion of scientific matters.'[1]

The meetings from which the Society took its rise are described in an early account by Dr. John Wallis as beginning in London about the year 1645. They were usually held at Gresham College, and were devoted to the discussion of new scientific discoveries. They may, indeed, have started much earlier, for there is evidence that almost from the beginning of the century Gresham College, with its professors of geometry and astronomy, provided a focus for a good deal of informal scientific discussion. About 1649 some of the company moved to Oxford, where similar meetings were held, first at William Petty's lodgings, and then at the lodgings of Dr. John Wilkins, Warden of Wadham College and afterwards Bishop of Chester. In 1651 this group formed the Philosophical Society of Oxford, which continued in existence until 1690.

Shortly before the Restoration several of the Oxford philosophers rejoined the London group at Gresham College. Here Christopher Wren had been appointed in 1657 Professor of Astronomy, and it was after one of his lectures, in November 1660, that a group of people gathered, as was their wont, 'for mutuall converse', and decided to form themselves into a society 'for the promoting of experimentall philosophy'. Two years later the new body received its charter as the Royal Society. At the outset its activities led to a good deal of misunderstanding and ridicule: even Charles II, its patron, laughed heartily at its experiments in 'weighing the air'.[2] Before long, however, it established its reputation, and played an increasingly important part in the rapid advance of experimental science. Isaac Newton, Lucasian Professor of Mathematics at Cambridge, was elected a Fellow in 1672, dedicated his *Principia Mathematica* to the Society in 1687, and in his later years became its President.[3]

---

[1] D. Stimson, 'Amateurs of Science in 17th Century England', in *Isis*, Vol. XXXI (Bruges 1939–40), p. 40.

[2] S. Pepys, *Diary*, 1 Feb. 1664.

[3] The most recent accounts of the early history of the Society are by Sir Henry Lyons, *The Royal Society, 1660–1940* (Cambridge 1944), Chs. i–ii; and Sir Harold Hartley (ed.), *The Royal Society: its Origins and Founders* (1960). See also J. Ward, *Lives of the Professors of Gresham College* (1740), pp. x–xix; R. T. Gunther, *Early Science in Oxford*, Vol. I (Oxford 1921), pp. 9–12; D. Stimson, *op. cit.*; and F. R. Johnson, 'Gresham College: Precursor of the Royal Society', in *Journal of the History of Ideas*, Vol. I (1940), pp. 413–38.

A Plan for Universal Adult Education

The ferment of new ideas out of which the Royal Society arose produced also the first systematic proposals for adult education. Among the educational reformers of this period, and among the constructors of utopias, the concept of universal education, long ago foreshadowed by Sir Thomas More, was almost a commonplace,[1] and the need for such education was clearly implicit in the famous declaration of Colonel Thomas Rainborough, the Leveller, during the Army debates at Putney in 1647: 'the poorest he that is in England hath a life to live, as the greatest he; and therefore . . . every man that is to live under a government ought first by his own consent to put himself under that government'.[2]

From the education of children to the education of adults, however, seemed a less obvious step then than it seems to us now: indeed the first stood in the way of the second, for the educational theorist who propounded a perfect system of schooling for children saw no necessity to provide for adult education. Only a few of the utopians— Gott, Winstanley, and Harrington—perceived that there might be things worth learning that were not dreamt of in the philosophy of the school child.

Samuel Gott, in *Nova Solyma* (1648), outlines a scheme for the education of children of all classes under the control of 'prudent men of experience, who can be questioned and consulted—who are, so to speak, Inspectors and Director of Education'. He adds:

And besides these, we have public discourses held frequently in all parts of the land, not only of a religious nature, but on ethics, the family life, and such topics. And so, you see, our education gains an entrance to the family circle.[3]

James Harrington, in his learned and ingenious but now almost unreadable fantasy, *Oceana* (1656), interests himself in the possibility of adult education in political matters, but the provision he suggests for it is not very extensive. Among the numerous elected assemblies provided for in his elaborate constitution was one to be known as 'the academy of the provosts', which was to assemble every day

---

[1] Here too the ideas of Comenius exerted a powerful influence. Among educational reformers who advocated universal education we may count, during the Commonwealth period, William Petty, Samuel Hartlib, John Dury, Charles Hoole, and (more hesitantly) John Milton. Among utopias of this period which propounded the same idea were the anonymous *Chaos* (1641), Samuel Gott's *Nova Solyma* (1648), James Harrington's *Oceana* (1656), and Peter Cornelius's *A Way Propounded to make the Poor Happy* (1659), as well as Gerrard Winstanley's *Law of Freedom*, which is dealt with in more detail below.

[2] A. S. P. Woodhouse (ed.), *Puritanism and Liberty* (1938, 2nd edn. 1950), p. 53.

[3] W. Begley (ed.), *Nova Solyma, the Ideal City* [by Samuel Gott] (1902), Vol. I, p. 96.

towards evening in a fair room for the discussion of affairs of state, freely and without undue ceremony, with all who chose to attend.[1] In addition a member of the senate was to address the people weekly on some aspect of the constitution. This latter provision has sometimes been taken by modern readers to imply a quite extensive system of popular education, but in fact the phrase 'the people' is here used in a technical sense: it means merely the elected legislative assembly.[2]

Gerrard Winstanley, in his *Law of Freedom in a Platform, or True Magistracy Restored* (1652), was the first to attempt a comprehensive view of the place of adult education in society; and his approach is of particular interest and significance because he places the new secular or humanist concept of adult education, with its emphasis on science, within the traditional framework of religious instruction. Winstanley was a Wigan man who became a cloth merchant in London, was ruined by the Civil War, turned to politics, and became one of the leaders of the group known as the Diggers, who believed in the common ownership of land. In a series of pamphlets he developed a theory of communism which was a curious blend of rationalism and mysticism, and which, as Professor Sabine has remarked, 'stood quite by itself in the political philosophy of the seventeenth century. It spoke with the authentic voice of proletarian utopianism, giving expression to the first stirring of political aspiration in the inarticulate masses and setting up the wellbeing of the common man as the goal of a just society'.[3]

Winstanley's study of the Bible had led him to the belief that God was the spirit of reason, which dwelt in every man and manifested itself in all the works of creation.

To know the secrets of nature is to know the works of God. And to know the works of God within the creation is to know God Himself, for God dwells in every visible work or body.[4]

In Winstanley's projected commonwealth, consequently, the main function of the clergy (elected annually in each parish) was adult education—the exposition of the works of God. The traditional teaching of the church he regarded as a mere fraud, a means of preserving the privileges of the clergy and the landowners. The

---

[1] J. Harrington, *The Commonwealth of Oceana*, ed. H. Morley (1887), pp. 134, 140.
[2] *Op. cit.*, pp. 181–2, 185–6.
[3] G. H. Sabine, *A History of Political Theory* (1937, 3rd edn. 1951), p. 419. Professor Sabine has produced a complete edition of Winstanley's works (Ithaca 1941), and there is also a useful selection edited by L. Hamilton (*Gerrard Winstanley: Selections from his Works*, 1944).
[4] Winstanley, *Selections*, ed. Hamilton, p. 163.

chosen minister in each parish, he says, may read to the people on the Sabbath three things:

First, the affairs of the whole land, as it is brought in by the postmaster, as it is related in his office hereafter following.

Secondly, to read the law of the Commonwealth; not only to strengthen the memory of the ancients, but that the young people also, who are not grown up to ripeness of experience, may be instructed, to know when they do well and when they do ill . . .

And thirdly, because the minds of people generally love discourses; therefore, that the wits of men both young and old may be exercised there may be speeches made in three-fold nature.

First, to declare the acts and passages of former ages and governments, setting forth the benefits of freedom by well-ordered governments . . .

Secondly, speeches may be made of all arts and sciences, some one day, some another, as in physics, surgery, astrology, astronomy, navigation, husbandry, and such like. And in these speeches may be unfolded the nature of all herbs and plants from the hyssop to the cedar, as Solomon writ of.

Likewise men may come to see into the nature of the fixed and wandering stars, those great powers of God in the heavens above; and hereby men will come to know the secrets of nature and Creation, within which all true knowledge is wrapped up, and the light in man must arise to search it out.

Thirdly, speeches may be made sometimes of the nature of mankind, of his darkness and of his light, of his weakness and of his strength, of his love and of his envy, of his sorrow and of his joy, of his inward and outward bondages, and of his inward and outward freedoms, etc. . . .

He who is the chosen minister for that year to read, shall not be the only man to make sermons or speeches; but everyone who hath any experience and is able to speak of any art or language, or of the nature of the heavens above or of the earth below, shall have free liberty to speak when they offer themselves, and in a civil manner desire an audience and appoint his day. Yet he who is the reader may have his liberty to speak too, but not to assume all the power to himself, as the proud and ignorant clergy have done, who have bewitched all the world by their subtle covetousness and pride.

And everyone who speaks of any herb, plant, art or nature of mankind is required to speak nothing by imagination, but what he hath found out by his own industry and observation in trial.

And because other nations are of several languages, therefore these speeches may be made sometimes in other languages and sometimes in our mother tongue; that so men of our English Commonwealth may attain to all knowledges, arts and languages . . .[1]

[1] *Op. cit.*, pp. 161–2. H. P. Smith, 'Adult Education Emerges', in *Rewley House Papers* Vol. III, No. V (1956–7) has interesting comments on Winstanley.

Lectures and Classes

Projects such as these, however interesting to look back upon, were of course too remote from the realities of the time to have any practical effect on the development of adult education, though they may have done something to familiarise people with the general concept. When we turn to consider the formal provision actually made at this time for secular adult education we find our information very patchy and incomplete, but it is evident that broadly speaking the pattern was rather similar to that which was already developing in the sixteenth century, with the main emphasis upon science and modern languages.

From the researches of Professor Taylor we know that the number of teachers of mathematics, astronomy and navigation increased in quite remarkable fashion during the early decades of the century. Already by 1616 it could be claimed that in London 'Never were there better or nearer helps to attain [mathematical knowledge] than at present, in this City'; and before the middle of the century there were teachers also in the provinces, for example at Cambridge, Bristol and Hull.[1]

Much of the instruction was evidently given privately, either individually or in classes,[2] and during the early part of the century public lecture courses seem to have been few. The lectures at Gresham College, however, continued to flourish, and Sir George Buck, writing in 1615, refers to 'a Lecture of Cosmography read in the Black Friars, in the house of Adrianus Marius'.[3]

From the same author we learn of the extensive provision made in London at this time for the teaching of foreign languages, probably in the main by means of private instruction:

There bee also in this Cittie Teachers and Professors of the holy or Hebrew Language, of the Caldean, Syriake, and Arabike or Larbey Languages, of the Italian, Spanish, French, Dutch [German] and Polish Tongues. And here be they which can speake the Persian and the Morisco, and the *Turkish* and the Muscovian language, and also the Sclavonian tongue, which passeth through 17 Nations. And in briefe divers other Languages fit for Ambassadors and Orators, and Agents for Merchants,

---

[1] E. G. R. Taylor, *The Mathematical Practitioners of Tudor and Stuart England* (Cambridge 1954), pp. 58, 79–80.

[2] William Oughtred (1575–1660), rector of Albury near Guildford for fifty years, taught mathematics free of charge to all comers, his pupils including many of the most distinguished scientists of the century.

[3] *The Third Universitie of England* [London], appended to J. Stow, *Annales*, 1615 (1631 edn., p. 1080).

and for Travailers, and necessary for all Commerce or Negotiations what-soever.[1]

This quotation makes clear the principal purpose for which such instruction was required. As far as the modern languages named are concerned, it was doubtless given either by resident foreigners or by schoolmasters whose main business was the teaching of children.[2] No doubt similar provision existed elsewhere, especially in the ports.

It is reasonable to suppose that courses and classes of the kind just described continued throughout the century, but unfortunately we have no further information about them until the 'nineties, except at Oxford and Cambridge, where members of the universities resorted to private lecturers to make up the deficiencies of university teaching. Robert Boyle's assistant, Peter Sthael of Strasburg, for example, was lecturing on chemistry at Oxford in the early 'sixties and again in the 'seventies, and during his first period his pupils included such distinguished figures as John Wallis, Christopher Wren, John Locke, and Anthony Wood.[3]

The first really public courses on chemistry that we know of were delivered by George Wilson, at his house in London, from about 1690 until his death in 1711. In 1691 he published a text-book for the use of the gentlemen who attended.[4] In 1698 Charles Cox, M.P. for Cirencester, established in London a series of free public lectures in mathematics: these were given, until 1707, by a city clergyman, Dr. John Harris, afterwards for a time Secretary of the Royal Society, and author of the first important English *Dictionary of Arts and Sciences* (1704). The fact that these lectures, originally held in St. Olave's Vestry, were subsequently transferred to the Marine Coffee House in Birchin Lane—an establishment much frequented by those con-nected with shipping—is an indication of the special interest of those attending.[5]

An interesting series of public lectures was that inaugurated under a bequest from Robert Boyle, who died in 1691. Boyle was an ardent Christian as well as a scientist, and the Boyle lectures were established, with an annual endowment of £50, for the purpose of 'proving the Christian religion against notorious Infidels, viz. Atheists, Pagans,

---

[1] *Op. cit.*, p. 1082.
[2] For the teaching of French and Italian in schools at this period see F. Watson, *The Beginnings of the Teaching of Modern Subjects in England* (1909), Chs. xi–xii.
[3] Gunther, *op. cit.*, Vol. I, pp. 22–5; P. Allen, 'Scientific Studies in the English Univer-sities of the Seventeenth Century', in *Journal of the History of Ideas*, Vol. X (1949), pp. 219–53; G. H. Turnbull, 'Peter Stahl', in *Annals of Science*, Vol. IX (1953), pp. 265–70.
[4] F. W. Gibbs, 'George Wilson (1631–1711)', in *Endeavour*, Vol. XII (1953).
[5] T. Cooper, 'John Harris', in *D.N.B.*; Taylor, *op. cit.*, pp. 138, 284, 419; A. Ellis, *The Penny Universities: a History of the Coffee Houses* (1956), pp. 126–7.

Jews, and the Mahometans . . .' The first series of eight, in 1692, was delivered by Richard Bentley, afterwards Master of Trinity College, Cambridge, who sought to demonstrate from Newtonian physics the existence of an intelligent creator; and a number of eighteenth-century divines similarly attempted to enlist the discoveries of science in the defence of Christianity. The Boyle lectures have been given annually, with few exceptions, to the present time.[1]

Coffee-Houses

In the general diffusion of knowledge and ideas, as distinct from formal adult education, the coffee-houses which became so numerous from the Restoration onwards played an important part. The custom of coffee-drinking was introduced from the Near East during the Commonwealth, the first coffee-house being established by a Jew named Jacob at Oxford in 1650, and the second by a Greek, Pasqua Rosée, in London in 1652. The houses spread with great rapidity throughout the country, and Charles II in 1675 attempted in vain to suppress them. By the end of the century there were over 2,000 coffee-houses in London, and in the provinces there were houses at Oxford and Cambridge, Bristol, Exeter, Plymouth, Warwick, Yarmouth, King's Lynn, Ipswich, Tunbridge Wells, Chester, Sheffield, Edinburgh and Glasgow, and probably in many other towns.[2]

Before the Revolution of 1688, the coffee-houses were mostly temperance establishments, conducted under strict rules, and priding themselves on their orderly and democratic character. Any man who paid his penny, whatever his rank, knight or commoner, bishop or curate, rich merchant or poor apprentice, was entitled to take the first vacant seat, to expect civil conversation from his neighbour, and to participate in any discussion that might be going on. It would, of course, be unrealistic to suppose that the conversation was always at a high and serious level. Most of it must have been mere gossip, but a good deal of serious discussion obviously did take place on the political, religious, literary and scientific topics of the day, and some of the London coffee-houses were intellectual centres which brought together many of the best minds of the day. One such was the Grecian, in Devereux Court, where the members of the Royal

---

[1] L. T. More, *Life and Works of the Hon. Robert Boyle* (1944), pp. 132–3; N. Hans, *New Trends in Education in the Eighteenth Century* (1951), pp. 162–3. Bentley gave the Boyle Lectures again in 1694, and John Harris in 1698.

[2] For a general account of the coffee-houses, see Ellis, *Penny Universities*; and for this period especially, the earlier accounts by W. C. Sydney, *Social Life in England, 1660–1690* (1892), pp. 409–24; and E. F. Robinson, *The Early History of Coffee Houses in England* (1893). Most writers on this subject are indebted to the store of history and anecdote gathered in Vol. II of J. Timbs, *Club Life of London* (1866).

Society used to forgather after their meetings; another was Will's in Russell Street, the haunt of poets, playwrights and critics, where Dryden presided almost nightly from 1660 until near the close of the century, like Jonson at the Apollo Club fifty years earlier. John Houghton, a Cambridge man and a fellow of the Royal Society, compared the coffee-houses with universities:

Coffee-houses make all sorts of people sociable, the rich and the poor meet together, as also do the learned and unlearned. It improves arts, merchandize, and all other knowledge; for here an inquisitive man, that aims at good learning, may get more in an evening than he shall by Books in a month: he may find out such *coffee-houses*, where men frequent, who are studious in such matters as his enquiry tends to, and he may in short space gain the pith and marrow of the others reading and studies. I have heard a worthy friend of mine (now departed) who was of good learning (and had a very good esteem for the universities, and they for him) say, that he did think, that *coffee-houses* had improved useful knowledge, as much as they have, and spake in no way of slight to them neither.[1]

The same conceit had been expressed in a broadside of 1667:

There is the Colledge, and the Court,
  The Country, Camp and Navie;
So great a Universitie,
  I think there ne're was any;
In which you may a Scholar be
  For spending of a Penny.[2]

After the Revolution the character of the coffee-houses changed. The sale of intoxicants became common, gaming was introduced, and open tables gave way to boxes for private conversation. Many coffee-houses, also, became practically the exclusive preserve of particular cliques, trades or professions; and in some of the more fashionable the patrons posted their servants at the entrance to keep out undesirables, thus preparing the way for the select clubs of the following century.

The First Debating Societies

Occasionally the coffee-houses provided the setting for specifically educational ventures, such as Sthael's lectures on chemistry (delivered at Tillyard's Coffee House in Oxford) and Harris's lectures on mathematics. They were also a natural home for clubs and societies

[1] J. Houghton, *Husbandry and Trade Improv'd* (1692–1703, 2nd edn. ed. R. Bradley 1727), Vol. III, p. 132. Printed also, in an abridged form, in the *Philosophical Transactions* of the Royal Society, Vol. XXI (1699), p. 317.
[2] *News from the Coffee House*, reprinted by Ellis, *op. cit.*, pp. 264–6.

of all kinds. Miles's Coffee House, at the sign of the Turk's Head in New Palace Yard, became in 1659 the meeting-place for what has been called 'the first debating club in England'.[1] This was the Rota Club founded by James Harrington and intended particularly to popularise the ideas of rotation of public offices, and voting by ballot, which had been expounded in his *Oceana*. The members met nightly round a specially constructed oval table, with an opening in one side for Miles to serve the coffee, and the vote after each debate was taken by means of a ballot-box.

John Aubrey, who was a member of the Club, described it as 'a philosophicall or political club, where gentlemen came at night to divert themselves with political discourse, and to see the way of balloting'. He also remarks that the quality of the debates was very high:

> The discourses in this kind were the most ingeniose, and smart, that ever I heard, or expect to heare, and bandied about with great eagernesse: the arguments in the Parliament howse were but flatt to it.

Samuel Pepys, who was one of many distinguished visitors, was surprised to note that a motion which had been carried 'by the voices' was defeated when put to the ballot.

The meetings ceased in February 1660, when Monk came to power to pave the way for the Restoration: 'upon generall Monke's comeing-in', says Aubrey, 'all these aierie modells vanished'.[2] This short-lived enterprise none the less illustrates the growing interest in the discussion of public affairs, which was to become in due time one of the mainsprings of adult education.

So far we know of only one seventeenth-century successor to Harrington's debating society. Among the posthumous papers of the philosopher John Locke, who died in 1704, was one entitled, 'Rules of a Society, which met once a week, for their improvement in useful Knowledge, and for the promoting of Truth and Chrstian Charity'. These rules provided that the Society should meet from six to eight in the evening, and that those only should be admiitted

---

[1] In 1764 an anonymous author, OPSINOUS, published a history of a famous eighteenth-century debating club, the Robin Hood Society, tracing its history back, with a wealth of circumstantial detail, to the year 1613. This story is repeated by some modern writers, but is now thought to be spurious. See R. J. Allen, *Clubs of Augustan London* (Harvard Univ. P. 1933), pp. 129–36, and below, pp. 92–3.

[2] The subsequent history of the founder of the Club was unfortunate, for he was cast into prison in 1661 on a charge of conspiracy, and though he was eventually released and lived till 1677, his mind was permanently enfeebled. See J. Aubrey, *Brief Lives*, ed. A. Clark, Vol. I (Oxford 1898), pp. 288–94; S. Pepys, *Diary*, 17 Jan. 1660. Cf. Robinson, *Early History of Coffee Houses*, pp. 96–103; and Ellis, *Penny Universities*, pp. 37–42. Ellis finds traces of similar gatherings at Oxford and Cambridge.

who were prepared to confirm that they loved all men, of what profession or religion soever; that no man should suffer harm for his opinions or way of worship; and that they loved and sought truth for truth's sake and would endeavour to communicate it to others. Members were to take it in turn to preside, and at each meeting each member in turn was to give his opinion on the question proposed for the evening, 'and no weighty Question to be quitted, till a majority of two-thirds be satisfy'd, and are willing to proceed to a new one'. No question was to be proposed contrary to religion, civil government or good manners.

We know that Locke was fond of forming discussion clubs, which usually met informally in the evenings over a bottle of wine to hear and discuss papers by the members on scientific and philosophical matters—it was one such gathering early in 1671 that gave rise to his *Essay on the Human Understanding*.[1] The society here referred to first met in London soon after the Revolution, but we have no details of its subsequent history.[2]

A Coffee-House Museum

Don Saltero's Coffee-House, opened in Cheyne Walk by James Salter in 1695, was unique in possessing a 'museum of curiosities'. The first public museum in England had been established earlier in the century by John Tradescant, gardener, naturalist, and traveller, who in 1625 was commissioned by the Duke of Buckingham to purchase rare beasts, birds, shells, and other curiosities from merchants trading abroad. Evidently he was also collecting on his own account, and when, after Buckingham's assassination in 1625, he entered the royal service as a gardener, he created at South Lambeth a botanic garden and collection of rarities. His son John Tradescant inherited his tastes, and in 1637 was in Virginia gathering plants, shells, and the like for the Lambeth collection. The father died about this time, and the son seems to have succeeded him in the post of gardener to Queen Henrietta Maria.

A catalogue of the Musaeum Tradescantianum, which the younger Tradescant published in 1656, shows that the museum (popularly known as 'Tradescant's Ark') comprised in addition to the botanic garden a vast and miscellaneous collection of curiosities—stuffed birds and animals, fish, shells, insects, minerals, fossils, weapons and

---

[1] H. R. Fox Bourne, *Life of John Locke* (New York 1876), Vol. I, pp. 247–9; M. Cranston, *John Locke* (1957), pp. 117, 140.
[2] See the Dedication to [P. Des Maizeaux (ed.)], *A Collection of several Pieces of Mr. John Locke* (1720), in which the Rules were first printed. They have been reprinted in *Rewley House Papers*, Vol. III, No. III (1954–5), pp. 62–3.

clothing, utensils, coins and medals, 'in wonderful variety and incongruous juxtaposition'. A supposed 'dragon's egg' from Turkey, a stuffed dodo from Mauritius, and a cloak of phoenix feathers, were among the items. It was regarded at that time as the most extensive collection in Europe, and was much visited. After the death of John Tradescant junior in 1662 it passed, after some litigation, into the hands of Elias Ashmole, and ultimately (1683) became the nucleus for the Ashmolean Museum at Oxford. The botanic garden was still in existence at Lambeth as late as 1749.[1]

Salter claimed to be a descendant of John Tradescant, and his museum, like that of the Tradescants, was a miscellany of marvels true and false. As he himself said:

> Monsters of all sorts are seen:
> Strange things in nature as they grew so;
> Some relicks of Sheba Queen,
> And fragments of the fam'd Bob Crusoe.

Richard Steele poked fun at these absurdities in the *Tatler* of 1700. None the less the museum proved a great attraction, and remained popular for over a century.[2]

Apart from the Ashmolean Museum, Don Saltero's was the only permanent public museum at this time. It would, however, be very misleading to regard it as typical of the scientific knowledge of the period. This was pre-eminently the age of the *virtuoso*—the cultured gentleman with a catholic interest in science, antiquities and the arts. Sometimes this interest was of a rather dilettante kind, but there were many wealthy individuals who devoted time and money to the building up of extensive and often carefully classified collections of natural history, antiquities, curiosities from abroad, and other objects of interest.[3]

One of the earliest collectors was Robert Hubert, or Forges, who for thirty years before the Commonwealth accumulated natural rarities from abroad. In 1664 he exhibited his collection 'at the place called the Musick House at the Miter, near the west end of St. Paul's Church', and in 1666 it was acquired by the Royal Society as a nucleus for the collection of natural and artificial

[1] The fullest account is in R. T. Gunther, *Early Science in Oxford*, Vol. III (Oxford 1925), pp. 280–92. See also the articles on the Tradescants by G. S. Boulger in *D.N.B.*; D. Murray, *Museums, their History and Use*, Vol. I (Glasgow 1904), pp. 107–9; Watson, *Teaching of Modern Subjects*, pp. 207–11. A 'physic garden' had been established at Oxford in 1621—D. Mathew, *The Age of Charles I* (1951), p. 220.

[2] *Op. cit.*, pp. 154–8; see also Timbs, *Club Life of London*, Vol. II, pp. 44–8; and *The Tatler*, No. 34, 28 June 1700. The collection was dispersed in 1799.

[3] A Society of Virtuosi was founded in 1689, and was still in existence in 1732—L. Cust, *History of the Society of Dilettanti* (1898), pp. 6–7.

curiosities which the Society was forming at Gresham College. In 1691 John Conyers, an apothecary and antiquarian of Shoe Lane, issued proposals for placing his museum of rarities on public display. The movement was, however, by no means restricted to the capital. Ralph Thoresby (1658–1725), the historian of Leeds, was an industrious collector; while in Scotland Sir James Balfour (1600–57) formed a splendid library and museum of Scottish antiquities, and his younger brother Sir Andrew Balfour an equally fine collection of medicine and natural history. Sir Andrew's collection was afterwards presented to the University of Edinburgh to form a public museum, but was allowed to perish through neglect.

The greatest *virtuoso* of them all, of course, was Sir Hans Sloane, President of the College of Physicians and of the Royal Society, whose long career as a collector extended to the middle of the eighteenth century, and whose vast accumulations of material eventually formed the starting-point of the British Museum. Salter was actually an old servant of Sloane's, and it was the gift of some of Sloane's unwanted specimens that launched him on his career as keeper of a museum.[1]

Concerts and 'Musick Houses'

In connection with coffee-houses we must also mention that incomparable character, Thomas Britton, the 'musical small-coal man'. A Northamptonshire man, Britton established himself in business as a coal-merchant in Clerkenwell about 1677. In the daytime he was to be seen, in blue smock and with a sack of coal on his shoulder, hawking his wares in the streets; but his evenings were given up to books and music. Over the stable in which he conducted his business was a long low room, accessible only by a ladder-like staircase from outside. This Britton converted into a concert-room, and here for thirty-six years, from 1678 onwards, he arranged concerts of vocal and instrumental music every Thursday evening.

One contemporary says that those attending formed a club, with a yearly subscription of 10s. and coffee at a penny per dish; but Thoresby in his *Diary* says the concerts were free. Perhaps there was a subscription for regular members only. Thoresby records (June 1712):

In our way home called at Mr. Britton's, the noted small-coal man, where we heard a noble concert of music, vocal and instrumental, the best in town, which for many years past he has had weekly for his own enter-

[1] On all this see Murray, *Museums, their History and their Use*, Vol. I, Chs. viii–ix and xi–xii.

tainment, and of the gentry &c., gratis, to which most foreigners of distinction, for the fancy of it, occasionally resort.

Handel and other eminent musicians of the day, professional and amateur, could be heard at Britton's concerts, and leaders of fashion such as the Duchess of Queensberry were in attendance. As a contemporary put it, 'anybody that is willing to take a hearty Sweat, may have the Pleasure of hearing many notable Performances'.

Britton was also interested in books, and in chemistry, for which he constructed a small but excellent laboratory. His scientific studies, however, did not prevent him from being very superstitious, and he is said to have died of fright, in 1714, as a result of a trick played on him by a ventriloquial blacksmith of Leicester Square. He left a fine collection of musical instruments and a library of about 1,400 volumes.[1]

The provision of public concerts marks a notable event in the development of musical education. Before the Civil War the chief public musical performances were those given in the theatres by way of prologue to the plays. When the theatres were closed under the Commonwealth, music was driven into the taverns, and soon after the Restoration we begin to hear of 'musick houses', i.e. taverns making a special feature of music, in various parts of the metropolis. The earliest appears to have been the one at the Mitre which we have already had occasion to mention. It was established by Robert Hubert, who was a music-lover as well as a collector of curiosities; and it was burnt down in the Great Fire of 1666. These music-houses remained popular until the end of the century.

In 1672 John Banister, a teacher of the violin who had at one time been leader of the King's band, announced that a performance of music by 'excellent Masters' would be given daily in his Music School in Whitefriars. Banister thus became the first to establish the public concert with an admission fee. The tavern atmosphere still lingered, however, for the audience sat at small tables, alehouse fashion, and in return for his shilling the customer was entitled to call for what he pleased. Britton, by supplying only coffee, took another step towards the separation of the public concert from the tavern, a separation which was to be completed in the following century.[2]

---

[1] There is an excellent account of Britton by W. B. Squire in *D.N.B.*

[2] Sydney, *Social Life in England, 1660–1690*, pp. 381–3; H. A. Scott, 'London's Earliest Public Concerts', in *Musical Quarterly*, Vol. XXII (1936); R. Nettel, *The Orchestra in England* (1946), Introduction. A vivid description of a music-house at Wapping at the close of the century is to be found in Ned Ward, *The London Spy* (ed. A. L. Hayward, 1927), p. 246.

The Freedom of the Press

The coffee-houses were particularly important as agencies for the dissemination of news and information. In order to understand their significance we must glance briefly at the history of the press from the late sixteenth century onwards.

Government control of printing, which was in essence an extension of the right of censorship exercised by the medieval Church, grew up from the time of the Reformation onward, and before the close of the sixteenth century had developed into a tripartite system in which the state collaborated with the Church and with the Stationers' Company—the official organisation of the printing trade, incorporated in 1557—to suppress opinions regarded as seditious or heretical. The various regulations were consolidated in a Star Chamber decree of 1586. In 1621 the control over books and pamphlets was extended to the *corantos* which began to appear in that year. These were weekly news-sheets concerned principally with foreign affairs—the ancestors of the modern English newspapers.

As the gulf between government and people steadily widened, however, breaches and evasions of the law became increasingly frequent and the secret presses poured forth a stream of unlicensed books and pamphlets. By 1640 the controls had virtually broken down, and the abolition of the Star Chamber in 1641 opened up a period of confusion and uncertainty in which unlicensed printers sprang up on every hand, and religious and political controversialists had practically a free field. It was at this time that there appeared the first domestic news-sheets. In November 1641 one Samuel Pecke, a scrivener, produced the first number of a weekly journal called *The Heads of Several Proceedings in Both Houses of Parliament*, or *Diurnall Occurrences*, and this enterprise quickly found many imitators, on the royalist as well as on the parliamentary side. Thomason, in London, collected over 7,000 newspapers between 1640 and 1661.[1]

In 1643 the censorship was reimposed, and the powers formerly exercised by the Crown under the royal prerogative were assumed by Parliament. The problem of enforcement remained difficult, but throughout the years 1643–60 the press was never entirely free. It was at this period that there arose the first clearly formulated demands for the liberty of the press. The Levellers put the case in a petition to Parliament in 1649:

If Government be just in its Constitution, and equal in its distributions,

[1] G. K. Fortescue (ed.), *Catalogue of the Pamphlets, Books, Newspapers and Manuscripts collected by George Thomason, 1640–1661* (1908), Vol. I, Preface, p. xxi.

it will be good, if not absolutely necessary for them, to hear all voices and judgments, which they can never do, but by giving freedom to the Press, and in case any abuse their authority by scandalous pamphlets, they will never want Advocates to vindicate their innocency.[1]

But of course the classic statement (though little known in its own time) was that made five years earlier in John Milton's *Areopagitica: a Speech . . . for the Liberty of Unlicensed Printing*:

Though all the winds of doctrine were let loose to play upon the earth, so truth be in the field, we do injuriously by licensing and prohibiting to misdoubt her strength. Let her and Falsehood grapple; who ever knew truth put to the worse in a free and open encounter?[2]

During the Restoration period provincial presses were still forbidden outside Oxford, Cambridge and York; there were no provincial newspapers, and the only newspaper available (apart from a few trade papers in London) was the officially licensed *London Gazette*.[3] Even in the capital the press was still hampered by restrictions of a variety of kinds. To begin with there was the fearsome apparatus of control imposed by the Printing Act of 1662, which included a censorship of books and newspapers, and strict regulations governing the number of presses, printers, and booksellers. If this machinery failed the government could resort to the use of the royal prerogative, or to the medieval law of treason (two printers were hanged under this law before the century came to a close) or to the law of seditious libel, which could be employed to repress any written or printed criticism of the government. In addition there was a complete ban on the publication of any report of the debates in Parliament.

In Scotland, though the regulations were different, the various civil and ecclesiastical controls were at this period just as irksome as in England, especially those exercised by the Privy Council and, after 1671, by the King's Printer. The publication of books was severely hampered, and the emergence of a native newspaper press was long rendered impossible.[4]

---

[1] Quoted F. S. Siebert, *Freedom of the Press in England, 1476–1776* (Univ. of Illinois, Urbana, 1952), p. 201.

[2] J. Milton, *Prose Works*, ed. J. D. St. John (1901), Vol. II, p. 96. On the development and regulation of the press in Tudor and Stuart times see H. R. Fox Bourne, *English Newspapers* (1887), Vol. I, Ch. i; J. B. Williams [J. G. Muddiman], *A History of English Journalism* (1908); H. G. Aldis in *Cambridge History of English Literature*, Vol. IV, Ch. xix; and W. M. Clyde, *The Struggle for the Freedom of the Press from Caxton to Cromwell* (Oxford 1934).

[3] This famous title was assumed in 1666, but the paper was established at Oxford in 1665, the plague year, as the *Oxford Gazette*.

[4] W. J. Couper, *The Edinburgh Periodical Press* (Stirling 1908), Vol. I, Introd. §§2–7; and the same author's paper, *Mrs. Anderson and the Royal Prerogative in Printing* (reprinted

In England the restrictions did not prevent daring printers and booksellers from producing and printing unlicensed books and pamphlets; and the ban on the printing of Parliamentary news was to some extent overcome by the issue of handwritten 'newsletters'. This was a practice that had its origins before the Civil War, after the establishment in 1637 of the first public postal system. During the Restoration period Henry Muddiman, the first editor of the *Gazette*, developed the system on an extensive scale, his letters being copied by clerks and circulated to the gentry and other well-to-do people throughout the country at a subscription of £5 a year.

On the whole, however, the circulation of news remained a hazardous business, and it was from this fact that the coffee-houses derived much of their importance in the life of the times. It was, indeed, because of the freedom of speech allowed there that Charles II attempted to suppress them: his Attorney-General, Sir William Jones, described the coffee-house as 'in the nature of a common assembly, to discourse of Matters of State, News and GREAT PERSONS'.[1] During the period of the Titus Oates plot, later in the same reign, it is said that the London coffee-houses were paying four or five shillings a week to the writers of news-letters.[2]

After the Revolution the restrictions on the press were gradually eased. The Printing Act was allowed to lapse in 1694, the King's prerogative powers fell into disuse, and for a time the only serious menace to the freedom of the writer was the law of seditious libel. In these circumstances newspapers rapidly increased in number. The reign of William III saw the appearance of the first provincial papers, the *Worcester Postman* (1690), the *Stamford Mercury* (1695) and the *Norwich Post* (1701); and the accession of Queen Anne was quickly followed by the advent of the first successful London daily newspaper, the *Daily Courant*. During the same period there appeared, in 1699, the *Edinburgh Gazette*, the first Scottish newspaper to achieve any degree of permanence. The Scottish Privy Council, however, continued to exercise a harsh censorship, and it was not until the abolition of this body, following the Union of 1707, that home news could safely be printed.[3]

from *Proceedings* of the Royal Philosophical Society of Glasgow, 1918). The main Scottish printing centres were Edinburgh, Aberdeen and Glasgow. The presses here were mainly occupied with official publications, Bibles, school-books, etc., though there were short-lived experiments in newspaper production from 1641 onwards.

[1] Ellis, *Penny Universities*, p. 89.

[2] J. B. Williams [J. G. Muddiman], *The King's Journalist* (1923), p. 219. This book gives a discursive account of Henry Muddiman and other journalists of the time.

[3] For the history of the English press during this period see Fox Bourne, *English Newspapers*, Vol. I, Chs. ii–iii; Williams, *History of English Journalism*, pp. 172–98 and App. B., and *The King's Journalist*; and Siebert, *Freedom of the Press*, Chs. xii–xiv.

5

The Eighteenth Century

THE EDUCATION OF THE ILLITERATE

The S.P.C.K. and Adult Education

ON 8th November, 1700, a Mr. Taylor of Wigan, a local correspondent for the Society for Promoting Christian Knowledge, reported that he was designing 'to put into practise yᵉ method yᵉ Society suggested of Teaching Servants to read at nights'. A fortnight later he was able to write that he had 'agreed with their Usher to teach Servants to Read in the Evenings, and that there is a prospect of good Success therein.'[1]

In March 1701, another correspondent, Mr. Joseph Margetts, of Kempston in Bedfordshire, sent an interesting report on the teaching work of John Pierson and John Reynolds:

> The former teaches gratis 15 or 16 poor Children to read, & instruct's them in the Church Catechism without Exposition, brings them to Prayers as often as there is any, & twice in the Week meet's another Company of adult persons (about 8 in number) in the Town, & hears them read, & train's them up in BP. William's Exposition of the Church Catechism. The latter instruct's Gratis another Company every night at his House, in the Catechism, in Reading and Serious Principles, & indeavours to brings them to an awful sence of God & man.[2]

In February 1702, Rev. Samuel Wesley, of Epworth (the father of John Wesley), sent an account of a Religious Society which he had formed for the young farmers there, on the lines of the Religious Societies of London. It had been agreed that the first care of the society should be 'to set Schools for the Poor, wherein Children (or if need be, Adult Persons) may be instructed in the Fundamentals of Christianity by men of known and approv'd piety'. Wesley had previously reported that the people of this district were 'so extreme Ignorant, that not one in 20 can say the Lord's Prayer right, nor one in 30 the Belief . . .'[3]

---

[1] W. O. Allen and E. McClure, *Two Hundred Years: the History of the Society for Promoting Christian Knowledge* (1898), p. 85.
[2] *Op. cit.*, p. 63.   [3] *Op. cit.*, pp. 89–93.

These modest entries in the records of the S.P.C.K. mark a new phase in religious adult education in this country. We have seen Puritan ministers, as early as the reign of Elizabeth, making a beginning in the formal instruction of adults by teaching them to read, but here for the first time we see the Church of England, not indeed directly but through an agency recognised for the purpose, putting its hand to the work. It was a step long prepared by history, and yet, it would seem, only reluctantly taken, for in spite of these early examples, and in spite of a recommendation in favour of night schools for adults issued by the S.P.C.K. in 1711,[1] the initiative does not seem to have been generally followed up, at least in England— in Wales and Scotland the story was different. Time may reveal examples to the contrary, but so far we know no instance of an adult school under S.P.C.K. auspices other than those already cited. To all appearances the adult school idea lay dormant in England until revived by the Sunday school movement towards the close of the century.[2]

Adult schools, however, were not the only form of adult education in which the S.P.C.K. engaged in its earlier years. The Society busied itself, for example, in the distribution of religious literature, not excluding such unpromising recipients as the London hackney-coach men and the sailors of the Royal Navy. The former were favoured with copies of *A Kind Caution against Swearing*; the latter received also *The Seamen's Monitor, Against Drunkenness*, and *Persuasives to the Observation of the Lord's Day*.[3] It is easy to see the amusing side of this, but one cannot withold one's admiration from the missionary to the Navy who reported from Spithead:

> That the service of God is wholly laid aside in some ships, by the contrivance of the Seamen. That a Captain ha's commanded him in the middle of his Sermon to leave off in the King's name: and that he ha's desir'd him in God's name to sit down & hear him.[4]

The Society also assisted in the movement for the formation of religious libraries which had been initiated by Thomas Bray. During the early years of the century a special S.P.C.K. committee established a lending library for the clergy in each of the four Welsh dioceses;

[1] *Op. cit.*, p. 143.
[2] There may, however, have been adult schools under secular auspices, at least in the towns. One such is recorded in Birmingham in 1747—J. A. Langford, *A Century of Birmingham Life* (1868), Vol. I, pp. 32–3.
[3] Allen and McClure, *op. cit.*, p. 124, note; H. P. Thompson, *Thomas Bray* (1954), p. 41. For S.P.C.K. publications generally see W. K. L. Clarke, *A History of the S.P.C.K.* (1959), pp. 80–5.
[4] Allen and McClure, *op. cit.*, p. 107.

and individual members of the Society were active in distributing small collections of books to the rural parishes for the use of the poorer clergy. After Bray's death in 1730 the work was carried on by a body known as the Associates of Dr. Bray, and by the end of the century the total of Bray libraries approached two hundred.[1]

The principal energies of the Society, however, were at first concentrated on the promotion of charity schools for children. By the end of George I's reign (1727) many hundreds of such schools had been established in England, supported by public subscription and providing usually a four-year course, with reading, writing, and perhaps arithmetic for the boys, and reading and needlework for the girls. The curriculum was heavily charged with religious instruction, and the teaching as a rule stereotyped and unimaginative, but these schools, and the similar though less numerous charity schools established by the Dissenters, must have made a considerable contribution to English popular education. By the middle of the century the movement had lost a good deal of its impetus, but many of the schools survived to become 'National' or 'British' schools in the nineteenth century.[2]

The Welsh Circulating Schools

In Wales, where 95 S.P.C.K. schools, and the like number of Dissenting schools, were established between 1699 and 1737, Rev. Griffith Jones, Rector of Llanddowror in Carmarthenshire, was still far from satisfied. Though a supporter of the S.P.C.K., he felt that the new schools were useless to the majority of the people. The course was too long; the fees, though modest, were too high; and English, which was the usual medium of instruction in South Wales, was a foreign language. He therefore set himself to raise subscriptions for schools of a new type, in which education should be free, should be given in Welsh, and should be limited to the barest essentials, i.e. reading and the catechism. His first experiment was made at Llanddowror in 1731–2, and by 1737 the 'Circulating Welsh Charity Schools' had been built up into a regular organisation.

Griffith Jones's system is described in his annual report for 1742–3:

Where a Charity School is wanted and desired, or like to be kindly received, no pompous Preparations or costly Buildings are thought of,

---

[1] Central Council for the Care of Churches, *The Parochial Libraries of the Church of England* (1959),pp. 18–24 and 63 sqq; T. Kelly, *Early Public Libraries* (1966), pp. 104–12, 202–3. See also above, pp. 45–6. The work of the Associates still continues on a smaller scale, since 1922 in association once more with the S.P.C.K.

[2] The fullest account is in M. G. Jones, *The Charity School Movement in the XVIII Century* (Cambridge 1938), Pt. I. Cf. Clarke, *op. cit.*, Ch. iv.

but a Church or Chapel, or untenanted House of convenient Situation, is fixed on; and publick Notice given immediately, that a *Welch* School is to begin there, at an appointed Time, where all Sorts that desire it are to be kindly and freely taught for Three Months; (though the Schools are continued for Three Months longer, or more, when needful; and then removed to another Place where desired). The People having no Prospect of such an Opportunity, but for a limited Time, commonly resort to them at once, and keep to them as closely and diligently as they can: though some can afford to come but every other Day, or in the Night only, because the Support of themselves and Families requires their Labour. The Masters are instructed, hired and charged to devote all their Time, and with all possible Diligence, not only to teach the Poor to Read, but to instruct them daily (at least twice every Day) in the Principles and Duties of Religion from the Church Catechism . . .

The teachers were either selected by the local clergy, or specially trained at Llanddowror, and they were paid according to the number and progress of their pupils. Textbooks were provided by the S.P.C.K., which printed yearly thousands of cheap Welsh Bibles, Prayer Books, Catechisms, and pious tracts, for sale to those who could afford to buy, and for free distribution to those who could not.

The schools spread with great rapidity throughout Wales. By 1750 there were 142 schools, and from 1757 until Jones's death in 1761 there were never fewer than 200 schools. From the annual reports it appears that during the whole period from 1737 to 1761 there were over 3,000 schools, in about 1,600 different centres, with over 150,000 day scholars, and about the same number of evening scholars—stupendous figures for a backward country with a population of some 400,000. If only two-thirds of those who attended learned to read, Griffith Jones's achievement was still remarkable.

A distinctive feature of these Welsh charity schools was that they were attended by adults as well as children. 'Poor and low People of various Ages, even from *Six* Years old to *Seventy*, and sometimes Parents and Children together, resort to these Schools', reported Griffith Jones, and the Vicar of Trelech in Carmarthenshire describes a visit to the school there, at which he was 'agreeably surprized to see there an *Old Man* seventy one Years of Age, with his Spectacles on his Nose, and the Church Catechism in his Hand, with five other Poor People far advanced in Years, who came there with their little Children to be taught to read the Word of GOD . . .' It seems not unlikely, in fact, that half the pupils attending were adults, though the proportion naturally fell as the years went by.

After Griffith Jones's death the schools were carried on for eighteen years by one of his most zealous supporters, Mrs. Bridget Bevan of Laugharne, and seem to have been more successful than ever. When Mrs. Bevan in turn died, in 1779, she left the charity money and the bulk of her personal estate to form a fund for the continuance of the work, but a niece disputed the will, an action in Chancery followed, and by the time judgment was finally given in favour of the will, in 1804, the schools had long since perished.[1]

The Scottish Highlands

Scotland also had its charity schools. The Society in Scotland for Propagating Christian Knowledge, founded in 1709 on the model of the English S.P.C.K., had by the close of the century established over 300 schools, chiefly in the Highlands, where the need was greatest. The Society operated in close collaboration with the Church of Scotland, and planted its schools in parishes where, though a parish school existed, supplementary provision was needed. This was frequently the case in the Highlands and the Islands, where parishes were so vast that a single school, even if efficient, could not cater for the needs of the scattered population. In these areas the new schools were rarely fixed for long in any one centre: they stayed for a few months, or even for two or three years, and then moved on. In the Scottish phrase they were 'ambulatory' schools, and it seems likely that it was from this practice that Griffith Jones derived the idea of his circulating schools. The Highland schools also resembled the Welsh schools in that the work of the teacher was not limited to children. 'Night schools for servants and adults, who could not leave their work in the day-time, were within his province, and on Saturday afternoons, when his pupils enjoyed holiday, he was bidden to visit the old and the sick who could not come to church.'[2]

Until 1766 the Society insisted that the children should be taught in English, but since this was an unknown tongue in many parts of the Highlands, Gaelic books were provided for the older people. In 1767 the Society printed 10,000 copies of a Gaelic translation of the New Testament, by James Stuart of Killen, in the hope that by

---

[1] For Griffith Jones and his schools see T. Kelly, *Griffith Jones, Llanddowror* (Cardiff, Univ. of Wales Press, 1950), and authorities there cited.

[2] Jones, *op. cit.*, pp. 188–9. For details see *An Account of the Rise, Constitution and Management of the Society in Scotland for Propagating Christian Knowledge*, by a Member of the Society (Edinburgh 2nd edn. 1720), pp. 36, 42–3; and reports on *The State of the Society in Scotland for Propagating Christian Knowledge* published in Edinburgh in 1729 and 1741.

learning to translate it 'the children will make more progress in the English language'.[1]

Towards the close of the century many factors were contributing to break down the ignorance and isolation of the Highlands, and in this transformation the charity schoolmaster played a leading part. 'With the Bible in one hand and the three R's in the other he penetrated to the most remote and backward parts, teaching and preaching as he went, and, as in Wales, he left behind him men and women who could read the Bible and could, moreover, teach others to read it too'.[2]

The Bray libraries did not extend to Scotland, but a similar scheme for the Highlands was sponsored by the Church Assembly in 1704, thanks mainly to the initiative of James Kirkwood, an ejected Scottish episcopalian minister who, after some years in England, became in 1702 Scottish correspondent for the S.P.C.K. Kirkwood's original scheme, as set forth in his *Overture for the Founding and Maintaining of Bibliothecks in every Parish throughout this Kingdom* (1699), was an exceedingly ambitious one, envisaging a free public lending library in each parish, containing at least one copy of every valuable book extant. The money required for the purchase, printing and binding of the books, he suggested, could be raised by a levy on all Church incomes; in each parish the reader or schoolmaster would act as librarian. This proposal was ignored by the Assembly, but when, with the assistance of his friends in the S.P.C.K., Kirkwood collected for the purpose books and subscriptions to the value of over £650, the Assembly gladly accepted the gift, and in 1704–5 distributed 77 libraries among the presbyteries and parishes of the Highlands and Islands. In 1709 the presbyteries which had not received libraries were urged to raise funds for the purpose locally.

These libraries were small but carefully chosen collections (less than 100 volumes mostly), which included not only theology but also history, medicine, astronomy, and agriculture; and the books might be borrowed by any Protestant, subject to a deposit of one quarter more than the value of each book borrowed. For a time the libraries must have been a great boon, but like the English parish libraries they were not adequately maintained and were allowed to fall into disuse. By 1826 most of them had disappeared.[3]

---

[1] Copies of an Irish Bible by William Bedell, Bishop of Kilmore, were distributed by the Church Assembly in 1698, but this version was not fully intelligible to the Scots.

[2] Jones, *op. cit.*, p. 210. Ch. vi of this work gives the fullest account of the Scottish charity schools. Cf. J. Mason, 'Scottish Charity Schools of the Eighteenth Century', in *Scottish Historical Review*, Vol. XXXIII (1954).

[3] D. Maclean, 'Highland Libraries in the Eighteenth Century', in Glasgow Bibliographical Society, *Records*, Vol. VII (1918–20); J. Minto, *History of the Public Library Movement* (1932), pp. 25–33; T. Kelly, *Early Public Libraries* (1966), pp. 113–14.

The Methodist Societies

Alongside all these special activities the normal preaching and pastoral work of the churches never ceased, though in England at least some of the fire and enthusiasm of earlier times died out of it. In the Established Church, as the religious passions of the seventeenth century gradually abated, there developed a more tolerant and latitudinarian spirit which was in itself wholly commendable, but which could and sometimes did lead to scepticism, indifference, and neglect of duty—a neglect rendered all the easier by the ancient evils of clerical poverty, pluralism and non-residence. In the Dissenting churches the work of the ministry was probably more effective, but even here something of the old fervour was lost when the stimulus of persecution disappeared.

In this changed atmosphere the Church of England Religious Societies did not flourish so easily as in the seventeenth century, but though beset by various difficulties they continued their work until in the 'thirties and 'forties the new and explosive force of Methodism arose to provide a new outlet for religious zeal.[1] The Methodist Societies founded by John Wesley and his disciples in England, though not restricted, as the Religious Societies had been, to members of the Church of England, were basically similar in purpose; and the Calvinistic Methodist Societies founded in Wales by Howell Harris and Daniel Rowlands were directly modelled on the older Societies.[2] Later, under Methodist influence, similar societies were founded by Evangelical clergymen within the Church of England, for example by Rev. Samuel Walker of Truro in 1754.[3]

The courage, the enthusiasm, and the emotional appeal of the Methodist preachers made a tremendous impact, especially on the working classes—in the mining areas, in the ports and in the rapidly growing industrial centres of the North of England. In Wales, where the older forms of Dissent had made little headway, the movement achieved even more striking successes and became part of a great

---

[1] See authorities cited above, p. 39. The figures for the number of societies in the eighteenth century given in J. Chamberlayne's *Magnae Britanniae Notitia* are worthless, the entry on this subject being carried forward unchanged in successive editions from 1704 to 1755.

[2] The relationship between the Methodist Societies and the earlier groups is carefully examined in the two volumes by J. S. Simon: *John Wesley and the Religious Societies* (1921), and *John Wesley and the Methodist Societies* (1923). The attempt of Dr. D. E. Jenkins, in the Introduction to his edition of Josiah Woodward's *Account of the Religious Societies* (Denbigh 1935), pp. 15–16, to demonstrate that Howell Harris began his societies in ignorance of the English precedents seems to me to fly in the face of the evidence.

[3] For this and other Evangelical societies see G. C. B. Davies, *The Early Cornish Evangelicals* (1951), pp. 66–70.

national awakening centred on the revival of the ancient Welsh language and literature.

The success of Methodism was significant for adult education in many ways, and first and foremost because of the great moral reformation which it brought about in those who came under its influence. The change was so dramatic that it would be difficult to credit if there were not ample evidence for it; but it is certain that thousands of working men and women, who, because of the poverty and hopelessness of their situation, had become idle, drunken, and dissolute, were given new hope and put on the way to being honest, sober, and industrious citizens. 'If any doubt it', declared a Methodist writer in 1785, 'let them go to Kingswood and Cornwall; let them go to Newcastle, Wednesbury and Whitehaven; let them go to Leeds, Sheffield, Manchester and Liverpool; let them go to Birmingham, Wolverhampton and Chester; let them go to Norwich, Bath and Bristol; and they will soon be satisfied that multitudes are now sober, holy Christian men'.[1]

Methodism and Adult Education

The employing classes, of course, approved and applauded, and because of this some historians of the working class have been inclined to look on the Methodist activities with suspicion. Yet we cannot reasonably doubt that the change was equally of benefit to the workers themselves. It brought an immediate improvement in their material condition, and opened up to the more intelligent amongst them the possibility of self-improvement. A rather striking example comes from Cornwall, when Rev. Richard Warner, who toured the country in 1808, reported that the brutal behaviour and debauchery which some years ago kept the tin-miners in a state little better than savagery were now, thanks to the good work of the Wesleyan Methodists, of rare occurrence. These men worked their mines on a profit-sharing basis, with the help of machinery, and Warner comments on their relatively high level of education: 'there are scarcely any of them who are not acquainted with the lower branches of arithmetic . . . it is rare to meet with a good miner who is not also a decent practical geometrician'.[2]

The process of self-improvement was greatly assisted by the structure of the Methodist Societies themselves, which when the Methodists at length separated from the Church of England became the

---

[1] T. Olivers, *A Defence of Methodism*, quoted W. J. Warner, *The Wesleyan Movement in the Industrial Revolution* (1930), pp. 176–7.
[2] R. Warner, *A Tour through Cornwall* (Bath 1809), pp. 297–301.

basis of their church organisation. The lowest unit in the organisation was the class-meeting, which incidentally provided a model for
later forms of working-class political organisation.[1] The weekly
meeting for mutual examination and encouragement in the faith
was a great training-ground in the arts of democracy. Even the
humblest and most illiterate might aspire to the position of class-
leader, and many a working man rose from class-leader to local
preacher, from local preacher to itinerant minister. Women also
had the opportunity of leadership in the early days of the movement,
but this practice did not persist.

Dr. W. J. Warner has made a revealing analysis of some sixty of
the regular Methodist preachers of the period prior to Wesley's
death in 1791. These preachers were not drawn from the ranks
of unskilled labour, nor on the other hand from the middle
classes: they belonged to the intermediate group of skilled artisans,
self-employed tradesmen, and small farmers. A few only had
acquired the rudiments of a classical education. The majority had
had an elementary education only, either at home, or at a charity
school, or at a private school of some kind. Dr. Warner stresses that
for these men their formal schooling was merely a starting-point.

Under the impact of Methodism, and especially the constant goading
of Wesley, their education was a continuous growth. The assiduity with
which many of these leaders undertook to improve the standard of their
intellectual life is one of the notable features of the revival . . . Some of
them became men of impressive learning, and many more evidenced
intellectual distinction in other ways.[2]

Throughout his career Wesley did his utmost to promote the
education of his followers. He encouraged the establishment of
Methodist charity schools on lines similar to those of the S.P.C.K.,
and at Kingswood, near Bristol, he took a personal share in founding
such a school, in 1739, for the children of the poor colliers of the
district. In his plan for this school he also included provision for ar
adult school. 'The older people', he wrote in his Journal, 'being not
so proper to be mixed with children (for we expect scholars of all
ages, some of them grey-headed), will be taught in the inner rooms,
either early in the morning, or late at night, so that they may work
unhindered.'[3]

[1] See below, pp. 135, 140.
[2] Warner, *Wesleyan Movement in the Industrial Revolution*, p. 253. For the opportunities of
leadership opened up by Methodism see Ch. viii of this work, and also R. F. Wearmouth,
Methodism and the Common People of the Eighteenth Century (1945), pp. 217–68.
[3] W. J. Warner, *op. cit.*, pp. 226–7. It is not clear whether this adult school ever came
into existence. There is no reference to it in an account of the school given by Wesley in
1783 (*Works*, 11th edn. 1856, Vol. XIII, pp. 286–7).

Wesley's main effort in adult education, however, was directed, like that of the S.P.C.K., towards the provision of books. He was convinced that no one could be 'a thorough Christian' without wide reading, and he urged his preachers to devote to reading at least five hours a day. If their time was occupied in travelling they must do as he did—ride with a slack rein and read on horseback. He also enjoined them to stuff their saddle-bags with books for the laity, and in order to provide suitable literature he embarked on what came to be an extensive publishing business. Unlike the S.P.C.K., he did not limit himself to religious works, but produced in vast numbers cheap abridged editions of the classics, tracts on social and economic problems, little manuals of useful information about medicine and etiquette, and a variety of other popular works. He also published a magazine, the *Arminian Magazine* (afterwards the *Methodist Magazine*), with a similarly wide range of interest. It was not long before these publications found their way into many a humble working-class home.[1]

Effects of the Industrial Revolution

Methodism also played its part in the great new movement for popular education which marked the closing decades of the eighteenth century—the Sunday-school movement. This movement has frequently been linked by educational historians with the development of the factory system,[2] and though the correlation is not strictly accurate, since at this stage the factory system was restricted mainly to the textile areas, it is true that the Sunday schools were in a very real sense a response to the social and economic changes brought about by the Industrial Revolution. This latter term has fallen out of favour with modern historians because it is thought to exaggerate the abruptness of the transformation that took place, and it is clear that the beginnings of many of the processes involved can be traced back almost indefinitely into the past. No one denies, however, that the latter half of the eighteenth century, and especially the two closing decades, saw a tremendous quickening of the pace of change.

The most dramatic change, and from our point of view the most significant, was in the size and distribution of population. In 1700 England and Wales had a population of about 5½ millions, and

---

[1] *Op. cit.*, pp. 230–2; H. F. Mathews, *Methodism and the Education of the People, 1791–1851* (1949), pp. 30–2 and Ch. vi; R. D. Altick, *The English Common Reader* (Chicago Univ. P. 1957), pp. 35–8.
[2] Notably and very strikingly by F. Smith, *History of English Elementary Education, 1760–1902* (1931), Ch. ii.

Scotland about another million. By 1801 the respective figures were about 8,900,000, and 1,600,000. The reasons for this increase are obscure, but it was at least partly due to a sharp fall in the death-rate, as a result of improved medical knowledge and improved sanitation and water-supplies; and there is general agreement that the increase was most rapid as the century neared its close. Even more striking than this general increase, however, was the shift of population to the new industrial areas of the North and Midlands, and the concentration of great masses of people in the manufacturing towns. The population of Manchester jumped during the century from about 8,000 to 95,000; of Liverpool from 5,000 to 78,000; of Birmingham from 5,000 to 73,000; of Leeds from 8,000 to 53,000; of Sheffield from 5,000 to 45,000; of Nottingham from 9,000 to 28,000; of Glasgow from 12,000 to 84,000.

This remarkable growth and concentration of population created a tremendous educational problem. One has the impression that up to the middle of the century at least the facilities for working-class education were better than they had ever been, and that except in the more remote rural areas it was only among the unskilled labour-ing classes that any very considerable proportion of adult illiterates was to be found—at any rate among the men; the proportion of illiterates among women was undoubtedly higher. But the educational machinery of this period— grammar schools, private schools, charity schools, dame schools—was quite inadequate to cope with the vast and sudden influx of population into the new industrial towns, and one suspects that in these areas there was a sharp deterioration in the position before the close of the century.[1] It was at this time that the idea of universal education, which had seemed so utopian in the seventeenth century, came to be looked on as a matter of urgent practical policy. It was now advocated not only by radicals such as Tom Paine, but by such respectable writers as Adam Smith and T. R. Malthus.[2] In the main, however, the motives behind the new educa-tional movement were religious and humanitarian, deriving not from theoretical considerations but from the ignorance and squalor in which the poor were seen to be living under the new economic conditions.

[1] As noted above, Altick, *English Common Reader*, pp. 35–6, thinks the initial deterioration took place in the late seventeenth century, and that the literacy rate may have declined still further during the eighteenth century. I do not think he makes a convincing case for this view, but he may well be right in the belief that 'by 1780 the national literacy rate was scarcely higher than it had been during the Elizabethan period'.

[2] A. Smith, *Wealth of Nations* (1776), Bk. V, Ch. i, Pt. III, Art. ii; T. Paine, *Rights of Man*, Vol. II (1792), Ch. v; T. R. Malthus, *Essay on the Principle of Population* (1798), Bk. IV, Ch. ix.

At a later date Lancaster and Bell were to find a solution to the problem by adapting mass-production methods to education, but in the meantime the answer was found in the Sunday school.

The Sunday School Movement

From one point of view the Sunday school may be regarded as a development of the catechetical teaching which, though much neglected by the eighteenth-century clergy, was still enjoined by the 59th canon; and we actually have examples of the teaching of reading in Sunday catechetical schools in South Wales as early as 1697.[1] Historically, however, the Sunday schools had little to do with catechising: they were a substitute for the day schools, a way of providing instruction in reading for children who could not be spared, during the week, from the labour of home, field, or factory.

There is no need here to enter into the question of exactly when and where Sunday schools originated. It is known that there were isolated examples for some years before Robert Raikes started his first school among the chimney-sweeps' children in Sooty Alley, opposite the city prison in Gloucester, in 1780; but it was Raikes, the cheery, talkative, flamboyant, warm-hearted Raikes, who launched the Sunday schools as a movement, using his position as editor and proprietor of the *Gloucester Journal* to give publicity to the cause. His first editorial on the subject appeared in 1783, and from this time the schools spread with astonishing rapidity. Church and Dissent combined in enthusiastic support, and in 1785 an undenominational national organisation, the Sunday School Society, was established to systematise and co-ordinate the work. Already in 1784 Manchester and Salford claimed 1,800 pupils, and Leeds the same. Birmingham, starting a little later, had 1,400 pupils in 1785. By 1787 Raikes claimed that there were a quarter of a million children in the schools.[2]

In Wales the movement had its roots partly in the circulating schools of Griffith Jones.[3] These schools, which had fallen into decay after the death of Bridget Bevan in 1779, were revived in North Wales from 1785 onwards by Thomas Charles, Calvinistic Methodist minister of Bala. Charles was a somewhat reluctant convert to the idea of Sunday schools, but began to organise them in

[1] At the Independent Churches at Neath and Tirdwncyn (near Swansea)—D. Evans, *The Sunday Schools of Wales* (1883), p. 161.
[2] Jones, *Charity School Movement*, pp. 142–54; G. Kendall, *Robert Raikes* (1939).
[3] The first recorded Welsh Sunday school was an adult school conducted by Jenkin Morgan, in 1770, in connection with a circulating school at Crawlom, near Llanidloes—Evans, *op. cit.*, p. 158.

1787 as a supplement to his day schools, and soon they became the dominant feature of his work. By 1798, when the Sunday School Society came to his assistance, he and his collaborators had already established over 100 schools in North Wales.[1] In Scotland, on the other hand, the Sunday schools were looked on with disfavour at this time as poaching on the preserves of the parish schools.[2]

It was characteristic of the Sunday schools both in the North of England and in Wales that they were attended by adults as well as children, and in Wales this became an accepted tradition which has survived to our own day. It was not long before special schools for adults were established in connection with the Sunday schools. As early as 1790 this was happening in Manchester, where schools for teaching reading to grown-up people were held on Sunday evenings.[3] In Wales, where from the beginning there seem to have been week-day evening schools for adults in connection with Charles's circulating schools, separate adult Sunday schools were eventually established in 1811.[4]

Hannah and Martha More

The combination of child and adult education is seen also in the pioneering work of Hannah and Martha More, from 1789 onwards, among the farm labourers, miners, and industrial workers of Cheddar, Shipham, Nailsea, and other villages of the Mendips. Here was a part of the country almost as completely cut off from English civilisation as the mountains of Wales or the Highlands of Scotland. The people were for the most part poverty stricken and illiterate; a dozen parishes together had no resident clergyman; the local landowners were indifferent to education, or openly hostile. It was into this half-savage region that the two dauntless middle-aged ladies determined to penetrate—Hannah, once a well-known figure in the literary world of London, and Martha, her sister. Deeply religious, they were closely linked with the Evangelical group known as the Clapham Sect, and two members of this group, William Wilberforce and Henry Thornton, provided most of the money needed for their educational work.

In successive summer campaigns from their home at Cowslip Green, near Bristol, the two sisters visited the Mendip villages in

---

[1] D. E. Jenkins, *Life of the Rev. Thomas Charles of Bala* (Denbigh 1908, 2nd edn. 1910), Vol. II, p. 286. In the three volumes of this work Charles's educational activities are described in painstaking detail. Cf. Jones, *op. cit.*, pp. 314–21.

[2] H. G. Graham, *Social Life in Scotland in the Eighteenth Century* (1901), p. 537.

[3] A. P. Wadsworth, 'The First Manchester Sunday Schools', in *John Rylands Library Bulletin*, Vol. XXXIII (Mar. 1951), p. 315.

[4] See below, p. 149.

turn. They established Sunday schools, day schools, and evening schools, organised benefit clubs for the women, distributed Bibles, catechisms, and other religious works, procured clergy, filled the once empty churches, civilised the whole region. Their formal work in adult education was slight, being restricted to evening readings of an oppressively pious kind, but the influence on the adult community of this work of general religious and educational reclamation was obviously immense.

Martha More's Journal, afterwards published as *The Mendip Annals*, tells the story of this gallant enterprise, and illustrates the kind of opposition that had to be overcome. One wealthy farmer roundly declared that he did not want his ploughmen made wiser than himself. 'If property is not to rule, what is to become of us?' he asked. His wife added that 'The lower class were fated to be poor, and ignorant, and wicked; and that, as wise as we were, we could not alter what was *decreed*.'[1] In dealing with such opposition the appeal to self-interest was more powerful than the appeal to religion. In approaching the farmers of Cheddar, Martha relates,

we . . . said that we had a little plan which we hoped would secure their orchards from being robbed, their rabbits from being shot, their game from being stolen, and which might lower the poor-rates.[2]

The *Annals* also illustrate, rather pathetically, the limitations that could govern the work of well-educated and well-meaning social reformers in those days. Here is Hannah More's description of the schools:

My plan for instructing the poor is very limited and strict. They learn of week-days such coarse works as may fit them for servants. I allow of no writing. My object has not been to teach dogmas and opinions, but to form the lower classes to habits of industry and virtue.[3]

In an address to the women of Shipham in 1801, Hannah reminds them that the scarcity of the times

has been permitted by an all-wise and gracious Providence, to *unite* all ranks of people *together*, to shew the *poor* how immediately they are dependent upon the *rich*, and to shew both *rich* and *poor* that they are all dependent on *Himself*. It has also enabled you to see more clearly the advantages you derive from the government and constitution of this country—to observe the benefits flowing from the distinction of rank and fortune, which has enabled the *high* so liberally to assist the *low* . . .[4]

[1] A. Roberts (ed.), *The Mendip Annals* (1859, 2nd edn. 1859), pp. 210, 212.
[2] *Op. cit.*, p. 17.
[3] *Op. cit.*, p. 6.
[4] *Op. cit.*, p. 243–4.

The poor did not always find such arguments convincing. 'They have so little common sense', wrote Martha, 'and so little sensibility, that we are obliged to beat into their heads continually the good we are doing them.'[1]

The same Tory and Evangelical ideas governed Hannah More's brief but successful incursion into popular publishing. *Village Politics* (1792) was her first effort in this direction. It was designed as an antidote to Tom Paine's *Rights of Man*, and sold by the thousand. Later she embarked on the production of a regular series, known as the *Cheap Repository Tracts*, in which she imitated the lively style, and also the format, of the popular chap-books or broadsheets. She later explained that

as an appetite for reading had . . . been increasing among the inferior ranks in this country, it was judged expedient, at this critical period, to supply such wholesome aliment as might give a new direction to their taste, and abate their relish for those corrupt and inflammatory publications which the consequences of the French Revolution have been so fatally pouring in on us.[2]

These tracts soon became familiar in every corner of England. Over a hundred were produced during the years 1795 to 1798, fifty of them written by Hannah More herself, and the sales ran into millions.[3]

The Birmingham Sunday Society

Interesting developments in connection with Sunday school work took place in Birmingham. Here, as in most places, the schools began on an inter-denominational basis, but quickly divided on sectarian lines. The two Dissenting schools, the Old and New Meeting Sunday Schools, established in 1787, met in the houses of the teachers, and the pupils had to be dismissed as soon as they could limp through the New Testament. In 1789 a group of teachers from the two schools organised the Sunday Society to provide instruction in writing, arithmetic, and other useful knowledge for the young people dismissed in this way. This work was disrupted by the Birmingham riots of 1791, but in 1796 the society was reconstituted as the Brotherly Society, whose objects were 'to provide gratuitous Teachers for the Old and New-Meeting Sunday-schools, to superintend the

---

[1] *Op. cit.*, p. 67.

[2] H. More, *Works* (1801), Vol. V, pp. vii–viii.

[3] The best biography is M. G. Jones, *Hannah More* (Cambridge 1952): see especially Chs. vi–vii. See also E. M. Howse, *Saints in Politics* (Toronto Univ. P. 1952), Ch. v; Altick, *English Common Reader*, pp. 73–7.

management of the SICK CLUB connected with those schools; and to aid the general promotion of knowledge and virtue.' For this latter purpose the members formed themselves into classes meeting weekly for instruction in 'Reading, Writing, Arithmetic, Drawing, Geography, Natural, Civil and Sacred History, and Morals; or, in short, whatever may be generally useful to a manufacturer [i.e. craftsman], or as furnishing principles for active benevolence and integrity'. This Society was still flourishing twenty years later, and had at that time 45 members.[1]

The claim advanced by some writers[2] that the Birmingham Brotherly Society was the first mechanics' institute is not a very plausible one, especially as most of those under instruction were adolescents. There were, however, other activities associated with the Birmingham Sunday Schools which do foreshadow some of the institutes' activities. For example the group of young men who established the Sunday Society had already, some years previously, formed themselves into a mutual improvement society for the study of science. They constructed apparatus, gathered a small lending library, and gave occasional lectures to young men connected with the manufactures of the town. In 1794–5 Thomas Clark, one of their members, gave a course of lectures on natural philosophy, in his own house, to a group of mechanics from the Eagle Foundry, who came to be known as the 'Cast Iron Philosophers'. Another interesting venture was the Artizans' Library established in 1799, which grew out of a Sunday school organised by Messrs. T. and S. Carpenter.[3]

These developments are of special interest because they provide a link between mere literacy education and the higher forms of adult education which, as we shall see in the next two chapters, had long been developing among the skilled workers.

The Nottingham Adult School

Shortly before the close of the century came a notable event in the movement towards the formation of adult schools. All those we have had occasion to notice hitherto, from 1700 onwards, arose as subsidiaries to the teaching of children: they were connected either

---

[1] James Luckcock, a local manufacturer who played a leading part in the organisation, appended an account of it to his *Moral Culture* (Birmingham 1817), from which these quotations are taken. See also W. Matthews, *A Sketch of the Principal Means which have been employed to ameliorate the Intellectual and Moral Condition of the Working Classes at Birmingham* (1830), pp. 5–15. Joseph Priestley was appointed junior minister at the New Meeting in 1780 (see below, pp. 105–6).

[2] Notably by J. W. Hudson, *History of Adult Education* (1851), pp. 29–31.

[3] Mathews, *op. cit.*, pp. 7–8, 15–18

with day schools or with Sunday schools. In 1798, for the first time, there was established in Nottingham an adult school independent of any other organisation, in order to meet the needs of young women employed in the lace and hosiery factories. Its origin is succinctly described by two modern historians of the adult schools:

In 1798 . . . an Adult Sunday School for Bible reading and instruction in the secular arts of writing and arithmetic was opened in a room belonging to the Methodist New Connexion in Nottingham, by William Singleton, himself a Methodist. He had help from a Quaker tradesman, Samuel Fox, who afterwards became especially identified with the school. Before long it came, indeed, to be principally conducted by Mr. Fox and the employés in his grocer's shop. It was a thing understood in the old-fashioned Quakerish economy, that all the shop assistants, male and female—they were principally women—should help at the Adult School on First-day morning. To this end Samuel Fox closed his premises earlier on Saturday night, and in order that they might arrive punctually at Meeting, he provided a nine o'clock breakfast for the teachers at his own house, after they had completed their two hours of teaching. The school came in later years to be specially helpful in the training of 'Sabbath School' teachers, but it was originally designed for the instruction of working women, and although a men's class was soon added, Mr. Fox appears always to have been specially interested in the success of the women's side.[1]

This school, which survived until quite recently, is looked on in the adult school movement to-day as 'the first adult school'. So in a sense it was, but its establishment did not, as it happened, lead to the creation of a movement. That came a little later, and the initiative came, not from Nottingham, but from Bristol.

[1] J. W. Rowntree and H. B. Binns, *A History of the Adult School Movement* (1903), p. 10. Cf. G. C. Martin, *The Adult School Movement* (1924), pp. 12–16.

6

The Eighteenth Century

COFFEE-HOUSES, CLUBS, AND SOCIETIES

ADULT education has commonly been regarded as essentially a phenomenon of the nineteenth and twentieth centuries, and for that reason its rise has been explained almost exclusively in terms of the Industrial Revolution and the rise of democracy. It will have been seen from the previous chapters how incomplete and misleading this view is. In its religious forms, the origins of adult education go back to the very beginnings of organised religion; in its secular forms, it dates back at least to the Renaissance. It is true that most of the forms of adult education with which we have so far been concerned have been embryonic rather than fully developed; but if we seek the period in which adult education in the modern sense had its substantial beginning, that period must be, not the nineteenth century, but the eighteenth. Religious adult education, as we have observed in the last chapter, made a great leap forward in this century by undertaking for the first time the formal education of the adult illiterate; and in the secular field we find adult education not only becoming more varied and more widespread but also assuming, in many cases, a recognisably modern shape.

The distinction between religious and secular adult education is one which we have found it necessary to make hitherto, and which must still be made during the greater part of the eighteenth century. At the opening of the century, indeed, the new emphasis placed by the churches on the instruction of the poor tended to sharpen the distinction, for secular adult education was at this time mainly, though not exclusively, an affair of the literate middle and upper classes. Towards the close of the century, however, as secular adult education increasingly penetrated to the working classes, and the instruction given by the churches began to rise above the level of mere literacy, the two streams of adult education at last began to draw closer together.

Coffee-Houses and Clubs

Our survey of the development of secular adult education must begin with the coffee-houses, which, along with the clubs and the taverns, are so inseparably intertwined with the social and cultural life of this period. Coffee-house life in the capital in the later years of Queen Anne has been immortalised by Steele and Addison in the pages of the *Tatler* and the *Spectator*, and it is tempting to linger over the familiar names of these and later years. For our present purpose, however, we must be content merely to mention such famous establishments as Button's, where Addison himself held sway, and which succeeded Will's as the meeting-place of the 'wits'; the Grecian, favourite resort of lawyers and Fellows of the Royal Society, where a gentleman once killed another in a duel over a Greek accent; Slaughter's, the haunt of artists and sculptors; Truby's and Child's, beloved of the clergy; Jonathan's and Garraway's, the mart of merchants and stockjobbers; and Lloyd's, then as now the centre of marine insurance. By the middle of the century the habit of coffee-drinking had become widespread throughout the provinces, and although by 1800 the great days of the coffee-houses as places of fashionable resort were over, they long maintained their popularity among working people.

Alongside the coffee-houses, and eventually eclipsing them in popularity, there arose the clubs. These were not entirely a new phenomenon—their origin has been traced back to the fifteenth century—but from the beginning of the eighteenth century they sprang up in great profusion in the capital, and to a lesser extent in provincial cities. Many of them first met in the coffee-houses themselves, others in taverns or chocolate-houses,[1] a weekly dinner being a common practice. Eventually the most successful set themselves up in separate establishments. Among the most famous were the great political clubs, such as the Kit-Cat, which was Whig, and the Cocoa-Tree, which was Jacobite, but there were all sorts of other clubs—literary, theatrical, artistic, scientific, religious, anti-religious, sporting, and of course merely convivial. The coffee-houses, the clubs, and the taverns provided, as we shall see, the framework within which many of the more specifically educational activities of the period were to develop.[2]

[1] Cocoa was introduced into England about the same time as coffee, and chocolate-houses, though never so numerous as coffee-houses, became fairly common. By this period the difference was purely nominal, since a wide range of beverages was available at both.

[2] For the coffee-houses, clubs, and taverns of this period see J. Timbs, *Club Life of London* (1866); E. B. Chancellor, *The XVIIIth Century in London* [1920], Ch. iv; and A. Ellis, *The Penny Universities* (1956). Contemporary descriptions may be found in the *Tatler* and the *Spectator*, and also in Ned Ward, *The London Spy*, which was written between 1698 and 1703, and has been edited by A. L. Hayward (1927).

Newspapers and Books

It might be supposed that with the increase in the number of newspapers after 1694 the coffee-houses would have lost something of their importance as centres for the collection and dissemination of news, but this was far from being the case. It is true that newspapers multiplied during the eighteenth century. George Crabbe wrote a poem about them, called *The Newspaper*:

> For, soon as morning dawns with roseate hue,
> The 'Herald' of the morn arises too,
> 'Post' after 'Post' succeeds, and all day long
> 'Gazettes' and 'Ledgers' swarm, a motley throng.
> When evening comes she comes with all her train
> Of 'Ledgers', 'Chronicles', and 'Posts' again,
> Like bats appearing, when the sun goes down,
> From holes obscure and corners of the town.

This was written in 1785, the year in which *The Times* began its distinguished career under the title of the *Daily Universal Register*. By this time London had seven or eight major daily newspapers, and nine evening papers appearing thrice weekly, besides a few recently founded Sunday papers and a variety of weeklies and other periodicals; and there were also about fifty English provincial newspapers (mostly weeklies) and about a dozen papers in Scotland.[1] Dr. Johnson, who died two years before Crabbe's poem was published, had complained in *The Idler* that

Journals daily multiply, without increase of knowledge. The tale of the Morning Paper is told in the Evening, and the narratives of the Evening are bought again in the Morning . . . The most eager peruser of news is tired before he has completed his labour; and many a man who enters the coffee-house in his nightgown and slippers is called away to his shop or his dinner before he has well considered the state of Europe.[2]

In spite of Johnson the newspapers continued to increase in number, in circulation, and in influence. The leading papers were now no longer content to print the news: they also included leading articles, theatrical notices, sometimes book reviews and miscellaneous essays; and after 1771, thanks to the bold defiance of John

---

[1] Early English provincial newspapers included those at Bristol (1702), Exeter (1707), Newcastle (1710), Nottingham (1710), Liverpool (1712), Leeds (1718), and Manchester (1719) (see also above, p. 63). Birmingham did not have a newspaper until 1741. In Scotland the development came rather later than in England, and though newspapers became numerous in Edinburgh the only newspaper centres existing in 1785 outside the capital were Glasgow (1715), Dumfries (1721), Aberdeen (1747), and Kelso (1783).

[2] S. Johnson, *The Idler* (1761, 3rd edn. 1777), Vol. I, pp. 36–7.

Wilkes and others, the ban on reports of Parliamentary proceedings was allowed to lapse. The press still laboured, however, under two serious handicaps. One was the law of seditious libel, which was invoked, for example, against Wilkes in 1763 in connection with the famous No. 45 of his *North Briton*; the other was taxation. Newspaper taxes were introduced by the Tory government of 1712 as a substitute for the lapsed Regulation of Printing Act, and took three forms: a tax on newspapers as such, of ½*d*. or 1*d*. per copy according to size; a tax of 1*s*. each on newspaper advertisements; and a paper tax, applicable to books as well as newspapers, of up to 1*s*. 6*d*. per ream (shortly reduced to 9*d*. per ream). By the end of the century the newspaper tax had been increased to 3½*d*. or 4*d*. per copy, and the advertisement tax to 2*s*. 6*d*.[1]

In consequence of these taxes the price of newspapers rose from the 1*d*. which was usual before 1712 to 3*d*. in 1776, and to 6*d*. by 1800. Newspapers thus became something of a luxury, and only the well-to-do could afford to take more than one. The coffee-houses, where all the news of the day could be read for a penny, provided the answer, and people of all classes took advantage of them. A foreign visitor noted that 'workmen habitually begin the day by going to the coffee-house in order to read the latest news'.[2] Some houses also provided their patrons with current pamphlets: the poet Shenstone boasted that for a subscription of a shilling, at George's in the Strand, he could read 'all the pamphlets under a three shillings' dimension'.[3]

In 1729 the London coffee-house keepers actually proposed that they themselves should collect the news, for publication in a *Coffee House Gazette*. Nothing came of the scheme, but the newspaper proprietors, in opposing it, admitted that 'the collectors of News . . . gather up most of their Intelligence from Coffee houses.'[4]

The output of books, like that of newspapers, increased tremendously during this period. London, Edinburgh, and Glasgow were the main centres, but thanks to the abandonment of the printing

[1] The most recent full account of the newspaper press during the eighteenth century is to be found in H. R. Fox Bourne, *English Newspapers* (1887), Vol. I. There is a brief but illuminating survey in F. Williams, *Dangerous Estate* (1957), Chs. i–iii. W. J. Couper, *Edinburgh Periodical Press* (Edinburgh, 1908), cc. 7–12; and J. P. S. Ferguson, *Scottish Newspapers held in Scottish Libraries* (duplicated, Scottish Central Library, Edinburgh 1956) are valuable for the Scottish press. For newspaper taxes see F. S. Siebert, *Freedom of the Press in England* (Illinois Univ.P. 1952), Ch. xv.
[2] M. de Saussure, *A Foreign View of England in the Reigns of George I and II*, quoted in A. E. Dobbs, *Education and Social Movements* (1919), p. 102.
[3] Timbs, *Club Life in London*, Vol. II, p. 107.
[4] E. F. Robinson, *Early History of Coffee Houses in England* (1893), pp. 207–12; Ellis, *Penny Universities*, pp. 223–5.

regulations there were numerous small presses elsewhere, each making its modest contribution to the intellectual life of the neighbourhood. 'The introduction of the first printing press', it has been said, 'is not merely the commencement of a new skilled trade, but a new source and kind of intelligence. What the discovery of printing was in its earliest days, though in a diminishing degree as time passes, the first press is in the local centre.'[1]

Circulating Libraries and Book Clubs

The growing wealth of the commercial, and as the century progressed industrial, middle classes, led to an increasing demand in provincial towns for the amenities of civilised life, and among other things for books, newspapers, and periodicals.[2] The rudimentary public and parish libraries were quite unable to meet this demand, and the result was the rise of the subscription libraries. These were of two kinds, private and commercial, the former being organised by private societies, the latter by the booksellers.

The commercial circulating libraries were the first in the field. The earliest of which we have certain knowledge was that started by Allan Ramsay, poet, wigmaker, and bookseller, in his shop in the High Street of Edinburgh, apparently in 1726; and by 1735 circulating libraries were established in Bristol, Birmingham, Scarborough, and Bath. In London there are examples from 1661 onwards of booksellers hiring out their surplus stock: 'All sorts of Histories to buy, or let out to read by the week', advertised the Widow Page, at the Anchor and Mariner near London Bridge, in 1674. It is not until 1735, however, that we find mention of a distinct library for lending purposes. From that time onwards the number rapidly increased, and within the next twenty-five years the bookseller's circulating library became common in the larger provincial towns, and in the spas and watering places. By the end of the century there were said to be not less than a thousand in the country, including over a score in London.[3]

The circulating libraries throve on the issue of fiction, and were deplored by the godly as corrupters of morals. The private subscription libraries, on the other hand, were for the most part eminently

[1] Æ. J. G. Mackay, *Short Note on the Local Presses of Scotland* (Edinburgh Bibliographical Society Publications, Vol. III, 1897), p. 34.
[2] For the transformation of urban life during this period, first in the ports, and later in the industrial centres, see D. Marshall, *English People in the Eighteenth Century* (1956), pp. 257 sqq.
[3] The famous London Library was not one of these, being a nineteenth-century creation.

respectable. Here again the earliest known examples come from Scotland. The first, exceptionally, was a working-class subscription library, formed in 1741 by the miners of Leadhills in Lanarkshire, 'wholly at their own suggestion'; and this example was imitated in 1756 at Wanlockhead, just over the border in Dumfriesshire.[1] In the meantime middle-class subscription libraries had been formed in Dumfries (1745) and Kelso (1751).[2]

The prototype of the gentlemen's subscription library in England was formed at Liverpool in 1758, originating, it would appear, from the coming together of three gentlemen's reading societies. The entrance fee was £1 1s., the annual subscription 5s. In 1803 the library was moved to a newly-erected building and became known as the Lyceum.[3]

By that time the example of Liverpool had been widely followed elsewhere, especially, at first, in the North of England.[4] In general the aim of these libraries was to provide their members with the best of the 'polite literature' of the day, the emphasis being on belles lettres, history and antiquities, travels and natural history, and periodicals. Most of them were clubs as well as libraries, and some, for example in Liverpool, arranged regular meetings which were the centre of a vigorous intellectual life.[5]

The commercial circulating libraries have continued to this day to play an important part in the distribution of the lighter forms of literature, but the private libraries, with notable exceptions such as

---

[1] *Rewley House Papers*, Vol. III, No. III (1954–5), p. 7; G. W. Shirley, 'Dumfriesshire Libraries', in *Scottish Adult Education*, No. 26 (Aug. 1959).

[2] Sir J. Sinclair, *Statistical Account of Scotland*, Vol. X, (Edinburgh 1794) p. 597, remarks that Kelso possesses 'a public library, which has existed for upwards of forty years, and can now boast of a collection of the best modern authors ... together with a coffee house supplied with the London, Edinburgh and Kelso newspapers'. For Dumfries see Shirley, 'Dumfriesshire Libraries', *loc. cit.*

[3] P. Macintyre, 'Historical Sketch of the Liverpool Library', in *Transactions of the Historic Society of Lancashire and Cheshire*, Vol. IX (Liverpool 1856–7); P. Cowell, 'Origin and History of Some Liverpool Libraries', in *Transactions and Proceedings of the Library Association*, 6th Annual Meeting, 1883.

[4] Warrington (1760), Manchester (1765), Lancaster, Carlisle, Leeds, and Halifax (1768), Rochdale and Settle (1770), Sheffield (1771), Bradford (1774), Hull and Whitby (1775), Luddenden (a Yorkshire village library, 1776), Birmingham (1779). Others founded before the close of the century included Norwich (1784), Newcastle (1787), Worcester (1790), Coventry (1790–1), and York (1794). Scottish libraries included Ayr (1762), Duns (1768), Selkirk (1772), Glasgow (1779), Greenock (1783), Montrose (1785), Perth (1786), Dumfries (1792), and Edinburgh (1794).

[5] For the commercial circulating libraries of this period see A. D. McKillop, 'English Circulating Libraries, 1725–50', in *The Library*, 4th Ser., Vol. XIV (1933–4); and H. M. Hamlyn, 'Eighteenth Century Circulating Libraries in England', in *The Library*, 5th Ser., Vol. I (1947); for the private subscription libraries see F. Beckwith, 'The Eighteenth-century Proprietary Library in England', in *Journal of Documentation*, Vol. III (1947–8). A. Anderson, *The Old Libraries of Fife* (County Library, Kirkcaldy, 1953), includes an interesting account of subscription libraries in that county.

London, Leeds, and Birmingham, have for the most part succumbed to the competition of the free public libraries.[1]

Mention should also be made of a somewhat humbler form of organisation, which in its origins preceded the subscription libraries, and persisted alongside them throughout the century, namely the 'book club'. This was simply a small group of people who clubbed together to purchase books, which after they had served their turn were either divided among the members or sold. There were clubs of this kind at Salisbury in 1735,[2] at Sheffield in 1737 and at Birmingham in 1745.[3]

James Lackington, proprietor of the well-known bookshop in Finsbury Square, London, has some interesting comments, towards the close of the century, on the increase in the circulation of books, and on the beneficial effects of book clubs and subscription libraries. He writes:

I cannot help observing, that the sale of books in general has increased prodigiously within the last twenty years. According to the best estimation I have been able to make, I suppose that more than four times the number of books are sold now than were sold twenty years since. The poorer sort of farmers, and even the poor country people in general, who before that period spent their winter evenings in relating stories of witches, ghosts, hobgoblins, &c. now shorten the winter nights by hearing their sons and daughters read tales, romances, &c. and on entering their houses, you may see Tom Jones, Roderick Random, and other entertaining books, stuck up on their bacon-racks, &c. If *John* goes to town with a load of hay, he is charged to be sure not to forget to bring home 'Peregrine Pickle's Adventures'; and when *Dolly* is sent to market to sell her eggs, she is commissioned to purchase 'The History of Pamela Andrews'.[4] In short, all ranks and degrees now READ. But the most rapid increase of the sale of books has been since the termination of the late war [i.e. 1783] . . .

---

[1] At Liverpool the Lyceum Library was dispersed a few years ago, but the Athenaeum, founded in 1798 as a library and newsroom, still survives, primarily as a club.

[2] Organised by Samuel Fancourt, a Dissenting minister, who afterwards (from 1742) conducted first a book club and then a subscription library in London—A. Clarke, 'The Reputed First Circulating Subscription Library in London', in *The Library*, N.S., Vol. I (1900); A. D. McKillop, *op. cit.*, pp. 479–81.

[3] Beckwith, *op. cit.*, p. 83. For book clubs in Scotland later in the century see M. Plant, *The Domestic Life of Scotland in the Eighteenth Century* (Edinburgh 1952), p. 236. Robert Burns organised a book club, in 1788–9, among the tenant-farmers of Dunscore in Nithsdale—see his letter printed in Sinclair, *op. cit.*, Vol. III, p. 598.

[4] Lackington is here guilty of some rhetorical exaggeration, for 'the poor country people in general' were still much addicted to the penny 'chapbooks'—crude illustrated narratives of humour, romance, crime, supernatural events, and the like, which were hawked round by travelling chapmen. A collection of them has been edited by John Ashton, *Chap-books of the Eighteenth Century* (1882). R. D. Altick, *The English Common Reader* (Chicago Univ. P. 1957), p. 39, points out that any one of the novels mentioned would have cost several times what Dolly got for her basket of eggs.

I have been informed, that when circulating libraries were first opened, the booksellers were much alarmed, and their rapid increase, added to their fears, had led them to think that the sale of books would be much diminished by such libraries. But experience has proved that the sale of books, far from being diminished by them, has been greatly promoted, as from those repositories, many thousand families have been cheaply supplied with books, by which the taste for reading has become much more general, and thousands of books are purchased every year, by such as have first borrowed them at those libraries, and after reading, approving of them, become purchasers.

Circulating libraries have also contributed greatly towards the amusement and cultivation of the other sex; by far the greatest part of ladies have now a taste for books.[1]

Literary and Antiquarian Societies

An interesting feature of this growth of libraries and book clubs is that here almost for the first time we see Scotland and the English provincial towns taking the lead over London. This, however, is only one aspect of the rapidly emerging intellectual life of the provinces: we shall observe the same phenomenon in the spread o public lecturing and the growth of local societies. Many of the developments that took place were in the field of science, and will be dealt with in the next chapter, but there were interesting and important developments also in literature, music and the arts, and in political and religious discussion. In these the part played by coffee-houses and clubs is particularly marked.

Literary and theatrical clubs were common in London throughout the century, the most famous being the Literary Club, formed by Samuel Johnson and Joshua Reynolds in 1764, and meeting at the Turk's Head tavern in Gerard Street. From the standpoint of the development of literary taste this was of great importance: Macaulay declared that its verdicts on new books 'were sufficient to sell off a whole edition in a day, or to condemn the sheets to the trunk-maker or the pastry-cook'. We do not find, however, that clubs of this kind engaged in any specifically educational activity.[2] For this we have to turn to the provinces.

In 1709 a group of gentlemen at Spalding, in Lincolnshire, formed the habit of meeting regularly in a local coffee-house to read and

[1] J. Lackington, *Memoirs of the Forty-Five First Years of the Life of James Lackington* (1791, 9th edn. 1794), pp. 243, 247–8.
[2] The actor Charles Macklin, on his retirement from the stage in 1754, tried to establish a kind of literary and debating society, under the title of 'The British Inquisition', in the coffee-house which he opened in Covent Garden, but his vanity and incompetence brought the enterprise to an end within a year—*Memoirs of Charles Macklin* (1804), pp. 199 sqq.; cf. Timbs, *Club Life of London*, Vol. II, pp. 82–4.

discuss the latest issue of Steele's *Tatler*. Out of these meetings arose, in 1712, the Spalding Gentlemen's Society, 'for the supporting of mutual Benevolence, and their Improvement in the Liberal Sciences and Polite Learning'. The Society met on one afternoon each week. Political and other controversial topics were barred, but otherwise 'every member to communicate whatever is useful, new, uncommon or curious in any art or science'. In practice the interests of the Society seem to have been mainly literary and antiquarian, the leading figure for many years being Maurice Johnson, of the Inner Temple, who was one of the founders of the Society of Antiquaries on its revival in 1717.[1] For books the Society had resort to the 'public library' which had been established in the parish church in 1637, and new members were required to present a book by way of entrance fee.

Similar societies were established later in other market-towns of Lincolnshire and the adjoining counties—at Stamford (1721), Peterborough (about 1730), Lincoln, Wisbech, and Doncaster—and also at Worcester. Most of these faded out by the middle of the century, but the Spalding Society still survives.[2]

The combination of literary and antiquarian interests is seen also in the foundation in 1751 of the Society of Cymmrodorion, which had as its principal objectives 'the Cultivation of the *British* [i.e. Welsh] Language, and a Search into [Welsh] Antiquities'. It was created by the London Welsh at the instigation of that warm-hearted but imprudent Welshman, Richard Morris, clerk in the Navy Office, who died in poverty in 1779. The Society survived him by eight years.[3]

In Scotland, similarly, a Literary and Antiquarian Society was established at Perth in 1784. Doubtless there were other societies interested in literature here and there in the provincial towns— Glasgow, for example, had a Literary Society in 1752, Warrington in 1758, and Leicester in 1790[4]—and literary interests were also catered for by book-clubs and subscription libraries, and to a small

---

[1] See below, p. 109.
[2] For these societies see J. Nichols, *Literary Anecdotes of the Eighteenth Century*, Vol. VI, Pt. I (1812), pp. 1–162. For Spalding see also W. Moore, *The Gentlemen's Society at Spalding* (Pickering 1851, new edn., Cambridge 1909), and G. W. Bailey, *Spalding Gentlemen's Society*, reprinted from *Lincolnshire Magazine* (1937).
[3] The story of this Society, and its successors of the same name, is told in R. T. Jenkins and H. M. Ramage, *History of the Honourable Society of Cymmrodorion* (*Y Cymmrodor*, Vol. L, 1951).
[4] J. Strang, *Glasgow and its Clubs* (2nd edn. 1857), p. 21; W. B. Stephens, *Development of Adult Education in Warrington* (unpublished M.A. thesis, Exeter 1958), p. 60; F. S. Herne, 'An Old Leicester Bookseller', in *Transactions* of the Leicester Literary and Philosophical Society, N.S., Vol. III, Pt. II, Jan. 1893.

extent, at the end of the century, by the literary and philosophical societies at Manchester and Newcastle.

Musical Societies

In music the public concert had now definitely established itself, alongside the theatre and the opera, as a feature of the cultural life of the times; and though taverns continued to be used there were now concert-halls, assembly rooms, and pleasure-gardens such as Vauxhall, Ranelagh, and Marylebone, to provide a setting quite divorced from the old tavern atmosphere.[1] In London we hear of concert clubs, of which the most notable was the Academy of Antient Music, which met at the Crown and Anchor Tavern in the Strand under the guidance of Dr. Pepusch (1710–92).[2]

Musical societies in the provinces performed a similar function. In Edinburgh concerts were arranged by the Music Club, founded in 1721, and later by the Musical Society, which flourished from 1725 to 1801. Birmingham, Liverpool, Manchester, and Glasgow all had music societies in the second half of the century, and occasional concerts are recorded earlier. Many English towns also began to organise music festivals. The Three Choirs Festival, which brought together the combined choirs of the cathedrals of Gloucester, Worcester, and Hereford, began its long and celebrated career at Gloucester in 1724. Music festivals began in Liverpool in 1766, in Birmingham in 1768, and in Manchester in 1777, and Norwich had a festival in 1770.[3]

A modern historian of music, while admitting that the public concert brought music to the rising middle classes, regards its advent as a sign of decadence, a symptom of the breakdown of the organic musical culture of a former age, 'in which the unlettered peasants created melodies like *Greensleeves*, in which both the aristocrat and the artisan took active part in singing and playing madrigals and fancies of Byrd and Weelkes and Wilbye, and in which all classes heard the music of Byrd in their church services'.[4] Perhaps this is a severe judgment. At any rate musical activities of a less passive kind were to be found in all classes of society.

[1] H. A. Scott, 'London Concerts from 1700 to 1750', in *Musical Quarterly*, Vol. XXIV (1938); T. L. Southgate, 'Music at the Public Pleasure Gardens of the Eighteenth Century', in *Proceedings of the Musical Association*, 38th Session (London 1912).

[2] R. Nettel, *The Orchestra in England* (1946), p. 26. For a time the Academy had a rival in the Philharmonic Society at the Devil Tavern, founded 1728.

[3] Nettel, *op. cit.*, pp. 66–8, and *The Englishman Makes Music* (1952), p. 71; J. A. Picton, *Memorials of Liverpool* (Liverpool 1873, 2nd edn. 1903), Vol. I, p. 205; W. E. A. Axon, *Annals of Manchester* (Manchester 1886), pp. 99, 104; *Grove's Dictionary of Music and Musicians* (5th edn., ed. E. Blom, 1954), s.v. Edinburgh, Glasgow, Manchester, Norwich.

[4] W. Mellers, *Music and Society* (1946, 2nd edn. 1950), pp. 140–1.

The members of the Academy of Antient Music were performers as well as listeners. There was also the Madrigal Society, founded in 1741 by John Immyns, an attorney, and still flourishing. It consisted mainly of working men, who met in the Twelve Bells tavern off Fleet Street, and who learned their three, four, and five part madrigals by a system of solmisation.[1] More aristocratic was the Noblemen's and Gentlemen's Catch Club (1761), which met weekly while Parliament was in session.[2] In Manchester was founded in 1770 the Gentlemen's Concert Club, a group of twenty-six amateur players consisting, according to the later account by Sir Charles Hallé, entirely of flautists.[3] And farther north, in the Forest of Rossendale, was that interesting company of artisans, the Dean Larks (handloom-weavers mostly) who composed their own hymn-tunes and often made their own instruments. It is said that 'when the first printed copies of Handel's *Messiah* were brought to their village the Dean Larks met the cart and escorted it to its destination singing the *Messiah* choruses, which they already knew by heart'.[4]

Art Societies

An important aspect of the cultural history of this period was the development of the fine arts, and the rise of the great English school of painting and sculpture associated with such names as Reynolds, Gainsborough, Romney and Roubiliac. In Anne's reign painters and sculptors were 'an obscure and struggling confraternity' barely distinguished from craftsmen[5]; fifty years later the line between the artisan and the creative artist was clearly drawn, and the superior position of the latter was recognised by the establishment of the Royal Academy (1768). In no small measure this transformation was due to the influence of continental travel, which had now come to be regarded as an essential part of the education of the well-to-do English gentlemen. It was a group of young aristocrats, lovers of Italy, who about 1732 founded the Society of Dilettanti, which met at the Thatched House tavern in St. James's Street. The Society

[1] J. Hawkins, *History of Music* (1776, new edn. 1875), Vol. II, pp. 886–7; Nettel, *Englishman makes Music*, pp. 48–58. One member, a baker named Samuel Jeacocke, used to bake fiddles in sawdust for a week to improve the tone.
[2] Nettel, *op. cit.*, pp. 44–8.
[3] Axon, *op. cit.*, p. 99; Nettel, *Orchestra in England*, p. 193.
[4] P. Scholes (ed.), *Oxford Companion to Music* (1938 edn.), pp. 75–6. For a general account of music at this period see the chapter by Sir Henry Hadow in Vol. II of *Johnson's England*, ed. A. S. Turberville. T. Newbigging, *History of the Forest of Rossendale* (Rawtenstall 1867, 2nd edn. 1893), pp. 258–65, gives an interesting account of the Dean Larks.
[5] B. Williams, *The Whig Supremacy, 1714–1760* (Oxford 1939), p. 384. The portrait painter, the coach-painter, and the house painter alike belonged to the Painter-Stainer's Company—A. Shirley in *Johnson's England*, ed. A. S. Turberville, Vol. II, p. 55.

combined a boisterous conviviality with serious patronage of the arts, financing expeditions to study classical antiquities, and assisting promising young artists to travel abroad.[1]

The public exhibition of works of art began almost accidentally when in the 1740s William Hogarth, Allan Ramsay, Richard Wilson and others presented paintings to adorn the court-room of the newly established Foundling Hospital in London, thus forming a small collection of contemporary paintings which the public flocked to see. Later the London artists combined to arrange annual exhibitions: the Society of Artists began to exhibit in 1760, and a rival body, the Free Society of Artists, from 1762.[2] These privately organised exhibitions were eventually superseded by those of the Royal Academy, especially when the great exhibition gallery was opened in Somerset House in 1780.

At least one provincial town followed suit. In Liverpool various attempts were made from 1769 onwards to create an Academy of Art, and in 1773–4 courses of lectures were delivered on architecture, perspective, anatomy, and chemistry, but the wars with America and France made it impossible at this time to establish the Academy on a permanent footing. A number of successful exhibitions were, however, organised from 1774 onwards.[3]

Debating Societies

A feature of the second half of the century was the rise of public debating societies. It is said that as early as the reign of Queen Anne discussion clubs were meeting in London to debate the rationalist ideas on religion propounded by such writers as John Toland, Anthony Collins and Bernard Mandeville,[4] but these, like their seventeenth-century predecessors, must have been private gatherings. The first public debating society of which we have precise information is the Robin Hood Society.

The origins of this famous Society are obscure, but it appears to have been meeting at the Essex Head tavern in Essex Street as early as 1742, and from 1747 until its dissolution in 1773 it met weekly on Monday evenings at the Robin Hood tavern in Butcher's Row.[5]

---

[1] L. Cust (ed. S. Colvin), *History of the Society of Dilettanti* (1898), Chs. i–iv.

[2] The Society of Arts (see below, p. 98), not yet exclusively concerned with technological matters, sponsored some of the early exhibitions.

[3] Picton, *Memorials of Liverpool*, Vol. I, pp. 208–10; T. Kelly, *Adult Education in Liverpool* (Liverpool 1960), p. 11.

[4] R. J. Allen, *The Clubs of Augustan London* (Harvard Univ. P. 1933), p. 128.

[5] The anonymous author of a *History of the Robin Hood Society* (1764) traces the origin of the Society, with much circumstantial detail, to a secret society founded by Sir Hugh Middleton in 1613. N. Hans, *New Trends in Education in the Eighteenth Century* (1951),

The subject for discussion was determined week by week, and each person present might speak for five minutes. Among the subjects listed in a contemporary account we find: 'Whether the Doctrine of the Trinity can be justified either by Reason or by Scripture?' and 'Whether the Power lodged in a Prime Minister, be not too great to be entrusted with any Subject?'[1] That such subjects could be discussed at all is symptomatic of the growth of a more tolerant climate of public opinion. Religious and political fanaticism, however, had still not entirely loosened its grip: in 1763 the seventy-year-old Peter Annet, a well-known deist and a member of the Society, was pilloried and imprisoned for attacking the truth of the Old Testament. It is not, therefore, surprising that the freedom with which religious and political subjects were handled in the debates of the Society should have given grave offence, and should have led to its being denounced as blasphemous, atheistical, licentious, and seditious.

Membership was open to all at a charge of 6d. per meeting, which included free porter or lemonade. The normal membership was about fifty, and evidently included a considerable number of tradesmen and craftsmen. Caleb Jeacocke, who presided over the debates for many years with grave dignity and unshakeable firmness, was a wealthy city baker.[2] A writer in the *Gentleman's Magazine* states that the members were chiefly 'lawyers' clerks, petty tradesmen, and the lowest mechanics', and comments sarcastically on their 'amazing erudition' in the works of such deistical writers as Tindal, Collins, Chubb, and Mandeville.[3] In time interest or curiosity attracted all sorts of other people. Goldsmith occasionally attended; the young Burke tried out his 'prentice oratory there; and Boswell describes a visit made in 1762, when the applause accorded to his mediocre speech on the excise made him wonder whether he might some day be an orator.[4]

Other such societies evidently existed in the capital at this time,

pp. 168–71, accepts this account at its face value, but we have no independent evidence for so early an origin. R. J. Allen, *op. cit.*, pp. 129–36, has no hesitation in regarding the story as a fabrication for the purposes of controversy, and dates the origin of the Society to 1747 only. It seems reasonable to suppose, however, that in dealing with more recent events the author of the *History* is more reliable. I have therefore accepted his statement that the Society met at the Essex Head before its removal to the Robin Hood in 1747, and that Caleb Jeacocke, who retired from the presidency in 1761, had held office for 19 years, i.e. since 1742 (*History*, pp. 117, 128).

[1] *History of the Robin Hood Society*, pp. 69, 71.
[2] He was a brother of Samuel Jeacocke of the Madrigal Society (above, p. 91 note).
[3] *Gentleman's Magazine*, Vol. XXIV (1754), p. 154.
[4] See, in addition to the works already cited, Timbs, *Club Life of London*, Vol. I, pp. 196–8; T. MacKnight, *Life and Times of Edmund Burke*, Vol. I (1858), pp. 71–2; J. Forster, *Life and Times of Oliver Goldsmith*, Vol. I (1877), pp. 287–90; J. Boswell, *London Journal*, ed. F. A. Pottle (1950), p. 322.

amongst them a political debating society known as the Honourable Society of Cogers, which was founded in 1755 and still survives. The Cogers (the name is derived, somewhat dubiously, from *cogito*) are said in an early minute book to have been originally 'Citizens of London who met to watch the course of political events and the conduct of their representatives in Parliament'. They met at a tavern near Fleet Street, and John Wilkes is reputed to have been their second president.[1]

The excitement caused by the War of American Independence stimulated the formation of numerous discussion clubs, mostly, it would seem, working-class in character and radical-rationalist in outlook. Thus in October 1778 the Society for Free Debate at the Queen's Arms, Newgate Street, was discussing whether the laws governing English soldiers were dangerous to liberty, and whether Britain should give up the American Colonies or declare war on France. In November 1779 the Apollo Society 'for the discussion of all questions in history, literature, policy and theology', at the King's Arms in Soho, was discussing the desirability of a union with Ireland; and the same question was being debated at the Westminster Forum. In October 1780 the Disputing Club at the King's Arms, Cornhill, was considering whether governments should give rewards for virtue as well as punishments for vice.[2]

To what extent debating societies became popular in the provinces is not clear, but Birmingham at least had two such societies in the 'seventies. The Robin Hood Free Debating Society, founded in 1774, and meeting in the Red Lion tavern, looks like an obvious imitation of the London society. It was radical in tone, and working-class in membership: a visitor complained of the low standard of oratory of the poor apprentices and mean mechanics who attended it, and of their dirty clothing, which he thought particularly regrettable because ladies were permitted to attend. The Amicable Debating Society, established in the same year, was a rival and apparently more select organisation. Neither Society seems to have lasted long.[3]

Newcastle also, at the same period, had at least two debating societies, one of them founded by Thomas Spence, the land reformer;[4]

[1] P. Rayleigh, *The Cogers of Fleet Street* [1907] (originally published as *History of Ye Antient Society of Cogers* [1903]). For other societies see *History of the Robin Hood Society*, pp. 147, 191.
[2] W. C. Sydney, *England and the English in the Eighteenth Century* (2nd edn., Edinburgh 1891), Vol. II, pp. 163–4. A more middle-class affair, interested particularly in political questions, was the debating society at the Clifford Street Coffee-House, described by Timbs, *op. cit.*, Vol. I, pp. 169–71.
[3] J. A. Langford, *A Century of Birmingham Life* (Birmingham 1868), Vol. I, pp. 239–44.
[4] R. S. Watson, *History of the Literary and Philosophical Society of Newcastle-upon-Tyne* (1897), pp. 15–21.

and in Liverpool there were debating societies meeting in taverns and coffee-houses from 1768 onwards.[1]

David Williams, Dissenting minister and radical reformer, who established a school in Chelsea in 1773, was the centre of a great variety of adult educational activities. He formed a club (Benjamin Franklin was one of the members) for the discussion of rational religion, and a society for the rational improvement of education, lectured extensively on both these topics, and for twelve years (from about 1777) conducted a class in politics for adults 'of defective education'. In the preface to his published course of lectures in this subject he described how,

Perceiving the common academical mode of reading, and pronouncing observations or advice, had little effect, on memories not retentive; he formed the students into parties for and against the most celebrated writers on Political Œconomy: and converted to his purpose, a prevalent passion in Englishmen, which had often embarrassed him . . . To hesitate, to doubt, or to question established authorities, is more conducive to a habit of profitable reading, than the effort of committing opinions to memory.

This recognition of the value of discussion and criticism in an adult class is, as Dr. Hans has pointed out, an interesting anticipation of methods later used in the tutorial class.[2]

Political and Religious Reform Societies

Many of the debating societies continued in full vigour for many years—indeed, this kind of society became henceforth a permanent feature of English cultural life. In the 'eighties and 'nineties, however, much activity of this kind was absorbed into the political reform societies which became so common at this time, and which multiplied in the glow of liberal enthusiasm produced by the early phases of the French Revolution. The Society of the Friends of the People (1792), and the London Corresponding Society (1792), were both centred on the capital, but they maintained contact by correspondence and by visits of delegates with a host of local town and country associations—Constitutional Societies, Friends of the People, Revolution Societies, and the like, which sprang up throughout the country. Norwich, Sheffield, Manchester, and Edinburgh were the main centres outside London: it appears that in 1793 there were thirty or forty reform societies in Norwich alone.

[1] Kelly, *Adult Education in Liverpool*, p. 12.
[2] D. Williams, *Lectures on Political Principles* (1789), Preface; Hans, *op. cit.*, pp. 163–5. Williams is best remembered as the founder of what became the Royal Literary Fund, for the assistance of distressed authors.

Most of these societies were middle-class in character, including among their supporters members of Parliament, local notables, and a sprinkling of the aristocracy; but the London Corresponding Society, the creation of a Piccadilly shoemaker named Thomas Hardy, was a deliberate attempt to mobilise working-class opinion. The members paid 1*d.* a week, and were organised in divisions of thirty or more, sending delegates to a central committee. This method of organisation proved very successful, and the Society soon came to number some thousands of members.

With the political aspects of this movement we are not here concerned, and it will be sufficient to remark that, although the aims of the reform societies never extended beyond universal suffrage and annual parliaments, they inevitably came to be associated in the public mind with the excesses of the French Revolution, with the consequence that by 1799 they had all either been suppressed or faded out of existence. What is of particular interest is their work in education. The Society for Constitutional Information, the first in the field, concentrated on the distribution of reform literature, but the London Corresponding Society and similar societies elsewhere adopted more direct methods, organising lectures, debates, and discussions, and providing small libraries of books for circulation among the members. Tom Paine's *Rights of Man*, published in 1791–2 as a reply to Burke's *Reflections on the French Revolution*, and constantly printed and reprinted, was the Bible of the movement; but William Godwin's *Political Justice* (published in 1793 at three guineas) was also procured in this way, and read, in spite of its abstract and philosophical style. The Act of 1799 which suppressed the Corresponding Societies also forbade unlicensed lectures, debates, and reading-rooms open to the public on payment of a fee.[1]

A contemporary[2] describes another group of societies, which existed in London during the years 1795–8, whose interests were religious as well as political. They met in taverns, or wherever for a few weeks or months they could find a home, under such names as The Moral and Political Society, or The Friends of Morality. They organised lectures and debates (especially on Sunday evenings),

[1] 39 Geo. III c. 79. For a general account of the political reform societies see G. S. Veitch, *Genesis of Parliamentary Reform* (1913). The Radical publishing activities of this period, and the counterblasts from the loyalist side, are described in R. K. Webb, *The British Working Class Reader* (1955), pp. 38–44; and Altick, *English Common Reader*, pp. 69–77. The subject is also dealt with in J. F. and W. Horrabin, *Working Class Education* (1924), pp. 13–17; and B. Simon, *Studies in the History of Education, 1780–1870* (1960), pp. 180–3.

[2] W. H. Reid, *The Rise and Dissolution of the Infidel Societies in this Metropolis* (1800), pp. 10 sqq.

clubbed together to buy books and pamphlets, and debated hotly with open-air preachers. According to this witness, a very hostile one, their own views were strongly anti-religious, and their favourite reading was in the works of Voltaire, David Williams, and above all, Paine's *Age of Reason*, a critical examination of Christianity published in 1794–5. As some of the leaders of the London Corresponding Society were deists or atheists, there was probably some overlap in membership between these groups and the working-class political societies.

There was much that was crude and unsavoury in the work of these societies, but Francis Place, the Charing Cross tailor who was to be the organiser of so many reform movements, bears witness to their genuine educational value. Place was 22 when he joined the London Corresponding Society in 1794. He had been trained as a journeyman breeches-maker, and had educated himself by reading at bookstalls and by borrowing books for a trifling payment from a friendly book-seller. At this time he was out of work, and was scraping a scanty living as organiser to various trade clubs.[1] He says of the London Corresponding Society:

> The moral effects of the society were very great indeed. It induced men to read books, instead of spending their time at public houses; it induced them to love their own homes, it taught them to think, to respect them-selves, and to desire to educate their children . . . The discussions in the Sunday afternoon reading and debating associations held in their own rooms opened to them views to which they had been blind. They were compelled by these discussions to find reasons for their opinions, and to tolerate the opinions of others. In fact, it gave a new stimulus to a large mass of men who had hitherto been but too justly considered, as incapable of any but the very grossest pursuits and sensual enjoyments. It elevated them in society.[2]

[1] G. Wallas, *Life of Francis Place* (1898), Ch. i.
[2] Place MSS. (British Museum), MS. 27808, ff. 59–60. Cf. MS. 35143, ff. 92–4, and for the methods of discussion, based on the reading of a set text, MS. 35142, f. 237 note, and Webb, *British Working Class Reader*, pp. 36–7.

7

The Eighteenth Century

SCIENCE FOR THE CITIZEN

The Growth of Public Interest in Science

'PEOPLE have nowadays got a strange opinion', observed Dr. Johnson in 1766, 'that every thing should be taught by lectures. Now, I cannot see that lectures can do so much good as reading the books from which the lectures are taken. I know of nothing that can best be taught by lectures, except where experiments are to be shewn. You may teach chymistry by lectures:—You might teach making of shoes by lectures!'[1]

It was in fact precisely in the field in which experiments and demonstrations were needed, namely in the teaching of the sciences, that lecturing became so popular during this period. The public interest in science, which during the seventeenth century had been restricted in the main to the *virtuosi* of the Royal Society and their circle, had now become widespread among the educated classes.

In part this interest was vocational, a reflection of the growth of industry and the demand for technological improvement which marked the earlier phases of what we may still for convenience call the Industrial Revolution. This kind of interest, now no longer strongly represented in the Royal Society, found expression, in 1754, in the establishment in London of the Society for the Encouragement of Arts, Manufactures, and Commerce, afterwards the Royal Society of Arts. Founded at a meeting in a London coffee-house, at the instigation of William Shipley, an obscure drawing-master of Northampton, the Society at once enlisted wide support from the aristocracy, gentry, manufacturers, and professional classes, and sought to encourage 'ingenuity and industry' by awarding premiums for improvements in the various branches of trade, industry, and agriculture.[2]

In large measure, however, the public interest in science was an

---

[1] J. Boswell, *Life of Samuel Johnson*, ed. A. Napier (London 1884), Vol. I, p. 415.
[2] The history of the Society has been written by Sir H. T. Wood, *History of the Royal Society of Arts* (1913), and more recently by D. Hudson and K. W. Luckhurst, *The Royal Society of Arts, 1754–1954* (1954).

interest in the subject for its own sake, part of what has been called the 'insatiable curiosity' of the age.

'Natural philosophy', says E. J. Holmyard, 'had become a fashionable hobby, and since the qualitative sciences had not yet assumed that complexity which they were later to develop, any educated man with dextrous fingers could acquire without difficulty a sufficient command of the subject to experience the thrill of standing at the threshold of the unknown . . . The happy upshot was that parson and prelate, lawyer and scholar, author and schoolmaster, burgess and aristocrat, found their fingers burn with the itch to experiment . . .'[1]

Johnson himself was one of them, and had 'an apparatus for chymical experiments' in his study.

For this kind of interest the Royal Society continued to serve as the main focus, reinforced as the century went on by specialist bodies such as the Medical Society of Edinburgh (1734), the Physical Society of Edinburgh (1771), the Medical Society of London (1773), and the Linnaean Society (1788), and at a rather more popular level by the provincial literary and philosophical societies.

Science Lectures and Classes

Public lectures on science became so widespread that a detailed record is impossible. In London the Gresham lectures, which included astronomy, geometry, and physic, continued,[2] and there were also at the beginning of the century lectures on mathematics and chemistry which had begun in the 1690s. The most notable London lecturer of the first half of the century was Dr. John Theophilus Desaguliers, son of a Huguenot refugee. A Church of England clergyman and a leading figure in the English masonic movement, Desaguliers was keenly interested in mathematics and natural philosophy, and lectured on these subjects regularly from 1712 or 1713 until his death in 1744. In 1724 and 1725, for example, he advertised a course of mechanical and experimental philosophy, in twenty-two lectures,

Whereby any one, although unskilled in mathematical sciences, may be able to understand all those phenomena of Nature, which have been discovered by geometrical principles or accounted for by experiments; and mathematicians may be diverted in seeing those machines used and physical operations performed, concerning which they have read.

The course covered mechanics, hydrostatics, pneumatics, and optics, and was delivered on Monday evenings at a fee of two and a

[1] A. S. Turberville (ed.), *Johnson's England* (Oxford 1933), Vol. II, p. 244.
[2] Above, pp. 26–7, 52.

half guineas. There was also a separate morning course of sixteen lectures on astronomy. Desaguliers acquired such a reputation that he was asked to deliver his course to George I and his court at Hampton Court, and subsequently to lecture before George II and his Queen.

This example was quickly followed, and courses on natural philosophy became a regular feature of the life of the capital. Another distinguished lecturer in this field was William Whiston, who had succeeded Newton as Professor of Mathematics at Cambridge but had been deprived for heresy in 1710. During his Cambridge days he had collaborated with Roger Cotes, Professor of Astronomy, in a course of public lectures on hydrostatics and pneumatics at the Observatory at Trinity College (1707). His lectures in London began in the 1720s.

Courses on other subjects were less frequent, but some interesting examples are recorded. From 1721 to 1727 John Martyn, a London apothecary, afterwards Professor of Botany at Cambridge, was lecturing on botany to a newly formed Botanical Society of which he was secretary. The chairman was J. J. Dillen, who became Professor of Botany at Oxford.[1] In 1731, and again in 1732, Peter Shaw, afterwards a fashionable London physician, gave a series of twenty lectures for five guineas a time on chemistry and its practical applications, illustrated by experiments and demonstrations.[2]

In 1774 another medical man, Dr. Bryan Higgins, established in Greek Street, Soho, a school of practical chemistry which provided a three months' course for gentlemen interested in experimental inquiries. The subscription was ten guineas, and meetings were held every other day. Each meeting began with an address not exceeding half an hour by Higgins, supported by experiments or demonstrations, and followed by discussion. These courses continued until 1796, and were attended mostly by physicians, chemists, manufacturers, and others with a professional interest in the subject.

Science courses were also popular in the English provincial towns —not only, as we should expect, in the rapidly growing industrial centres of the North and Midlands, but also in ports, market-towns, and spas. At Newcastle-on-Tyne James Jurin, master at the Grammar School from 1709 to 1715, and afterwards famous as a physician, lectured on natural philosophy; and Isaac Thompson lectured on the same subject in 1739. Manchester had lectures in mathematics as

---

[1] G. S. Boulger, 'John Martyn', in *D.N.B.*
[2] F. W. Gibb, 'Peter Shaw and the Revival of Chemistry', in *Annals of Science*, Vol. VII (1951).

early as 1719,[1] and courses in natural philosophy were frequent there from the 1740s onwards. Scarborough, owing to the accident that Peter Shaw was in practice there for a few years, had a course in chemistry in 1733, and Birmingham had 'philosophical lectures' in 1747 and 1750.[2]

In the second half of the century one has the impression that there were science courses almost everywhere. Manchester, Newcastle, and Bristol seem to have been the most important centres, but a class of itinerant lecturers was now springing up who made regular tours of neighbouring towns. Thus in the 'sixties and 'seventies Benjamin Donn was lecturing in Bristol and district[3]; Adam Walker, of Manchester, was lecturing in Manchester, Liverpool, Leeds, Halifax, York, Birmingham, 'and many small towns in the North', as well as in London, and James Ferguson, self-educated son of a Scottish day labourer, undertook tours which included Bristol, Bath, Derby, Manchester, and Newcastle.[4] The usual subject for these provincial courses was natural philosophy, a title which was often used as a convenient omnibus term for the physical sciences. More specific courses were also given, however, in mathematics, astronomy, and chemistry.[5] Though popular in character, and often illustrated by rather spectacular experiments, models and demonstrations (somewhat in the manner of the present-day Royal Institution lectures for school children), the courses were usually quite solid and systematic in the presentation of their scientific material, and their appeal was as much to the general interest of the subject as to any professional or vocational value it might have for the audience. The audiences were usually middle-class, and included a considerable number of ladies.

We may fairly say, in fact, that these lectures have their place in the remote ancestry of University Extension teaching rather than in that of the technical colleges. The prototype of these latter, or at least of the evening institutes, was to be found in the evening classes in mathematics for craftsmen and mechanics which started about

---

[1] See below, p. 104.
[2] J. A. Langford, *A Century of Birmingham Life* (Birmingham 1868), Vol. I, pp. 33-4.
[3] An interesting account of itinerant lecturers in the Bristol area, by Eric Robinson, was printed in *The Listener*, 12 Dec. 1957.
[4] Other centres at which lectures are known to have been given during the latter half of the century are Exeter, Taunton, and Stourbridge; Leicester, Nottingham, Etruria, Chesterfield, and Gainsborough; and in the North, Warrington, Lancaster, Kendal (which had the privilege of lectures from the young John Dalton), Rotherham, and Sheffield. For the last two see M. Brook, 'Dr. Warwick's Chemistry Lectures and the Scientific Audience in Sheffield (1799–1801)', in *Annals of Science*, Vol. XI (1955).
[5] The best known itinerant lecturer on chemistry was John Warltire, the friend and collaborator of Joseph Priestley: see D. McKie, 'Mr. Warltire, a good chymist', in *Endeavour*, Vol. X (1951)

the same time—in Newcastle from the 1750s, in Salford from 1772, in Leicester in 1788, and in Soho, London, from 1789.[1]

Anderson's Institution, Glasgow

The subject of public science lectures in Scotland at this period is one that still awaits investigation, but in Edinburgh and Glasgow, at least, something was being done. The blind Scottish scientist Henry Moyes, who afterwards lectured extensively on chemistry and natural philosophy in England, Ireland, and America, began his lecturing career in Edinburgh in the 1770s, and lectured there again at intervals in his later career.[2]

In Glasgow a science course was given for many years under the auspices of the University. It was not, it seems, uncommon at this period for lectures at the Scottish universities to be attended by students from outside the walls.[3] At Glasgow, however, under the statutes of 1727, the Professor of Natural Philosophy was obliged to give, in addition to his normal academic courses, a course in experimental philosophy specially designed for the general public. John Anderson, who held the chair from 1757 until his death in 1796, turned this into a course in applied science for the benefit of 'the Manufacturers and Artificers in Glasgow'. The course met morning and evening on Tuesdays and Thursdays throughout the University session, at a fee of £1 1s. At a time when Glasgow was rapidly rising into importance as a commercial and industrial centre, such a course was inevitably very popular, and Anderson claimed that it was attended by 'Town's people of almost every rank, age and employment'. He was particularly anxious to secure the attendance of working mechanics, and is said to have distributed free tickets to 'gardeners, painters, shopmen, porters, founders, bookbinders, barbers, tailors, potters, glassblowers, gunsmiths, engravers, brewers, and turners'.[4]

Anderson spent a considerable part of his academic career in quarrelling with his University colleagues, and when he died he bequeathed his estate for the establishment of a rival university. The funds proved quite inadequate for this purpose, but his trustees made a beginning by founding in 1796 a body known as Anderson's Institution, which ultimately became, after many vicissitudes, the

---

[1] The best general account of science lectures and classes at this period is in N. Hans, *New Trends in Education in the Eighteenth Century*, Ch. vii. See also T. Kelly, *George Birkbeck* (Liverpool 1957), pp. 25, 58–9.

[2] J. A. Harrison, 'Blind Henry Moyes', in *Annals of Science*, Vol. XIII (1957).

[3] For examples of this, at Glasgow and Edinburgh, see A. Kent (ed.) *An Eighteenth Century Lectureship in Chemistry* (Glasgow 1950), pp. 4, 33, 84, 112.

[4] Kelly, *op. cit.*, pp. 20–2, and authorities there cited.

Glasgow Royal College of Science and Technology which we know to-day.

Thomas Garnett, a Yorkshire doctor, was chosen as first professor, with the duty of conducting morning and evening lectures on natural philosophy and chemistry, with particular reference to arts and manufactures, for the ladies and gentlemen of Glasgow. In 1799 Count Rumford founded the Royal Institution in London on very similar lines, and Garnett went off to be first professor there. His place at Glasgow was taken by another Yorkshire doctor, George Birkbeck, with whose achievements here and elsewhere we shall have to deal in a later chapter.[1]

Working-Class Scientific Societies

The general interest in science was reflected also in the formation of scientific societies. The earliest of these, it is interesting to note, were quite specifically working-class in character. The Spitalfields Mathematical Society, founded in 1717, had a membership limited to the square of eight, and seems to have consisted almost entirely of working men, principally weavers. The Society met from 8 to 10 on Saturday evenings, at first in taverns, later in its own rooms. During the first hour each member was to employ himself in some mathematical exercise, or forfeit one penny; and if he refused to answer a question in mathematics asked by another he was to forfeit twopence.[2] The second hour was occupied, at least from 1746, in experiments in natural philosophy, and a collection of apparatus ('air-pumps, reflecting telescopes, reflecting microscopes, electrical machines, surveying instruments, etc.') was acquired for this purpose. A considerable library was also formed, and members were allowed to borrow instruments and books on giving a note of hand for their value.

The eighteenth-century members of the Society included one or two men of real distinction, for example Thomas Simpson, who became in 1743 Professor of Mathematics at the Royal Military Academy at Woolwich, and John Dollond, founder of the famous firm of optical instrument makers.[3] Dollond, who spent most of his

---

[1] Kelly, op. cit., pp. 22–6, and authorities there cited.

[2] J. Timbs, Club Life of London (1866), Vol. II, pp. 160–1. This probably represents the early practice of the Society. The fullest account is by H. H. Cawthorne, 'The Spitalfields Mathematical Society (1717–1845)', in Journal of Adult Education, Vol. III (1928–9), and from this it appears that by 1783 the rules were a little different and the fines much heavier.

[3] S. Smiles, The Huguenots (4th edn. 1870), pp. 323–4. Smiles also mentions a weaver named Edwards as having become a professor at Woolwich but this is incorrect. Another source suggests that Edwards entered Government service at Chatham, but I have been unable to discover anything further concerning him.

life as a weaver before joining his son in an optical business, studied not only mathematics but also anatomy, natural history, astronomy, optics, divinity, and ecclesiastical history, and in order to pursue his studies learned Latin, Greek, French, German, and Italian.[1] He invented the achromatic telescope, and in the year of his death (1761) was elected a Fellow of the Royal Society.

The Society absorbed another local mathematical society in 1772, and a Historical Society in 1783. By the early years of the nineteenth century it was beginning to attract professional as well as working-class members, and to concentrate on lectures instead of individual study. From 1826 onwards trade depression, the decline of hand-loom weaving, and the competition of the mechanics' institutes led to a decline, and in 1845 the Society was itself absorbed by the Astronomical Society.

Why weavers should be particularly interested in mathematics is not clear. Perhaps it is because their trade accustomed them to working with mathematical patterns, and at the same time allowed them ample opportunity for reflection. However this may be, the same phenomenon is observable, at this period, among the weavers of Lancashire and Yorkshire, who were particularly interested in geometry. Where the seventeenth-century Kidderminster weaver had placed some work of devotion on the loom before him, the northern weaver placed a geometrical problem to occupy his spare thoughts. In 1718 the Manchester weavers formed a mathematical society on lines similar to those of the Spitalfields society, and at their request John Jackson, afterwards described as 'the Father of the Lancashire School of Geometers', gave in 1719 a series of public lectures on the subject. The society flourished throughout the eighteenth century, and in 1794 had an offshoot in the Oldham Mathematical Society.[2]

It should be said that the interests of the Spitalfields weavers, many of whom were Huguenots or of Huguenot descent, were by no means confined to mathematics. A witness before the Royal Commission on Handloom Weavers testified in 1840 to the extraordinary wealth of cultural societies that had formerly existed in this district. After referring to the Mathematical Society and the Historical Society, he went on:

There was a Floricultural Society, very numerously attended, but now extinct. The weavers were almost the only botanists of their day in the metropolis. They passed their leisure hours, and generally the whole

---

[1] A. M. Clerke, 'John Dollond', in *D.N.B.*

[2] T. T. Wilkinson, 'The Lancashire Geometers and their Writings', in *Memoirs of the Manchester Literary and Philosophical Society*, 2nd Ser., Vol. XI (1854).

family dined on Sundays, at the little gardens in the environs of London, now mostly built upon, in small rooms, about the size of modern omni-buses, with a fire-place at the end. There was an Entomological Society, and they were the first entomologists in the kingdom. The society is gone. They had a Recitation Society for Shakspearian readings, as well as reading other authors, which is now almost forgotten. They had a Musical Society, but this is also gone. There was a Columbarian Society which gave a silver medal as a prize for the best pigeon of a fancy breed . . . They were great bird fanciers, and breeders of canaries . . . Their breed of spaniels, called Splashers, . . . were of the best sporting blood . . .[1]

How many of these activities dated back to the eighteenth century is not clear, but the Floricultural and Entomological Societies were probably early in date,[2] and there were Spitalfields weavers in the Madrigal Society founded in London in 1741.[3]

We do not know to what extent working-class mutual improve-ment societies for the study of science existed in other centres, but we have already had occasion to notice one such society, interested particularly in natural philosophy, at Birmingham in the 'eighties and 'nineties.[4]

The Lunar Society

The gentlemen's societies formed in the East Midlands from 1712 onwards[5] paid a certain amount of attention to science, and we have remarked also the formation of a Botanical Society in London in 1721. In Scotland a Philosophical Society, for the improvement of arts and sciences, was established in Edinburgh in 1739. The forma-tion of the great provincial literary and philosophical societies, however, belongs to the late eighteenth and early nineteenth cen-turies. It is a development characteristic particularly of the North, and is clearly associated in part, though by no means exclusively, with the new interest in applied science arising from the Industrial Revolution.

In England an interesting precursor of the literary and philosophi-cal societies was the famous Lunar Society of Birmingham, which included such well-known figures as Matthew Boulton and James Watt, partners from 1775 onwards in the manufacture of steam-engines at Boulton's Soho works; Erasmus Darwin, the Lichfield physician and grandfather of Charles Darwin; Richard Lovell

[1] Royal Commission on Handloom Weavers, *Reports of Assistant Commissioners*, Part II (1840), pp. 216–17. The workers of Birmingham also had their allotments and summer-houses on the fringe of the city—see Langford, *Century of Birmingham Life*, Vol. II, p. 283.
[2] See Smiles, *op. cit.*, p. 323.   [3] See above, p. 91.
[4] Above, p. 79.   [5] Above, pp. 88–9.   [6] Above, p. 100.

Edgeworth, educationist and inventor; Josiah Wedgwood the potter; and Joseph Priestley, scientist and Unitarian minister. This group corresponded with, and often received visits from, most of the famous scientists of the day, and there has consequently been a tendency to suppose that the circle of the Society was much wider than in fact it was.

Actually it comprised a dozen or more people, meeting privately once a month in one another's homes, to discuss the latest scientific discoveries and to conduct scientific experiments. The name arose from the fact that, to make the homeward journey easier, the members customarily met at the time of the full moon. The Society seems to have had its origins in informal gatherings for discussion, about the year 1768, but it does not seem to have taken formal shape until about 1775.

The 'Lunatics', as they were inevitably christened, were particularly interested in chemistry: it was at this period that Priestley was publishing the results of his experiments on the composition of air and other gases, and that Watt was identifying the constituent elements of water. A letter from Watt to Darwin, inviting his presence at a meeting in January 1781, gives a good idea of the kind of discussion that went on:

For your encouragement there is a new book to be cut up, and it is to be determined whether or not heat is a compound of phlogiston and empyreal air, and whether a mirror can reflect the heat of the fire. I give you a friendly warning that you may be found wanting whichever opinion you may adopt in the latter question; therefore be cautious. If you are meek and humble, perhaps you may be told what light is made of, and also how to make it, and the theory proved by synthesis and analysis.[1]

The Society continued in full vigour until 1791. In that year the excitement caused by the French Revolution led to riots in Birmingham, in which Priestley, as a known sympathiser with the Revolution, was the principal victim. Both his chapel and his house were burnt, his fine library and laboratory destroyed, and he himself driven from the city, to find ultimate refuge in America. His departure, and the deaths of other leading members, led to a gradual decline of the Society, which had its last known meeting in 1799.[2]

[1] H. C. Bolton (ed.), *Scientific Correspondence of Joseph Priestley* (New York 1892), p. 201.
[2] S. Smiles, *Lives of the Engineers*, Vol. V, Boulton and Watt (rev. edn. 1874), Ch. xv; H. C. Bolton, *op. cit.*, App. II; H. Pearson, *Doctor Darwin* (1930), Ch. vii; A. Holt, *Life of Joseph Priestley* (1931), Chs. vii, ix, x; R. E. Schofield, 'Membership of the Lunar Society of Birmingham', in *Annals of Science*, Vol. XII (1956). An interesting account of the members of the Society, and their connections with other similar societies and with the dissenting movement in education generally, is given in B. Simon, *Studies in the History of Education, 1780–1870* (1960), pp. 17–38.

Literary and Philosophical Societies

Erasmus Darwin, meantime, had left Lichfield to take up residence in Derby, where he brought together a group of the local gentry, professional men and manufacturers to form the Derby Philosophical Society (1784). Though less distinguished than the Lunar Society, it had a longer life, perhaps because from the first it devoted considerable attention to the building up of a library, including the publications of all the leading scientific societies of Great Britain and France. It survived until 1857, when it was amalgamated with the Derby Museum.[1]

Literary and philosophical societies were also formed at Liverpool in 1779,[2] and at Leeds in 1783,[3] but these proved short-lived. It was the Manchester Literary and Philosophical Society, founded in 1781, which became the model for many societies of this type. It had its origin in private informal gatherings, rather like those of the Lunar Society, at the house of Dr. Thomas Percival, a medical man and a noted social reformer, but unlike the Lunar Society it developed into a public institution, with regularly appointed officers and order of procedure, and many of the papers read before it were published in its official *Memoirs*.

Amongst the founders was Dr. Thomas Barnes, minister of Cross Street Presbyterian (afterwards Unitarian) Chapel, and it was here that most of the early meetings of the Society were held. Of the other founders more than half were medical men or apothecaries. The activities of the Society covered a wide range of interests[4]—literature, history, economics, mathematics, medicine, and so forth—but it was for its work in science that the 'Lit. and Phil.' won the greatest reputation. This was in considerable measure because of the work of John Dalton, who joined in 1794, and during his fifty years' membership read 116 papers and served successively as Secretary, Vice-President and President.[5]

---

[1] E. Robinson, 'The Derby Philosophical Society', in *Annals of Science*, Vol. IX (1953).
[2] B. B. B. Benas, 'Centenary of the Historic Society of Lancashire and Cheshire', in the Society's *Transactions*, Supplement to Vol. C (Liverpool 1950), p. 9.
[3] E. K. Clarke, *History of 100 Years of the Leeds Philosophical and Literary Society* (Leeds 1924), p. 2 note.
[4] The rules provided that the subjects of conversation should include natural philosophy, chemistry, literature, civil law, general politics, commerce and the arts, but religion, 'the practical branches of physic', and British politics were excluded—R. A. Smith, *A Centenary of Science in Manchester* (*Memoirs of the Lit. and Phil. Soc. of Manchester*, 3rd Ser., Vol. IX, London 1883), p. 29.
[5] F. Nicholson, 'The Literary and Philosophical Society, 1781–1851', in *Memoirs*, 8th Ser., Vol. LXVIII (1923-4); C. L. Barnes, *The Manchester Literary and Philosophical Society* (Manchester 1938); H. J. Fleure, 'The Manchester Literary and Philosophical Society', in *Endeavour*, Vol. VI (1947). Robert Owen was an early member, and his autobiography (*Life of Robert Owen*, 1857-8, new edn. 1920, pp. 50-3) gives an impression of the meetings.

For at least four years (1783–7) the Society sponsored an evening College of Arts and Sciences for young business and professional men, but this project failed owing to lack of support.[1]

In 1793 the Newcastle Literary and Philosophical Society was formed, largely on the model of that at Manchester. As at Manchester, the medical profession took a leading part in its establishment, but the principal founder was the Unitarian minister, Rev. William Turner, who long served as one of the joint secretaries of the Society, and was for thirty years (from 1803) its official lecturer on natural philosophy and allied subjects.[2] The next thirty or forty years saw similar developments in many English provincial towns.[3]

An important point, though space does not permit us to enlarge upon it, is the influence of the dissenting academies upon this movement for scientific education. Being free from the statutes and traditions that bound the English universities and grammar schools, these academies were able to break away from the narrow classical curriculum and develop a broader discipline better suited to the practical needs of the professional man, the merchant, and the manufacturer. Thus they taught English literature, modern languages, history, and geography, and they commonly placed a great deal of emphasis on experimental science. The names of Joseph Priestley, John Dalton, Thomas Percival, Thomas Barnes, and William Turner, all of them associated with dissenting academies either as teachers, or as pupils, or both, may serve as pointers to the extent to which these institutions helped to provide leadership for the new scientific movement in adult education.[4]

There has always been in adult education a strong strain of non-conformity, both religious and political. It is significant, too, that of the six persons just named five were Unitarians, the exception being John Dalton, who was a Quaker. Of all the dissenting sects the Unitarians were the most forward, both in this and the succeeding century, in seeking to promote the cause of adult education.

In Scotland scientific activity was concentrated mainly in the

[1] The scheme was due to Thomas Barnes, who in the previous year (1782), had propounded a plan for a museum of chemistry and the mechanic arts, with a curator to give lectures—an interesting anticipation of the mechanics' institute idea. See Smith, *op. cit.*, pp. 163–70; and H. J. Thompson, *Owens College* (Manchester 1886), pp. 2–10.

[2] See R. S. Watson, *The Literary and Philosophical Society of Newcastle-upon-Tyne* (1897), especially Ch. iii.

[3] See below, p. 113. Leicester had a short-lived philosophical society, about 1788–90, founded and presided over by Richard Phillips (afterwards Sir Richard Phillips), the Radical bookseller—F. S. Herne, 'An Old Leicester Bookseller', in *Transactions* of the Leicester Literary and Philosophical Society, N.S., Vol. III, Pt. II (Jan. 1893).

[4] For the influence of the Warrington Academy on the Manchester Literary and Philosophical Society, see H. McLachlan, *Warrington Academy* (Chetham Society, 2nd Ser., Vol. CVII, Manchester 1943), pp. 114–28.

universities of Edinburgh and Glasgow, which by the end of the century had shaken off the iron grip of Calvinism and had become the centres of a great intellectual Renaissance. Many societies, scientific and non-scientific, sprang up within the universities themselves—the Speculative Society of Edinburgh is a famous example—but public scientific societies arose only in the capital. Some of these have already been mentioned.[1] The Physical Society of Edinburgh, founded in 1771, was incorporated in 1788 in the Royal Physical Society of Edinburgh, and devoted itself mainly to the study of natural history. The Philosophical Society of Edinburgh, founded in 1739, was moribund for many years but was reconstituted in 1783 as the Royal Society of Edinburgh. Like the Manchester Literary and Philosophical Society it was intended to have both a literary and a scientific side, but the scientific interest quickly became dominant.[2]

The Development of Public Museums

It will be appropriate to conclude this survey of scientific education in the eighteenth century with a brief reference to the gradual development of public museums. We have referred in earlier chapters to the primitive collections established by the Tradescants at South Lambeth and by Don Saltero in Cheyne Walk. Don Saltero's coffee-house museum continued to attract customers, and found imitators as the century went on. In 1756 a Mr. Adams, at the Royal Swan in Kingsland Road, was exhibiting a collection of rarities which included (perhaps out of compliment to the proprietor) 'Adam's eldest daughter's hat', and 'Adam's key of the fore and back door of the Garden of Eden'; and in 1772 James Cox, of Spring Gardens, Charing Cross, was advertising a museum of jewellery, mechanical contrivances, and curiosities.[3]

In the meantime the formation of more scientific private collections continued, and the reconstitution of the Society of Antiquaries in 1717 provided facilities for more systematic study and discussion within this particular field.[4] Some of the private collections were

---

[1] Above, pp. 99, 105.

[2] J. Kendall, 'The Royal Society of Edinburgh', in *Endeavour*, Vol. V (1946).

[3] Timbs, *op. cit.*, Vol. II, pp. 46–7. The religious items in the catalogues of these early museums remind one of the lists of relics preserved in medieval churches, e.g. the list for St. Mary's, Warwick, in 1445 (*Victoria County History, Warwickshire*, ed. W. Page, Vol. II, 1908, p. 128).

[4] This revival had its origins in private meetings in various London taverns from 1707 onwards, and the Society's meetings were initially held at the famous Mitre Tavern in Fleet Street—see J. Evans, *A History of the Society of Antiquaries* (Oxford 1956), Chs. iii–v. About 1739 William Stukeley, the antiquary, founded an Egyptian Society which met in a London tavern (*ibid.*, p. 94).

thrown open free of charge to the public, and became while their owners lived virtually public museums. This was notably the case with the collection formed by the wealthy London physician Richard Mead (1673–1754), who converted his spacious house in Great Ormond Street into 'a repository of all that is curious in nature or in art'. Later in the century, from 1775 to 1783, Sir Ashton Lever was exhibiting in Leicester Square the museum which he had formed at his home at Alkrington Hall, near Manchester. James Parkinson, who subsequently acquired the collection by purchasing a ticket in a lottery, continued to exhibit it for some years near Blackfriars Bridge.

It is about this time that we hear of the first public museum in the provinces, namely at Lichfield. It was formed by Richard Greene, a relative of Dr. Johnson, who visited it in company with Boswell in 1776. 'Sir,' said Dr. Johnson, 'I should as soon have thought of building a man of war, as of collecting such a museum.'[1] In Scotland, though small collections of science, natural history, and antiquities were formed in the Universities of Edinburgh, Glasgow, and Aberdeen, and by professional bodies such as the Faculty of Advocates, the serious and systematic formation of a museum was first undertaken in 1780 by the Society of Antiquaries of Scotland, formed in Edinburgh in that year. This ultimately became the National Museum of Antiquities.

The outstanding event in museum history in the eighteenth century, however, was unquestionably the foundation of the British Museum, created in 1753 by the purchase for the nation of the magnificent collections of the late Sir Hans Sloane, and opened to the public, at Montagu House, in 1759. Many years were to pass before the full potentialities of the Museum could be realised, and a French visitor to the natural history collection towards the close of the century described it as 'rather an immense magazine, in which things have been thrown at random, than a scientific collection'[2]; but in time to come it was to be a great instrument of public instruction, illustrating 'the phenomena of the universe and the activities of man more completely perhaps than any other single institution in the world'.[3]

The establishment of the British Museum was also a portent in library history, for along with the Sloane museum the government

[1] J. Boswell, *Life of Samuel Johnson*, ed. A. Napier (1884), Vol. I, p. 415.
[2] Faujas de Saint-Fond, quoted in D. Murray, *Museums, their History and Use*, Vol. I (Glasgow 1904), p. 212. His account was first published in 1797.
[3] G. Davies, *The Whig Supremacy, 1714–1760* (Oxford 1939), p. 372.

acquired Sloane's great library of 50,000 books and 3,516 manuscripts, and these, with the addition of the Harleian and Cottonian manuscripts, and a large collection of books and manuscripts from the royal library, laid the foundation of the great British Museum Library which we know to-day.

8

The Nineteenth Century

THE AGE OF MECHANICS' INSTITUTES

BY the first half of the nineteenth century adult education was flourishing in a great variety of forms and at all levels of society, but the characteristic feature of the period was the tremendous interest in the teaching of science. We have seen this interest developing, in the form of public lectures and scientific societies, from the seventeenth century onwards, and we have observed how it received a new impetus as a result of the importance of applied science in the Industrial Revolution. This new impulse continued into the early nineteenth century, but the technological interest, though it helped to loosen the purse-strings of hard-headed northern manufacturers for the endowment of local societies, was not the only one: there was also a keen interest in science for its own sake. Whatever the motive, the urge to study science inevitably found its chief outlet in adult education, because the provision for science in the public educational system was so completely inadequate. At the outset of the century the grammar schools and the two ancient universities were still almost untouched by the modern scientific movement; the dissenting academies were fading out; and the foundation of the University of London—the first to give adequate recognition to scientific studies, was a quarter of a century away. Only in some private schools, and in the Scottish universities, was a serious scientific education to be had.[1]

Middle-class Scientific and Cultural Societies

In these circumstances we find, during the first half of the century, new scientific societies, both specialist and non-specialist, springing up everywhere. Among the specialist societies were some of a national character, such as the Geological Society (1807), the Royal Astronomical Society (1820), the Zoological Society (1826), the Royal Geographical Society (1830), the Royal Botanic Society (1839), and

[1] See D. S. L. Cardwell, *The Organisation of Science in England* (1957), Ch. iii. Cf. Sir E. Ashby, *Technology and the Academics* (1958), Chs. i–ii.

the Chemical Society (1841). All these subjects were, of course, embraced within the scope of the Royal Society, but until after 1820 this was still much more a gentlemen's club than a learned society.[1] Outside London there were geological societies from Cornwall (1814) to Edinburgh (1834), natural history societies from Orkney (1837) to Suffolk (1848), philosophical societies or institutes from Cambridge (1819) to Aberdeen (1840).[2] These last usually aimed at covering the whole range of the sciences, the oldest and most comprehensive being the Glasgow Philosophical Society (1802), which included not only all the physical and biological sciences but even statistics and domestic economy.

The study of science was also pursued in a more general cultural context. In London bodies such as the London Institution (1805), the Philomathic Institution (1807), and the Russell Institution (1808), showed a catholic interest in science, letters, and sometimes art, while in many English provincial towns the pattern was set by the literary and philosophical societies founded at Manchester and Newcastle in the previous century. Societies of this name (or occasionally 'philosophic and literary society') were established in Liverpool (1812), Leeds (1820), Sheffield and Hull (1822), Whitby (1823), Bristol (1824), Halifax (1830), Leicester (1835), and Barnsley and Rochdale (1833); and there were similar bodies, under other names, in Warrington (1811), Plymouth (1812), Nottingham (1824), Bath (1825), Elgin (1836), Gloucester (1838), and Ipswich (1842).

The character of these societies is typified in the statement of the objects of the Leeds Philosophical and Literary Society, namely 'the promotion of Science and Literature, by the reading of Papers, the delivery of Lectures, the formation of a Museum, the collection of a Library, and the establishment of a Laboratory fitted up with Apparatus'.[3] Essentially they were societies for the mutual improvement of their own members. There were, however, some scientific societies which aimed to influence a wider public. Such was the Royal Institution in London, whose foundation in 1799 has been noted above, and which was established 'for diffusing the knowledge and facilitating the general and speedy introduction of new and

---

[1] The death in 1820 of Sir Joseph Banks, the amateur naturalist who had been President since 1778, marked the turning point in the Society's history, but it was not until 1860 that the scientific Fellows outnumbered their colleagues. See Sir H. Lyons, *The Royal Society, 1660–1940* (Cambridge 1944), Ch. vii.

[2] In many instances, as in Suffolk, the study of natural history was associated with that of archaeology, though archaeology also had its own societies, for example the Sussex Archaeological Society and the Cambrian Archaeological Association, both founded in 1846.

[3] A. Hume, *Learned Societies and Printing Clubs of the United Kingdom* (1847), p. 3.14

useful mechanical inventions and improvements, and also for teaching, by regular courses of philosophical lectures and experiments, the application of these discoveries in science to the improvement of arts and manufactures, and in facilitating the means of procuring the comforts and conveniences of life'.

As it happened, the Royal Institution did not develop on such severely technological lines as this statement of aims would suggest. An attempt to provide residential technical education for young mechanics (1801) had to be abandoned because it was thought by many to have 'a dangerous political tendency', science for the working classes being associated in the public mind, at this period, with scepticism, radicalism, and the French Revolution. Henceforth for many years the main feature of the Institution's activities lay in its public lecture-courses, which, delivered by such men as Humphry Davy, Michael Faraday, and Sidney Smith, attracted brilliant and fashionable audiences. The future of the Institution, however, was being shaped not in the lecture-room but in the laboratory; for the chemical and electrical researches of Davy, who was Professor of Chemistry from 1802–12, and of Faraday, who held the same office from 1833 until his death in 1867, won both for themselves and for the Institution an international reputation.

The Liverpool Royal Institution, which was for a time one of the major provincial organisations devoted to the diffusion of learning, was in part inspired by the London body, but was uncompromisingly cultural in character. Its aim was declared to be 'the promotion of literature, science and the arts', and the leading figure in its early years was that remarkable man William Roscoe, who for a generation was at the centre of every great cultural movement in Liverpool, and had won world acclaim by his *Life of Lorenzo de' Medici* (1796).[1] Professors were appointed in a variety of subjects, an elaborate programme of morning and evening lectures was arranged, a library, a natural history museum and an art gallery were formed, and classical and mathematical schools were started for boys. In addition the Institution provided a meeting place for other cultural organisations such as the Literary and Philosophical Society and the Philomathic Society.

These admirable enterprises met with varying success. The boys' school (the two schools were quickly formed into one) proved most valuable, and survived until 1892, when the competition of newer

[1] Lawyer, banker, historian, art connoisseur, and minor poet, Roscoe was the son of a Liverpool market-gardener, and largely self-taught. There is a fascinating *Life* by his son Henry Roscoe (2 vols. 1833).

schools led to its closure. The lectures seem to have been popular at first, but proved such a drain on the Institution's finances that they had to be abandoned in 1839. The art gallery, though enriched by paintings from the Roscoe collection which are now among the most precious possessions of the Walker Art Gallery, was frequented mainly by students. The museum was more popular, especially on open days when the public were admitted free of charge: on one such day in 1840 over 11,000 people were admitted.

All the departments of the Institution's work, however, were throughout handicapped by inadequate financial resources, and this led to its decline when faced with the competition of municipal institutions later in the century.[1]

The Royal Manchester Institution, also for the promotion of literature, science and the arts, was established on similar lines in 1823. The interest in applied science which had inspired the original Royal Institution was, however, reflected in such bodies as the Scottish Society of Arts (1821), the Royal Cornwall Polytechnic Society (1833), and the Liverpool Polytechnic Society (1838).

To this long list of scientific societies must be added one more— the British Association, an itinerant congress of scientists modelled on the Gesellschaft deutscher Naturforscher und Ärzte. It was founded in 1831, in part as a result of dissatisfaction with the Royal Society, and its object was to promote discovery, to direct general attention to scientific matters, and to 'make it easier for scientists to meet.[2]

Origins and Precursors of the Mechanics' Institutes

The existence of these institutions provided a focus for much of the public lecturing on science that had hitherto been carried on

---

[1] See below, p. 215.

[2] The story of the middle-class cultural societies of the early nineteenth century has been strangely neglected. Hume, *Learned Societies*, cited above, is the best general reference work, but is very incomplete. Information regarding some societies may be had in J. W. Hudson, *History of Adult Education* (1851), and in an article in the *Quarterly Review*, Vol. XXXIV (1826), pp. 153 sqq., and there is a useful list in the *Encyclopaedia Britannica* (11th edn. 1910–11) s.v. Societies, Learned, but for the most part details have to be sought from local sources, or from the histories of individual institutions, e.g. H. B. Woodward, *History of the Geological Society of London* (1907); T. S. Moore and J. C. Philip, *The Chemical Society, 1841–1941* (1947); W. S. Porter, *Sheffield Literary and Philosophical Society* (Sheffield 1922); E. K. Clarke, *History of the Leeds Philosophical and Literary Society* (Leeds 1924); Halifax Literary and Philosophical Society, *Centenary Handbook* (Halifax 1930); H. B. Browne, *Chapters of Whitby History 1823–1946* (Hull 1946); H. B. Jones, *The Royal Institution* (1871); T. Martin, *The Royal Institution* (1942, 2nd edn. 1948); H. A. Ormerod, *The Liverpool Royal Institution* (Liverpool 1953). For the British Association see Cardwell, *Organisation of Science in England*, pp. 46 sqq.

Dates of foundation tend to vary in different accounts, according to whether the author is referring to the first conception of the society concerned or to some later and more formal stage in its establishment.

under other auspices, but a great deal of independent public lecturing still went on. A correspondent in *The Times* in 1815 referred to 'peripatetic philosophers, who give lectures for a guinea each course, in every village near London'.[1] The price here cited, about half that customarily charged in the big cities, suggests that the lecturers were now beginning to reach down to a more popular audience, and we have confirmation of this in references to itinerant lecturers, about this time, in small country towns such as Clitheroe, Settle, and Kirkcaldy.[2] Thus the ground was being prepared for the establishment of institutions similar in organisation to the literary and philosophical societies, but more popular in scope. In 1814, indeed, a Scottish schoolmaster, Dr. Thomas Dick of Methven, near Perth, actually suggested such a plan in a series of letters to the *Monthly Magazine*. His scheme was for the establishment of 'literary and philosophical societies, among the middling and lower ranks of the community', and he made a beginning at Methven by organising science classes and a popular library.

The answer to the need expressed by Dick was shortly to be found in the mechanics' institute movement. At the time that he wrote, many factors were converging to bring this movement into being. Just as the institutes may be regarded as a downward extension of middle-class literary and philosophical societies, so also they may be regarded as an upward extension of the movement for the elementary education of children, which drew widespread support in the early years of the century both from evangelical conservatism and from Benthamite liberalism, and found expression in the rapid extension of the monitorial schools initiated by Joseph Lancaster and Andrew Bell. From yet another point of view they may be looked on as an educational reflection of the new political and economic aspirations of the working classes—aspirations which were repressed during the French wars but found an outlet once more, in the post-war years, in trade unionism, in the socialist and co-operative movements, and in demands for parliamentary reform which eventually took shape in Chartism. And of course they may also be interpreted as a consequence of the Industrial Revolution.

This last factor is indeed often advanced as the sole cause of the mechanics' institute movement, and certainly its importance should not be underestimated. The unprecedented growth of population, the concentration of the working classes in the new urban areas, and

[1] *Times*, 9 Nov. 1815.
[2] Clitheroe 1810, Kirkcaldy 1817, Settle 1823–4. See T. Kelly, *George Birkbeck* (Liverpool 1957), p. 59. A fuller study would no doubt produce many more examples.

the increasing need for better-educated workmen in a period of rapid technological change, combined to create an environment in which it was easy for the mechanics' institutes to take root and flourish. It is, however, a mistake to link the movement, as is often done, specifically with the development of the factory system. Almost inevitably, we tend to associate 'mechanic' with 'machinery', but in the 1820s, when the first mechanics' institutes were founded, the power-driven factory was not at all extensively developed outside the textile areas, and the name 'mechanic' did not mean primarily a machine operative. In so far as it had a precise meaning, it meant, on the contrary, a craftsman, a 'tradesman' in the northern sense; but its meaning was often extended to cover all manual workers, or, more vaguely still, all who belonged to the 'working class'. In fact it was the skilled craftsman rather than the machine operative who at this period most needed to keep abreast of new inventions, new processes, and new materials, and it was to this group that the first efforts in the education of mechanics were directed.[1]

The mechanics' institute movement had its forerunners in the various working men's libraries, book clubs, and mutual improvement societies, which had their beginning, as we have seen, in the eighteenth century. The earliest of them, indeed, the Spitalfields Mathematical Society, was still flourishing at the outset of the nineteenth century, and others quickly followed, some of them even anticipating, very nearly, the actual title of mechanics' institute. The first example of this is recorded in 1810 in a manuscript in the Chester City Library, which bears the title 'Mechanic Institution established in Chester MDCCCX', and includes proposals issued by John Broster, a local bookseller and antiquarian, for the creation of a library and reading room for masters, workmen, and apprentices. Another example is found in the Mechanical Institution founded in London, in 1817, by Timothy Claxton, a journeyman mechanic. This was a mutual improvement society for instruction in 'all subjects connected with the arts, sciences, manufactures and commerce' and Claxton's plans included the formation of a library and a collection of models of machinery, but the society came to an end in 1820 before these proposals could be fully developed.[2]

In 1823, when the London Mechanics' Institution was formed,

---

[1] For an interesting discussion on this point at the time of the foundation of the London Mechanics' Institution see Kelly, op. cit., p. 86, and for later changes in meaning of the word 'mechanic' ibid., pp. 243–5.

[2] Claxton went in 1820 to Russia, and thence to the U.S.A., where he played a leading part in the establishment of mechanics' institutes. See his Hints to Mechanics (1839), Chs. i–iv.

there were said to be a number of mutual improvement societies meeting in the city, among them the City Philosophical Society in Dorset Street, Salisbury Square, which had been in existence about fifteen years.

In 1817 Samuel Brown, a merchant of Haddington, created a system of 'itinerating libraries'—small collections of books, chiefly religious, which were circulated among a score of centres in the Haddington area. From this there developed, in the following year, a small society of tradesmen for the study of such subjects as mechanics, chemistry, and geometry.[1] In Glasgow in 1821, at the suggestion of J. B. Neilson, manager of the Glasgow Gas Company and afterwards amous as the inventor of the hot-blast furnace, there was founded the Glasgow Gas Workmen's Library, which also developed, by 1824, into a mutual improvement society, with a library, laboratory, and workshop.[2]

In Liverpool, thanks mainly to the initiative of Egerton Smith, editor of the *Liverpool Mercury*, a Mechanics' and Apprentices' Library and Reading Room was successfully launched in July 1823; and a similar venture was inaugurated in Sheffield in December of the same year at the instance of T. A. Ward, editor of the *Sheffield Independent*. The Liverpool venture, it is interesting to observe, was inspired by an Apprentices' Library established in New York three years previously.[3]

The First Institutes

All these various enterprises indicate the climate of opinion within which the mechanics' institute movement was born, but the train of events leading directly to that movement developed independently, and may be traced back to Glasgow in the year 1800. Dr. George Birkbeck, son of a Quaker banker of Settle, in Yorkshire, had just completed his medical training at Edinburgh when in 1799 he was appointed Professor of Natural Philosophy at Anderson's Institution, Glasgow. During his first session he found it necessary to have a new set of apparatus constructed for his lectures, and on one occasion his attention was arrested, he tells us, by the inquisitive countenances of a circle of operatives gathered round a model of a centrifugal pump which was being made for him in a tinman's shop.

[1] [S. Brown], *Some Account of the Itinerating Libraries and their Founder* (Edinburgh 1856). Brown was a great-uncle of John Brown of the *Horae Subsecivae*.

[2] *Glasgow Mechanics' Magazine*, Vol. II (1824–5), pp. 191–2, 376–80.

[3] For further details regarding these forerunners of the mechanics' institutes, see Kelly, *op. cit.*, Ch. iv; and M. Tylecote, *Mechanics' Institutes of Lancashire and Yorkshire* (Manchester 1957), Ch. i. T. A. Ward of Sheffield was also a leading figure in the establishment of the Sheffield Literary and Philosophical Society.

I beheld, through every disadvantage of circumstance and appearance, such strong indications of the existence of unquenchable spirit, and such emanations from 'the heaven lighted lamp in man', that the question was forced upon me, Why are these minds left without the means of obtaining that knowledge which they so ardently desire, and why are the avenues of science barred against them because they are poor? It was impossible not to determine that the obstacle should be removed . . .

In complete ignorance, therefore, of anything of the kind that had been attempted before, Birkbeck decided to offer, free of charge, a special course of lectures, 'abounding with experiments, and conducted with the greatest simplicity of expression and familiarity of illustration, solely for persons engaged in the practical exercise of the mechanical arts'. He was not optimistic, he explained, that such a course would contribute much to scientific discovery, but he was convinced

that much pleasure would be communicated to the mechanic in the exercise of his art, and that the mental vacancy which follows a cessation from bodily toil, would often be agreeably occupied, by a few systematic ideas, upon which, at his leisure, he might meditate.

The subject of his choice was 'the mechanical properties of solid and fluid bodies'—not, the modern adult educationist would think, a best-selling title, but such was the zeal of the working men of Glasgow for knowledge, and such Birkbeck's skill as an expositor, that 75 mechanics attended on the opening night, and by the fourth Saturday evening the audience had risen to 500. The course appears to have lasted for three months, and was repeated annually until Birkbeck left Glasgow in 1804, to settle eventually in London.[1]

Birkbeck was succeeded as professor by Dr. Andrew Ure, who later became well-known as a writer on applied science, and also as the author of that remarkable *apologia* for the Industrial Revolution, *The Philosophy of Manufactures* (1835). Under his direction the mechanics' class was successfully maintained for many years, and in 1821 it inspired Leonard Horner of Edinburgh (afterwards first warden of London University) to take the lead in establishing the Edinburgh School of Arts. This, in spite of the name, was the first fully-fledged mechanics' institute. Its first aim was to provide for working men systematic courses of lectures 'in such branches of physical science as are of practical advantage in their several trades' —notably chemistry, mechanics, and mathematics—but the other characteristic features of a mechanics' institute quickly developed:

[1] Kelly, *op. cit.*, pp. 26–41.

classes for more elementary instruction; a library; and a collection of models and apparatus for experiments.

No doubt in imitation of the Edinburgh venture the Haddington mutual improvement society transformed itself, apparently early in 1823, into the Haddington School of Arts,[1] but the next great step forward was taken later in that year at Glasgow. Here the mechanics' class at Anderson's Institution, which had long formed almost a self-contained unit, at length decided in July 1823 to break away and form an independent body, to be known as the Glasgow Mechanics' Institution. The new institution leased a disused chapel as a lecture-room, appointed a paid lecturer, organised courses in natural philosophy, chemistry, mechanics, and mathematics, and began to gather a library and a museum of apparatus. Over a thousand students were enrolled in the first year. Unlike the Edinburgh School of Arts, which was from the first financially assisted and firmly controlled by leading citizens of the town, the Glasgow Mechanics' Institution determined to be completely self-supporting, and the system of management adopted was so democratic that even the lecturers were elected by the general body of members.[2]

The London Mechanics' Institution

The *Glasgow Free Press* carried the news of these developments to London, where J. C. Robertson, editor of the newly founded *Mechanics' Magazine*, and Thomas Hodgskin, his associate editor, took the initiative in proposing the establishment of a London Mechanics' Institution. Birkbeck, now a successful London physician, was one of the first to come forward when the proposal was made known, and played such a prominent part both in the preliminary proceedings and in the later history of the Institution that he came to be regarded, not unjustifiably, as its founder.

At the very outset Robertson and Hodgskin sought also the assistance of Francis Place. This was a decision pregnant with consequence, for although Place was invaluable in organising working-class support he also brought in the middle-class Whigs and Radicals —Henry Brougham, J. G. Lambton (afterwards Lord Durham), J. C. Hobhouse, Sir Francis Burdett, Jeremy Bentham, James Mill, George Grote—and thus gave, not only to the London Mechanics' Institution,

[1] This society, though short-lived (it eventually became a subscription library) is of interest because among its early pupils was Samuel Smiles, whose *Self-Help* was to be one of the great classics of working-class adult education.

[2] Neither the Edinburgh School of Arts nor the Glasgow Mechanics' Institution has an adequate history. For Glasgow, however, see A. H. Sexton, *The First Technical College* (Glasgow 1894); and J. Muir (ed. J. M. Macaulay), *John Anderson and the College he Founded* (Glasgow 1950).

but to the whole mechanics' institute movement, a reputation
for radicalism which took more than a quarter of a century to live
down.

The preliminary negotiations were marked by a bitter dispute over
an important question of principle: should an appeal be launched
for subscriptions from the well-to-do? Place said emphatically yes,
for by no other method could working men secure the funds needed
to establish the Institution on a satisfactory basis. Birkbeck, in the
chair, supported him. Robertson and Hodgskin said no: 'If the
money were placed on the table before them,' declared Robertson,
'they ought to reject it, as they would the greatest evil.' Hodgskin,
who became known in later years as one of the pioneers of English
socialism, had written in the initial manifesto announcing the
Institution that

Men had better be without education—properly so called, for nature
of herself teaches us many valuable truths—than be educated by their
rulers; for then education is but the mere breaking in of the steer to the
yoke; the mere discipline of a hunting dog, which, by dint of severity, is
made to forego the strongest impulse of his nature, and instead of devour-
ing his prey, to hasten with it to the feet of his master.

After repeated and acrimonious debates reaching far into the
night, the victory went to Birkbeck and Place, and it was agreed that
a subscription should be launched. At the same time, however, it
was written into the constitution that two-thirds of the managing
committee must be working men. Here, too, were fateful decisions,
for the attempt of the London mechanics to combine self-government
with the support of the well-to-do was widely imitated elsewhere.
In the end, of course, money talked, and the result was that the
institutes, instead of serving as instruments of political, social, and
economic emancipation as Robertson and Hodgskin would have
wished, became on the whole supporters of the existing social order.
It should, however, be said that had the policy of working-class
independence been rigidly adhered to, the institutes could hardly
have become either so widespread, or so successful educationally, as
they in fact were.

In December 1823, the London Mechanics' Institution was for-
mally inaugurated, with Birkbeck as its first president—a post which
he held till his death in 1841. The object of the Institution, declared
the *Rules and Orders*, was 'the instruction of the Members in the
principles of the Arts they practise, and in the various branches of
science and useful Knowledge'. To this end, there were to be lectures

on science, literature and the arts (especially science); classes to teach the various branches of mathematics and their applications; a reference library, lending library, and reading room; a museum of 'machines, models, minerals, and natural history'; and a workshop and laboratory. In his opening address Birkbeck declared:

All intention of interference with political questions we do therefore disclaim . . . If indirectly we shall be supposed to exercise any influence,— and education may extend the views of the Mechanic,—I am persuaded we shall invigorate the attachment which must ever exist to every wise and well-constructed system of legislation . . .

Thus respectability was ensured, and Birkbeck sealed the victory of the established order, a year later, by advancing £3,700 towards the cost of creating a lecture theatre in Chancery Lane.[1]

Early Successes and Difficulties of the Institutes

From Edinburgh, Glasgow, and London as centres the mechanics' institute spread with astonishing rapidity, especially in London— where a whole cluster of institutes grew up in the suburbs—in the industrial counties of the North of England, in the Forth-Clyde valley, and in the seaports. At least 13 new institutes came into existence in 1824, and about 70 in 1825. By 1826 there were over 100. Among major institutions founded during this early phase were Greenock (1823); Ipswich, Manchester, Leeds, Newcastle, and Aberdeen (all in 1824); Plymouth, Bristol, Portsmouth, Birmingham, Derby, Liverpool, Warrington, Bolton, Halifax, and Stirling (1825); and Swansea (1826). In London a special group of institutes, known as Literary and Scientific Institutions, sprang up to cater for commercial and professional people. Elsewhere 'Mechanics' Institution' was usually the formal title, though a few institutes adopted other names: 'School of Arts', 'Literary, Scientific and Mechanics' Institution', 'Society for the Diffusion of Useful Knowledge', and so forth.

A powerful factor in this rapid growth was an enthusiastic pamphlet by Henry Brougham entitled *Practical Observations upon the Education of the People*, which was published in 1825 and ran through twenty editions before the end of the year. Brougham appealed to the employers to come forward generously to assist the new movement, and many of them did so. Alexander Galloway, the well-

---

[1] Kelly, *George Birkbeck*, Ch. v. For the general account of the mechanics' institutes that follows I have drawn heavily on Book II of this work. For a lively and penetrating account of the Lancashire and Yorkshire institutes see the pioneering work by Dr. Mabel Tylecote cited at p. 118 above.

known engineer, was a prominent supporter of the London institute and we find also George Stephenson at Newcastle, Marc Isambard Brunel at Rotherhithe, Josiah Wedgwood at Hanley, Benjamin Heywood the banker at Manchester, Charles Hindley the cotton manufacturer at Ashton-under-Lyne, and so on. Professional men, especially doctors and journalists, played a leading part in many centres. In general the political complexion of the movement was Whig, its religious complexion Nonconformist, with the Unitarians as particularly strong supporters in some places. The Tories and the Church either stood aside or were openly hostile. Their criticisms have been quoted so often as hardly to bear repetition: perhaps the most extreme was that of the anonymous writer in the *St. James's Chronicle*, that "A scheme more completely adapted for the destruction of this empire could not have been invented by the author of evil himself.'

Not all mechanics' institutes, by any means, were the result of patronage from above. Many, like that at Glasgow, were created by the efforts of the working men themselves. This was the case, for example, at Keighley, where the institute was created by a joiner, a painter, a tailor, and a reed-maker; at Kendal, where the institute began as a working men's library; at Morpeth, where it began as a mutual improvement society; and at many other centres, including Birmingham, Halifax, and Aberdeen. In most cases, however, it became necessary to seek financial support from outside in order to secure the buildings and equipment that were essential for effective educational work. This happened even at Glasgow, where at the outset the members were fervent in their determination to be self-supporting.

The motives that inspired the middle-class founders of the early institutes were as various as the ways in which the institutes originated. Employers such as Alexander Galloway sought better educated and more industrious workmen; politicians such as Brougham hoped the institutes would provide training in self-government; philanthropists such as William Wilberforce hoped they would alleviate the poverty and misery of the working classes; parsons such as Rev. E. Higginson, of Derby, looked to them to establish 'respect for the laws and a ready obedience to them; that due subordination of rank on which the well-being of every gradation in society depends; and the faithful discharge of all those duties which we owe to the whole community'. Only a minority of people regarded the institutes, as Birkbeck did, primarily as agents of cultural education, as a means of liberating the mind and enriching the understanding.

As for the workers who flocked into the institutes in such large numbers, their motives were much the same as those of their predecessors in the mutual improvement societies or book clubs of the eighteenth century. 'Self-improvement' was the slogan, and self-improvement covered both a genuine intellectual interest in learning for its own sake, and a desire to acquire knowledge as an instrument of personal advancement. There were also, however, not a few working men—men such as Henry Hetherington and William Lovett in London, and G. J. Holyoake in Birmingham, whose motives were in part social and political, and who saw in the institutes a means towards a radical reconstruction of society.

In 1826 the onward movement of the institutes suffered a sharp check. One reason for this lay in the onset of economic depression, to which throughout their history the institutes always showed themselves exceedingly sensitive. There were, however, other reasons, and the most important was that the average English working man, ill-educated as he commonly was, and tired at the end of a long day's work, just could not absorb the long and systematic courses of lectures on chemistry, mechanics, hydrostatics, and the like which nearly all the institutes attempted in the early days. This was so even when the lecturer was competent and took pains to explain and illustrate his material, but such lecturers were scarce, and at £4 or £5 a lecture too expensive for the smaller institutes.

In Scotland the position was different. Here, thanks to the development of the parish school system, a high proportion of working men had a sound basic education, and generations of theological discourse had produced an intellectual toughness and discipline that were lacking south of the Border. In Scotland, in consequence, the major institutes, such as Edinburgh, Glasgow, and Aberdeen, were able to maintain systematic science courses for many years. In England, however, many of the early members gave up in despair. Those who remained were the skilled workers, and the places of those who withdrew were taken, if taken at all, by clerks, shopkeepers, and the like.

The institutes suffered also from their exclusive pre-occupation with scientific education. A great many people were not really interested in science: they were interested in literature, or in politics and economics, which were almost universally barred as controversial. And many, after a twelve-hour day, wanted something more in the nature of relaxation and social life. But the early institutes made no concessions to such weakness: newspapers were excluded from the reading rooms, and fiction from the libraries. So the average working man returned to his public-house, or his club, or his mutual improvement society.

A Nation-wide Movement

For some years the movement remained in the doldrums, while the more active elements in the working classes devoted themselves to other causes—socialism, co-operation, trade unionism. By the early 1830s the first phase in these latter movements was fading out, the worst of the slump was over, and the mechanics' institutes resumed their forward march. By 1841 there were over 300 institutes in existence. London and industrial Lancashire and Yorkshire were still the main centres, but the movement had now spread also to the Midlands, and there was a scattering of institutes in the rural areas, especially in the region of Bristol, Bath, and Gloucester. In these rural districts, where the needs of the industrial workers were less in evidence, the title 'Literary and Scientific Institution' was often adopted, but 'Mechanics' Institution' continued to be common in the North.

In some centres, notably Manchester and Glasgow, an attempt was made to attract the unskilled workers by the establishment of institutes of a very popular kind. In the Manchester area these institutes were called Lyceums, and provided newsrooms, popular lectures, cheap concerts and coffee-parties, and elementary classes, all for a subscription of 2s. per quarter as compared with the 5s. per quarter which was common in the ordinary mechanics' institutes. These ventures flourished for a time, but achieved no permanent success.

The very severe economic depression of the early 'forties, and the growth of Chartism, brought a further check in the development of the movement, and it was not until about 1845 that a new advance began. By 1850 the institutes were again booming everywhere, and in 1851 there seem to have been close on 700 of them. About a quarter of the institutes at this time were in Lancashire or the West Riding of Yorkshire, but there was now scarcely any sizeable town without its mechanics' institute or similar body, and many were situated in quite small villages. In Scotland and Wales the spread was much less marked: in Scotland the main concentration was still in the Forth-Clyde valley; in Wales it was in the southern industrial region.

The variety of institutes at this time was astounding. There were large urban institutes, such as Liverpool, Manchester, and Leeds, with handsome buildings and some thousands of members; and at the opposite extreme there were tiny village institutes, with a handful of people meeting in a hired room. There were industrial institutes, for example for miners, weavers, pottery workers, ironworkers, railway workers, quite often for the employees of a single firm. There were Church of England institutes (for the Church had by this time decided to fight the devil with his own weapons); there were also Nonconformist institutes and temperance institutes. In many parts of the country, too, the institutes were now organised into unions for mutual assistance, and three of these unions—the Yorkshire Union, the Lancashire and Cheshire Union, and the Northern Union (for Northumberland and Durham)—proved valuable and enduring instruments of co-operation.

Other Contemporary Movements

Nor is this the whole story. Alongside the institutes there sprang up a host of other bodies very similar in purpose and organisation. In the North of England, and especially in the West Riding of Yorkshire, there were large numbers of working-class mutual improvement societies, which in the smaller centres of population fulfilled many of the functions of mechanics' institutes: indeed in the annual reports of the West Riding Union, and its successor the Yorkshire Union, from 1838 onwards, the two types of organisation figure side by side, and appear virtually indistinguishable. The 'mutual instruction classes' which were numerous in Aberdeenshire at the time of the 1851 census were on similar lines.[1]

A special kind of mutual improvement society was that which arose under the auspices of the Young Men's Christian Association. In its origin the Y.M.C.A. was a religious society, not dissimilar in spirit from the societies of the seventeenth and eighteenth centuries, though differing from them in its non-denominational character. It was founded in London in 1844 on the initiative of a young draper's assistant, George Williams, and its purpose was then defined as 'the improvement of the spiritual condition of young men engaged in the drapery and other trades, by the introduction of religious services among them'. Within a year, however, in order to widen the appeal of the Association and bring in young men who might not in the first instance be attracted by the religious approach, the definition was altered to read: 'the improvement of the spiritual and mental condition of young men engaged in houses of business, by the introduction

---

[1] An account of these classes is given in I. J. Simpson, *Education in Aberdeenshire before 1872* (1947), pp. 203–4. In 1850 there was an Aberdeen and Banffshire Mutual Instruction Union, embracing ten clubs.

of family or social prayer, Bible classes, Mutual Improvement Societies, or any other plan strictly in accordance with the Scriptures'.

In 1848, in accordance with the new policy, a library and reading room were opened in Gresham Street, and here lectures and classes were also organised. The annual report for 1850 recorded that there were already 500 members, and classes had been held in French, German, Greek, Hebrew, arithmetic, mathematics, book-keeping, history, essay-writing, and psalmody. In addition the Association organised each winter a series of large-scale popular lectures. From 1849 these were held at Exeter Hall, which ultimately (1881) became the headquarters of the London Association. All this, of course, was the beginning of what soon became, first a national movement, and then, linking up very often with similar movements in other countries, an international movement. By 1851 there were already eight London societies, and, in various parts of the British Isles, sixteen provincial branches.[1]

The success of the mechanics' institutes also had its impact on middle-class adult education. The Literary and Scientific Institutions established in London in the 'twenties to cater for commercial and professional workers were imitated in the provincial 'Athenaeums', of which the prototype was the Manchester Athenaeum, founded in 1836. In practice these institutions soon came to be monopolised by employers and professional men, combining club facilities with a form of adult education more popular in character than that offered by the literary and philosophical societies.

Were the Mechanics' Institutes a Failure?

It was widely held in the mid-nineteenth century, and is still widely believed, that the mechanics' institutes were a failure.[2] It is alleged that they failed to attract the working people; that they failed to accomplish any serious educational work; and that in any case they were dead by the middle of the century. These statements are only partly true.

[1] The most useful account of this phase of the Y.M.C.A. is in L. L. Doggett, *History of the Young Men's Christian Association* (New York 1922), Pt. I, Ch. ii. See also G. J. Stevenson, *Historical Records of the Young Men's Christian Association* [1884], pp. 1–49; J. E. Hodder Williams, *The Father of the Red Triangle: the Life of Sir George Williams* (1918), Chs. iii–vii. For the precursors of the movement, and for parallel developments outside London, see Stevenson, *op. cit.*, pp. 6–10; *Fifty Years' Work amongst Young Men in all Lands* (Y.M.C.A. Central International Committee, 1894), pp. 171–6; Z. F. Willis, 'The Y.M.C.A. and Adult Education', in *Journal of Adult Education*, Vol. III (1928–9), pp. 36 sqq.; and C. P. Shedd and others, *History of the World's Alliance of Young Men's Christian Associations* (1955), Chs. i–ii.
[2] The most recent criticism (better informed than most) is R. D. Altick, *The English Common Reader* (Chicago Univ. P. 1957), Ch. ix.

It is true that the institutes failed to capture and hold the interest of the masses of the working people, i.e. the unskilled workers: in this respect they anticipated the experience of a number of other adult education movements. It is clear from surviving lists of members' occupations, however, that they did continue to attract the skilled manual worker, especially in the North of England and in Scotland. In general, as I have observed elsewhere, their membership was 'very like that of the Workers' Educational Association in the early twentieth century, i.e. skilled manual workers, with a sprinkling of shopkeepers, shop assistants, and business and professional people, the general picture being upper working-class—lower middle class'. It was only in large cities such as Manchester that clerical workers predominated.

It is also true that the educational programmes of the institutes underwent a radical change after the first few years. Those which survived the crisis of 1826, and those which were founded later, virtually abandoned (except in Scotland) the attempt to provide serious and systematic lecture-courses in science, and substituted miscellaneous programmes of single lectures and occasional short courses on a great variety of topics—science, history, literature, antiquities, phrenology, and so forth—interspersed in some cases with musical entertainments, ventriloquial performances, and other diversions. It is also true that the later institutes paid much more attention to social activities, such as parties, concerts, 'soirées', excursions, exhibitions, even cricket matches. What is overlooked is that the genuine educational work of the institutes had now been transferred from the lecture-room to the classroom, where instruction could be given in smaller groups, and, if necessary, at a much more elementary level. Manchester in 1839, for example, had 1,015 pupils in classes, of whom 635 were learning writing, grammar, or arithmetic, and the remainder mathematics, drawing, music, and French. And in 1851 Huddersfield (a really working-class institute) had 600 members in regular attendance at classes in reading, writing and arithmetic, music, elocution, composition, shorthand, geography, history, drawing, French, German, grammar, geometry, bookkeeping, literature, chemistry, and natural philosophy.

Some institutes sought to reinforce their adult instruction by establishing day schools for the children of members. This was notably the case at Liverpool and Leeds, where the boys' and girls' high schools founded by the mechanics' institutes still survive.

The museums which many institutes attempted to form were in the main a failure, and the collections of apparatus for experimental purposes rusted unused. The libraries and reading rooms, however, were most valuable instruments of education. The libraries were not, of course, very big—the largest in 1841 were in London (7,000 volumes) and Liverpool (6,000 volumes), and the smaller institutes rarely had more than a few hundred miscellaneous volumes. But even these collections were of great value in the days before public libraries came into existence.

For the belief that the mechanics' institutes were dead by 1850 there is no justification, but the story of their subsequent development must be reserved for a later chapter.

Literature, Art, and Music

Though science was the great catchword of this age, as of our own age, literature, art, and music were by no means unrepresented in the field of adult education. Literature might be squeezed out, or thrust into a subordinate place, in the middle-class literary and philosophical societies, but it figured regularly, and almost from the beginning, in the programmes of mechanics' institutes. Many of these indeed, as we have observed, adopted after the initial phase the name 'literary and scientific institute', and literary institutes and literary societies flourished in villages and market towns.[1]

Art was given an important place in mechanics' institutes and similar bodies because of its importance in industrial design—a consideration which led the government, following the report of a Select Committee on Arts and Manufactures appointed in 1835, to sponsor the establishment of special Schools of Design in London and a number of provincial centres. The Normal School of Design in London became eventually the Royal College of Art, and the provincial schools, developing for the most part independently of the mechanics' institutes, were absorbed under the auspices of the Department of Science and Art into the country's system of technical education.

Clearly, however, there was also a great deal of interest in art for its own sake. Lectures and short courses on the history of art and architecture were common, and the lectures and classes conducted by Benjamin Haydon from 1835 to 1839 were a highlight in the early history of the London Mechanics' Institution. 'Lectured at the Mechanics' with great applause . . .' he wrote in his diary in 1836. 'They are of a different race to the audiences at the Royal

---

[1] The 1851 Census includes in its list of 'literary and scientific institutions' nearly seventy literary institutes and literary societies in England and Wales, besides a few in Scotland.

Institution.'[1] He afterwards lectured in all the principal towns of England and Scotland.

The day of public art galleries was not yet, though the National Gallery had its beginnings in 1824; but from time to time exhibitions were arranged under the auspices of local bodies, for example the Birmingham Academy of Arts, founded for this purpose in 1814.[2]

Facilities for hearing and studying music were everywhere increasing. For the middle-class concert-lover there was now in London and in the great provincial centres a considerable choice of subscription concerts, both choral and orchestral, both amateur and professional. London had the Concert of Antient Music, founded in 1776; the Philharmonic Society, founded in 1813; and the Sacred Harmonic Society, founded in 1832; besides English and Italian opera.[3] Birmingham had its Choral Society and its Music Festival; Manchester its Choral Society and its Gentlemen's Concerts (of which Sir Charles Hallé was appointed conductor in 1849). Liverpool had by 1851 'ten or a dozen public halls all of which were used intermittently, and some principally, for concerts'.[4] Nor should we suppose that such activities were restricted to the large towns: Warrington, for example, had a Musical Society, for choral and orchestral work, founded in 1834.[5]

These were middle-class ventures. The working classes could attend the occasional cheap concerts arranged by mechanics' institutes and similar bodies; or they could combine music with refreshments in a public house or in one of the casinos, music saloons, or 'penny singing rooms' which seem to have been common in the northern industrial towns.[6]

It was at this time that brass bands became popular. The still famous Besses o' th' Barn Band, whose members rose at four in the morning in order to put in an hour's practice before going down the pit at six, won a competition at Manchester as early as 1821.[7] The great feature of the period, however, was the development of working-class choral singing. Mr. Nettel links this development with the social changes brought about by the Industrial Revolution: 'the

---

[1] B. R. Haydon, *Autobiography and Memoirs*, ed. T. Taylor (1926), Vol. II, p. 600; Kelly, *op. cit.*, pp. 130–1.

[2] J. A. Langford, *A Century of Birmingham Life* (Birmingham 1868), Vol. II, pp. 365 sqq.

[3] See the chapter on 'Music' by E. J. Dent in G. M. Young (ed.) *Early Victorian England* (1934), Vol. II; and R. Nettel, *The Orchestra in England* (2nd edn. 1956), pp. 87–99, 130–40.

[4] Young, *op. cit.*, Vol. I, pp. 238–9; Nettel, *op. cit.*, pp. 161–70.

[5] W. B. Stephens, *Development of Adult Education in Warrington during the Nineteenth Century* (unpublished M.A. thesis, Exeter Univ. 1958), p. 30.

[6] Young, *op. cit.*, pp. 234–5. There is an interesting though disapproving account of a singing-room at Preston in J. Kay, *Condition of Poor Children* (1853), App. V.

[7] R. Nettel, *The Englishman Makes Music* (1952), pp. 133–4.

influx of workers during the nineteenth century to the new industrial towns from the old rural areas meant that they entered the century a nation of folk singers but that their descendants emerged from it a nation of choirsingers'.[1]

The spread of choral societies is particularly noticeable from the 1830s onwards. Thomas Cooper, afterwards noted for his educational work among the Chartists, gives a vivid description of a society which he organised, about 1836, in Lincoln, which performed Handel's *Messiah* and other works before crowded audiences in one of the city churches. 'My heart and brain were soon on flame', he writes, 'in the worship of Handel's grandeur, and with the love of his sweetness and tenderness.'[2]

From 1838 we have a description of a music school organised by the Strutts, the great Derbyshire cotton-spinners, among their factory-workers at Belper. The passage is worth quoting at length because it illustrates the relationship between music and other forms of adult education.

William Strutt, the philosopher, commenced the Mechanics' Institute at Derby, and supplied it with lectures on most of the sciences. Mr. Joseph Strutt, with eminent taste, has collected one of the finest galleries of pictures and statues in this part of the country, which is open to all admirers of the arts, on being introduced. John, the son of Mr. George Strutt, who resides at Belper, . . . has formed a musical society, by selecting forty persons, or more, from his mills and workshops, making a band of instrumental performers and a choir of singers. These persons are regularly trained by masters, and taught to play and sing in the best possible manner. Whatever time is consumed in their studies, is reckoned into their working hours. On the night of a general muster you may see five or six of the forge-men, in their leather aprons, blasting their terrific notes upon ophicleides and trombones.[3]

The Sol-fa Movement

The choral movement received a great impetus in the 1840s as a result of the popularisation of the sol-fa notation and the introduction of new methods of class teaching. The pioneers in this work were John P. Hullah, a composer and organist, and John Curwen, a

---

[1] R. Nettel, *Music in the Five Towns, 1840–1914* (1944), p. 1. But see above, p. 91, for a village choral society in the eighteenth century.

[2] T. Cooper, *Life* (1877 edn.), p. 107. For Cooper see below, pp. 142–4.

[3] W. Gardiner, *Music and Friends*, Vol. II (1838), pp. 511–12. I am indebted for this quotation to Nettel, *Englishman Makes Music*, p. 94. Nettel's account also includes striking evidence from the writings of George Hogarth (1835) and J. P. Hullah (1841) as to the important place occupied by choral music in the life of the industrial towns and villages, especially in the North of England (see pp. 92, 104–5).

Congregational minister. Hullah's methods were based on those used by Guillaume Wilhem in Paris for the instruction of large classes of working people. In February 1841 he opened a singing school at Exeter Hall, London. It was intended for teachers in day and Sunday schools, but all sorts of other people flocked in, and 'class after class was formed of persons who attended for the purpose of learning singing on their own account'. Schoolteachers paid 15s. for a course of sixty lessons, 'mechanics and persons in a still more humble sphere' 8s. or 10s. Soon there was a demand for elementary instruction in other subjects, and classes were successfully launched in writing, arithmetic, and drawing.[1]

Hullah's teaching work in London continued for more than twenty years, and he also lectured and taught extensively in the provinces. In 1843, for example, he conducted 'the first great meeting of the Lancashire and Cheshire Workmen's Singing Classes' in the Free Trade Hall, Manchester, with 1,500 performers'.[2] His methods were spread by his pupils, and soon thousands of people were learning to sing on the Hullah system. One of his disciples in the North was Joseph Mainzer, a German priest who had long experience of teaching music to working men in Paris.[3] Another was a Mr. Constantine, who in 1843 was doing a weekly round of classes embracing Blackburn, Lancaster, Ulverston, Ambleside, Kendal, Casterton, and Preston. In several of these places he taught more than one class: at Ulverston he had a class of 50 ladies and gentlemen, a class of 40 children, and a mixed class of 100; at Blackburn his three classes included a very large one consisting chiefly of factory hands.[4]

John Curwen, who as a minister was principally interested in improving the quality of singing in churches and Sunday schools, began in 1841 to propagate the familiar tonic sol-fa notation, which remained in extensive use until the first World War. This was an adaptation of a method pioneered by Sarah Ann Glover, a Norwich schoolteacher: it was simpler than Hullah's notation, for the principle of the 'movable Doh' dispensed with the necessity for accidentals. For many years there was rivalry between the two systems, especially after 1872, when Hullah was appointed by the Committee

---

[1] Unfortunately the existence of these supplementary classes proved fatal to a move made in the House of Lords in 1842 for a grant in aid of Hullah's work (the first proposal for government aid to adult education), for the Bishop of London was suspicious of the establishment of classes without provision for religious instruction—[F. R. Hullah], *Life of John Hullah* (1886), pp. 35–6. Cf. J. L. and B. Hammond, *The Bleak Age* (1934), pp. 116–17.

[2] W. E. A. Axon, *Annals of Manchester* (Manchester 1886), p. 222.

[3] He was author of *Singing for the Million* (1842).

[4] Hullah, *op. cit.*, pp. 33–4.

of Council on Education as inspector of music in training schools, but it was Curwen's system which carried the day. The publishing business which he founded in 1844 made music in the new notation cheaply available; the Tonic Sol-fa Association and the *Tonic Sol-fa Reporter* spread a knowledge of his methods; and eventually (1879), a Tonic Sol-fa College provided training for teachers. In the last resort, however, it was the superior simplicity of his method that commended it, and opened up an understanding of music to many thousands of people to whom the ordinary staff notation would have remained for ever a mystery. This was particularly so in Wales, where the introduction of the tonic sol-fa system was largely responsible for the remarkable development of vocal and choral singing from the early 1860s onward.[1]

[1] See J. S. Curwen, *Memorials of John Curwen* (1882), and for Wales L. S. Jones, *Church and Chapel as Sources and Centres of Education in Wales during 1850–1900* (unpublished M.A. thesis, Liverpool University 1940), Ch. ix. For the sol-fa movement generally, see Nettel, *Englishman Makes Music*, Ch. vi.

9

The Nineteenth Century

THE RADICAL OPPOSITION

ALTHOUGH the mechanics' institutes stand out as the typical form of working-class adult education in the first half of the nineteenth century, they were by no means the only one. As in the later eighteenth century, the various working-class radical movements also gave rise to educational activities, which developed almost independently of the mechanics' institutes, if not in actual opposition to them. The dichotomy between the two forms of adult education should not be overstressed, for some of the working-class leaders, e.g. Francis Place, William Lovett, and Henry Hetherington in London, and George Jacob Holyoake in Birmingham, participated actively in the work of the institutes, and many others availed themselves of the facilities the institutes offered. It was at the London Mechanics' Institution, too, that Thomas Hodgskin found a platform for the anti-capitalist lectures which were afterwards published as *Popular Political Economy*. In general, however, the institutes were so anxious to avoid the taint of Radicalism that they rigorously excluded any treatment of politics or political economy. They repeatedly proclaimed, in the words of Bacon, that 'Knowledge is Power', but the kind of knowledge so many of the workers wanted had to be sought elsewhere. Thomas Coates, in a report published in 1841, pictures the institutes as saying to the eager mechanic:

We explain to you the physical sciences; we demonstrate to you the atomic theory; we show you the orbit of the planets, but the nature and advantages of our political Constitution, a question which every newspaper more or less raises . . . shall not be taught or discussed here— nevertheless the Chartists in the next street handle it quite freely, and will spare no pains to induce you to adopt their opinions.[1]

The various working-class movements of the early nineteenth century, from the Hampden Clubs to the Chartists, were indeed shot through with educational idealism, and though at present our know-

[1] Society for the Diffusion of Useful Knowledge, *Report of the State of Literary, Scientific and Mechanics' Institutions* (1841), p. 31.

ledge of their activities is scrappy and inadequate, enough is known
to make it clear that their contribution to adult education was by no
means negligible.[1]

Hampden Clubs and Other Political Societies

Of the Hampden Clubs, which were founded in 1812 by the
veteran Parliamentary reformer Major John Cartwright, and became
popular among working-class Radicals during the troubled years
after the war, we have an interesting account in the autobiography
of Samuel Bamford:

Hampden clubs were now established in many of our large towns, and
the villages and districts around them. Cobbett's books were printed in a
cheap form; the labourers read them, and thenceforward became deliberate and systematic in their proceedings. Nor were there wanting men
of their own class, to encourage and direct the new converts; the Sunday
schools of the preceding thirty years, had produced many working men
of sufficient talent to become readers, writers, and speakers in the village
meetings for parliamentary reform; some also were found to possess a
rude poetic talent, which rendered their effusions popular, and bestowed
an additional charm on their assemblages: and by such various means,
anxious listeners at first, and then zealous proselytes, were drawn from
the colleges of quiet nooks and dingles, to the weekly readings and discussions of the Hampden clubs.[2]

The Hampden club of Bamford's native town of Middleton, near
Manchester, was founded in 1816, and rented for its meetings a
disused Methodist chapel. This connection with Methodism was not
accidental, for Methodism provided a high proportion of the leaders
of the independent working-class movements of this period,[3] and
these movements took over and adopted for their own purposes the
Methodist plan of the weekly class-meeting and the small weekly
subscription. [4]

This was the case with the numerous parliamentary reform
societies—the Unions of Political Protestants, the Northern Political
Union, and similar bodies—which flourished in the years of unemployment and repression between 1816 and 1822. The classes provided speedy and easy contact between the leaders and the rank and
file, facilitated the collection of funds, and also served as a means of

---

[1] Since this chapter was written a useful account of the educational aspects of these
movements (particularly valuable on the work of the Chartists) has been provided by
B. Simon, *Studies in the History of Education, 1780–1870* (1960), Chs. iv–v.
[2] S. Bamford, *Passages in the Life of a Radical* (2nd edn. Manchester n.d.), Vol. I, pp. 7–8.
[3] Cf. S. Webb, *The Story of the Durham Miners* (1921), pp. 23–4.
[4] This point is clearly established by Dr. R. F. Wearmouth in *Some Working-Class
Movements of the Nineteenth Century* (1948).

propaganda and education. At Hull, for example, the members of the Union of Political Protestants, formed in 1818, were divided into classes of twenty, each meeting weekly to read 'Cobbett, and Sherwin's *Registers*, Wooler's *Black Dwarf*, and other works, calculated to diffuse political knowledge'. At Newcastle, where there was a similar arrangement, the class leader was expected to select the material for reading, and conduct the discussion: he was to 'encourage the members to make remarks', and to 'repress any violent or improper expression'. The works recommended here included, in addition to those mentioned above, Cartwright's *Bill of Rights* and Bentham's *Reform Catechism*.[1] The government's alarm at the proceedings of some of these societies was reflected in one of the Six Acts of 1819, which repeated the prohibition of 1799 on unauthorised lectures, debates, and reading-rooms open to the public.[2]

The Early Co-operative Movement

These early attempts to secure parliamentary reform proved fruitless, and after 1823 the movement died down until the eve of the Reform Bill. In the meantime the working people sought a remedy for the evils that beset them in co-operation and trade unionism. The first successful co-operative society was established in London in 1824; by 1830 there were said to be three hundred of them, and by 1832 between four and five hundred. These early societies were founded under the influence of the utopian socialist ideals of Robert Owen. They functioned usually as trading associations or producers' co-operatives, but the ultimate objective was the formation of independent co-operative communities settled on the land, and in the plans for these communities the provision of education, both for children and for adults, played a prominent part.

In the meantime the co-operators did their utmost to educate themselves. The London Co-operative and Economical Society and the Edinburgh Practical Society (two short-lived pioneer groups founded in 1821) both made provision for adult education and the education of members' children; the London society organised lectures and discussions; the Westminster society arranged lectures on science; the Birmingham society held debates and organised a library.[3] In London there also came into existence, in 1829, the British Association for the Promotion of Co-operative Knowledge,

---

[1] Wearmouth, *op. cit.*, pp. 31–49.
[2] 60 Geo. II c. 6.
[3] F. Hall and W. P. Watkins, *Co-operation* (Manchester 1937), p. 61; H. J. Twigg, *Outline History of Co-operative Education* (Manchester 1924), pp. 6–7.

which attempted to serve as a central organisation for propaganda and education.

In Brighton the leading members of the co-operative society were men who had attended classes in science conducted at the Mechanics' Institute by Dr. William King, a local physician, and from 1828 to 1830 King published a monthly periodical, the *Co-operator*, in order to enlighten the working classes on the principles of co-operation. In one of his later issues he wrote:

> But, above all things, . . . let Co-operators compete with each other in the improvement of their minds; let them form classes for this purpose; let them have common reading-rooms and libraries; let them learn how to keep common accounts, the principles of book-keeping, and the dealings of trade. These are the first steps in learning, and which are most useful to themselves. When they have accomplished this, then let them extend their reading to other subjects, and never cease till they have dissipated those mists of ignorance in which they are at present enveloped.[1]

Only one co-operative community actually came into existence in Great Britain during these years. It was created by Abram Combe (founder of the Edinburgh Practical Society) at Orbiston, near Motherwell, in 1825, and had to struggle against many difficulties, but its members had provided themselves with a library and a theatre before the mortgage was foreclosed in 1827.[2]

The Early Trade Unions

The trade unions which came into existence in such numbers, in all parts of the country, in the years following the repeal of the Combination Acts in 1824, and especially from 1829 onwards, were concerned primarily with specific economic grievances. Educational activities, consequently, did not figure in their programmes to any considerable extent. The union leaders, however, had 'largely drunk of the new gospel of Owenite Co-operation',[3] and many of the co-operative societies were in fact formed by trade groups, the most grandiose effort in this direction being the Grand National Building Guild formed by the Operative Builders' Union, at Owen's suggestion, in 1833. The Guild aimed at reorganising the building industry on co-operative lines, and its objectives included the 're-education' of the members and the instruction of their children.[4] The fact is

---

[1] *The Co-operator*, 1 Dec. 1829, reprinted in T. W. Mercer, *Co-operation's Prophet* (Manchester 1947), p. 130.
[2] F. Podmore, *Robert Owen* (1906), Vol. II, Ch. xv.
[3] G. D. H. Cole, *Robert Owen* (1925), p. 202.
[4] *Op. cit.*, pp. 204–7; G. D. H. Cole, *Short History of the British Working Class Movement*, Vol. I (1925, 2nd edn. 1927), pp. 119–22.

that among the working-class leaders of this period, trade unionism, co-operation, and political Radicalism were all facets of the same movement, and that movement was inspired by Owen's belief in the infinite power of education to perfect the character of man and his moral and material well-being.

The climax of this first phase of trade unionism came with the creation in 1834 of the Grand National Consolidated Trades Union. The unions, however, were still not strong enough to face the combined hostility of government and employers, and before the end of the year the movement had suffered disastrous defeat. With the collapse of the trade unions came also the collapse of many of the early co-operative societies. Robert Owen turned back to his ideal of community living, and the working-class leaders turned increasingly to political action.[1]

The London Working Men's Association

Political Radicalism was by no means entirely dormant during the developments just described in the co-operative and trade union field. In 1831, when the British Association for the Promotion of Co-operative Knowledge came to an end, many of its leading members, including William Lovett and Henry Hetherington, formed a new body known as the National Union of the Working Classes, with headquarters at the Rotunda in Blackfriars Road. The excitement attendant on the passing of the Reform Act of 1832, and the disappointment at the failure of the Act to emancipate the working classes, brought recruits flocking in, and similar bodies were quickly formed in the provinces, for example in Manchester, Blackburn, Macclesfield, Bristol, Norwich, and Brighton. The aims of the new movement were originally economic as much as political, but under the influence of Lovett and others the emphasis came to be on the political objectives, which included five of what later became the six points of the People's Charter: universal suffrage, vote by ballot, equal representation, annual Parliaments, and no property qualification for members.

In London, and in some centres at least in the provinces, the members of the Union were organised in classes on the Methodist model: in London there were over one hundred classes of twenty-five members each. Lovett tells us that the most useful meetings were those of the classes:

---

[1] There is a useful account of all this in G. D. H. Cole, *A Century of Co-operation* (Manchester [1944]), Ch. ii.

The class meetings were generally held at the house of some member. The class leader was the chairman and some subject, either for conversation or discussion, was selected. Sometimes selections were made from books. The works of Paine, Godwin, Owen, Ensor, and other Radical writers were preferred. The unstamped periodicals of the day were also subjects of conversation and discussion, and in this manner hundreds of persons were made acquainted with books and principles of which they were previously ignorant.[1]

After the trade union fiasco of 1834, the National Union was reborn in 1836 as the London Working Men's Association, with Lovett as secretary and Hetherington as treasurer. These two men, craftsmen both, Lovett a cabinet-maker and Hetherington a printer, were in many ways typical of working-class leadership at this period. Radicals, Owenites, and freethinkers, they were both largely self-educated, and they had both taken full advantage of the facilities offered by the London Mechanics' Institution. And they were both dedicated men, prepared to suffer hardships and imprisonment in the great cause of uplifting the condition of the working masses. Hetherington, as we shall see, was the great champion of a free press; Lovett was above all the champion of education.

Under Lovett's influence the Working Men's Association gave a high priority to educational activities. The aims of the members included the following:

To devise every possible means . . . to remove those cruel laws that prevent the free circulation of thought through the medium of a *cheap and honest press*.

To promote, by all available means, the education of the rising generation . . .

To collect every kind of information appertaining to the interests of the working classes in particular and society in general, especially statistics regarding the wages of labour, the habits and conditions of the labourer . . .

To meet and communicate with each other for the purpose of digesting the information required . . .

To publish their views and sentiments . . . to create a moral, reflecting, yet energetic public opinion; so as eventually to lead to a gradual improvement in the condition of the working classes, without violence or com motion.

To form a library of reference and useful information; to maintain a

---

[1] Wearmouth, *Working-Class Movements*, p. 69. For a general account of the Union see pp. 50–84 of this work, and also W. Lovett, *Life and Struggles of William Lovett* (1876, new edn., ed. R. H. Tawney, 1920), Ch. iv. For the 'unstamped periodicals' see below, pp. 161–2. One of them, the *Poor Man's Guardian*, published by Henry Hetherington, acted as the unofficial organ of the movement.

place where they can associate for mental improvement, where their brethren from the country can meet with kindred minds . . .[1]

Like the National Union, the London Working Men's Association quickly found imitators, and soon there were Working Men's Associations in many parts of the country, including Scotland. The political aims of these Associations were expressed in the People's Charter, which embraced the famous six points of parliamentary reform.[2] This document, drawn up by Lovett and his colleagues, and published in 1838, became the rallying point of the Chartist movement during the bitter struggles of 1839–42 and again during the brief revival of 1848.

The Educational Activities of the Chartists

The tangled story of Chartism need not be repeated here. It was never a united movement, and as time went on it split into a variety of local or ideological groupings. Lovett's movement, though it had taken the initiative, fell into the background after the failure of the great petition of 1839, and the centre of the stage was occupied by the National Charter Association, founded in 1840 under the leadership of Feargus O'Connor. This had its main centre in Manchester, and drew its strength, not from the skilled workers who had chiefly been represented in Lovett's Association, but from the half-starved handloom weavers and factory operatives of the northern industrial cities, suffering at this time in the grip of an economic depression of unexampled severity. In the Midlands Birmingham became the centre, from early 1842 onwards, of the Complete Suffrage Union, a kind of middle-class Chartist movement headed by Joseph Sturge, a Quaker corn-miller. Scotland was divided: both O'Connor and Sturge had followers there, and this country was also the most active centre of Christian Chartism, a movement which united Chartist principles with a kind of primitive Christianity. The most important of the Christian Chartist churches, however, was at Birmingham, under the leadership of Arthur O'Neill and John Collins.

Most of the Chartist groups used lectures and discussions as a means of propaganda; reading rooms for Chartist newspapers and other literature were common; and the system of organisation in classes was extensively adopted from 1839 onwards.[3] It would be an illusion to suppose that these classes were usually, or indeed often,

---

[1] Lovett, *Life and Struggles*, Vol. I, pp. 94–5.
[2] I.e. the five previously put forward by the National Union, plus a sixth, 'payment of members'.
[3] For the Chartist class-meetings see Wearmouth, *op. cit.*, pp. 126–43.

engaged in serious educational work, but the amount of adult education accomplished by Chartist groups is none the less impressive.

The most comprehensive plans for education came, as might be expected, from Lovett. His proposals were first expounded in a tract on National Education published in 1837, and were afterwards more fully set forth in a little work entitled *Chartism*, prepared by himself and John Collins in 1840, while the two were serving a term of imprisonment in Warwick gaol for Chartist activities in Birmingham. His scheme provided for the creation throughout the kingdom of *'Public Halls* or *Schools for the People'*, which in the daytime would be used for infant, primary and secondary education, and in the evenings would be used by adults 'for *public lectures* on physical, moral and political science; for *readings, discussions, musical entertainments, dancing'*, and other forms of recreation. Each hall was to include baths, a small museum, and a laboratory or workshop. The plan also envisaged the establishment of small district circulating libraries of 100–200 volumes, 'containing the most useful works on politics, morals, the sciences, history, and such instructing and entertaining works as may be generally approved of', to be sent in rotation to the various towns and villages.[1]

Unfortunately Lovett lacked the means to carry this admirable scheme into effect. Convinced from past experience that the working people alone were too poor to be effective, he founded in 1841 a new body, the National Association for Promoting the Political and Social Improvement of the People. This was intended to attract the support of all classes, but it never caught the popular imagination in the same way as the Working Men's Associations had done, and the only concrete result of Lovett's efforts was the establishment of the National Hall, Holborn—a disused chapel which for fifteen years served as a centre for public meetings, lectures, classes, and concerts. A Sunday school was established in 1843, and a day school, under Lovett's direction, in 1848.[2]

The most widespread and effective educational work accomplished by the Chartists was that carried out under the auspices of Christian Chartism, for the Chartist churches were everywhere associated with educational work. Thus the church at Birmingham 'consisted of a political association which studied democratic thought as laid down in the works of Cobbett, Hunt, Paine, and Cartwright, and a Church

---

[1] Lovett, *Life and Struggles*, Vol. II, pp. 253–5. A similarly comprehensive educational scheme, including provision for the appointment of lecturers on political economy in every district, was proposed in an Edinburgh Chartist newspaper, the *True Scotsman*, in 1839— L. C. Wright, *Scottish Chartism* (Edinburgh 1953), pp. 78–9.

[2] Lovett, *op. cit.*, Vol. II, pp. 292–4, 326–8, 342, 368–72.

whose purpose was to further temperance, morality, and knowledge. It had schools for children and for young men, and a sick club.'[1] In Deptford there was a Working Men's Church where the members were reported to be studying the New Testament in Greek.[2] In Scotland the Chartist churches were associated with 'evening classes, libraries, debating and dramatic societies, and schemes for liberal education'.[3] Quite a number of them established day schools, and in the village of Partick (now a suburb of Glasgow) there was a Chartist Education Club whose members met nightly for mutual instruction in reading, writing, arithmetic, grammar, and geography. Aberdeen had a Chartist Mutual Instruction Society on similar lines.[4]

Other Scottish Chartist organisations also developed educational work. Coupar Angus had a Mutual Improvement Society which also functioned as a co-operative group. At Dundee, on the other hand, politics was associated with poetry. One group here met in the dark workshop of James Gow, the weaver-poet; another in the more respectable surroundings of a coffee-house. Neither group was exclusively working-class: a number of well-to-do Dundee citizens belonged to both.[5]

Thomas Cooper

The most remarkable individual effort in the story of Chartist adult education was that accomplished by Thomas Cooper in Leicester. Cooper was not exactly a self-educated man, for thanks to the self-sacrifice of his mother, who was the widow of a journeyman dyer, he was enabled to stay at school until he was fifteen. The only career that opened up to him, however, was that of a shoemaker, and the story of his efforts to extend his education, while pursuing this humble occupation in Gainsborough, is one of the heroic narratives in the history of working-class self-improvement:

I thought it possible that by the time I reached the age of twenty-four I might be able to master the elements of Latin, Greek, Hebrew, and French; might get well through Euclid, and through a course of Algebra; might commit the entire 'Paradise Lost,' and seven of the best plays of Shakespeare, to memory; and might read a large and solid course of history, and of religious evidences; and be well acquainted also with the current literature of the day.[6]

[1] M. Hovell, *The Chartist Movement* (Manchester 1918), p. 200.   [2] *Op. cit.*, p. 203.
[3] Wright, *Scottish Chartism*, pp. 101–2.   [4] *Ibid.*
[5] *Op. cit.*, pp. 106, 152–3. Gow illustrates once more the persistent association between handloom weaving and adult education. The association between weaving and poetry is equally notable.
[6] See Cooper's autobiography, *The Life of Thomas Cooper*, first published 1872 (1877 edn., p. 57).

Sundays, he tells us, he devoted to Milton and theology. As to the weekdays,

> Historical reading, or the grammar of some language, or translation, was my first employment on week-day mornings, whether I rose at three or four, until seven o'clock, when I sat down to the stall.
>
> A book or a periodical in my hand while I breakfasted, gave me another half-hour's reading. I had another half-hour, and sometimes an hour's reading, or study of language, at from one to two o'clock, the time of dinner—usually eating my food with a spoon, after I had cut it in pieces, and having my eyes on a book all the time.
>
> I sat at work till eight, and sometimes nine, at night; and, then, either read or walked about our little room and committed 'Hamlet' to memory, or the rhymes of some modern poet, until compelled to go to bed from sheer exhaustion—for it must be remembered that I was repeating something, audibly, as I sat at work, the greater part of the day—either declensions and conjugations, or rules of syntax, or propositions of Euclid, or the 'Paradise Lost,' or 'Hamlet,' or poetry of some modern or living author.[1]

For four years he pursued this intensive course of study, acquiring amongst other subjects a knowledge of Latin, Greek, French, and Italian, and even some Hebrew; until at length in 1827 a physical breakdown put an end alike to his studies and to his shoemaking. Afterwards he became by turns schoolmaster, Methodist preacher, and journalist, and it was while working in the last capacity that he became acquainted with the Leicester Chartists (a branch of O'Connor's National Charter Association), and at the same time with the wretched condition of the Leicester stocking-workers. He at once threw himself heart and soul into the Chartist movement, and quickly assumed a leading position in the local organisation. He devoted himself particularly to the cause of education: he edited a succession of Chartist journals; organised an adult Sunday school with classes named after such Radical heroes as Algernon Sydney, John Hampden, George Washington, William Cobbett, and so on; and lectured on two or three evenings a week:

> I lectured on Milton, and repeated portions of the 'Paradise Lost,' or on Shakespeare, and repeated portions of 'Hamlet,' or on Burns, and repeated 'Tam o'Shanter;' or I recited the history of England, and set the portraits of great Englishmen before young Chartists, who listened with intense interest; or I took up Geology, or even Phrenology, and made the young men acquainted, elementally, with the knowledge of the time.[2]

These meetings were held in the Shakespearean Rooms in the

[1] *Op. cit.*, p. 59.   [2] *Op. cit.*, p. 169.

Amphitheatre, and early in 1842 Cooper organised his followers into the Shakespearean Brigade of Leicester Chartists, with himself as general and various 'commissioned officers' serving under him. Two weaver-poets composed hymns which were collected in the Shakespearean Chartist Hymn Book. One of them, to the tune 'New Crucifixion', began:

> Britannia's sons, though slaves ye be,
> God, your creator, made you free; . . .[1]

By July 1842 the Brigade claimed to have 2,600 members, but by this time the trade depression had become so severe that the adult school had to be abandoned. 'What the hell do we care about reading, if we can get nought to eat?' was the brutal comment of one working man. In April 1843 Cooper was sentenced to two years' imprisonment for seditious conspiracy, and on his release he settled in London. After his departure the educational work of the Leicester Chartists, though it continued for some years, never again attained the same proportions or the same success.[2]

Cooper ultimately repented of the scepticism of his Chartist years, and ended his life as a Baptist preacher, but before that he was for several years a writer and lecturer. Among the places at which he regularly lectured in London were the National Hall in Holborn (Lovett's establishment), the John Street Literary and Scientific Institution off Tottenham Court Road, and the Hall of Science in City Road.[3] The two last were Socialist institutions, and serve to remind us that the educational work of Robert Owen and his followers by no means came to an end with the collapse of the early co-operative movement.

The Owenites

After the débâcle of 1834 Owen at once adjusted his sights. In the following year he founded the Association of All Classes of All Nations, whose objects, as defined in a Conference at Manchester in 1837, included the propagation of Owenite ideas by means of public meetings, lectures, discussions, and cheap publications. Special 'social missionaries' were appointed to lecture on the subject throughout the country, and since local authorities were often

---

[1] *Op. cit.*, p. 166.

[2] Cooper's own narrative (especially Ch. xiv) should be read alongside the more critical account in A. T. Patterson, *Radical Leicester* (Leicester 1954), Chs. xvi and xviii. The educational aspects of Chartism are explored in an unpublished M.A. thesis by R. A. Jones, *Knowledge Chartism* (Birmingham Univ. 1938).

[3] For a list of the many historical, literary, musical, and political subjects on which he lectured see his *Life*, pp. 345–6.

unwilling to lend public rooms for Socialist meetings the Owenites erected their own halls, usually called 'Social Institutions' or 'Halls of Science'. By 1840 such halls had been erected, or were being erected, in London, Manchester, Liverpool, Sheffield, Huddersfield, Leeds, Bradford, Halifax, Birmingham, Coventry, Glasgow, and many other towns. George Jacob Holyoake, the well-known co-operator, was appointed lecturer at the Worcester Hall of Science in 1841, and afterwards served as a social missionary, first in Sheffield, and afterwards (1845) in Glasgow.[1]

During the late 'thirties and early 'forties Socialism often worked in close alliance with Chartism, for a great many Chartists were also Socialists, and indeed a great part of the money for building the Halls of Science came from the Chartists and other reformers.[2] Thomas Coates reported in 1841:

The Chartist and the Socialist zealously diffuse their opinions far and wide; they have created halls, and established places of meeting in which they discourse to thousands; they invite persons of adverse opinions to listen to and freely discuss the expositions of their principles: the Socialists, especially, comprise in the plan of their societies some of the most useful and attractive objects of the Mechanics' Institutions; they have lectures on the sciences, they have music, and in some cases other classes, and they add to these the occasional attraction of tea-parties, accompanied by dancing.[3]

Coates adds the interesting comment that there were fewer members in the Socialist institutions in London than in the mechanics' institutes, but the attendance was much greater.

Friedrich Engels, writing in 1844, and with special reference to Manchester, gives as might be expected a glowing picture of the enthusiasm of the workers for 'sound education' (as distinct from the prejudiced education provided by the mechanics' institutes):

This is proved by the popularity of lectures on economics and on scientific and aesthetic topics which are frequently held at working-class institutes, particularly those run by Socialists. I have sometimes come across workers, with their fustian jackets falling part, who are better informed on geology, astronomy and other matters, than many an educated member of the middle classes in Germany.[4]

[1] G. J. Holyoake, Sixty Years of an Agitator's Life (1892), Vol. I, pp. 133–40, 205.
[2] For the link between the two movements see Podmore, Robert Owen, Vol. II, pp. 454–5.
[3] Society for the Diffusion of Useful Knowledge, Report of the State of Literary, Scientific and Mechanics' Institutions, pp. 29–30. An interesting study of the activities of a Chartist hall is J. Salt, 'The Sheffield Hall of Science', in The Vocational Aspect, Vol. XII (1960).
[4] F. Engels, The Condition of the Working Class in England (1844, ed. W. D. Henderson and W. H. Chaloner, Oxford 1958), p. 272.

Engels also praises the enterprise of the Socialists in making available to the workers in cheap editions, not only the writings of progressive English authors, but also translations of Continental philosophers such as Helvetius, Holbach, and Diderot, Strauss's *Life of Jesus*, and Proudhon's *Property*.[1]

As time went on the Owenites increasingly took on the character of a religious sect, preaching a form of secular ethics, and holding services modelled on those of the Church of England. By 1842 the Association of All Classes had been transformed into the Rational Society: this was active for some years, but gradually faded out after the collapse in 1845 of an attempt to establish an Owenite community at Queenwood in Hampshire. Holyoake in Glasgow was the last Owenite missionary.[2]

In the meantime, in 1844, the Rochdale Equitable Pioneers' Society, making use of the simple principle of a dividend on purchases, had launched the co-operative movement on what was to prove a new and more profitable line. The Pioneers were firm believers in the Owenite ideal of education, and from an early date the activities of the little store in Toad Lane included discussion groups, a newsroom, and a library. In 1853, after a series of *ad hoc* grants, they decided to devote $2\frac{1}{2}$ per cent of their profits to educational purposes.[3]

[1] *Op. cit.*, pp. 272–3.
[2] For details of this later phase of Owenism see Podmore, *Robert Owen*, Vol. II, Chs. xix–xxiii.
[3] Twigg, *Co-operative Education*, pp. 12–13. For the history of the library see C. Stott, 'Early Rochdale Libraries', in Rochdale Literary and Scientific Society, *Transactions*, Vol. XVIII (1932–4), pp. 107–8.

IO

The Nineteenth Century

FUNDAMENTAL EDUCATION

WHEN we add together all the various institutions so far described in the last three chapters, and when we take into the reckoning also the great miscellany of other educational or semi-educational bodies which space has not permitted us to describe—the reading rooms and subscription libraries, the farmers' clubs and agricultural societies, the parish institutes, the working men's institutes, and so forth, it is clear that for the literate adult at least the facilities for further education were, by the middle of the century, many and varied.[1]

The Extent of Working-Class Education

But how many adults were literate? This is a question on which the evidence is plentiful but also confused and contradictory. If one considers the schools which were available to the masses of the people, it is difficult to imagine that they taught anybody anything, yet we know that somehow they did. If one considers the wretched housing and working conditions of the people, similarly, it is difficult to imagine how they found time or energy to learn anything in adult life, yet again we know that somehow they did. In an earlier work I put forward the view that by 1840 most adults in England and Wales (more men than women) had had some kind of schooling, in day school, Sunday school, or evening school, or at home; that the rate of literacy varied from one part of the country to another, and of course from one social class to another; that on the average about three-quarters of the adult population had some knowledge of reading, and about three-fifths some knowledge of writing, but that a much smaller proportion had any real competence in these arts, and less than half had any competence in arithmetic or more advanced subjects. As far as the working classes were concerned, we may suppose that the clerical and skilled manual groups usually had

---

[1] The 1851 Census, which is by no means complete, lists 1,017 'literary and scientific institutions' in England, 40 in Wales, and 221 in Scotland. See *Census of Great Britain, 1851. Education: England and Wales. Religious Worship and Education: Scotland* (*1854*).

a fair grounding in the three Rs, but of the inferior grades—factory operatives, unskilled labourers, and agricultural workers—a considerable proportion, perhaps half in the worst slum areas, were quite illiterate. In Scotland the urban workers seem to have been at least as well educated as their English counterparts, and the rural population, thanks to the now widespread parish school system, distinctly better.[1]

I was encouraged to discover that another student, after careful analysis, had reached very similar conclusions,[2] and on the whole I think this estimate still stands, though in the light of further reading I am disposed to feel that it erred in attempting too great a measure of precision. It would be wrong, of course, to ignore the black spots. The dirt and disease, the poverty and ignorance, which characterised life in the jerry-built cottages and rat-infested cellars of some of the new industrial areas, especially in the 'thirties and 'forties, are too familiar to the student of social history to need repetition here. In general, however, the educational picture is rather better than has commonly been supposed, and there can be no doubt that during the half-century now under review there was, in fact, a steady improvement in adult literacy, as a result of the improved facilities for basic education both at the child and at the adult level.[3]

Day school education made a great leap forward early in the century owing to the spread of the monitorial system which had been developed by Andrew Bell and Joseph Lancaster. The Church of England took up the cause of Dr. Bell, the Nonconformists the cause of Lancaster, who was a Quaker, and monitorial schools came into existence all over the country: hundreds were founded in the 'thirties and 'forties. By 1851 the Census counted in England and Wales 15,518 public day schools, with 1,422,982 scholars, besides 30,524 private day schools with 721,396 scholars.[4] 'The inference appears inevitable', says the census report after a careful analysis of the figures, 'that very few children are *completely* uninstructed; nearly all, at some time or another of their childhood, see the inside of a schoolroom, although some do little more.'[5]

---

[1] T. Kelly, *George Birkbeck* (Liverpool 1957), App. X. The contrast between the factory operative and the skilled artisan is well brought out in J. M. Ludlow and Lloyd Jones, *The Progress of the Working Class, 1832–1867* (1867), pp. 13–19.
[2] R. K. Webb, 'Working Class Readers in Victorian England', in *English Historical Review*, Vol. LXV (1950), and 'Literacy among the Working Classes in Nineteenth Century Scotland', in *Scottish Historical Review*, Vol. XXXIII (1954).
[3] The most recent study is in R. D. Altick, *The English Common Reader* (Chicago Univ. P. 1957), Ch. vii.
[4] *Census of Great Britain, 1851. Education: England and Wales*, p. xliv. The endowed grammer schools are included under public day schools.
[5] *Op. cit.*, p. xxx.

In Scotland the proportion of school children to total population was rather higher than in England, and, as we should expect, the proportion of public schools to private schools was considerably higher. The census showed 3,349 public day schools with 280,045 scholars, but only 1,893 private day schools with 88,472 scholars.[1]

The Sunday schools also increased rapidly in numbers. As in the case of the day schools, the decades 1831–51 were years of particular activity in the founding of new schools, and by 1851 there were in England and Wales, according to the census, 23,514 schools, reckoning 2,407,642 scholars, and in Scotland 3,803 schools with 292,549 scholars. These schools, which commonly had two sessions each Sunday, played an important part in the education of children, especially in Wales and industrial Lancashire and Yorkshire, where day school facilities were least adequate—one giant school in Stockport had some 5,000 scholars. In these same areas the Sunday schools also included a great many adult scholars: it was estimated that in the manufacturing districts up to 25 per cent of the scholars were over 15; in Wales the proportion sometimes exceeded 50 per cent. Many of the schools also maintained libraries, weekday evening classes, and mutual improvement societies.[2]

The Rise of the Adult School Movement

Rev. Thomas Charles of Bala, who, as we have noted in an earlier chapter,[3] had taken a leading part in promoting Sunday schools in North Wales, embarked in 1811 on a new experiment. Finding some adults averse from attending school with the children, he established a school exclusively for adults. A few years later he reported:

the first attempt succeeded wonderfully, and far beyond my most sanguine expectation . . . The report of the success of this school soon spread over the country, and, in many places, the illiterate adults began to call for instruction. In one county . . . the adult poor, even the aged, flocked to the Sunday Schools in crowds; and the shopkeepers could not immediately supply them with an adequate number of spectacles. Our schools, in general, are kept in our chapels; in some districts, where there are no chapels, farmers, in the summer time, lend their barns. The adults and

---

[1] *Census of Great Britain, 1851. Religion and Education: Scotland*, p. 36.
[2] For Stockport see W. I. Wild, *History of the Stockport Sunday School* (1891); and for Wales, D. Evans, *Sunday Schools of Wales* (1883), Chs. x–xii. G. J. Holyoake, about 1837, taught at the Unitarian Sunday School at the New Meeting House at Birmingham (Priestley's chapel), which had classes in logic and mathematics. Only the Unitarians, however, gave such secular instruction on Sundays—Holyoake, *Sixty Years of an Agitator's Life* (1892), Vol. I, pp. 47–8.
[3] Above, pp. 75–6.

children are sometimes in the same room, but placed in different parts of it . . . As the adults have no time to lose, we endeavour (before they can read) to instruct them without delay in the first principles of Christianity.[1]

Charles died in 1814, and early in the following year it was reported that in North Wales

the Sunday Schools for Adults and Children are very much increased and such is the present state of this country that a Man that cannot Read is ashamed of himself and 30 years ago it is well known that 9 out of 10 of the peasants in the country could not read—the late Mr. Charles of Bala was the Instrument to effect all this change.[2]

The spread of the schools led to a great demand for Welsh Bibles, and Charles was one of the founders, in 1804, of the British and Foreign Bible Society, which by the year of his death had supplied Welsh Bibles and Testaments to the number of 100,000. It is said that when the first consignment of 250 New Testaments arrived at Bala in 1806, the people from miles around went out to meet them, unharnessed the carrier's cart, and themselves dragged the precious burden into the town, where every copy was immediately disposed of.[3]

The discovery that many of the poor people of Bristol were unable to read the Bibles offered by the Society led to the foundation there, in 1812, of an Institution for instructing Adult Persons to read the Holy Scriptures. The lead in the work was taken by William Smith, doorkeeper of a Methodist chapel in the city, Thomas Martin, a Methodist minister, and Stephen Prust, a tobacco merchant. People of all denominations gave their support, and within little over a year there were 9 schools for men, with 300 scholars, and 9 for women, with 301 scholars, besides 4 other adult schools under separate auspices. The annual report for 1816 showed 24 schools for men and 31 for women, with a total membership of 1,581.[4]

From Bristol as centre the movement spread rapidly across the south of the country into the Midlands and South Wales, and to a lesser extent into the industrial centres of Northern England. Among

---

[1] T. Pole, *History of the Origin and Progress of Adult Schools* (Bristol 1814, 2nd edn. 1816), pp. 3–4. Cf. D. E. Jenkins, *Life of the Rev. Thomas Charles of Bala* (Denbigh 1908, 2nd edn. 1910), Vol. III, pp. 396–7. The exact location of Charles's first adult school is unknown, but another account by him, quoted in part by Evans, *Sunday Schools of Wales*, p. 175, makes it clear that it was not, as stated by Hudson, *History of Adult Education*, and others, at Bala itself. The original of this account is printed in *First Annual Report* of the Society for the Support of Gaelic Schools (2nd edn. Edinburgh 1812), pp. 62–3.

[2] Jenkins, *op. cit.*, Vol. III, p. 560.

[3] Evans, *op. cit.*, pp. 301–8; Jenkins, *op. cit.*, Vol. III, pp. 68–9.

[4] Pole, *op. cit.*, p. 22. J. W. Hudson, *History of Adult Education* (1851), p. 7, gives for 1816 a total of 63 schools with 1,857 scholars. Presumably these figures are drawn from the report for the following year.

major centres of population where the work was taken in hand within the next four years were London, Plymouth, Birmingham, Liverpool, Leeds, and Newcastle, and there were many smaller centres, often unknown to us by name, in which schools were established. In Buckinghamshire and Berkshire an association of Church of England clergy had established, by 1814, no fewer than 57 schools in the area within a radius of about ten miles of Great Marlow. In Nottingham, where the original adult school of 1798 still flourished, there were at this date 8 or 9 schools, besides others in the surrounding area. Perhaps the most surprising example is the village of Walton-le-Dale, near Preston, which by 1817 had 8 schools and its own textbook. Here and in many other places the schools were held in private houses, and came and went as the need dictated, so that any precise computation of numbers will always be impossible. From the information now available, however, it appears that between 200 and 300 adult schools must have been founded in the five years following the creation of the Bristol society. In addition schools were shortly opened, in many places, for the instruction of prisoners in gaols and houses of correction.[1]

Characteristics of the Schools

In a number of places, e.g. Bristol, Leeds, York, and Yarmouth, the Quakers were active in the work. At Bristol one of the members of the managing committee of the schools was an American-born Quaker physician, Dr. Thomas Pole, whose *History of the Origin and Progress of Adult Schools* is one of our main sources for the early history of the movement, and did much at the time to spread a knowledge of the work throughout England and Wales. An address by Pole printed in this volume typifies the mixture of pious and prudential motives among the middle-class patrons of these schools:

We are now called upon to become instrumental in opening windows to admit celestial light into the habitations of darkness and ignorance;

[1] The primary authorities are Pole, *op. cit.*; [C. Goddard], *An Account of the Origin, Principles, Proceedings and Results of an Institution for Teaching Adults to Read, established in the contiguous parts of Buckinghamshire and Berkshire, in 1814* (Windsor 1816); and J. F. Winks, *History of Adult Schools* (Loughborough 1821). The last, a rare work of which there are copies in the Leicester City Library and a transcript at the National Institute of Adult Education, includes a detailed account of the work of an adult school founded by Winks (a draper's assistant) at Gainsborough in 1820. Thomas Cooper, the Chartist, took part in this venture as a youth, and describes it in his *Life*, though his narrative suggests a rather later date (1877 edn., pp. 46–7).

Hudson, *op. cit.*, uses Pole but also contains later information. G. Currie Martin, *The Adult School Movement* (1924), the standard modern account, is confused and unsatisfactory on this period. For the schools at Walton-le-Dale, and also for a hitherto unknown school at Chorley, see T. Kelly, 'An Early Lancashire Adult School', in *Transactions* of the Historic Society of Lancashire and Cheshire, Vol. CX (Liverpool 1959).

that those who sit in the valley of the shadow of death may be brought to the saving knowledge of the Lord, 'to sing forth the honour of his name, to make his praise glorious'. . .

But when the good seed hath been sown, and when the poor have indeed tasted that the Lord is gracious, and have experienced that in keeping his commands there is great reward, how changed will be the state of our favoured isle! The lower classes will not then be so dependent on the provident members of society as they are now, either for the comforts or necessaries of life. Industry, frugality, and economy will be their possession. They will also have learned better to practice meekness, Christian fortitude, and resignation. Our poor's-rates will thus be lightened; our hospitals, alms-houses, dispensaries, and other pubic charities less encumbered: the generous efforts of the well-disposed will thus become a legacy of blessing to succeeding ages; whilst those whom Divine Wisdom has seen fit to place in the humbler stations of life, will recount with gratitude the favours conferred upon them, and give praise to Him from whom is derived every good and perfect gift.[1]

As the Quaker historians of the movement have pointed out, schools founded under such auspices had none of the democratic character of the adult schools of the later nineteenth century.[2]

Most of the schools of this period were in effect non-denominational Bible classes. They met usually on Sunday mornings and afternoons, under voluntary teachers, and as a general rule their sole aim was to teach reading. Indeed in many cases the scholars were turned out as soon as they could read in the New Testament. The textbooks used were based almost exclusively on Biblical examples and vocabulary: thus in one textbook the spelling lessons for words of more than two syllables included such words as *pha-ri-see, se-pul-chre, sy-na-gogue, righ-te-ous-ness*, and *a-bo-mi-na-tion*.[3] The rules drawn up by Pole (based on those used at Bristol), provided that as soon as the pupils could read 'distinctly and readily in the Bible', they should be dismissed.[4]

A few adult schools, e.g. at Bristol, Sheffield, and Edgbaston, ventured to teach writing as well as reading, but this was generally

[1] Pole, *op. cit.*, pp. 15, 19. The first edition of Pole's *History* is the first work, so far as I know, to use the term 'adult education' (see especially p. 40). A life of Pole by E. T. Wedmore was published as a supplement to the *Journal of the Friends' Historical Society* (1908).

[2] J. W. Rowntree and H. B. Binns, *History of the Adult School Movement* (1903), p. 13.

[3] The textbook published by the Bristol Adult School Society, *Lessons for the Instruction of Adults* (4th edn. 1814), was widely used. A primer under the same title was produced by the Walton Adult School Society (2nd edn. 1817), and to avoid confusion the Bristol Society later changed the title of its book to *The Original Collection of Lessons for the Instruction of Adults* (9th edn. 1827). See Kelly, 'Early Lancashire Adult School', *ut supra*, and Martin, *Adult School Movement*, pp. 40–5, 59.

[4] These rules are printed in Pole's *History*, and reprinted in Martin, *op. cit.*, Appendix A.

looked at askance as a secular occupation unsuited to the Sabbath. None, as far as we know, followed the example of the pioneer Nottingham school of 1798 in teaching arithmetic on Sundays. Where writing and arithmetic were taught, it was usually, as at Chorley, in supplementary evening classes during the week.

We have no information regarding adult schools of the English type in Scotland, but Gaelic schools established in the Highlands, on the Welsh circulating school model, from 1811 onwards, accepted adults as well as children. A special society was formed in Edinburgh to promote such schools, and Pole quotes from its fifth report (1816) an account of a school at Glencalvie whose 60 pupils included a veteran of 116—surely the oldest adult scholar on record![1] By 1849 there were 60 Gaelic schools in the Highlands and Islands, with 2,280 pupils of whom 242 were over 20 years of age.[2]

Decline and Recovery

By 1830, perhaps by 1825, what we may call the Bristol phase of the adult school movement was on the wane. In some centres, e.g. Bristol itself, Bath, and London, the work continued into the 'thirties and 'forties, but evidently with diminishing numbers. In Bristol there were 36 schools in 1834, 25 in 1843, 18 in 1849; in Bath, which had had 20 schools in 1815, there were 7 in 1846. In many other centres the schools fulfilled their immediate function and quickly disappeared.

Where the work survived, or where new schools were founded, there was evidently a demand for a wider range of subjects. A school established at Greengate, Salford, in 1824, was a pioneer in this respect, offering, in addition to the usual elementary subjects, chemistry and mathematics. In Manchester a reading school for adults, which existed in connection with Mr. Roby's Congregational Chapel as early as 1824, was transformed by 1849 into evening classes for writing, arithmetic, grammar, geography, and drawing. At Christ Church, Birmingham, an adult school established about 1827 was by 1849 teaching not only reading but also writing (for men) and sewing (for women). At Bristol a Sunday adult school formed by the Scripture Knowledge Institution in 1834, to teach reading, changed its meetings in 1840 to weekday evenings and began to teach writing also. At Romsey an adult school begun by

---

[1] Pole, *op. cit.*, p. 41; Hudson, *History of Adult Education*, pp. 11–12. Cf. Evans, *Sunday Schools of Wales*, pp. 319–21.
[2] Hudson, *op. cit.*, p. 22.

the parochial clergy in 1848 offered instruction on three evenings a week in writing and arithmetic.[1]

Birmingham in the 1840s saw a revival of Sunday adult school work on traditional lines, but this revival owed its inspiration, not to Bristol, but to the original school at Nottingham. The leading figures in the new venture were two Quaker business men, Joseph Sturge and William White. Sturge, a liberal-minded man who had distinguished himself in the anti-slavery movement and was also for a time a leading member of the Complete Suffrage Union, was impressed by the work of the Nottingham School on a visit in 1842. His adult Sunday school in Severn Street, Birmingham, was begun in 1845 as a school for older boys, but adults began to attend in 1846, and were formed into a separate class, which quickly grew to large numbers. A sister school for women and girls was formed in 1848. It was in that year that William White became associated with the work. He served as teacher of the first class in the men's school from 1848 until his death in 1900, and was greatly influential in persuading Quakers throughout the country to take an active part in the work of adult education.[2]

The Severn Street school so far responded to the new age as to teach writing as well as reading, and there were from about 1850 weekday evening classes in arithmetic, grammar, and geography. But a deputation of the teachers who visited Nottingham in 1846 were still shocked by the idea of teaching arithmetic on the Sabbath: 'we imagine,' they said, 'that persons who learn arithmetic on First-day will soon think it no harm to keep their accounts or even transact business on that day.'[3]

Rowntree and Binns estimated that in 1845 'the total number of men and women in adult schools throughout the country was well under five hundred, probably it was not half that figure'.[4] Hudson, in 1849, put the number of adult poor learning to read in England at 800, and in Scotland at 300; but he estimated that in Wales there were 2,000 in adult evening schools, besides some 3,000 in Sunday schools.[5]

---

[1] In this and the preceding paragraph I have sought to interpret the scraps of information provided by Hudson, *op. cit.*, pp. 12–25, and Martin, *op. cit.*, Chs. iii–iv, but much more research is needed before a full and consecutive narrative can be presented. F. Hill, *National Education* (1836), Vol. I, pp. 199–202, gives an account of the adult school at Edgbaston at that date.

[2] H. Richard, *Memoirs of Joseph Sturge* (1864), pp. 549–55; S. Hobhouse, *Joseph Sturge* (1919), pp. 166–72; O. Morland, *William White* (1903), Chs. iii–iv; W. White, *The Story of the Severn Street and Priory First-day Schools* (1895), pp. 7–25.

[3] Rowntree and Binns, *op. cit.*, p. 13 note.

[4] *Op. cit.*, p. 18.

[5] Hudson, *op. cit.*, p. 21.

Night Schools

Such is, in broad outline, the story of the adult school movement in the first half of the nineteenth century, as derived from the traditional sources. It is, however, by no means the whole story. If we look at the 1851 Census we find that it records, for England and Wales, no fewer than 1,545 evening schools for adults, with 39,783 pupils[1]; and for Scotland 438 schools with 15,071 pupils.[2]

These figures clearly have little or no relation to those just cited, but they do represent a vast and hitherto unrecognised extension of the provision for the elementary education of adults. Most of the schools were held in day school premises, and a great many were probably private ventures by day school teachers.[3] Nearly all made a charge for admission, from 1*d.* per week upwards. The counties in which schools were most numerous were Lancashire (314) and the West Riding of Yorkshire (237)—precisely the areas in which, at the same period, the mechanics' institutes were flourishing. In Scotland, similarly, the main concentration was in the Forth–Clyde valley, Lanarkshire alone accounting for nearly 40 per cent of the schools.[4] For Wales, where the Sunday school continued to be the main instrument of adult education, only 36 schools are recorded.[5]

The kinds of people who attended these schools are clearly indicated in the Census figures. In England and Wales the principal occupations stated were artisans (14,405), agricultural labourers (6,709), factory hands (4,418), and domestic servants (1,317), and with the exception of a handful of clerks and shopkeepers all the rest were manual workers of one kind and another. There were 27,829 men and 11,954 women. In Scotland, where the proportion of women was rather higher (5,571 women to 9,500 men) the principal

---

[1] *Census of Great Britain, 1851. Education: England and Wales*, pp. lxviii–lxix. The statistical tables are at pp. ccviii sqq.

[2] *Op. cit., Religion and Education: Scotland*, pp. 76–81.

[3] Sometimes such classes were conducted by the parish clergy—see A. T. Hart, *The Country Priest in English History* (1959), pp. 48–51; D. McClatchey, *Oxfordshire Clergy 1777–1869* (Oxford 1960), pp. 157–620. Charles Kingsley, in 1848, had a night school for thirty men in his rectory at Eversley in Hampshire; in 1850 he added a weekly lecture on English history—F. Kingsley (ed.), *Charles Kingsley: his Letters and Memories of his Life* (1876, new edn. 1883), pp. 61, 96. In London an 'Institution of Evening Classes for Young Men' was established in 1848—Viscount Ingestre, *Meliora* (1852–3), Vol. II, pp. 1 sqq.

[4] Occasional examples of evening schools in the rural areas of Scotland are recorded from the late eighteenth century onwards. See J. C. Jessop, *Education in Angus* (1931), pp. 295–6; I. J. Simpson, *Education in Aberdeenshire* (1947), p. 202.

[5] The Welsh figures may, however, be understated: in 1847 we find 59 night schools for adults recorded in Carmarthenshire, Glamorganshire, and Pembrokeshire, and 47 in North Wales—Committee of Council on Education, *Reports of the Commissioners of Inquiry into the State of Education in Wales* (1847), Pt. I, pp. 490–2; Pt. III, p. 320.

occupations stated were the same, but the order differed slightly, viz., artisans (4,386), factory operatives (2,397), agricultural labourers (561), domestic servants (553).

The principal subjects studied were, in England and Wales, writing (1,410 schools), reading (1,305), geography (344), grammar (339), history (172), mathematics (135), arithmetic (127), and religious knowledge (108). A great variety of other subjects, however, appear in the list: no fewer than 32 schools, for example, offered instruction in the ancient languages. In Scotland writing (403 schools) again headed the list, and the other most popular subjects were arithmetic (384), reading (347), grammar (168), geography (105), book-keeping (94), and mathematics (42). History and religious instruction here came very low on the list.

We should, perhaps, be a little cautious about accepting these figures at their face value. One wonders, for example, about the relationship of these evening schools for adults with the all-age evening schools which are known to have existed at an earlier date. Such schools are recorded in the 'thirties and 'forties in many parts of the country—in Birmingham, in Norwich, in the Lancashire industrial towns, and in the mining districts of Durham, Northumberland, and South Wales.[1] They catered mainly for adolescents, but the number of adults attending was often quite considerable. Thus in Salford, which had 28 evening schools (besides 9 attached to Sunday schools), we read that

> In these Schools, reading, writing and accounts form the principal objects of instruction; . . . The Scholars are principally young men, who pay for their instruction from their own earnings . . . In some of these Schools, there were several Scholars above twenty-five years of age; and your Committee found one old man of sixty, who had learned to read within a few months.[2]

The 1851 Census remarks that the number of evening schools for children 'must be far from inconsiderable',[3] but does not attempt to enumerate them. Are we to infer that by this date evening schools for children and evening schools for adults had become clearly separated? It would be surprising if this were the case, and if it was not, the question arises whether some of the evening schools recorded as for adults did not in fact include adolescents as well.

[1] See M. E. Sadler (ed.) *Continuation Schools in England and Elsewhere* (Manchester 1907, 2nd edn. 1908), pp. 52–3; and the reports of the Manchester Statistical Society on the state of education in Manchester, Salford, Liverpool, Bury, and Pendleton (1834–8).

[2] Manchester Statistical Society, *Report of a Committee on the State of Education in the Borough of Salford in 1835* (1836), p. 15.

[3] *Education: England and Wales*, p. lxvii.

Yet even if we allow for some exaggeration from this cause the figures remain impressive, and it is astonishing that this large and varied body of work—complementary in many ways to the work of the mechanics' institutes, should so long have remained unknown. Clearly the adult evening schools must be assigned a most important role in the story of early nineteenth-century adult education. It was in these schools, perhaps more than anywhere else, that the illiterate or semi-literate adult acquired the elements of education.

II

The Nineteenth Century

THE INSTRUMENTS OF ADULT EDUCATION

THE last three chapters have described the emergence during the first half of the nineteenth century of a great variety of adult educational institutions. More were to come, but before we continue the narrative it will be useful to consider the remarkable development, especially in the fifty years centring on 1850, in what may collectively be called the instruments of adult education—newspapers, books, libraries, museums, art galleries. These years witnessed a phenomenal expansion of the newspaper press, several successful ventures in the provision of cheap educational literature, the launching of the public library movement, and the first tentative steps towards a more effective provision of museums and art galleries.

The Struggle for a Free Press

It has been remarked that 'much more than political constitutions, statistics of economic progress or demonstrations of national unity, the state of a country's newspapers discloses which rung of the ladder of civilisation has been reached'.[1] In 1800, in spite of the increase in the number of newspapers described in an earlier chapter, the press was still by modern standards a weak and ineffective instrument. Hand-printing, primitive communications, heavy taxation, and the poverty and inadequate schooling of the masses, all combined to limit its circulation, and not a single daily paper had a circulation exceeding 5,000. Because of the precarious financial basis on which they rested, newspapers were in general venal and corrupt—even *The Times*, in its early years, was in receipt of a government subsidy of £300 per annum—and any editor who dared to take an independent line lived under the constant threat of the law of seditious libel.

The operation of this law was strikingly illustrated in 1810, when William Cobbett was fined £1,000 and sent to prison for two years for protesting against the flogging of militiamen; and again in 1813, when Leigh Hunt and his brother John were fined £500 each and

[1] F. Williams, *The Dangerous Estate* (1957), p. 5.

imprisoned for two years for an attack on the Prince Regent. It was, however, in the turbulent years following the Napoleonic Wars that the struggle against the libel law was fought and won, and the most notable protagonists were two London publishers and booksellers: William Hone, formerly a solicitor's clerk, and Richard Carlile, once a journeyman tinman. Both hailed from the West country— Hone from Somerset and Carlile from Devon. Both were at this period Radicals and free-thinkers, and Carlile remained so until his death in 1843; but Hone, who died a year earlier, devoted himself increasingly to literary and antiquarian research, and died a devout Christian.[1]

It was in 1817 that Hone was brought to trial, three times on three successive days, on charges of blasphemous libel arising out of the publication of political parodies on the Catechism, the Lord's Prayer, the Ten Commandments, the Litany, and the Athanasian Creed. He conducted his own defence, speaking for six hours on the first day, seven on the second, and eight on the third, and Harriet Martineau has vividly described how the shabby, middle-aged, ailing bookseller, so mild yet so persistent, braved and eventually overcame even the fiery Lord Chief Justice Ellenborough. From the heap of tattered volumes that surrounded him, he demonstrated that Martin Luther was a parodist, that Bishop Latimer was a parodist, that Mr. Canning was a parodist; that parody was not necessarily intended to ridicule the thing parodied. In defiance of the judges, the three successive juries acquitted him, and he clinched his victory by publishing a full account of the trials.[2]

The failure of these proceedings was a bitter lesson to the government, and the lesson was driven home by the courage and obstinacy of Carlile. It was Carlile, actually, who published the *Parodies* in respect of which Hone was tried—Hone had published them originally but had withdrawn them. For this offence Carlile languished eighteen weeks in gaol before freed by Hone's acquittal. In 1819 he was sentenced to a fine of £1,500 and three years' imprisonment for publishing the works of Tom Paine, but his wife took over his business and continued to sell his publications. In 1821 she went to join her husband in Dorchester gaol, and Carlile's sister, Mary Anne, took her place; and when she in turn was imprisoned a

---

[1] Of Hone, who is best remembered for his *Everyday Book* and similar compilations, there is a biography by F. W. Hackwood (*William Hone, his Life and Times*, 1912). G. J. Holyoake wrote *The Life and Character of Richard Carlile* (1870), and also the article on him in *D.N.B.*

[2] H. Martineau, *History of the Thirty Years' Peace* (1849, new edn. 1877). Vol. I, pp. 164–70.

succession of volunteers came forward to carry on the work and suffer for the cause. Carlile's boldness and determination brought him many sympathisers. Every prosecution increased the sale of his works, and every trial was fully reported in his periodical the *Republican*, which he edited from prison. Since he and his coadjutors steadfastly refused to pay the fines imposed on them, these had to be commuted into additional terms of imprisonment, and it was not until 1825 that he himself was released.

By this time the Tory government of Lord Liverpool was convinced that libel trials of this kind were useless: they merely served to publicise the libels. In 1831 one further attempt was made to muzzle the Radical press, this time by the Whig government of Lord Grey. Carlile was brought to trial in January, and Cobbett in February, for having written in support of the agricultural labourers of Kent and adjoining counties, who had been driven by their desperate conditions to rioting and machine-breaking. Carlile was found guilty, and had to serve nearly another three years in prison; but in Cobbett's case the jury failed to agree, and the prosecution had to be abandoned.

This was the end. The libel laws, though not repealed, were allowed to fall into disuse, and the reformed Parliament of 1834 shelved the question by remitting it to a Select Committee which never reported.[1]

'*Taxes on Knowledge*'

This victory over the libel laws, so important in the development of English political freedom, was shortly followed by a partial victory in the matter of the newspaper taxes—the 'taxes on knowledge', as Edwin Chadwick christened them in the *Examiner*. In 1830 these taxes were threefold: a tax of 4*d.* per copy on newspapers; a tax of 3*d.* per lb. on paper; and a duty of 3*s.* 6*d.* on each advertisement. Cobbett, in 1816, found a way of evading the newspaper tax by printing a special edition of his weekly *Political Register* giving comment but no news. The stamped edition of the *Register* cost 1*s.* 0½*d.*; the unstamped edition without news cost 2*d.* This *Twopenny Trash* achieved the stupendous sale of 40–50,000 copies per week, and found a number of imitators, notably T. J. Wooler's *Black Dwarf*, which began in 1817.

The loophole that Cobbett had discovered was stopped by one of

---

[1] The best general account of this struggle is W. H. Wickwar, *The Struggle for the Freedom of the Press, 1819–1832* (1928). For the restrictive effect on the press of the libel law as affecting private individuals see C. Knight, *Passages of a Working Life* (1864–5), Vol. I, pp. 134–5.

the Six Acts of 1819, which rendered liable to duty 'all pamphlets and papers containing any public news, intelligence of occurrences, or any remarks or observations thereon, or upon any matter in Church or state . . .'[1] Lord Ellenborough's defence of this act was revealing. 'It was not', he said, 'against the respectable press that this bill was directed, but against a pauper press which, administering to the prejudices and passions of a mob, was converted to the basest purposes . . . If he was asked whether he would deprive the lower classes of all political information, he would say he saw no possible good to be derived by the country from having statesmen at the loom and politicians at the spinning-jenny.'[2]

For the next ten years the cheap press practically disappeared, and it was not until July 1831, in the political excitement preceding the passing of the Reform Bill, that Henry Hetherington deliberately challenged the government by issuing a penny weekly, unstamped, called the *Poor Man's Guardian*, bearing on its front page the legend: 'A weekly newspaper for the people, established contrary to "Law", to try the power of "Might" against "Right".'[3]

This was the beginning of the great 'battle of the unstamped', which was carried on relentlessly for five years. Hetherington found many allies, amongst them Richard Carlile, and unstamped periodicals began to pour from the presses. London was the main centre of production but some provincial cities, e.g. Manchester and Leeds, had their own unstamped press. The government retaliated by fining and imprisoning printers, publishers and newsvendors, and by confiscating stocks and printing presses. Hetherington himself was thrice imprisoned.

The working-class Radicals soon found that they were not alone in the struggle. Middle-class liberal opinion had begun to bestir itself in the matter of the newspaper taxes as early as 1830, and at length in 1835, when the Whigs had just come into power again under Lord Melbourne, a society was formed to work for repeal. Its leading figures were George Birkbeck and Francis Place, allies in the cause of reform since the foundation of the London Mechanics' Institution ten years previously; and its supporters included about thirty members of Parliament, amongst them Joseph Hume, J. A. Roebuck, and Edward Bulwer (afterwards Lord Lytton). Under pressure from this group the government at length decided to compromise, and in 1836 the stamp duty on newspapers was reduced to

[1] 60 Geo. III c. 9.
[2] H. R. Fox Bourne, *English Newspapers* (1887), Vol. II, pp. 227–8.
[3] For Hetherington see above, p. 139.

$1d.$[1] The taxes on advertisements and paper were reduced about the tame time—the advertisement tax to $1s.$ $6d.$ in 1833, the paper tax to $1\frac{1}{2}d.$ per lb. in 1836.

The result of this partial victory was disappointing in the extreme. The new stamp duty law was rigorously enforced, so that the cheap unstamped press virtually disappeared. It is true that the issue of stamped papers doubled within ten years, and new Sunday papers of a popular kind, such as the *News of the World*, began to build up a large circulation. The stamped papers, however, usually $5d.$ instead of $7d.$ as hitherto, were still far beyond the reach of the working man, who could only peruse them in reading rooms, coffee-houses, and taverns. Moreover, since payment of the tax conferred the right of free postage throughout the country, the London papers, with their superior news service, had a great advantage: until 1853 England had not a single successful daily paper outside London, and Scotland had only two, both published in Glasgow.[2] The greatest advantage of all was reaped by *The Times*—'a towering Everest of a paper with sales ten times those of any other daily, combining leadership in circulation, in news services . . . in advertisement revenue, commercial profit and political influence to an extent no other newspaper anywhere in the world has done before or since.'[3]

By the middle of the century the demand of the Radical reformers for social justice and intellectual emancipation was reinforced by the growing need of commerce and industry for cheap and efficient national and local newspapers, and in 1849 a new campaign was started for the abolition of the remaining taxes on the press. This time the lead was taken in Parliament by men of the Manchester free trade school—Richard Cobden, John Bright, and above all T. Milner Gibson. Among their supporters were William Ewart, the pioneer of the public library movement, and two stalwarts of the earlier struggle, J. A. Roebuck and Joseph Hume. On the working-class side we find many familiar names—Henry Hetherington, Francis Place, G. J. Holyoake, William Lovett. A new name is that of C. D. Collet, who was secretary of the Association for Promoting the Repeal of the Taxes on Knowledge, and afterwards wrote a detailed narrative of these events.[4]

[1] For this phase of the newspaper tax agitation see T. Kelly, *George Birkbeck* (Liverpool 1957), pp. 164–73, and authorities there cited.

[2] Williams, *Dangerous Estate*, p. 100. The first successful English provincial daily was the *Northern Daily Times*, begun in Liverpool in 1853.

[3] *Ibid. The Times* also led in the application of new printing techniques. It was the first to introduce steam printing in 1814, and printing from a rotating cylinder in 1848.

[4] The *History of the Taxes on Knowledge* (2 vols. 1899, abridged edn. in Thinker's Library 1933).

This time there were no martyrdoms, but the campaign was long and hard-fought, and some of the veterans—Hetherington, Place and Hume—died before victory was achieved. The taxes were defended, of course, on fiscal grounds, but the essentially political character of the opposition was revealed in a speech in the Commons by the Whig prime minister, Lord John Russell, in 1850, in which he roundly declared that he could give no countenance to plans for encouraging such abominations as popular newspapers or popular education in this country.[1] Cobden saw this clearly. 'So long as the penny lasts', he told John Cassell in 1850, 'there can be no daily press for the middle or working class . . . the governing classes will resist the removal of the penny stamp, not on account of the loss of revenue, . . . but because they know that the stamp makes the daily press the instrument and servant of the oligarchy.'[2]

It was only by slow stages that the opposition was overcome. The advertisement tax was the first to go, in 1853; the newspaper tax was abolished in 1855, and the paper duty in 1861.[3] The effect of the abolition of the penny stamp duty was quite astonishing. It broke the monopoly of the London press, and above all of *The Times*. 'It was', says Francis Williams, 'as though a spell had been broken.'[4] In London the appearance of the *Daily Telegraph*, price 1*d.*, claiming to cater not only for the highest classes but 'for the million', was a portent of a new age of journalism. Within six years its circulation was double that of *The Times* (now selling at 3*d.*); within another ten years it was selling 240,000 copies, and claimed the largest circulation in the world. In the provinces, meantime,

Morning papers at 2*d.* or 1*d.* sprang into existence in every great city in the country. Manchester, Liverpool, Birmingham, Bradford, Leeds, Newcastle, Nottingham, Sheffield, Darlington, Plymouth, and other English towns found themselves within a matter of weeks or even days possessed of strong daily organs of local opinion. Edinburgh and Aberdeen joined Glasgow in the possession of a daily press. So did Belfast. Never in history has there been so sudden and tremendous a flowering of the press.[5]

Among the new provincial dailies were some which had formerly existed as weeklies or bi-weeklies, for example the *Manchester Guardian*, which had been founded as a Radical weekly in 1821 and had

---

[1] Fox Bourne, *op. cit.*, Vol. II, p. 212.
[2] *Op. cit.*, Vol. II, p. 210. Cf. J. Morley, *Life of Richard Cobden* (1879, 11th edn. 1903), p. 885.
[3] The best short account of the campaign is in Fox Bourne, *op. cit.*, Vol. II, Ch. xx.
[4] *Dangerous Estate*, p. 99. Chs. vii and viii of this work give a vivid description of the developments which followed the abolition of the duty.
[5] *Op. cit.*, p. 105.

become a bi-weekly after the reduction of the stamp duty to 1*d*.
Papers such as this now launched out into competition with the
London press, and began to provide a full coverage not only of local
but of national and foreign news.

The number of newspapers in the United Kingdom jumped from
563 in 1851 to 1,294 in 1867. The advance of the press was aided by
technical progress—the development of railways and the electric
telegraph, the creation of a world-wide news network organised by
P. J. Reuter, the invention of stereotypes and the horizontal rotary
press, improvements in paper-making. By all these changes speed
of production, and speed in the transmission of news, were enormously increased. The middle and working classes now at last had
available to them a press that was both cheap and efficient.

The Cheap Literature Movement

From newspapers we turn to books and periodicals. Here, amid
many interesting commercial and technical developments tending
towards the multiplication and popularisation of reading material,
we may single out the cheap literature movement which was such a
striking feature of the period from the mid-'twenties onward. This
developed at two levels. At the higher level series such as Constable's
Miscellany, Murray's *Family Library*, Lardner's *Cabinet Library*, and
Cadell's *Waverley Novels*, brought sound literature within range of the
pocket of the prosperous clerk or mechanic. All these made their
appearance between 1827 and 1830, Constable's *Miscellany* at 3*s*. 6*d*.
a volume, the others at 5*s*. a volume—dear enough for those days,
but cheap compared with the typical three-volume novel at half a
guinea a volume.[1] At the lower level a sustained effort was made by
the Society for the Diffusion of Useful Knowledge, and by publishers
such as Charles Knight and the Chambers brothers, to provide
useful and attractive literature for the working masses.

These developments were not entirely new, for there had been a
number of eighteenth-century experiments in cheap popular literature. It will be sufficient here to recall the publishing ventures of the
S.P.C.K. and John Wesley, and the *Cheap Repository Tracts* of Hannah
More, which were themselves designed as an antidote to the cheap
publication of the works of Tom Paine. The nineteenth-century
movement was more varied in character, and on the whole less
deliberately propagandist in tone, though as we shall see the element
of propaganda was by no means absent.

---

[1] R. D. Altick, *The English Common Reader* (Chicago Univ. P. 1957), pp. 268–9, 273–4.

Charles Knight and the Diffusion of Useful Knowledge

One of the leading personalities concerned was Charles Knight, who superintended the publications of the Society for the Diffusion of Useful Knowledge. 'Pray, sir, what do you travel in?' he was asked while on a tour of the manufacturing districts. 'In Useful Knowledge, sir,' was Knight's reply. The son of a bookseller and printer at Windsor, Knight served an apprenticeship to his father, and had considerable journalistic experience before setting up in London as a publisher, at the age of 32, in 1823. For nearly ten years he had aspired to be 'a popular educator'. The rapid advances in the education of the poor, he argued in 1819, had created '*a new power* entrusted to the great mass of the working people', but this power had come under the influence of 'cheap publications almost exclusively directed to the united object of inspiring hatred of the Government and contempt of the Religious Institutions of the country'. Religious tracts, 'often either fanatical or puerile' in tone, could do little to counteract this influence: it was essential to provide a healthy, wholesome alternative literature to meet the intellectual wants of the working classes. In 1825 Knight devised a plan for a *National Library* of cheap books on history, science, art, and miscellaneous literature.[1]

Knight was thus admirably fitted to act as the agent for the Society for the Diffusion of Useful Knowledge, which was founded by Brougham in 1826, avowedly as the ally of the mechanics' institutes and similar organisations intended for the education of the working classes. He brought together under his chairmanship a team which included Lord John Russell, Lord Auckland, Lord Althorp, James Mill, Henry Hallam, Rowland Hill, William Allen, Leonard Horner, Augustus de Morgan, and many other distinguished scholars and men of affairs. Knight, whose own business had suffered shipwreck in the depression of 1826, was appointed in 1827 as superintendent of the Society's publications, and from 1829 onwards acted also as publisher.

The operations of the Society extended over twenty years, and represented the most comprehensive and systematic attempt up to this time to provide cheap educational literature for the masses. The *Library of Useful Knowledge*, launched in 1827 with a comprehensive preliminary *Discourse on the Objects, Advantages, and Pleasures of Science* from the pen of the omniscient Brougham, comprised a series of fortnightly pamphlets, each of 32 closely printed pages, selling at 6*d*. each. These were not scissors-and-paste affairs: each pamphlet was

---

[1] Knight, *Passages of a Working Life*, Vol. I, pp. 225–6, 234–7, Vol. II, p. 37.

an original and authoritative work, which had passed the scrutiny of a most exacting committee. The subjects of this series were mainly scientific, but the *Library of Entertaining Knowledge*, published from 1829 onwards in half-volumes at 2*s.* each, was intended to have a wider appeal, and paid more attention to literature, history, and the arts. In 1832 came the *Penny Magazine*, a weekly 8-page miscellany of literature, history, science, and the arts, which had the then novel attraction of being illustrated by woodcuts. Other ventures included almanacks, maps, a *Quarterly Journal of Education* which ran for five years (1831–6), a *Farmer's Series*, a *Library for the Young*, a *Gallery of Portraits*, and above all a *Penny Cyclopaedia*, launched in 1832 and finally completed in 1844, in 27 volumes. This was a heroic enterprise which involved Knight, as publisher, in a loss of over £30,000, including, as he pointed out, £16,500 in paper duty.[1]

The fate of these publications was similar to that of the formal lectures arranged in the early years of the mechanics' institutes. The volumes of the *Library of Useful Knowledge* were too scientific and too difficult for the average working man; and even the *Library of Entertaining Knowledge*, which included such works as A. T. Malkin's *Historical Parallels* and Sir Henry Ellis's *Elgin Marbles*, was by no means easy reading. The *Penny Magazine*, too, assumed a background of knowledge and ideas which few of those for whom it was intended actually possessed. The result was that the Society's publications found their readers not among the poor but among the relatively well-to-do—skilled craftsmen, clerks, and shopkeepers.

The Society also incurred some unpopularity because (again like the mechanics' institutes) it refused to treat of politics.[2] Economic issues were indeed dealt with, but in a harsh *laissez faire* spirit which showed little understanding of the working man's difficulties and aspirations. This was particularly evident in one of Knight's own contributions, written in 1830 at the time of the agricultural disturbances in the southern counties, and published in the series known as *The Working Man's Companion*. It was entitled *Results of Machinery, Namely, Cheap Production and Increased Employment Exhibited.* 'When there is a glut of labour', it advised the workers, 'go at once out of the market; become yourselves capitalists'—a remark which even the *Quarterly Review* thought notable 'for its singular infelicity'.[3] A further

---

[1] *Op. cit.*, Vol. II, pp. 203, 331 sqq. The amount published each week had to be increased after the first year, and in the end the weekly parts were costing 4*d.*

[2] A Society for the Diffusion of Political Knowledge, founded by Brougham and Knight in 1834, met with no success. See R. K. Webb, *The British Working Class Reader* (1955), pp. 92–3.

[3] *Quarterly Review*, Vol. XLVI (Jan. 1832), quoted Webb, *op. cit.*, p. 119.

volume on *The Rights of Industry* (1831), was 'especially addressed to working men, to exhibit their rights in connexion with their duties by proving that the interests of every member of society, properly understood, are one and the same'.[1]

The *Results of Machinery* was a great success in some quarters: those benevolent employers, the Strutts of Derbyshire, ordered a gross.[2] But it can hardly be wondered at if the ungrateful working man turned from this sort of thing in disgust.

In spite of such difficulties, the Society achieved at the outset a remarkable success. The early volumes of the *Library of Useful Knowledge* sold close on 30,000 copies, and the *Penny Magazine* began with a sale of 200,000. These circulation figures, however, were not maintained: already by 1835 the sales of the *Library of Useful Knowledge* had fallen to 4,000, and by the mid-'forties the sales of the *Penny Magazine* had fallen to 40,000. The Society began to get into financial difficulties, and after an ill-advised attempt to produce a *Biographical Dictionary*, which never got beyond the letter A, was eventually forced to wind up its activities in the year 1846.

The Society was not by any means such a complete failure as has sometimes been made out. Its publications, though they missed the mass market aimed at, certainly found purchasers, and must be credited with a substantial contribution to popular education. The Society assumed too high an intellectual level in its readers; on the other hand it performed a lasting service by its insistence on high standards of scholarship from its authors. Above all, as a recent critic has observed, it publicised 'the *idea* of cheap, enlightening literature',[3] which henceforth had a permanent place in English publishing.[4]

Apart from his work for the Society, Knight himself made an extensive contribution to cheap literature both as publisher and as author. When the Society failed he made an attempt to carry on the *Penny Magazine* under his own name, but had to give up after six months. This failure, however, was more than compensated by the success of his *Weekly Volumes*, a miscellany of works on literature,

---

[1] Knight, *Passages of a Working Life*, Vol. II, p. 168.
[2] Webb, *op. cit.*, p. 117.
[3] Altick, *English Common Reader*, pp. 271–2.
[4] The fullest contemporary account of the Society is to be found in Knight, *Passages of a Working Life*, Vol. II. For modern accounts see F. A. Cavenagh, 'Lord Brougham', in *Journal of Adult Education*, Vol. IV (1929–30), and T. C. Jarman, 'Charles Knight', *ibid.*, Vol. VI (1932–4). Webb, *British Working Class Reader* (especially pp. 66–73, 77–80, 114–22) and Altick, *English Common Reader* (especially pp. 269–83, 332–8) deal critically with the subject in relation to the general background of popular literature in this period. Peacock's satire of the Society in his *Crotchet Castle* (1831) has often been quoted.

history, natural history, and so forth, published at a shilling each and intended particularly for book clubs and reading societies. The series was continued with great success for two years, and then for a further two years on a monthly basis. Other notable works included the *Pictorial Bible*, the *Pictorial Shakespeare*, the *Pictorial History of England, London, Half-hours with the Best Authors*, and the *English Cyclopaedia* (1853)—a remodelled version of the old *Penny Cyclopaedia*. All these were issued in parts, usually monthly.

William and Robert Chambers

Less ambitious than the Society for the Diffusion of Useful Knowledge, but in the long run more successful, were the brothers William and Robert Chambers of Edinburgh. Concerning these two notable brothers it would be possible to write at great length, for William's life of himself and his brother is among the most interesting and entertaining biographies of the century. Of his many good stories concerning their boyhood at Peebles one is worth quoting for the light it throws on cultural life in a small Lowland town in the opening years of the century.

Newspapers were scarce in Peebles at this time. William and Robert's father, who was a small tradesman, subscribed to a newspaper club to purchase the twice weekly *Edinburgh Star*; among the cottagers the news of the campaigns against Napoleon circulated at third or fourth hand. It was in these circumstances that one Tam Fleck, who happened to possess an ancient copy of L'Estrange's translation of Josephus,

struck out a sort of profession by going about in the evenings with his Josephus, which he read as the current news; the only light he had for doing so being usually that imparted by the flickering blaze of a piece of parrot coal. It was his practice not to read more than from two to three pages at a time, interlarded with sagacious remarks of his own by way of footnotes, and in this way he sustained an extraordinary interest in the narrative. Retailing the matter with great equability in different households, Tam kept all at the same point of information, and wound them up with a corresponding anxiety as to the issue of some moving event in Hebrew annals . . .

'Weel, Tam, what's the news the nicht?' would old Geordie Murray say, as Tam entered with Josephus under his arm, and seated himself at the family fireside.

'Bad news, bad news,' replied Tam. 'Titus has begun to besiege Jerusalem—it's gaun' to be a terrible business'.[1]

---

[1] W. Chambers, *Memoir of William and Robert Chambers* (1872, rev. edn. n.d.), p. 25.

A curious fact about the Chambers brothers is that although they were not twins (William was born in 1800, Robert in 1802), they were both born with six fingers to each hand and six toes to each foot. William was operated on successfully, but Robert was lame for the greater part of his life. Both boys had a decent education as education went in those days, that is to say, they were flogged through the burgh school and the grammar school; they supplemented their schooling with the help of the local circulating library and also, astonishingly, with the help of a set of the *Encyclopaedia Britannica*— a rash but treasured investment of their rather improvident father.

In 1813 the father became bankrupt and the family emigrated to Edinburgh, where the two boys eventually established themselves as booksellers, and by prodigies of industry and economy won their way through to success. William added printing to his bookselling business. Robert, who had a taste for learning and had the advantage of a period of additional schooling at an Edinburgh classical academy, took to authorship, and while still a young man won a considerable reputation with his *Traditions of Edinburgh* (1824). Eventually the brothers joined forces to form the well-known publishing firm of W. and R. Chambers.

Robert continued his literary labours throughout his life, his best-known works including a *History of the Rebellion of 1745–6* (1828); the *Cyclopaedia of English Literature* (1844); the *Life and Works of Robert Burns* (1851); and the *Book of Days* (1863). The labour of preparing this last shattered his health. After his death in 1871 it was revealed that he was also the author of the anonymous *Vestiges of Creation* (1844), which in some respects anticipated Darwin's *Origin of Species*. His elder brother William also wrote a little, but in the main devoted himself to the business side of the enterprise. The fitting climax of his story came in 1865, when he was elected Lord Provost of Edinburgh.

It was in 1832 that the brothers became partners in the publication of *Chambers's Edinburgh Journal*. This was a weekly miscellany intended for popular reading, and published at $1\frac{1}{2}d$.; and it anticipated the *Penny Magazine* by eight weeks. The aim of the two journals was very similar, but Chambers's was more literary in character, and though it did not at once attain the stupendous sales of the *Penny Magazine*, it proved to have the greater staying power: indeed as a monthly, with the modified title of *Chambers's Journal*, it survived into our own day. William Chambers thought this was because a society could not compete with private enterprise, but the greater zeal of the Scots for education may have had something to do with it. At any rate *Chambers's*, in spite of the fact that it was not illustrated, seems to have been more popular than the *Penny Magazine* with working people. We occasionally read of an English artisan making sacrifices to obtain the *Penny Magazine*, but in Scotland we are told that *Chambers's* was read by factory hands, shepherds, even milk-boys, as well as in the drawing-rooms of the well-to-do. The wife of the poet Allan Cunningham reported, for example, that it was very popular in the hills of Galloway:

> The shepherds, who are scattered there at the rate of one to every four miles square, read it constantly, and they circulate it in this way: the first shepherd who gets it reads it, and at an understood hour places it under a stone on a certain hill-top; then shepherd the second in his own time finds it, reads it, and carries it to another hill, where it is found like Ossian's chief under its own gray stone by shepherd the third, and so it passes on its way, scattering information over the land.[1]

The Chambers brothers also carried through a great many other educational enterprises. The first, after the Journal, was *Chambers's Information for the People*, begun in 1833. This was followed by the *Educational Course, Papers for the People*, and finally *Chambers's Encyclopaedia* (1859–68).[2]

Harriet Martineau

The year 1832 was indeed a notable year in the history of cheap publishing. It saw not only the advent of *Chambers's Journal* and the *Penny Magazine*, but also renewed activity on the part of the S.P.C.K., which launched the *Saturday Magazine* as a rival to the *Penny Magazine*, and appointed a Committee of General Literature to sponsor cheap books with a Christian tendency. The results were disappointing: within a few years the Committee became merely a producer of school books, and in 1837 the *Saturday Magazine* was handed over to its publisher, Parker, who brought it to an end in 1844.[3]

Another notable event of 1832 was the publication of the first of Harriet Martineau's famous *Illustrations of Political Economy*. Miss Martineau, who collaborated with Knight in some of his enterprises, had been born in 1802 into a Unitarian family at Norwich, where her father was a cloth-manufacturer. Shy, awkward, exceedingly plain, and increasingly deaf, she had an unhappy childhood, and in her early twenties misfortune was piled on misfortune: within two years

---

[1] W. Chambers, *Memoir*, p. 245.
[2] The chief sources are the *Memoir* and W. Chambers, *Story of a Long and Busy Life* (1884). See also Webb, *op. cit.*, especially Ch. iii; and Altick, *op. cit.*, especially pp. 280–1, 32–9.
[3] Webb, *op. cit.*, pp. 73–4, 77–8.

she lost her eldest brother, her father, and her fiancé, and the family business was ruined. Thus thrown virtually upon her own resources, she took to authorship as a means of making a living, and the reading of Mrs. Jane Marcet's *Conversations on Political Economy* inspired her to attempt a series of tales which would present the truths of that great science (by which she meant the truths of *laissez faire* economics) in a popular and readable form.

The *Illustrations of Political Economy* make sad reading to-day, because of the amount of 'instruction' it was felt necessary to mingle with the stories; but they were not without their merits, for the authoress took pains to acquaint herself with the details of working-class life and the views of working-class people, and she had considerable narrative power. At any rate the monthly tales immediately became popular—indeed fashionable, for they found their way even into the hands of the young Princess Victoria. Brougham discovered with indignation that the Society for the Diffusion of Useful Knowledge had rejected one of the tales as too dull, and at once persuaded the Society to commission the authoress to write four tales on *Poor Law and Paupers* in preparation for the Poor Law Amendment Act of 1834. With these, and five *Illustrations of Taxation*, Harriet Martineau produced in all thirty-four volumes in the space of two and a half years.

With her numerous later writings it is not necessary here to deal, though her *History of the Thirty Years' Peace, 1816–1846*, published by Knight in 1849, is still interesting and valuable. After a long illness from which she was cured by mesmerism, she settled in 1846 at Ambleside in the Lake District, where amongst other activities she undertook for many years a yearly series of lectures to the mechanics of Ambleside and their families.[1]

John Cassell

Another interesting character in this gallery of popular educators was the publisher John Cassell, a younger contemporary of Knight and the Chambers brothers. Like the latter he was a self-made man. Born in Manchester in 1817, the son of an innkeeper, he was thrust out into the world at an early age, after a brief and inadequate schooling, to become in turn factory hand, carpenter, and (at the age of 19) temperance advocate. For some years in the 1830s, as a big, rough, raw-boned lad, he stumped the country with a bag of

---

[1] H. Martineau, *Autobiography* (2 v. Windermere 1857, 3 v. London 1877), especially Vol. I, and for the Ambleside lectures Vol. II, pp. 301 sqq. The most recent biography is V. Wheatley, *Life and Work of Harriet Martineau* (1957).

tools on his back, combining odd jobs of carpentry with lectures on the virtues of temperance. In 1841 he married, and with his wife's help established himself in business in London as a wholesale tea and coffee merchant, his object being to provide cheap and attractive beverages as an alternative to alcoholic liquors.

This, however, was only one method of combating drunkenness: the other was education. In his early London days he is said to have startled a temperance meeting at Exeter Hall by suddenly exclaiming, 'I have it! The remedy is Education! Educate the working men and women, and you have a remedy for the crying evil of the country. Give the people mental food and they will not thirst after the abominable drink which is poisoning them'.[1]

It was not long, therefore, before he ventured on the field of publishing, beginning anonymously the *Teetotal Times* in 1846, and going on under his own name to publish a Radical weekly, the *Standard of Freedom*, in 1848. Henceforth for some years he was a most prolific publisher of books and periodicals 'calculated to advance the social and moral well-being of the working-classes.'[2] Thus between 1850 and 1854 his publications included the *Working Man's Friend* (a penny weekly), *John Cassell's Library* (monthly volumes of 144 pages each at 6d.), French, German, and Latin dictionaries (in 3d. numbers, forerunners of the present *Cassell's Dictionaries*), *Cassell's Natural History* (in 1s. parts), *Uncle Tom's Cabin* (the first English edition, in 2d. numbers), *Cassell's Illustrated Family Paper* (a penny weekly which survived in different forms until 1932), and the *Popular Educator* (another penny weekly). This last was perhaps his greatest educational enterprise. Begun in 1852, and completed in five volumes in 1854, it consisted mainly of formal lessons in languages, the sciences, and the arts. Here, for a penny a week, it was claimed, the diligent working man could acquire sufficient learning to see him through London 'matric'. The *Popular Educator* was immensely popular: it was reprinted endlessly, and had sold over a million copies when it was replaced by the *New Popular Educator* in 1887. At one stage, in the 'fifties, Cassell organised 'co-instruction societies', where students of the book could meet to read essays and compare progress.

Unfortunately, though he had a flair for the popular taste, Cassell had no flair for financial management, and by 1855 he was bankrupt. The business was taken over by Petter and Galpin, printers, who after three years took Cassell into partnership. In this capacity he at once launched out on new ventures, notably the *Illustrated*

---

[1] S. Nowell-Smith, *The House of Cassell, 1848–1958* (1958), p. 9.
[2] *Op. cit.*, p. 22.

Family Bible, which sold in penny numbers at the rate of 300,000 a week. In 1865 he died of cancer.[1]

The labours of Cassell and his predecessors all went to swell the ever-growing flood of popular literature. Already in 1864, as Charles Knight penned his autobiography, he was able to point with justifiable pride to the advances made in his own lifetime, as reflected in the figures for new publications. The increase was due to a great many factors—the increasing public taste for reading, the enterprise of the cheap publishers, technical improvements in printing and illustration, improved communications—especially the railways with their accompanying bookstalls—improved domestic lighting, and so on. Knight recognised that sound literature had not yet entirely eradicated 'the diseased taste, which appears to be now common to the sanded kitchen and the carpeted drawing room', for sensational fiction—the circulating library novels of the well-to-do, the cheap novels and magazines of the poorer classes—but he had a firm Victorian confidence that this would eventually be achieved.[2]

Libraries before 1850

Library provision in the first half of the nineteenth century was extensive (much more extensive than is generally realised) but inadequate. Information regarding it has to be gleaned from many sources, but by far the most important source is the 1849 Report of the Select Committee on Public Libraries, which led to the passing of the Public Libraries Act of 1850.

The British Museum, the great national library, was a superb collection, but ill-catalogued and accessible only to readers who could produce a recommendation from some person of standing. The handsome new reading room which was provided in 1838 closed at 4 p.m. (earlier on dark days because there was no artificial lighting) and was thus virtually inaccessible to working people.[3] London also had a number of old foundation libraries—Sion College, Dr. Williams's Library, and Archbishop Tenison's Library—but these were mainly theological in character. The reading room of Tenison's Library was occupied by a private subscription library.[4]

The only provincial cities which had public libraries were Manchester, Preston, and Glasgow. Chetham's Library at Manchester was regarded by the trustees as primarily a library for scholars: it

---

[1] For a readable account of all this see Nowell-Smith, *op. cit.*, Chs. i–iv.
[2] Knight, *Passages of a Working Life*, Vol. III, pp. 175–84.
[3] G. F. Barwick, *The Reading Room of the British Museum* (1929), p. 87.
[4] House of Commons, Select Committee on Public Libraries, *Report* (1849), p. 136. (This Report is cited henceforth as C.P.L.)

was 'emphatically a library of folios', principally theological.[1] At Preston a free public library was founded and endowed by Dr. Shepherd in 1757, but was reported to be 'little used'.[2] Stirling's Library in Glasgow was founded in 1785, under the will of Walter Stirling, as 'a public library for the citizens of Glasgow', but its use was long restricted to persons paying a substantial subscription. It was not until 1849 that it was at last made freely available to the citizens.[3] The various 'town libraries' and 'public libraries' recorded in other English and Scottish towns were for the most part not public libraries in our sense at all, but were maintained by subscriptions and restricted to the use of subscribers.[4]

In many English towns substantial and often valuable libraries were attached to the cathedrals. The 1849 Report records 34 such libraries, of which half a dozen or so were fairly freely accessible to 'respectable inhabitants'.[5] They were, however, primarily theological in character. The same applied, though in less degree, to the old seventeenth- and eighteenth-century parochial libraries. The Committee had information regarding 163 of these still surviving in England and Wales, and 16 in Scotland. Most of them were in a state of neglect and decay, but there were exceptions: that at Langley Marish in Buckinghamshire was well cared for[6]; and that at Beccles in Suffolk had been rescued to form the nucleus of a town library.[7]

These, however, were not the only parish libraries. Churches, nonconformist chapels, and allied organisations such as Sunday schools, ragged schools, and domestic missions often had small libraries of more recent growth, sometimes supplemented by cheap supplies from the Religious Tract Society. This Society, between 1832 and 1849, distributed in England and Wales over 4,000 libraries of about 100 volumes each, mostly to schools and churches, 'wherever an agency can be found'.[8] In Leeds, where the vicar, Dr. W. F. Hook, took an active interest in adult education, there was a library in almost every church and chapel.[9] In Oxfordshire in 1834 free parochial lending libraries existed in 23 market towns and villages.[10]

---

[1] C.P.L., p. 74.
[2] W. J. Hudson, *History of Adult Education* (1851), p. 155.
[3] C.P.L., pp. 18–19.
[4] There were some exceptions, e.g. the library left for the use of the people of Gainsborough by 'Nathaniel Robinson, mercer', which Thomas Cooper was so delighted to discover in the 1820s. It had, he says, 'been thrust aside into a corner, and almost forgotten'—Cooper, *Life* (1872, new edn. 1877), p. 51.
[5] C.P.L., p. vi.
[6] There is an interesting description of it as it was in 1860 in Knight, *Passages of a Working Life*, Vol. III, Ch. ix.
[7] C.P.L., p. 148.   [8] C.P.L., p. 168.   [9] C.P.L., p. 128.
[10] D. McClatchey, *Oxfordshire Clergy 1777–1869* (Oxford 1960), p. 162.

In many parts of the country village libraries were being promoted, in the 1840s, by the clergy and by local landowners and manufacturers. We hear of this development in the Midlands, in Buckinghamshire, in the Scottish Lowlands, and in Aberdeenshire.[1] In most cases these were very small collections, and the interest in them was quickly exhausted. (An apparent exception is the Dukinfield Village Library in Cheshire, which by 1851 had some 1,700 volumes,[2] but Dukinfield was by this time a considerable industrial township.) In Scotland the system of circulating libraries established by Samuel Brown in the Lothians, and afterwards copied in the Highlands, continued to operate in 1849, but on a much reduced scale; and a similar scheme had just been launched in Peeblesshire.[3]

More important than all these little libraries, were the libraries of the cultural societies which were so numerous at this time—literary and philosophical institutions, mechanics' institutions, mutual improvement societies and the like. Indeed, in the absence of a public library service, practically every society tried to provide its members with books: there were Oddfellows' libraries, farmers' club libraries, benefit society libraries, co-operative society libraries, and many more. The libraries of mechanics' institutes were particularly important, because they were fairly easily accessible to middle- and working-class people, and they provided a wider range of books than was available in libraries formed under religious auspices. By the middle of the century, too, most of them provided fiction as well as more serious works, and most witnesses before the Select Committee agreed (rather disapprovingly) that fiction was the main demand.

Unfortunately the stocks of societies of this kind were not impressive. The holdings of mechanics' institutes ranged from over 15,000 volumes at Liverpool to a shelf of books in a village institute, and the average was under 1,000 volumes—many of them unattractive presentation volumes—'dull, heavy books', Samuel Smiles called them in his evidence before the Select Committee.[4]

Working men's libraries of various kinds were common, and within their limits useful. There were old and well-established ones such as the Mechanics' and Apprentices' Libraries at Liverpool and

[1] C.P.L., pp. 86, 89–90, 96, 200–2. Cf. G. W. Shirley, 'Dumfriesshire Libraries', in *Scottish Adult Education*, No. 26 (Aug. 1959); I. J. Simpson, *Education in Aberdeenshire before 1872* (1947), p. 205.
[2] Hudson, *History of Adult Education*, p. 222.
[3] C.P.L., pp. 111–16; cf. above, p. 118.
[4] T. Kelly, *George Birkbeck* (Liverpool 1957), p. 267; C.P.L., p. 127. Cf. C. W. Baker, 'Mechanics' Institutions and Libraries', in Central Society of Education, *First Publication* (1837); W. A. Munford, *Penny Rate* (1951), Appendix; and the same author's paper on 'George Birkbeck and the Mechanics' Institutes' in C. B. Oldman and others, *English Libraries 1800–1850* (1958). The figures given above are for 1851.

Sheffield; and there were others which came and went with bewildering rapidity. In some of the mining districts, and in Nottingham, the workmen formed libraries of their own because the local mechanics' institutes and other bodies refused to admit controversial religious and political works. At Nottingham between 1835 and 1844 six such 'operatives' libraries' were formed, five meeting in public houses and one in a temperance institute.[1] Working men's libraries were also provided, in many places, by coffee-houses. In London, in 1849, there were said to be about 2,000 coffee-houses, largely frequented by working people, and according to William Lovett about a quarter of these had libraries—some as many as 2,000 volumes.[2]

Finally there were the various kinds of circulating libraries. Private circulating libraries varied from the select gentlemen's subscription library to the working man's book club, an outstanding example in the former category being the London Library, founded by Thomas Carlyle and his friends in 1841.[3] Commercial circulating libraries varied from the fashionable Minerva Library at two guineas a year to the small 'shop library' supplying cheap fiction at 1d. a volume.[4]

This list of libraries sounds very impressive, but the total book supply, particularly for the poorer classes, was very inadequate. Free public libraries, even for reference, were very few, and the free public lending library was virtually non-existent. There was, therefore, a good deal of truth in the indictment delivered by George Dawson, a well-known public lecturer, before the Select Committee:

The fact is, we give the people in this country an appetite to read, and supply them with nothing. For the last many years in England everybody has been educating the people, but they have forgotten to find them any books.[5]

The first rate-aided public library in the country was established, not under the Public Libraries Act of 1850, but under the Museums Act of 1845, which permitted local authorities in towns of 10,000 or more inhabitants to levy a $\frac{1}{2}d.$ rate for the foundation and maintenance of a public museum. Canterbury in 1847 used this Act to acquire the museum and library of the Philosophical and Literary Institution[6], and Warrington in 1848 brought together a local sub-

---

[1] C.P.L., pp. 80, 157–8; W. H. Wylie, *Old and New Nottingham* (1853), pp. 350–1.
[2] C.P.L., p. 177. The coffee-houses continued, of course, the tradition of supplying newspapers. See on this Webb, *British Working Class Reader*, pp. 33–4.
[3] S. Nowell-Smith, 'Carlyle and the London Library', in Oldman and others, *English Libraries, 1800–1850*.
[4] Altick, *English Common Reader*, pp. 216–19.
[5] C.P.L., p. 85.   [6] J. J. Ogle, *The Free Library* (1897), p. 11.

scription library and the museum of the Natural History Society.[1] Salford, in 1849, set about doing the same sort of thing in a building already available.[2]

The Public Libraries Act, 1850

The Act of 1850 was passed mainly on the initiative of William Ewart, a Liverpool man who was at this time M.P. for Dumfries.[3] It extended the operation of the Museums Act to embrace public libraries. The adoption of the Act was made subject to the approval of two-thirds of the ratepayers in a special poll, and it permitted expenditure only on premises and maintenance, not on books. A similar Act for Scotland and Ireland was passed in 1853.

The first municipality to adopt the Act was Norwich in 1850; the first to open a public library under the Act was Winchester in 1851. Other authorities which adopted the Act, or secured special local acts, by 1854, were Brighton, Manchester, Bolton, Ipswich, Oxford, Liverpool, Blackburn, Sheffield, and Cambridge.

An amending act of 1855 raised the permissible level of expenditure to a 1*d.* rate, and permitted expenditure on 'books, newspapers, maps, and specimens of art and science' as well as premises and maintenance (in Scotland these changes had been made in the previous year). The machinery for adoption was also simplified, and the population limit reduced to 5,000. In spite of these improvements, however, progress was at first very slow, and only 35 authorities had adopted the Act by 1869.[4]

Art Galleries and Museums

Public art galleries, with the exception of the National Gallery in London, were virtually non-existent in the early nineteenth century, though occasional exhibitions were arranged, and there were some collections in the hands of private societies, for example the Liverpool Royal Institution, which were from time to time open to the public.

Public museums, at the outset of the century, were almost as scarce. London, of course, had the British Museum, and also

[1] J. P. Aspden (ed.), *Warrington Hundred* (Warrington 1947), pp. 95–9; G. A. Carter, 'Warrington and the Public Library Movement', in *The Fortnightly* (Dec. 1950). The public were admitted free of charge to read in the library, but for more than forty years books for home reading were issued only to subscribers.

[2] T. Greenwood, *Public Libraries* (1886, 4th edn. 1894), p. 139; C.P.L., p. 246.

[3] Ewart's part is described in W. A. Munford, *William Ewart, M.P.* (1960), pp. 127 sqq.

[4] On all this see J. Minto, *History of the Public Library Movement* (1932), Chs. v–vii and xi; Munford, *Penny Rate*, Chs. ii–v. E. Edwards, *Free Town Libraries* (1869), Ch. iv, gives much detail concerning the early public libraries.

Parkinson's museum, near Blackfriars Bridge, which an American visitor in 1800 thought of more value to the public than the British Museum because it was so much more easily accessible.[1] In Scotland there were museums of antiquities at Edinburgh and Perth. A surprising number of museums of one kind or another, however, came into existence in the years preceding the Museums Act of 1845.

In London Parkinson's museum shortly fell into neglect, and was sold off in 1806. Some of the material, however, was purchased for the museum which had been opened in Piccadilly in 1805 by William Bullock, a Liverpool goldsmith. This was rehoused in 1808 in the specially erected Egyptian Hall, and was built up at a cost of £30,000 into an extensive and attractive collection under the name of the London Museum. It was sold in 1819, when Bullock went off to Mexico. In the main it was a collection of natural history, and considerable trouble was taken over the method of display. Thus in one room

The visitor was introduced through a basaltic cavern, similar in style to the Giant's Causeway or Fingal's Cave, into an Indian hut, situated in a tropical forest, in which were displayed most of the quadrupeds described by naturalists. In addition to these there were correct models . . . of the trees and other vegetable productions of the torrid climes. The whole was assisted by an appropriate panoramic effect of distance . . .[2]

The museums outside London dated for the most part from the 1820s or later, and most of them were in England, where over 40 museums are known to have existed before 1845. More than 30 of these were museums attached to the universities, or to literary and philosophical societies, natural history societies, antiquarian societies, and the like, and the extent to which they were accessible to the public varied from place to place, but if later practice is any guide probably most of them were fairly frequently open to non-members at a small charge.[3] The remaining museums in England were, or afterwards became, town museums, controlled by the local council. In Wales the only recorded museum at this time was that of the Royal Institution of South Wales at Swansea; and Scotland, apart from university museums and the old-established museums in Edinburgh and Perth, had only five.

The museums of this period, whether private or municipal, were nearly always small, and of course the methods of arrangement and

[1] See above, p. 110, and D. Murray, *Museums, their History and their Use*, Vol. I (Glasgow 1904), p. 177.
[2] T. Greenwood, *Museums and Art Galleries* (1888), pp. 41–2; cf. Murray, *op. cit.*, p. 178.
[3] The most detailed information on this point is in Ch. xxviii of Greenwood, *op. cit.*, and reflects the practice in 1888.

display were poor by modern standards. In a great many cases they were collections of local antiquities and curiosities, with a few more exotic items presented by returned travellers. Canterbury, for example, had a collection of Roman and Saxon relics, Worcester a museum of geology, botany, and archaeology, Plymouth a collection illustrating petrology, ornithology, and entomology, and Tynemouth a collection of curiosities brought by sailors. George Dawson, giving evidence before the Select Committee on Public Libraries, spoke very disparagingly of town museums: 'they often consist of two or three cases of stuffed birds, an Indian canoe, and two or three matters of that kind, but there is little scientific arrangement; you could not study by them.'[1]

The Museums Act of 1845, referred to above, made possible the establishment of rate-aided museums, but the local authorities were slow to avail themselves of this power. Only a handful of public museums, e.g. Canterbury, Ipswich, Leicester, Salford, Warrington, and Winchester, came into existence between 1845 and 1850, and the next twenty years brought only another dozen. It was not until the 1870s and 1880s that the movement for free rate-supported museums really began to get under way, and right up to 1880 more museums were being founded by private societies than by public authorities.

One notable development was a direct outcome of the Great Exhibition of 1851. This Exhibition gave a tremendous stimulus to the development of technical education, and among other things it led to the establishment, in 1853, of the Department of Science and Art, incorporating the Department of Practical Art created in the previous year. The new Department functioned at first under the President of the Board of Trade, and later (1856) under the Lord President of the Council. Its purpose was 'to increase the means of industrial education and extend the influence of Science and Art upon productive Industry,' and the proposals made to this end included 'museums by which all classes might be induced to investigate those common principles of taste which may be traced in the works of excellence of all ages'.[2] The result was the opening, in 1857, of the South Kensington Museum, out of which developed, in 1899, the important collections now known as the Science Museum and the Victoria and Albert Museum.

The Ipswich Museum, opened in 1847, offers an interesting example successful of a provincial museum. An account written in 1850 describes it as a 'really noble and useful institution':

[1] C.P.L., p. 85.
[2] *The Science Museum: the First Hundred Years* (H.M.S.O. 1957), p. 1.

Vast stores of objects in natural history, animal and vegetable, with an extensively classified series of mineral productions, were collected and placed in commodious premises, consisting of a fine and lofty room, surrounded by a gallery . . . Large handsome cases have been erected around and up the centre of the principal room and along the galleries, and these contain the various specimens scientifically arranged by the curator . . . The Museum has a valuable collection of birds, foreign and British, numerous specimens of four-footed animals and reptiles, as well as geological and minerological productions. In addition to these, many specimens of works of art, and a small but extremely valuable library of books, and specimens of the ingenuity of the inhabitants of other climes, have been presented to the institution . . .

At its anniversary, a dinner and soirée are held, and there is a gathering of men of science unequalled in any provincial town, except at the meetings of the British Association . . .

From the commencement of the institution it was laid down as a fundamental principle, that the Museum should be more particularly for the benefit of the working classes, and to carry out that principle the public are admitted free during one day in the week—Wednesday—and also on Wednesday and Friday evenings.[1]

The response of the public was excellent, the attendance averaging 600 for every day and evening the museum was open to the public. An attempt to organise classes for the study of natural history and other sciences, however, was a failure, and few working people attended the public lectures given by distinguished visiting scientists.

In 1881 a special building was erected for the museum, library, and school of art. By 1888 the museum claimed to possess 'one of the finest local geological collections in Europe', besides a fine herbarium and collection of local ornithology and entomology; and weekly public lectures during the winter were attracting an average audience of 500. By this time the museum was entirely free and rate-supported.[2]

---

[1] J. Glyde, jun., *The Moral, Social and Religious Condition of Ipswich* (Ipswich, 1850), pp. 176–9.
[2] Greenwood, *op. cit.*, pp. 72–4.

The Nineteenth Century

WORKING MEN'S COLLEGES AND INSTITUTES

OWN to the middle of the nineteenth century it seemed that the great middle-class effort to educate the workers had been only a partial success. It had, it appeared, reached only the upper crust of the working classes, leaving the great proletarian masses almost untouched. The middle classes themselves constantly lamented this fact. To us, from the vantage point of more than a century later, after the failure of repeated attempts at mass adult education, it seems that they underestimated the extent of their achievement. At the lowest level the adult schools (religious and secular) and the adult classes in Sunday schools, provided many illiterate or semi-literate men and women with the basic tools of education. At a higher level the mechanics' institutes, the workmen's libraries, the cheap books and periodicals, not only assisted working men of exceptional intelligence and enterprise to make the most of their abilities: they also helped to diffuse knowledge and ideas among a much wider section of the working population. In this latter field the efforts of the middle classes were reinforced by the efforts of the workers themselves—the mutual improvement societies, the Chartist reading rooms, the co-operative discussion groups, and so forth. And in the background of all this the Sunday schools and the cheap day schools, inadequate as they were, were helping to lay the foundation for a more literate generation in the future.

None the less it must be admitted that there were grave weaknesses in the approach of the middle classes to adult education. Except in the adult schools, they commonly overestimated the education of working people; they often underestimated their intelligence; and they completely failed to understand the fierce flame of political and social idealism that burned in the breasts of their leaders. The middle classes were for the most part too patronising, too dogmatic, too conservative in their social and economic outlook, too austere and utilitarian. They saw education as harnessed to a particular purpose —religious salvation, social order, economic prosperity, as the case might be. They forgot about the need for recreation; they forgot about the joy of education: the joy that possessed Thomas Cooper the shoemaker as he ploughed his way through the dusty volumes of the old town library at Gainsborough[1]; the joy that possessed John Clare the peasant-boy as he sat down in the lee of a wall to read Thomson's *Seasons*.[2] As William Chambers remarked apropos of the Society for the Diffusion of Useful Knowledge, 'they made no provision for the culture of the imaginative faculties'.[3]

The Sheffield People's College

It was the realisation of this last weakness that led Rev. R. S. Bayley, minister of the Howard Street Independent Chapel in Sheffield, to found in 1842 the Sheffield People's College. Bayley had lectured at the Mechanics' Institute, and had felt that its studies were too narrow in scope and purpose, and lacked any integrating principle. His so-called College was, to begin with, a whitewashed, unplastered garret, in which classes were held by candlelight at 6.30 in the morning and 7.30 in the evening. The classes were open to both men and women at 9*d.* per week, and the distinguishing feature of the curriculum was that besides including the usual elementary subjects, e.g. English grammar, Euclid, geography, and drawing, it laid great stress on the humane studies—literature and composition, history, logic, Greek, Latin, and modern languages. In this respect the College did pioneer work comparable with that done by the Dissenting academies of the eighteenth century in the field of secondary education, for although these subjects were not new in working-class adult education they had never before been given the dominant place.

The People's College was a great venture of faith on Bayley's part, reflecting his belief that 'among the toiling masses of the town there might be a latent perception of the beautiful, an ardent love of the true', and that 'the necessity to labour for a living did neither insure the absence of taste to appreciate the higher branches of knowledge, nor preclude the possibility of acquiring them'.[4] He was evidently a man of immense energy and wide if rather superficial knowledge. He did practically all the teaching himself, with the help of monitors trained up from among the students; he also wrote and

---

[1] Above, p. 174 note.
[2] R. D. Altick, *The English Common Reader* (Chicago Univ. P. 1957), p. 252.
[3] W. Chambers, *Memoir of William and Robert Chambers* (1872, rev. edn. n.d.), p. 235.
[4] G. C. Moore Smith, *The Story of the People's College, Sheffield, 1842–1878* (Sheffield 1912), p. 54. This is the standard account of the history of the College.

printed five special textbooks, and for a time even edited a monthly college journal.

Moore Smith has preserved interesting particulars regarding Bayley's methods of teaching.[1] In literature his method was to drill the students in selected specimens. 'When you have fully mastered them,' he would declare, 'you will be competent readers as long as you live.' Composition he taught by making the students write essays which were then subjected to unsparing class criticism. In moral knowledge it was his habit to propound a question, make each student answer, and then send the students home to write what they could for the next meeting.

At first the College was very successful, but in 1846, as the result of a quarrel, Bayley was expelled from his church, and two years later he left Sheffield for London. This misfortune nearly extinguished the College. A small band of students came to the rescue, and re-organised it as a self-governing and self-supporting institution, but without Bayley's inspiration the humane studies languished, and the old heresy of vocational interest cropped up again. In 1853 the committee recorded its view that 'there was something more required for the artisans of Sheffield than a purely mental discipline, . . . and that to be really a College for the People, it must include in its curriculum classes that would have a direct bearing on the industrial pursuits that distinguish the town'.[2] So Latin and Greek were missing from the syllabus for the following year, and The Application of Chemistry to the Sheffield Trades took their place. The students began to take the Society of Arts examinations, and the College was virtually absorbed into the growing body of technical education. It maintained a modest but useful existence till 1874, when the building was demolished.

The London Working Men's College

This Sheffield experiment was important not only for its own sake but also because it inspired a greater and longer-lived institution—the London Working Men's College, founded in 1854. This venture was closely connected in its origins with the movement known as Christian Socialism, which was born in 1848 amongst a group of people in London—university and professional people mostly—under the leadership of Frederick Denison Maurice. The French Revolution of February of that year, and the Chartist demonstrations of 10th April, shocked these people into a realisation of the deep gulf that still separated the middle and working classes, and the need to

---

[1] *Op. cit.*, pp. 18–19.   [2] *Op. cit.*, p. 62.

establish a new relationship. They found the answer in Socialism—not a secularised Socialism like that of Robert Owen, but a Socialism deeply rooted in the Christian tradition, a Socialism whose purpose was to raise all men to the status of manhood, and unite all classes in the pursuit of higher spiritual ideals.

Maurice has been described as 'incomparably the greatest, alike in life, in vision, and in achievement', among the churchmen of the nineteenth century.[1] At this time he was a man of 43, Professor of English Literature and History, and of Theology, at King's College, London. He was deprived of his chairs in 1853 after the publication of his *Theological Essays*, but was afterwards, from 1866 until his death in 1872, Professor of Moral Philosophy at Cambridge. Of those associated with him in the early phase of the Christian Socialist movement the best-known were younger men in their twenties: the scholarly J. M. F. Ludlow, a barrister who had been born in India and educated in France; Charles Kingsley, parson and novelist; and that cheerful extrovert, Thomas Hughes, whose fame as the author of *Tom Brown's Schooldays* may well lead us to forget that he was also at one time a Liberal M.P., and that he ended his days as a county court judge. Ludlow was the intellectual power of the movement, and Maurice was its prophet.

In 1848 and the years immediately following, the Christian Socialists were active in the pursuit of their new ideal. They began with social work of various kinds: house-to-house visiting, infant and evening schools, Bible classes, and working men's co-operative associations—in which last they placed a confidence which was by no means justified by earlier experiments of the kind. They also worked hard to spread their ideas through the press. Two short-lived journals, *Politics for the People* and the *Christian Socialist*, and a series of *Tracts on Christian Socialism*, were but indifferently received, but Kingsley's two Christian Socialist novels, *Alton Locke* and *Yeast*, were fiercely denounced in all the respectable reviews, and met with a corresponding success. *Yeast* exposed the miseries of the agricultural labourer, while the hero of *Alton Locke* (said to have been based on Thomas Cooper) was a working tailor.

Experience convinced the Christian Socialists, as it has convinced many reformers before and since, that the social problem was at root one of education; and in 1853 the news of the Sheffield experiment, coming about the same time as the expulsion of Maurice from his position at King's College, led to the decision to establish a Working Men's College with Maurice as Principal. Not all those concerned

---

[1] C. E. Raven, *Christian Socialism, 1848–1854* (1920), p. 75.

in the launching of this enterprise were Christian Socialists, but the influence of the group was very strong. Maurice, Ludlow, and Hughes took part in the actual foundation, and Kingsley, though prevented from doing so by his parochial duties in Hampshire, was an active helper.[1]

The name 'College' was deliberately chosen, because the founders wished the new institution to be, in a real sense, a community of teachers and students, like the Oxford and Cambridge colleges with which they were themselves familiar. 'The name college,' Maurice explained, '. . . implies a Society for fellow work, a Society of which teachers and learners are equally members, a Society in which men are not held together by the bond of buying and selling, a Society in which they meet not as belonging to a class or caste, but as having a common life which God has given them and which he will cultivate in them.'[2]

In contrast to the mechanics' institutes, the curriculum of the new College was to emphasise the humane studies. Mathematics, languages, drawing and the like were not to be excluded, but they were to be taught from a liberal point of view. 'The aim was not to enable bright young men from the working class to get on in the world, but rather to provide opportunities for the enrichment of personal life for all who cared to make the necessary effort.'[3]

The College duly opened in 1854 at 31 Red Lion Square. It was open to all men and youths over 16 who were competent in the three Rs. Maurice's aim was that the College should ultimately become self-governing and self-supporting, but he insisted that the content and method of teaching should be firmly in the hands of the teachers. These were a most distinguished band. Maurice himself taught theology and history; Ludlow taught law and languages; F. J. Furnivall the philologist taught English grammar; Ruskin, D. G. Rossetti, Burne-Jones, and other Pre-Raphaelites taught art; and other teachers and lecturers during the early years included Kingsley, G. Lowes Dickinson, George Grove, Leslie Stephen and Frederic Harrison. Hughes found a niche for himself in superintending the boxing class and the volunteer corps, and generally promoting the social life of the College. All these gave their services without fee. As M. E. Sadler remarked, 'In the long history of adult education in England, there is no chapter comparable with this.'[4]

In spite of this galaxy of talent, the results of the early years' work of

[1] J. F. C. Harrison, *History of the Working Men's College, 1854–1954* (1954), Ch. ii.
[2] *Op. cit.*, p. 21.   [3] *Op. cit.*, p. 26.
[4] M. E. Sadler (ed.), *Continuation Schools in England and Elsewhere* (Manchester 1907, 2nd edn. 1908), p. 44. On the early art classes see J. Llewelyn Davies, *The Working Men's College, 1854–1904* (1904), Ch. v.

the College were fundamentally a disappointment. The men who joined the classes were very much the same as those who a generation earlier had joined the London Mechanics' Institution, that is to say, about half of them were manual workers—small craftsmen mostly— and the rest were clerks, shopmen, and lower-paid professional workers.[1] And the subjects they wanted to study, apart from the elementary subjects, which the College did not at first provide, were also much the same. 'The most numerously attended classes were those on Languages, English Grammar, Mathematics, and Drawing; while the weakest were the Humanities (history, literature, law, politics) and the Physical Sciences.'[2] In 1855 an adult school was started to prepare illiterate students for entry, and two years later an elementary class was created to form a bridge between the adult school and the College.

None the less the College did differ from the mechanics' institutes. It was much more successful in creating a genuine corporate and social life, and it did succeed in inspiring at least some of the students with the feeling that learning is a great adventure of the spirit, and not just the mechanical acquisition of new knowledge.

As the years went by weaknesses revealed themselves in the government of the College, and financial difficulties arose as the result of the acquisition of new premises in Great Ormond Street, to which the College moved in 1857. These difficulties came to a head in the decade following Maurice's death in 1872, when Hughes reluctantly took over the principalship. Thanks, however, in large measure to the energy of R. B. Litchfield, the youngest of the original founding members, the constitution and finances were reorganised, and the College re-established on a sound basis. In the 'eighties and 'nineties the system of teaching and examinations was also put on a much more systematic footing. The College continued to rely on the services of voluntary teachers, and continued to proclaim its ideal of liberal education for working men, but the curriculum was broadened to include commercial and technical subjects such as shorthand and book-keeping, carpentry and plumbing, on the ground that these subjects attracted working men to the College. George Tansley, a devoted student and teacher of the College, was the leading spirit in all this, and was rewarded by seeing the student enrolments rise to over 1,000 before the close of the century. But clearly the new policy had its dangers.[3]

[1] Harrison, op. cit., pp. 49–50.   [2] Op. cit., pp. 58–9.
[3] The only satisfactory history is that by Harrison already cited. For the motives that originally inspired the movement see J. F. D. Maurice, Learning and Working (1855), and F. Maurice (ed.), Life of Frederick Denison Maurice (1884).

Colleges for Women

A feature of the College was that women were never admitted to full membership of the classes, though in the early days there were a few separate classes for women, and for some years they were permitted to share in the singing classes. In 1864 the Working Women's College was founded in Queen Square, Bloomsbury. Many of those concerned favoured mixed classes, and would have welcomed an amalgamation with the Men's College; and when this was refused it was decided, in 1874, to change the name to 'The College for Men and Women'. A minority party, however, clung to the original idea and established a new 'College for Working Women' in Fitzroy Street. This breakaway institution proved the more successful of the two. Its students were shop assistants, domestic workers, milliners, nurses, teachers, and the like, and its curriculum included domestic subjects such as dressmaking, cookery, and hygiene as well as academic subjects. The College for Men and Women closed its doors in 1901, but the College for Working Women still continues. For many years its leading spirit was Frances Martin, and after her death in 1922 the name 'Frances Martin College' was adopted in recognition of her work.[1]

Provincial Colleges

From London the idea of the Working Men's College quickly spread to the provinces, and between 1855 and 1868 a dozen or more colleges were founded in England and two in Scotland. Information regarding most of these institutions is difficult to come by. Many of them were short-lived—Ancoats in Manchester, Cambridge, Ely, Huntingdon, Wolverhampton, and the two Scottish colleges, Ayr and Prestwick, all perished within ten years of their foundation. At the main Manchester college, where a promising start was made in 1858 with much assistance from the staff of the recently founded Owens College, difficulties regarding premises led in 1861 to a merger between the Working Men's College and the Owens College evening classes.[2]

Several colleges which survived longer seem to have done so mainly as centres for vocational instruction, and faded out with the

---

[1] Harrison, *op. cit.*, pp. 108–10; R. M. Harris, 'Frances Martin College', in *Further Education*, Vol. I (1947–8). The College now operates, on a reduced scale, within the walls of the Working Men's College.

[2] J. Thompson, *The Owens College* (Manchester 1886), Ch. viii; T. Kelly, *Outside the Walls* (Manchester 1950), pp. 7–8; C. D. Legge, 'Manchester Working Men's College', in *Manchester Guardian*, 11 Jan. 1958. A. J. Scott, a friend of Maurice and first Principal of Owens College 1851–7, took a prominent part in the movement.

development of technical education later in the century. This, one suspects, was the case at Haley Hill (Halifax) (1855–early 1880s), Salford (1858–86), Boston (1859–92) and Ipswich (1861–90). The South London Working Men's College in Southwark, founded in 1868 with T. H. Huxley as its first principal, developed after his resignation in 1880 into a library and art gallery.[1]

The most successful of the provincial colleges, and the only one to survive into the twentieth century, was that at Leicester, which grew in 1862 out of night school work and took the name Working Men's College in 1868. Its founder was D. J. Vaughan, liberal churchman and educationist and friend of Maurice, and under his forty-three years' presidency the College, in spite of many concessions to vocational interests, managed to preserve something of the liberal ideal that had inspired Maurice's work in London. The motto which Vaughan gave to it was 'Sirs, ye are brethren'. In spite of the development of technical education it managed to retain its place and its distinctive function, and it ultimately became, under the name Vaughan College, an extra-mural centre for Leicester University College.[2]

Significance of the Movement

The Working Men's College movement, in spite of the very modest measure of success that attended it, was of fundamental importance in the history of adult education because for the first time it drew attention to the distinction between technical education and liberal studies. Hitherto adult education, whether elementary as in the adult schools or more advanced as in the mechanics' institutes, had been quite generalised in character. Any form of adult education was conceived to be good; any form of adult education would help people to live fuller lives, would make them better workers and better citizens. Maurice first saw clearly that

---

[1] C. Bibby, *T. H. Huxley* (1959), pp. 33–4.

[2] Atkins, E. (Ed.), *The Vaughan Working Men's College, Leicester, 1862–1912* (Leicester 1912); A. J. Allaway, *David James Vaughan* (reprinted from Leicestershire Archaeological and Historical Society, *Transactions*, Vol. XXXIII, Leicester 1957). For the later history see below, pp. 265, 280 note.

In this account of the provincial working men's colleges I have been much indebted to the assistance of my friend Mr. C. D. Legge, of Manchester University.

To avoid confusion it should perhaps be mentioned that the name 'People's College' was adopted at Nottingham (1846), Norwich (1849), and Warrington (1858), by institutions conducting evening classes designed chiefly for adolescents (the Nottingham and Warrington colleges also ran day schools). The Norwich People's College, which was already in decline by 1850, is said to have been originated by Bayley, but the others were not connected in any way with the working men's college movement. The People's College at Melbourne, Derbyshire, listed J. W. Hudson, *History of Adult Education* (1851), p. 223, is apparently to be identified with the Mechanics' Institution.

there was a real difference between 'the means of livelihood' and 'the means of life'.[1] As Dobbs has put it: 'It was necessary that education should start with the problem of social reconstruction and should be grounded on a deeper and more spiritual analysis than had underlain earlier movements. The new ideal was not information but the enrichment of personality.'[2]

This distinction, once made, was never lost sight of, and played a vital role in the subsequent development and organisation of adult education.

Working Men's Clubs and Institutes

It cannot be claimed that the working men's colleges were any more successful than the mechanics' institutes in attracting and holding the masses of the working people. Henry Solly, founder and first secretary of the Working Men's Club and Institute Union, declared that 'the main life and character of English working men, their wants and troubles, their strength and weakness, were almost a *terra incognita*, an unknown region, to the great majority of the middle and upper classes . . .'[3] The great fault of earlier institutions intended for the weekly wage-earner was, in his view, their failure to give a sufficiently prominent place to recreation as distinct from education.[4]

Actually, this discovery was not as new as Solly thought. The idea of combining entertainment and recreation with education had been tried out many times in lyceums and the more popular type of mechanics' institute in many places from the 'thirties onward. 'After a day of hard work a man wants refreshment and ease,' declared Sir Benjamin Heywood, President of the Manchester Mechanics' Institute in 1837, and in a new institute he founded in the working-class suburb of Miles Platting he took great pains to create a club-like atmosphere, 'to see if we cannot make it a match for the public house'.[5]

In Birmingham in 1846 'an intelligent "stockinger" of the name of Brooks' founded, under the auspices of the Ministry to the Poor, a People's Instruction Society which Charles Knight visited in 1848. He describes it as

a real working-man's club, which combined the recreative principle with

---

[1] The words are not Maurice's, but Lord Goschen's—see D. H. S. Cranage in R. St. J. Parry, *Cambridge Essays on Adult Education* (Cambridge 1920), p. 17.
[2] A. E. Dobbs, *Education and Social Movements, 1700–1850* (1919), p. 184.
[3] H. Solly, *These Eighty Years* (1893), Vol. II, p. 166.
[4] *Op. cit.*, pp. 160–1.
[5] B. Heywood, *Addresses at the Manchester Mechanics' Institution* (1843), pp. 92, 107–8.

that of mutual improvement; offered a well warmed and ventilated room, supplied with books and newspapers; could furnish wholesome food at the cheapest rate; and was wholly self-supporting by the payment of one penny a week from each of its numerous members.[1]

There had been other experiments of the same kind, and when the Club and Institute Union came to prepare its first report in 1863, it recorded no fewer than thirty pre-existing clubs which had been helped or brought into association with the Union during the year.[2]

The Union was established in 1862, largely on Solly's initiative, with the veteran Lord Brougham as President, and a distinguished list of vice-presidents. The idea of a national movement was suggested by Dr. David Thomas, a London Congregational minister, but Solly had long been working towards the same end. His interest in working-class conditions had first been keenly aroused when, as a young Unitarian parson at Yeovil in 1840, he had become associated with the local Chartist movement. Later, in London, he had come greatly under the influence of 'the great prophet', Maurice, and had been caught up in the foundation and subsequent activities of the Working Men's College. A strong temperance advocate, he had in various places of his ministry, and especially at Yeovil, Cheltenham, and Lancaster, attempted the formation of mutual improvement societies, but never with such success as he had wished. The idea of a *club* seemed to him the answer to his difficulties, and he now gave up his ministry to throw himself enthusiastically into the work of the Union.

The Union was formed, according to its opening manifesto, 'for the purpose of helping Working Men to establish Clubs or Institutes where they can meet for conversation, business, and mental improvement, with the means of recreation and refreshment, free from intoxicating drinks'.[3] During Solly's five years as full-time secretary, he spread the gospel indefatigably throughout the land, enlisted the aid of countless noblemen, clergy, members of Parliament, and other persons of eminence, and raised a substantial sum of money. Clubs sprang up on every side, and by 1867 nearly 300 were 'known to the Union'.

Unfortunately most of these clubs proved short-lived. Many reasons were advanced for this at the time—the admission of juveniles, resentment at the patronage of wealthy founders, and so

[1] C. Knight, *Passages of a Working Life* (1864–5), Vol. III, pp. 84–6.
[2] B. T. Hall, *Our Sixty Years: the Story of the Working Men's Club and Institute Union* (1922), pp. 23–4.
[3] *Op. cit.*, p. 14.

forth—but undoubtedly the principal reason was the exclusion of beer (and often of tobacco also). Very soon the rules had to be amended to allow of local option in this matter. Even Solly, staunch teetotaller as he was, was brought to recognise that it was better for a man to drink in moderation in his club than to excess in his pub. 'There is', he explained, 'a very large number of respectable working men who desire to have a pint of beer after the day's work is done, as much as a lady desires an afternoon cup of tea . . . They wish for no more, but they will take no less.'[1]

So beer won the day, and the clubs began to prosper. More important still, they became financially independent. Many years were to pass, however, before the Union became as strong as the individual clubs. The truth is that it was not, initially, a Union at all, but merely a society to which clubs could affiliate, and as there was no adequate arrangement for financing its work it was mainly dependent on charitable contributions. It was not until 1889 that, having shed its aristocratic supporters, it became a genuine Union, with each club as a member, making its due contribution to the expenses of the centre. From this time the Union steadily gathered strength. In 1889 there were 329 clubs in membership. By 1899 there were 683.

It is worthy of note that the club movement was predominantly associated with the capital and the English industrial areas. London, the home counties, Lancashire, Cheshire, Yorkshire, and the West Midlands accounted for 479 of the clubs existing in 1899, and there were hardly any clubs in Wales and Scotland.[2]

In these constitutional changes Solly had no part, for he had resigned the secretaryship in 1867. In spite of all his good qualities he was inclined to be dictatorial, and in nearly all the enterprises in which he engaged he sooner or later fell foul of his colleagues. He long continued to work for the propagation of the clubs, and for a short time in 1871–3 he acted as organising and travelling secretary, but after this he never again held office in the Union. He devoted the rest of his long life (he died in 1903 in his ninetieth year) to a variety of social and educational enterprises for the working classes. For a time he was deeply involved in a London Artisans' Club and Institute which he founded in Newman Street. He managed to secure 'a respectable niche' in the programme for 'lectures,

---

[1] *Op. cit.*, p. 207.
[2] *Op. cit.*, p. 113. The best account of the history of the Union is that given by Hall, but H. Solly, *Working Men's Social Clubs and Educational Institutes* (1867, 2nd edn. ed. B. T. Hall 1904), and Vol. II of Solly's autobiography, especially Chs. v–x, are also valuable for the earlier years.

discussions, readings and recitations',[1] but was pained to discover that many members did not appreciate his self-sacrifice in taking up residence on the premises. In 1873 he persuaded James Stuart, who was then engaged in launching the University Extension movement, to help him in an attempt to form a national Trades Guild of Learning, to promote lectures and classes among the members of trade unions; and when this failed he established an Artisans' Institute in St. Martin's Lane, with himself as principal, to experiment in a combination of technical training for crafts with other studies of a more liberal character. This prospered modestly for a few years, but in 1878 ill health and financial difficulties compelled him to give it up.[2]

The educational work of the Club and Institute Union during this period was never as extensive as Solly had hoped. 'It was not', says B. T. Hall, who became secretary in 1893, 'unwillingness on the part of the Union, or failure to find teachers, but the unwillingness of workmen to receive what was offered which was the difficulty.'[3] At the centre the Union conducted examinations in history and essay-writing, awarded prizes for debating, arranged lectures, and organised Saturday afternoon visits to places of interest. In the provincial clubs there were occasional lectures and classes. But only the circulating library, commenced in 1864, achieved any real degree of popularity: book-boxes were sent out to clubs at a fee of 5s. a year, and by 1893 the annual circulation of books had reached 10,000. 'Truth to tell', comments Hall, 'Education (of the pedagogic kind) was not the Union's work'.[4] It was not until Ruskin College and the Workers' Educational Association came into existence at the turn of the century that the Union found a way to provide for the minority of its members which desired serious further education.

The People's Palace

Two other institutions call for mention in a chapter devoted to working men's colleges and clubs. The first is that interesting institution, the People's Palace, opened in 1887 in the Mile End Road. This was an embodiment in bricks and mortar of a novelist's dream, for Sir Edmund Currie, who built it, took as his pattern the 'Palace of Delight' described in Sir Walter Besant's novel *All Sorts and Conditions of Men* (1882). Besant conceived the Palace as 'a centre of organised recreation, orderly amusement, and intellectual and

---

[1] Solly, *op. cit.*, Vol. II, p. 359.
[2] For Solly's later work see *These Eighty Years*, Vol. II, Chs. viii–xiii.
[3] Hall, *op. cit.*, p. 96.
[4] *Op. cit.*, p. 97.

artistic culture' for the East End of London, and so, to begin with, it was. It was furnished with 'a noble hall, a swimming bath, a splendid organ, one of the finest library buildings in London, a winter garden, art schools, and a lecture room', and at first all went well:

We started with all the things mentioned above, and with billiard-rooms, with a girls' social side, with a debating society, with clubs for all kinds of things—cricket, football, rambles, and the like; we had delightful balls in the great hall, we had concerts and organ recitals, the girls gave dances in their social rooms; there was a literary society; we had lectures and entertainments, orchestral performances and part singing; nothing could have been better than our start . . . The literary club proved a dead failure; not a soul, while I was connected with the Palace, showed the least literary ability or ambition. Still the successes far outweighed the failures.

Unfortunately the management of the Palace was shortly taken over by the Drapers' Company, who closed down most of the social activities and turned the place into a polytechnic—a development Besant never ceased to regret. It later became the East London Technical College, and is now Queen Mary College.[1]

Morley College

Across the river, in Lambeth, was an institution equally unusual in its origins—Morley College, which actually grew out of the Royal Victoria Theatre—the Old Vic. It was Emma Cons, friend of Octavia Hill and like her a pioneer in housing reform, who first conceived the idea of establishing in this slum area of London a centre for innocent and wholesome recreation. With the help of friends she took over in 1880 the Royal Victoria Theatre, at that time given over to melodrama of the lowest description, and haunted by thieves and prostitutes, and re-opened it as the Royal Victoria Coffee Hall. The theatre saloon was turned into a coffee tavern, and the programme comprised variety on Mondays and Saturdays, lectures and entertainment on Tuesdays and Fridays, choir and band practice on Wednesdays, and ballad concerts on Thursdays. All these things were offered at the lowest possible price—a few coppers, even as little as 1d. on some evenings.

For the first few years the Hall passed through a succession of financial crises, which it would not have survived had it not been for the support of Samuel Morley, a millionaire hosiery manufacturer and philanthropist from the Midlands, who became chairman of the managing committee in 1884. Emma Cons now proceeded to

---

[1] Sir W. Besant, *Autobiography* (1902), pp. 244-7.

develop the educational side of the work. She established a working men's club in 1884, and technical classes in association with the Science and Art Department in 1885. Morley died in 1886, and three years later the educational work was placed on a new and separate footing as the Morley Memorial College. Miraculously, it was still accommodated in the Old Vic building—above, below, and behind the stage.

In view of the pioneering work done by Emma Cons and others it was appropriate that the new College should from the first be open to women on an equal footing with men. Its primary aim was defined as

To promote by means of classes, lectures and otherwise, the advanced study by men and women belonging to the working classes, of subjects of knowledge not directly connected with or applied to any handicraft, trade or business.

Provision was also made for more elementary instruction for those who needed it, and for the promotion of social intercouse.

The College quickly established itself, and by the mid-'nineties there were over 1,100 students—mostly young, mostly male, and drawn from a variety of manual and clerical occupations. The leading figure during these years, apart from Emma Cons, was Caroline Martineau, who acted as unpaid Principal from 1891 till her death in 1902. Among many able teachers (paid or unpaid) was Graham Wallas, who first came to the College to deliver a University Extension course in 1893.

The opening of the nearby Borough Polytechnic in 1893 led to some falling off in student numbers towards the close of the century, but in 1901 there were 55 classes in 32 different subjects. In addition to elementary, technical and commercial classes the programme included a wide range of liberal studies, e.g. classical and modern languages; poetry, music, and art; history, geography, and geology; botany and biology; political economy and psychology; and also some practical classes, e.g. cookery, dressmaking, and woodcarving. There was also a vigorous social life, with a wide range of clubs and societies.[1]

Apart from the admission of women, the resemblance to the London Working Men's College is very striking. The motives of the founders were indeed rather different, for the Christian Socialist mystique had given way to a down to earth practical philanthropy; but the ultimate result was very much the same.

[1] The story is admirably told in a volume by Denis Richards, the present Principal, *Offspring of the Vic* (1958). See especially Chs. ii–viii.

13

The Nineteenth Century

CHANGING SCENES

AFTER the storm and stress of the first half of the nineteenth century, the second half was relatively peaceful. It was not, of course, entirely without its troubles: there was, for example, the cotton famine in Lancashire at the time of the American Civil War; and there were severe general trade depressions in the 'seventies and 'eighties. But between the Crimean War and the Boer War Britain was not involved in any major international conflict, and at home there was nothing that could be compared with the Chartist movement of the 'forties. The Parliamentary Reform Acts of 1867 and 1884, which at last enfranchised the ordinary householder, were passed without any of the agitation that had attended the Reform Act of 1832.

This was, moreover, the golden age of British capitalism. Both industry and commerce were rapidly expanding, and under a free trade economy British goods and British capital were finding their way into every corner of the globe. This advancing prosperity led to a great concentration of wealth in the hands of merchants and manufacturers. Not a little of this was used for the public benefit, as many of our civic buildings still testify; and some of it went also to support the growing body of professional workers—doctors, lawyers, teachers, and the like.[1] The working classes also had their share of prosperity: the real wages of skilled workers (also an increasing proportion of the population) actually doubled during the period 1850–1900. In part this was due to the development of trade unionism—a new unionism which, firmly based on individual crafts, had long forgotten the cloudy idealism of the Grand National Consolidated era.

In other ways, too, the condition of the working classes was improved. The protective legislation which had begun in the era after the first Reform Act was steadily extended, and a succession of

[1] Professional workers in England increased from $2\frac{1}{2}$ per cent of the occupied population in 1851 to $4\frac{1}{2}$ per cent in 1871.

factory acts, public health acts, housing acts, and local government acts gradually removed, or brought under control, the worst of the evils that had followed in the wake of the Industrial Revolution. The ten-hour day, which under the Ten Hours Act of 1847 had been restricted to the textile workers, was gradually extended and made effective during the next thirty years, and by the 'seventies many unions had won for their members a nine-hour day. Measures were taken for the control of insanitary conditions, and from the 'sixties onwards progressive municipalities made a beginning in the tremendous task of clearing or improving slum dwellings.

It was at this time that the main structure of local government, of which the foundations had been laid by the Municipal Reform Act of 1835, was completed. The County Councils Act of 1888 created the administrative counties and distinguished county and non-county boroughs; the Local Government Act of 1894 established parish and urban district councils. Some time was to pass, however, before these new organs were to gather to themselves all the functions appropriate to local government; in the meantime they were supplemented by a variety of *ad hoc* authorities.

The Development of Elementary and Technical Education

Social and economic changes inevitably brought educational change in their wake, for a country increasingly dependent on the skill of its manufacturers, in an increasingly competitive age, could no longer afford an educational system—if system it could be called —under which a large section of its working people received little or no schooling; which left technical education to voluntary effort; and in which universities almost completely out of touch with modern science and technology provided an antiquated education for a privileged *élite*. The transformation of the universities will be described in the next chapter: here we are concerned principally with the advances in elementary and technical education, which were achieved, surprisingly enough in this age of *laissez faire*, mainly by an extension of the powers of the state and the local authorities.

The Education Act of 1870 set up local School Boards to fill the gaps in elementary schooling left by voluntary effort. It is true that education did not become compulsory till 1876, nor free until 1891, and at the close of the century it was still possible for a child to finish his full-time schooling at 12, but substantially the 1870 Act spelt the end of illiteracy in England and Wales. In Scotland the comprehensive act of 1872 inaugurated a very similar development, but here education was at once made compulsory, to the age of 13.

Technical education, in 1850, was restricted to the provision made by mechanics' institutes and a few of the more advanced night schools. Very shortly, however, the Society of Arts and the government Science and Art Department took measures to promote more systematic teaching. The Society of Arts formed in 1852 a national union of mechanics' institutions, and from 1856 began to organise examinations at various centres in science and commerce. The Science and Art Department inaugurated in 1859 augmentation grants to teachers of science, and from 1861 organised examinations in the basic sciences. Later, in 1879, the newly established City and Guilds of London Institute began to examine in technological subjects, and from 1882 the Society of Arts was able to concentrate on commercial subjects.

The period 1850–90 saw, both in London and in the provinces, a rapid development of technical education in various forms, at various levels, and under various auspices. Many new institutions came into existence, and many existing institutions, such as mechanics' institutes and co-operative societies, were drawn into the work. This early phase in the history of technical instruction, preliminary to the development of a state system, has not been adequately studied, but the example of Warrington in Lancashire, by no means one of the larger industrial centres, illustrates what must have been happening in a great many places. The Warrington Mechanics' Institute was moribund by 1850, but between this date and 1891, when a local authority technical institute was established, there were at various times technical classes organised by the Museums Committee, by a College of Art which developed from the Mechanics' Institute, by an evening school in connection with the People's College, by a privately supported School of Science, and by the Recreative Evening Schools movement.[1]

Solly's Artizans' Institute in London, to which reference has been made above,[2] falls within the same context of developing technical education. In 1879 what is generally regarded as the first technical college was established by the City and Guilds Institute at Finsbury. In 1882 Quintin Hogg opened in Regent Street the first of what was to become a widespread system of polytechnics, designed for 'the promotion of industrial skill, general knowledge, health and well-being of young men belonging to the poorer classes'.

In the meantime the government had been contemplating action.

---

[1] W. B. Stephens, *Development of Adult Education in Warrington* (unpublished M.A. thesis, Exeter 1958), Chs. vii–viii.

[2] Above, p. 192.

The poor showing made by the British exhibits at the Paris Exhibition of 1867 caused widespread alarm, and after a Select Committee and two Royal Commissions on the subject Lord Salisbury's government eventually passed the Technical Instruction Act of 1889, which empowered county and county borough councils to establish Technical Instruction Committees and devote the proceeds of a 1d. rate to technical and manual instruction. Providentially the Local Taxation Act of the next year provided the new committees with ample resources in the form of the 'whisky money'—a fund derived from a tax on whisky originally intended to finance the closure of redundant public houses. In London substantial sums were also granted for the same purpose from parochial charities. By 1902, when the whisky money ceased to be available, the country's system of technical education was well under way.[1]

The Mechanics' Institutes after 1850

All these changes inevitably had their effect upon adult education, and particularly on working-class adult education. In this field the mechanics' institutes still represented, after the turn of the half-century, the most important and widespread activity. Far from being, as has long been supposed, moribund in 1850, they were at this time in the heyday of their growth, and as far as one can judge the peak of the movement was not reached until about 1860. Even after that date new institutes continued to be founded in large numbers, especially in the industrial areas.

By this time, however, a considerable cleavage was beginning to develop. In Scotland and the North of England, where the membership was still substantially working-class—craftsmen, clerks, operatives, shop assistants, and the like—and where there was a growing demand for skilled and educated workmen, the institutes tended to move increasingly in the direction of technical education, especially after the introduction of the Society of Arts and Science and Art Department examinations. In the South of England, where the middle-class element often predominated, the trend towards technical education was less strong, and here many of the institutes were just general literary and scientific societies, with the emphasis on the library, general lectures, and social activities rather than on classes.

[1] There is no adequate history of technical education, but C. T. Millis, *Technical Education: its Development and Aims* (1925), Chs. i–vi, gives much interesting detail, and there are shorter accounts in A. Abbott, *Education for Industry and Commerce* (1933), Chs. i–iii; and C. A. Bennett, *History of Manual and Industrial Education, 1870 to 1917* (Peoria, Illinois, 1937), Ch. viii. See also S. F. Cotgrove, *Technical Education and Social Change* (1958), Chs. i–iv; and for the polytechnics E. M. Wood, *The Polytechnic and its Founder Quintin Hogg* (1904, rev. edn. 1932).

In 1875 the mechanics' institutes were still vigorous: the institutes at Crewe and Nottingham, for example, played an important part in the inauguration of the University Extension movement. By 1900, however, it was clear that their day was past. Many had already disappeared, and others were but shadows of their former selves. The reason for this change was simply that the functions the institutes had formerly fulfilled were now increasingly being taken over by the local authorities. These functions had been many and various: continued elementary education, technical and art education, and library provision were the principal ones, but some institutes, for example Devonport, were also responsible for museums, and others, for example Leeds and Liverpool, had important day schools. Elementary education was provided after 1870 in public day schools, and continued education was available in government-supported evening schools. Technical and art education was provided after 1889 by the Technical Instruction committees; and the provision of public libraries and museums, though still far from adequate, was growing every year.

In some cases the local authorities set up new machinery which gradually superseded or absorbed that of the institutes, but there were very many instances in which the authorities simply took over the work, and often the premises, of the institutes, as going concerns. In this way many mechanics' institutes became technical colleges: such was, indeed, the origin of many of our most famous technical colleges and university institutions, e.g. at Leeds, Huddersfield, Manchester, Glasgow, and Edinburgh. The Leeds and Liverpool Colleges of Art likewise sprang out of the mechanics' institutes there. In other cases the institute library was taken over to form a public library, or the nucleus of one; and in a few cases public museums originated in the same way. Where the institutes ran secondary schools, these were taken over by the local authorities after the Education Act of 1902: here again Leeds and Liverpool provide notable examples.

Sometimes the transition from voluntary body to local authority was long delayed: at Crewe the institute technical classes were not taken over by the authority till 1912, and the library not until 1936. In general, however, the institutes which survived the first decade of the twentieth century (and about half a hundred still exist to-day) did so in virtue of the one function which public authority was not able to fulfil, that is to say, they survived as social clubs.[1]

[1] On all this see T. Kelly, *George Birkbeck* (Liverpool 1957), Bk. II, Ch. iii. Birkbeck College, London, Strathclyde and Heriot-Watt Universities, and Manchester University Institute of Science and Technology, all originated as mechanics' institutes.

Thus the end of the mechanics' institutes was not inglorious. They perished, indeed, for the most part, but they left behind them a legacy of useful public institutions.[1]

Evening Schools

The evening adult schools, of which we have seen there were a great many in 1851,[2] operated at a humbler level than the mechanics' institutes, being mainly concerned with the provision of basic education for men and women who, though not for the most part entirely without schooling, had forgotten what little they had learned. Unfortunately the subsequent history of these schools is tangled with the history of evening schools catering also for adolescents, which from 1851 became eligible under certain conditions for government grant. The 1851 Census had recorded in England and Wales 1,545 adult schools with close on 40,000 pupils. In 1858 there were said to be 2,036 evening schools, most of them attached to day schools, and three-quarters of them under the auspices of the Church of England; but from such figures as are available it appears that the majority of the 81,000 pupils (55,000 males and 26,000 females) were children or adolescents.[3]

These figures include both grant-aided and non-grant-aided evening schools, the latter being in a substantial majority. If, therefore, as seems to be the case, they are to be taken as representing the sum total of evening schools at this date, we must suppose either that there was a steep decline in the number of adults attending between 1851 and 1858, or that the figures for 1851 include, as has been suggested above, some evening schools catering for adolescents as well as adults.

The distribution of the schools is of interest. Lancashire, with 319 schools, was far ahead of all other counties; Middlesex had 181, Yorkshire 160. No other county reached the hundred mark, but Cheshire, Norfolk, Suffolk, Northamptonshire, Warwickshire, Wiltshire, and Somerset all had 50 or more. Wales had very few. As for the subjects taught, returns from 681 schools showed that the three

---

[1] It is interesting to note that some of the early experiments in the way of technical institutions had their social as well as their educational side. This was notably the case with Solly's Artizan's Institute, and with the original Regent Street Polytechnic. For the East London Technical College, originally the People's Palace, see above, pp. 192–3.

[2] Above, pp. 155–7.

[3] Royal Commission on the State of Popular Education in England [Newcastle Commission] *Report*, Vol. I (1861), pp. 39–51, 628–35, 658, 669. Precise ages are known only for some 13,500 pupils, of whom 49 per cent. were over 15 but only 11 per cent. over 20. G. C. T. Bartley, *Schools for the People* (1871), p. 415, after quoting the Newcastle Commission figures, says, 'As a rule, these Schools are for Adults, or those over the age of 17 or 18.'

R's and religious instruction were the main staple. A minority of schools taught also needlework, geography, grammar, and history, and a few only had classes in mathematics, science, music, and drawing.

Another feature of interest is the association of so many of these schools with the Church of England. Thanks to the ecclesiastical reforms of the 'thirties, the era of the working parson had now arrived. In the rural areas especially, the Church school now became 'the focal point in the village, where in the evening the adult population could meet for culture or entertainment'; and many parsons were tireless in organising night schools and other educational and social activities. 'The modern country clergyman', wrote a contemporary, 'is always on the go with his penny readings, harvest home festivals, church services, lectures, entertainments . . . His life is one long effort. He is always to be seen in a long single breasted coat, and slouched billy cock hat, hurrying at a half run from one end of the village to the other, intent upon some new scheme for what is called interesting the people.'[1]

For Scotland (where 438 schools had been recorded in 1851) we have no comparable statistics for this period. The report of the Argyll Commission remarks that evening schools are common in the industrial areas, but that on the whole the evening school system does not appear to have taken very deep root in Scotland. An interesting development in Scotland to which this report draws attention, however, is that in many remote parishes the young farmworkers 'take a winter now and then for their own improvement, leave "service" altogether, and go to the day school'. A few become so keen on their studies that they return each winter for several years.[2]

In England and Wales (mainly in England) the 'sixties saw a marked growth in the number of pupils in grant-aided evening schools, which seem to have gradually squeezed out the private establishments. The growth was particularly marked after the issue of the revised grant regulations of 1862, which defined the function of the evening school as continued elementary education for scholars over 11. The number of pupils in grant-earning schools rose from 14,000 in 1863 to 83,000 in 1870-1, after which date, however, the

[1] A. T. Hart and S. C. Carpenter, *The Nineteenth Century Country Parson* (Shrewsbury 1954), pp. 32-4. The 'penny readings' here referred to, i.e., readings from well-known authors, were a popular pastime in the late nineteenth century. See, for example, *Some Habits and Customs of the Working Classes*, by a Journeyman Engineer (1867), pp. 168-83, quoted H. P. Smith, *Literature and Adult Education a Century Ago* (Oxford 1960), pp. 17-34.
[2] Royal Commission on Schools in Scotland, *Second Report* (1867), pp. cxxiv-cxxix. Cf. I. J. Simpson, *Education in Aberdeenshire before 1872* (1947), p. 202.

development of elementary education in the day-schools caused a steady falling-away in numbers. In 1871 scholars over 18 were made ineligible for grant, and with this regulation the evening schools for the time being virtually disappeared from the sphere of adult education. The age limit was raised to 21 in 1876, and in 1893, after the evening schools had been reorganised to provide more advanced education, the limit was removed altogether, but the purpose of this change was primarily to provide for extended technical and professional instruction. Like so many other adult educational enterprises, the evening schools were being absorbed into the country's system of technical education.[1] We must, however, note the work of the Recreative Evening Schools Association, which was founded in 1885 by Dr. J. B. Paton of Nottingham. Though directed specifically to the needs of adolescents, this movement stressed the importance of practical, cultural, and recreational subjects, and thus pointed the way to a future in which the evening school would again have an important part to play in adult education.[2]

The Revival of the Adult Schools

In the meantime we must note a marked revival of the traditional adult school of the early nineteenth century. In a previous chapter we have traced the decline of the phase of widespread adult school activity which began at Bristol in 1812, and the subsequent revival of the work by Joseph Sturge of Birmingham in mid-century. From the confused narrative of the movement's historian[3] it is difficult to perceive very clearly the line of subsequent development, but it appears that for twenty years or more the spread of the revival was very slow, and confined almost entirely to the towns of the North and Midlands.[4] These schools, like those of the earlier period, were concerned in the first instance with the instruction of illiterates, and were attended mainly by working men and women. No longer, however, were the pupils turned out, as they had often been in the early days, as soon as they could read: on the contrary, a conscious effort was made to retain them. A spirit of fellowship gradually replaced the old atmosphere of patronage, and classes in basic subjects such

[1] M. E. Sadler, *Continuation Schools in England and Elsewhere* (Manchester 1907, 2nd edn. 1908), pp. 52–71.

[2] J. L. Paton, *John Brown Paton* (1914), Ch. xii; cf. Royal Commission on the Elementary Education Acts [Cross Commission], *Final Report* (1888), pp. 162–4, 320–3. On Paton see further below, Ch. xiv.

[3] G. C. Martin, *The Adult School Movement* (1924), especially Chs. iv–v.

[4] F. J. Gillman, *The Story of the York Adult Schools* (York 1907), p. 3, lists the oldest adult schools surviving at that date as Nottingham, Birmingham, Sheffield, Leominster, Huddersfield, York, Bristol, Leeds, Dewsbury, Doncaster, Settle, and Hitchin, all these except the first two being founded 1854–60.

as reading, writing, and arithmetic were accompanied, or followed, by classes for the study of the Bible and the discussion of religious problems. Many schools developed subsidiary activities: savings banks, sick funds, libraries or book clubs, temperance societies.

In considerable measure these differences were due to the fact that the adult schools of this period were predominantly under the aegis of the Quakers, operating through the Friends' First Day School Association, which had been founded in 1847. William White and Richard and George Cadbury at Birmingham, J. S. and Joseph Rowntree at York, and J. S. Fry at Bristol, were among the many Friends who entered the movement at this period. Very often these Quaker adult schools were associated with social missionary work among the poor. This was particularly the case at Birmingham, where in some of the slum areas derelict public-houses were bought and converted for adult school purposes. This and other aspects of the work are illustrated in a description of a class conducted by George Cadbury at Severn Street. He was appointed as teacher in 1863, and continued for half a century:

The class, which numbered some three hundred men, grew up with him from youth to manhood. It became not so much a class as a companionship of old friends, of which George Cadbury was less a teacher than an elder. It included a large proportion of intelligent working men from self-respecting homes; but many of the members came from the most degraded surroundings, and learned the rudiments of reading and writing in the elementary sections of the class. They were brought in from the slums or the public-houses, or even from the prison gate. For membership of the class had no meaning unless it was inspired by a missionary fervour. The members must go out into the highways and byways, down into the lodging-houses and the mean streets, and bring in those who were outside the Churches and all the civilizing influences of life.[1]

A passage from another Quaker biography, this time the life of J. S. Rowntree of York, illustrates the character of religious instruction in these schools:

He would take pains to use simple words, and if long words came into the lesson he would make sure that the meaning was really grasped. He followed the Socratic method, sometimes questioning an idea into the minds of his class and then questioning it out again . . . Whenever possible he used pictures or diagrams, or he would bring with him some object such as a locust, or an Eastern lamp, to illustrate the lesson. No one could

[1] A. G. Gardiner, *Life of George Cadbury* (1923), p. 44. The history of the Bedford Institute, established by the Quakers in Spitalfields in 1865, also illustrates the association of adult schools with missionary endeavour, though here the core of the work was a Sunday school. See A. T. Alexander, *Fifty Years' Story of the Bedford Institute* [1915].

feel more strongly than he did the difference between theology and life
... His care was to make the central meaning and truth of a Bible passage
clear, and then to press home the practical applications of the truth itself,
not his own opinions about the truth, or about the ways in which it
might be theologically stated. 'It was delightful', one man says, 'to hear
him talk about Old Testament characters, he made them so wonderfully
real.'[1]

The religious teaching in the Quaker schools was not in any way
denominational, but at Birmingham and in some other centres there
arose in association with the schools 'Christian Societies' which
organised a simple religious service on Quaker lines.

It might have been expected that the Education Act of 1870 would
mean the end of the adult school movement. Strangely enough,
however, the very period at which the effects of the act began to
show themselves, i.e. the 1880s, was for the adult schools the beginning of a new phase of expansion. In 1870 the total number of
students in Quaker adult schools was about 8,000, representing, say,
100 schools. In 1876 there were over 10,000. By 1886 the total
number of adult students had reached about 25,000, of whom
21,600 were in Quaker schools, the growth of the latter being
particularly marked in Yorkshire. After that date there was indeed
a decline in some places, but the general trend was upward. At the
end of the century there were in all 350 schools with 45,000 students,
29,000 being in Quaker schools.[2]

It will be seen that a characteristic feature of this new phase was
the development of non-Quaker schools. This was particularly the
case in Leicestershire, where in the 'eighties there were nearly
100 adult schools, mostly non-Quaker. A similar development,
though not on the same scale, took place in Yorkshire. As a result of
this development district unions of adult schools on an undenominational basis came into existence in the 'eighties and 'nineties in the
Midlands, Leicestershire, London, Somerset, and Norfolk, and in
1899 these unions joined with the F.F.D.S.A. in a National Council
of Adult School Associations.

The reason that the adult schools were able to develop in this way
was that they showed themselves responsive to changing conditions.
They did, it is true, continue to provide elementary instruction as
long as there was a demand for it (classes in writing continued as late
as 1914); but essentially they had ceased to be schools and had

---

[1] P. Doncaster, *John Stephenson Rowntree* (1908), p. 28.
[2] For these figures see J. W. Rowntree and H. B. Binns, *History of the Adult Schoo
Movement* (1903), pp. 25–6, 33.

become societies, with a wide and increasing variety of social and educational activities built round a central core of Bible teaching. This variety is strikingly illustrated by the case of the Scarborough adult school, which had a rowing club and a drum and fife band.[1] By 1890 reading and writing occupied a small place only, and in many places the class teacher had given way to an elected president.[2]

A writer in *One and All* in 1895 stressed the importance of 'first half-hour talks', lectures, discussions, debates, and social evenings; and another writer in the same journal in 1897 recommended adult schools to establish a connection with the local University Extension movement, to organise lectures, reading circles, and educational excursions, and to encourage systematic reading in connection with the school's own teaching.[3] It was in this spirit that the adult school movement entered the new century.

The Y.M.C.A.

As a result of these changes the work of the adult schools came in many ways to resemble that of the Y.M.C.A., which was also developing rapidly in the later years of the century, and had indeed now become an international movement. A district organisation began to develop in the 'sixties, a National Committee for England (afterwards the National Council) was established in 1882, and a British Committee, representing England and Wales, Scotland and Ireland, was formed in the following year. The succeeding decade witnessed a rapid growth, and by 1894, the jubilee year, there were in the British Isles 651 Y.M.C.A. branches with close on 850,000 members and associate members.

Like the adult schools, the Y.M.C.A. branches combined religious instruction, which was their basic work, with a considerable range of social and educational activities. Of course there were differences. The Y.M.C.A. had no denominational connections, and its main appeal was to a younger age-group than the adult schools, and to a rather higher social class—it will be remembered that it was originally directed to 'commercial young men'. Naturally, too, it placed more emphasis on physical and recreative activities suited to the needs of young people. The majority of branches, however, provided a library and reading room, and quite a number also organised lectures (including University Extension courses), literary and

[1] S. E. Robson, *Joshua Rowntree* (1916), p. 45.
[2] Rowntree and Binns, *op. cit.*, pp. 36–7.
[3] Hudson Shaw began Oxford University Extension lectures at Severn Street, Birmingham, in 1892—W. White, *The Story of Severn Street and Priory First-Day Adult Schools* (1895), p. 92.

debating societies, and classes in science, art, history, geography, music, classical and foreign languages, and commercial subjects.[1]

In 1877 the Y.M.C.A. was joined by a sister movement, the Young Women's Christian Association, which had grown from a fusion of two movements of that name which had been started independently in 1855, one by Mary Jane Kinnaird in London, the other by Emma Robarts of Barnet.[2] Their motive was Christian, but not primarily educational, the task they set themselves being the care and protection of friendless young women, especially inexperienced young women of the working classes coming unprepared from the country into the big cities. At this stage, therefore, the Y.W.C.A. was not significant as an agent of adult education: its concern was with such matters as food, lodging, and employment, and much of its energies went into the establishment of hostels.[3]

Adult Education in Wales

There do not appear to have been any adult schools of the English type in Scotland at this period, and there were very few in Wales. Here the all-age Sunday school continued to serve as the educational focus of the community.

On Sunday afternoons, while the children learned to read and write in the schoolroom, their fathers and grandfathers, their mothers and grandmothers plunged into the mysterious and controversial problems of Calvinist theology in their classes in the 'big chapel'. These were no light-hearted and superficial discussions, for the champions of the rival theories and arguments assembled for the Sunday School fully armed with quotations and references culled from serious pre-Sunday reading of commentaries and explanatory textbooks.[4]

In association with the chapel and the Sunday school there developed a variety of educational activities which provided the equivalent —indeed more than the equivalent—of the English adult school. These included adult reading classes, held on weekday evenings under the guidance of a minister or other qualified person for more

---

[1] G. J. Stevenson, *Historical Records of the Y.M.C.A.* [1884]; Z. F. Willis, 'The Y.M.C.A. and Adult Education', in *Journal of Adult Education*, Vol. III (1928–9), pp. 36 sqq.; R. S. Wort, *One Hundred Years, 1844–1944: the Story of the Y.M.C.A.* (1944), especially Ch. v. I am indebted for statistical information to Mr. G. R. Howe of the National Council of Y.M.C.A.s.

[2] Mary Jane Kinnaird was the wife of the Hon. Arthur Kinnaird, the banker, afterwards Lord Kinnaird. She was a close friend of Lord Shaftesbury, who was one of the Y.M.C.A.'s keenest supporters.

[3] J. Duguid, *The Blue Triangle* (1955), Chs. i–ii.

[4] C. R. Williams, *Fifty Years of Adult Education in South Wales* (South Wales District of the W.E.A. [Cardiff], 1957), p. 4.

advanced Biblical studies; literary societies for lectures and debates; public lectures; penny readings; 'chapel societies' which were rather like the Religious Societies of seventeenth- and eighteenth-century England; and competitive meetings organised on a regional basis for competitions in Bible-reading and essay-writing. Of all these the reading-classes and the competitive meetings were educationally the most important. The former, which were conducted on tutorial lines and involved preparatory reading by the members, laid the foundation for the later development of tutorial class teaching in Wales; and the essay competitions at the latter often led to the production of substantial and scholarly works, e.g. at the meeting organised by the Llandegai Sunday School in 1862 the prize-winning entry was an essay of 350 pages on The Antiquarian Remains and Memories of the Llandegai District.[1]

The periodical eisteddfods held in various centres for the encouragement of Welsh language, literature and music were an important factor in the cultural life of the country. The old medieval eisteddfod had died out in the sixteenth century, but the movement had been revived in the eighteenth century and had become widespread in the first half of the nineteenth century. At this period the eisteddfods were customarily held under the auspices of various secular organisations, such as the Cymreigyddion and Cymmrodorion societies. From the middle of the century onwards the clergy began to take an active and ultimately a dominating part, and in this way the eisteddfods became linked with the literary societies and competitive meetings centred on the churches. The annual national eisteddfod, held in alternate years in North and South Wales, began in the 'sixties and has had a continuous history since 1880.[2]

Co-operative Education

A striking feature of this period is the almost complete submergence of the radical strain in adult education. With the general improvement in conditions the working-class revolutionary movements of earlier years either disappeared or changed their emphasis. The Chartist movement died out altogether; the co-operative societies, reorganised on the Rochdale system of dividends on purchases, forgot their former socialistic fervour; and the trade unions, now

[1] For these activities see L. S. Jones, *Church and Chapel in Wales as Sources and Centres of Education* (unpublished M.A. thesis, Liverpool 1940), Ch. x.

[2] D. J. Jones, *Social Aspects of the Rise and Decay of Literary Culture in Mold and Holywell* (unpublished M.A. thesis, Liverpool 1929), pp. 30, 105 sqq.; University of Wales, Extension Board, *Survey of Adult Education in Wales* (privately published, Cardiff 1940), pp. 9–10; T. Parry and R. T. Jenkins, *Eisteddfod y Cymry: The Eisteddfod of Wales* (Bangor 1943).

firmly planted on a craft basis, became increasingly concerned with the sectional interests of their members. There was, indeed, a brief recrudescence of utopian Socialism in the 'eighties under the Marxist influence of the Social Democratic Federation, but the Socialism which eventually began to win the allegiance of the working classes, towards the end of the century, was a Fabian Socialism to be achieved by constitutional action—'a heap of reforms to be won by the droppings of a host of successive swallows who would in the end make a Socialist summer'.[1]

The educational work of the Chartists inevitably disappeared, and the trade unions, though their leaders constantly preached the virtues of knowledge, did not themselves undertake any substantial educational provision.[2] In the co-operative movement the tradition of adult education did indeed survive, but it was no longer a radical tradition. The discussions and debates in the early days of the Rochdale Pioneers had been concerned with co-operation as a principle of social organisation, and with schemes for social redemption, but in the later nineteenth century the educational work carried on by the societies was not very different from that carried on by other organisations catering for the working classes. Of Rochdale, which was outstanding for its educational work, G. D. H. Cole writes:

The Rochdale Society became the owner of the best library in the town, complete with branch libraries and reference libraries scattered all over its area. In 1877 it had fourteen libraries and a total of 13,389 volumes, apart from periodicals, of which it took in twenty-seven daily and fifty-five weekly issues, as well as a wide range of monthly and quarterly magazines. It had a laboratory and a large number of scientific and mathematical instruments, and it lent out for a charge microscopes complete with series of slides. The books in its library covered a wide range of subjects, including fiction; and it is interesting to observe that books on the social sciences formed one of the least numerous classes in its catalogue. The classes which it conducted were mainly in science, with a few in art . . .[3]

A list of the classes at this period bears out this last statement: they were in such subjects as mathematics, geometry, mechanical

[1] G. D. H. Cole and R. Postgate, *The Common People, 1746–1938* (1938), p. 411.
[2] When the Amalgamated Society of Carpenters and Joiners began in 1868 to organise technical classes for its members, the General Secretary, Robert Applegarth, thought this was 'probably the first instance, in the industrial history of the country, of a Trade Union undertaking to provide a plan for the education of its members'. Classes in technical drawing and building construction were organised at a number of branches, and prospered for a time—A. W. Humphrey, *Robert Applegarth* [1913], Ch. viii.
[3] G. D. H. Cole, *A Century of Co-operation* (Manchester [1944]), p. 231. A detailed account is given in A. Greenwood, *The Educational Department of the Rochdale Equitable Pioneers' Society* (Manchester 1877).

drawing, physiology, botany, magnetism, electricity, chemistry, physical geography, French and art. Most of these classes were supported by the Science and Art Department.[1]

Not all the societies by any means followed Rochdale's example in allocating a percentage of their profits to education. Only 230 out of 912 made grants to education in 1880, and 100 of these were in the North-West, which accounted for more than three-quarters of the total expenditure. Many of the grants were much less than the $2\frac{1}{2}$ per cent which was held up as an ideal, and much of what was appropriated for education was actually spent on social gatherings. In most cases, therefore, educational activity was limited to the provision of a library and newsroom, a few popular lectures, and perhaps one or two classes. A report of 1884 showed 47 lending libraries, 69 circulating libraries, and 194 newsrooms, with a total of 134 lectures and 2,253 students in classes.[2]

In short, only a minority of co-operative societies at this time made any significant contribution to adult education, and those which did operated rather in the manner of evening schools or mechanics' institutes than in any distinctively co-operative way. To say this is not to underestimate the great importance and influence of the societies in some areas, and especially in some of the Lancashire towns. It was among these societies, at Rochdale and Oldham for example, that the University Extension movement was to find some of its earliest and most ardent supporters.

From about 1885 a change came over the scene. On the one hand the educational work which some of the societies had developed was increasingly taken over by the local authorities. The technical classes gave way to classes promoted by the new Technical Instruction Committees; the libraries became less necessary as public libraries grew in numbers and efficiency. On the other hand we see in this period the beginnings of modern co-operative education, properly so called. This new movement owed much to the influence of a number of university men, especially James Stuart of Cambridge, the pioneer of University Extension, Arnold Toynbee of Oxford, the historian of the Industrial Revolution, A. H. D. Acland, first Oxford Extension secretary, and his successor M. E. Sadler.[3]

Stuart, who had given courses for the Rochdale Pioneers, urged at the Co-operative Congress at Gloucester in 1879 that the educational funds of the movement should be used to maintain special

1 Greenwood, *op. cit.*, pp. 10–13.
2 For these figures see H. J. Twigg, *Outline History of Co-operative Education* (Manchester 1924), Apps. X and XI.
3 Cf. H. P. Smith, *Labour and Learning* (Oxford 1956), pp. 60–1.

lecturers, 'peripatetic professors of a Co-operative University.'[1] At the Oxford Conference in 1882 Toynbee brought this suggestion forward again. He urged that,

however seemingly immersed in the petty business of the shop co-operators may be, their real aim and their real determination is to put an end to competition and the division of men into capitalists and labourers . . .

In the new educational setting of the time, he argued, the special function of the co-operative movement was the education of men as citizens,

because co-operators, if they would carry out their avowed aims, are more absolutely in need of such an education than any other persons, and because if we look at the origins of the co-operative movement we shall see that this is the work in education most thoroughly in harmony with its ideal purpose.[2]

This time the suggestion was taken up, a committee was appointed with Acland as secretary, and the ultimate outcome was that from 1887 onwards the Co-operative Union began to promote classes in co-operation and co-operative book-keeping, and later in industrial history and in citizenship. This work was still in its infancy when the end of the century came.

Another notable development was the emergence of women to a position of power and influence in the co-operative movement. The Women's Co-operative Guild was founded in 1883 on the initiative of Mrs. Arthur Acland, and grew rapidly under the leadership of Margaret Llewellyn Davies, who became secretary in 1889. The specifically educational work of the Guild, among working women, was often at a very humble level, but it did invaluable service in training its members to speak in public, to serve on committees, and to take their share in the formulation of policy not only in the co-operative movement but in other social, economic and political movements of the time; and it also did much to stimulate co-operative societies to a more active educational policy.[3]

Cultural Societies

There are other aspects of adult educational activity during the second half of the nineteenth century which cannot be dealt with

[1] J. Stuart, *Reminiscences* (1911), p. 167.
[2] Toynbee's address is printed in his *Lectures on the Industrial Revolution* (1884, new edn. 1908), pp. 239 sqq.
[3] Cole, *op. cit.*, Ch. xii.

here, because their history has never been fully explored. We must, however, make brief reference to the valuable part played by cultural societies of all kinds.

Of the middle-class literary and philosophical societies Hudson wrote in 1851: 'The Provincial Philosophical Societies of England have completed their career, they are the débris of an age passed away.'[1] This, however, proved too pessimistic a judgment. It is true that some societies were at this time in the doldrums, but Hudson himself admits that others, e.g. Newcastle, Scarborough, Hull, Huddersfield, Edinburgh, and Plymouth, were doing useful work, and the fact is that most of these societies survived, with varying fortunes, into the present century. In some cases the advance of public education led to a restriction of activities, e.g. Sheffield surrendered its museum to the town in 1875,[2] and Halifax in 1897.[3] On the other hand the establishment of local colleges sometimes brought a new accession of members. At Newcastle the society itself played an important part in bringing the local college into existence, and in 1896 it was reported that the society 'was never so strong, useful, and flourishing as it now is'.[4]

And what of all the other societies of late Victorian England—the literary societies, musical societies, dramatic societies, historical societies, antiquarian societies, geological societies, natural history societies, mutual improvement societies, and the rest? By this time they were so numerous that it would be impossible for us to relate their story even if the materials were available, but in sum their cultural influence must have been considerable, not least among working people. Even today some of the older workers in adult education remember students who in their younger days were members of such societies, and who, in virtue of the training there received, were afterwards able to play a most valuable part in the more formal work of University Extension and the W.E.A.

Newspapers and Books

What we have called in a former chapter the instruments of adult education—newspapers, books, libraries, museums, art galleries—continued to grow apace during the closing decades of the century.

[1] J. W. Hudson, *History of Adult Education* (1851), p. 167.
[2] W. S. Porter, *Sheffield Literary and Philosophical Society: a Centenary Retrospect* (Sheffield 1922), p. 38.
[3] Halifax Literary and Philosophical Society, *Centenary Handbook* (Halifax 1930), pp. 28–9.
[4] R. S. Watson, *History of the Literary and Philosophical Society of Newcastle-upon-Tyne* (1897), p. 326.

It must be confessed that developments in the press did little to contribute to popular enlightenment. Following the abolition of the newspaper taxes daily newspapers became, as we have seen, cheap and available to all, but they remained as stodgily middle-class as ever in contents and presentation, and working people, for the most part, did not read them. They preferred, instead, the more sensational Sunday papers, or periodicals of romantic or melodramatic stories such as the *Family Herald* and the *London Journal*. One of the penalties of the general improvement that had taken place in the political and economic position of the working classes was that the proletarian press of former times—the press of Cobbett, Hetherington, and Carlile, crude, realistic, hard-hitting—had completely disappeared.

When at last, in the 'nineties, a new working-class press appeared, it was under the direction of big business. It was directed, not as yet at the mass of the working people, but at the new literate population created by the Education Act of 1870, a lower middle and upper working-class public, the public of the bank clerks, shop assistants, skilled artisans, the public of the Kippses and Pollys. Its pioneer was Alfred Harmsworth, afterwards Lord Northcliffe. He began by exploiting, in weeklies such as *Answers, Home Chat, Boys' Friend*, and the like, the rich vein of popular interest which had been uncovered by George Newnes when he launched *Tit-Bits* in 1881. He went on to acquire, and revolutionise, the *Evening News*, using the new techniques first developed by T. P. O'Connor in the *Star* in 1888— bold headlines, short pithy paragraphs, concentration on 'human interest'. Finally in 1896, with the help of his brother Harold (afterwards Lord Rothermere), he embarked on his greatest venture— the halfpenny *Daily Mail*. This was a new phenomenon. It was 'the busy man's paper', the paper that claimed to give all the news for half the price. Before the century closed it was selling nearly a million copies.

The dominating position which the *Daily Mail* quickly acquired in the newspaper world can be compared only with that of *The Times* in the mid-nineteenth century; and in 1908, to complete his victory, Northcliffe acquired the great *Times* itself. For the new journalism which he did so much to popularise it can be said that it was based on a much more realistic assessment of the interests of the ordinary man and woman. It made the news warmer, more human, more interesting, and thereby created a new class of newspaper readers. The emphasis, however, was always upon large circulations, large profits, giving the reader what he wanted: such educational value as the new popular press had was purely incidental.[1]

Of books we can tell a more cheering story. The salient feature of late nineteenth-century publishing is the steady forcing down of book prices to meet the demands of an ever-growing public. The price of newly published works, long accustomed to depend for their main market on the circulating libraries, was most strongly resistant to this trend, but from the 'eighties new novels, hitherto 31s. 6d., began to be published instead at 5s. or 6s. And the price of cheap reprints, fiction and non-fiction, which in Bohn's editions, for example, had been 3s. 6d. or 5s. at mid-century, came down to 2s., 1s., 6d., 3d., even by the close of the century to 1d. W. T. Stead sold nearly 5,000,000 of his Penny Poets, and 6,500,000 of his abridged Penny Novelists, and George Newnes was offering unabridged texts of about 100 pages at the same price. 'The common reader in the last days of Victoria was more amply supplied with books than ever before.'[2]

The Public Library Movement

The circulating libraries suffered from this competition, but survived. The great giants of the trade at this time were Mudie's and W. H. Smith's; in 1900 they were joined by a new and successful competitor in Boots's Booklovers' Library. Increasingly, however, the provision of books for the serious reader was being taken over by the public libraries, which grew rapidly in number as the century drew to a close. The number of public authorities adopting the Libraries Acts between 1870 and 1879 was 48; between 1880 and 1889 there were 65, and between 1890 and 1899 there were 153.[3]

This rapid development was due partly to increased demand; partly to new Library Acts of 1893 (England and Wales) and 1894 (Scotland) which enabled urban authorities to adopt the Acts by resolution without the cumbersome procedure of a special meeting of ratepayers; and partly to the generosity of private benefactors. Notable among these were John Passmore Edwards, who in the 'nineties endowed numerous libraries in London and his native Cornwall; and the Scottish-American millionaire Andrew Carnegie, whose gift of a public library to his native town of Dunfermline in 1881 marked the beginning of a golden stream of benefactions which,

---

[1] For this section I am much indebted to F. Williams, *Dangerous Estate* (1957), Chs. ix–x. See also R. D. Altick, *The English Common Reader* (Chicago Univ. P. 1957), Ch. xv.

[2] Altick, *op. cit.*, Ch. xiii (the quotation is at p. 317).

[3] Ministry of Reconstruction, Adult Education Committee, *Third Interim Report: Libraries and Museums* (1919), p. 3. I have excluded the figures for Ireland.

extended to England in 1897, gave a tremendous impetus to library development.[1]

The libraries were improving, not only in quantity, but in quality. A body of theory and practice was gradually built up to meet the needs of this new public service, and by the 'eighties it was possible to provide a professional training with examinations conducted by the recently founded Library Association. The introduction of the open access system at the Clerkenwell Public Library in 1894 marked a great step forward in efficient service to the reader.[2]

These developments, unfortunately, were confined almost exclusively to the towns: the rural areas, where rateable values were usually insufficient to support a public library, were still in the main dependent on the old-fashioned village libraries, Sunday school libraries, and the like. This gap was not to be filled until the county library service was inaugurated in the present century. In the meantime a useful contribution was made in Yorkshire by an itinerating Village Library operated by the Yorkshire Union of Mechanics' Institutes. This scheme was modelled on the itinerating libraries established in the Lothians earlier in the century: boxes of fifty books were issued at six-monthly intervals to village groups of twenty-five subscribers, each of whom paid 1d. per week. The scheme was initiated by James Hole of Leeds in 1852, and was still rendering useful service forty years later.[3]

Art Galleries and Museums

Public art galleries and museums still lack their historian, but it is evident that their development was on similar lines to that of the public libraries, but moved at a much slower pace. During the period under review the local authorities remained on the whole reluctant to use the powers available to them, though there was some quickening after the Museums and Gymnasiums Act of 1891. Dependence on private benefactions was still considerable. Sir Henry Miers, in a report on museums published in 1928, saw the forty years from 1880 to 1920 as the richest period of museum development, but commented that of the public museums created during that period nearly half had originated in private collections, and only about

---

[1] W. A. Munford, *Penny Rate* (1951), Chs. v–vi. For dates of adoption in England and Wales see Board of Education, Public Libraries Committee, *Report on Public Libraries in England and Wales* (1927), pp. 235 sqq.
[2] Munford, *op. cit.*, p. 104.
[3] T. Greenwood, *Sunday School and Village Libraries* (1892); J. F. C. Harrison, *Social Reform in Victorian Leeds* (Thoresby Society, Leeds 1954), pp. 39–41.

one-third from the spontaneous action of corporations or groups of individuals.[1]

Contrasting events in Manchester and Liverpool may serve as an illustration of the kind of process that was going on in many places. In each city there was in the mid-nineteenth century a Royal Institution with a substantial collection of works of art. The Liverpool Royal Institution also had a valuable museum. At Manchester the Royal Institution in 1881 successfully negotiated the transfer of its art collection to the civic authorities, and the Institution building was converted into the City Art Gallery.[2] At Liverpool similar negotiations took place in 1850–1, but these proved abortive, and the local authority, aided by munificent benefactors, thereupon set to work to create for itself the institutions it needed—the William Brown Library and Museum (opened 1860), the Walker Art Gallery (1877), and the Picton Reading Room (1879). The end was inevitable: the Royal Institution, with its limited resources, could not indefinitely continue its museum and art gallery in competition with these new civic institutions. The Museum was disposed of, mostly to Nottingham and Bootle, in 1877 and 1886; and in 1893 it was agreed to transfer the art collections to the Walker Art Gallery.[3] Thus both at Manchester and at Liverpool the ultimate outcome was the same—the transference of private collections into public hands.

[1] Sir H. Miers, *Report on the Public Museums of the British Isles* (Carnegie U.K. Trust, Edinburgh 1928), p. 10. A valuable survey and description of the principal museums and art galleries of Great Britain, by A. B. Meyer, is to be found in *Annual Report of the Smithsonian Institution for 1903: Report of the U.S. National Museum* (Washington 1905), pp. 520–77.

[2] W. E. A. Axon, *Annals of Manchester* (Manchester 1886), p. 382.

[3] H. A. Ormerod, *The Liverpool Royal Institution* (Liverpool 1953), Chs. iv–v. The Institution ultimately passed (1948) into the possession of Liverpool University.

14

The Nineteenth Century

THE UNIVERSITIES ENTER THE FIELD

The Origins of University Extension

The most distinctive feature of adult education in this country in modern times has been the contribution of the universities. This contribution is commonly traced back to the work of James Stuart of Cambridge in the 'sixties, but it rests, of course, upon a much older and more broadly based movement.

By the middle of the nineteenth century the two ancient English universities had become a social and intellectual backwater in the life of the nation. They still provided the education of a gentleman for the sons of the aristocracy destined for a career in politics, the Church, or the law, but the great new stream of life which flowed from the Industrial Revolution passed them by. To the merchants, the manufacturers, the engineers, and the increasing body of middle-class professional people, they had little or nothing to offer. And of course the whole world of nonconformity was excluded by the religious tests.

The term 'University Extension', when it first came into use in the 1840s, meant primarily the extension of facilities for full-time university education. A start had already been made by the foundation of the University of London in 1826 and the University of Durham in 1832. London University was afterwards (1836) expanded to embrace King's College, founded in 1831, the original establishment taking the name of University College. In mid-century plans were propounded for the erection of new universities or university colleges, the affiliation of provincial institutions to existing universities, the establishment of professorships in non-university towns, and the award of exhibitions to poor but deserving students. Between 1850 and 1880, prodded by a series of Royal Commissions, and by internal critics such as Benjamin Jowett and Mark Pattison, the older universities did in fact carry out a series of reforms. The religious tests were modified in 1854 and abolished in 1871; new honours schools were established; the Oxford and Cambridge Local Examinations were inaugurated (1857–8); colleges were founded for women; and facilities were provided for non-collegiate students.[1] A similar wind of reform, at this time, was sweeping through the four ancient Scottish universities, which though they did not suffer from the social and religious exclusiveness of Oxford and Cambridge, had likewise been falling behind contemporary needs.

At the same time there were springing up in various parts of the country new institutions of university character—Owens College, Manchester, 1851; Durham College of Science, Newcastle (affiliated to Durham University), 1871; University College, Aberystwyth (the first college of the University of Wales), 1872; Yorkshire College, Leeds, 1874; University College, Bristol, 1876; Firth College, Sheffield, 1879; Mason College, Birmingham, 1880. In 1880 Owens College became the first constituent member of the new federal Victoria University, in which it was subsequently joined by Liverpool (founded in 1882) and Leeds.[2]

University Extension in the narrower sense of the extension of facilities for part-time university education was a part of this wider movement. The scheme was long prepared both in theory and in practice. On the theoretical side J. W. Gilbart, the banker, suggested in 1847 the establishment of societies in non-university towns to organise educational lectures, with lecturers paid by the government. There might, he thought, be two or three professors in each town, periodically visiting the smaller towns of the district, and engaging local lecturers to visit the villages.[3] William Sewell of Oxford proposed in 1850 the foundation of university professorships and lectureships in Manchester, Birmingham, and other large centres of population.[4] And in 1855 Lord Arthur Hervey of Cambridge (later Bishop of Bath and Wells), proposed the creation of four 'rural or circuit Professors, to be nominated by the University', to give courses on natural philosophy, geology, astronomy, and literature in literary, scientific, and mechanics' institutes. The professors would, he suggested, be fellows, and contributions from the institutes would provide an additional income of £400 a year each.[5]

---

[1] On all this see J. P. C. Roach, 'Victorian Universities and the National Intelligentsia', in *Victorian Studies*, Vol. II (Indiana University, 1959–60).

[2] On these colleges see further below, pp. 229–30.

[3] J. W. Gilbart, *Lectures and Essays* (1847), Preface.

[4] W. Sewell, *Suggestions for the Extension of the University submitted to the Rev. the Vice-Chancellor* (Oxford 1850).

[5] Lord Arthur Hervey, *A Suggestion for Supplying the Literary, Scientific, and Mechanics' Institutes of Great Britain and Ireland with Lecturers from the Universities* (1855). For these schemes see H. J. Mackinder and M. E. Sadler, *University Extension Past, Present and Future* (1890, 3rd edn. 1891), pp. 6–11; and R. D. Roberts, *University Extension under the Old and the New Conditions* (Cambridge 1908); and for Gilbart, *University Extension Journal*, Oct. 1906, pp. 8–9.

On the practical side we must place, first, the provision occasionally made by a number of universities for non-matriculated students. We have seen an example of this in John Anderson's courses at Glasgow in the eighteenth century,[1] and later we have another example at Cambridge, where for more than fifty years (1819–72) Professor Adam Sedgwick lectured on geology to an audience which regularly included not only university students but townspeople (women as well as men).[2] In the second place we must remember the long tradition of assistance by university people, in a private capacity, in adult educational activities of various kinds. In England this tradition can be traced back as far as Gresham College, and it found its latest expression in the work of Maurice and his friends at the London Working Men's College.

The most remarkable anticipation of University Extension, however, is to be found not in connection with any of the established universities, but in connection with the incipient university at Owens College. Here from the beginning evening classes were an important part of the College activities, and when the Manchester Working Men's College was founded in 1858 the staff of Owens College, from the Principal downwards, gave their wholehearted support and assistance. Among those who participated in the teaching was the young Henry Roscoe (afterwards Sir Henry Roscoe), a grandson of William Roscoe of Liverpool and at that time recently appointed as Professor of Chemistry at Owens College.

Eventually, as we have seen, in 1861, the classes of the Working Men's College were merged in the evening classes of Owens College, to which they brought a great accession of strength.[3] Roscoe, however, now embarked on Extension activities on his own account. He began, during the winter of 1862–3, with recreative evening lectures for unemployed cotton operatives, at this time in great distress owing to the cotton famine caused by the American Civil War.[4] Later, in 1866–7 and in 1870–9, he organised a whole series of Penny Science Lectures for working men, given by himself and

[1] Above, p. 102.
[2] Royal Commission on the University and Colleges of Cambridge, *Report* (1852), Evidence, p. 116; J. W. Clark and T. McK. Hughes, *Life and Letters of Adam Sedgwick* (Cambridge 1890), Vol. I, pp. 203–4.
[3] Above, p. 187.
[4] This was one of many efforts to provide education for the unemployed. Under the auspices of the Council of the Cotton Relief Fund, adult elementary schools were established throughout the cotton district in disused mills and other converted premises. At the suggestion of a member of a workers' delegation, attendance at these schools during the day-time was made a condition of relief, but they were also open in the evenings for instruction and recreation. During the winter of 1862–3 there were at one time 48,000 men and youths in attendance. There were also sewing classes for girls. See J. Watts, *The Facts of the Cotton Famine* (1866), pp. 200–12.

other distinguished scholars. They were described as 'illustrated by experiments and adapted to large audiences'. At first the lectures formed a consecutive series on scientific topics, later they were individual 'celebrity lectures'. T. H. Huxley, who, as Professor at the School of Mines, had been engaged in similar activities among the working men of London, gave the opening addresses in 1870 and 1871.[1]

James Stuart

The formal work of University Extension, in its modern sense, began under the auspices of the University of Cambridge in 1873, and arose out of two specific demands. One, to which the large audiences at lectures of the type given by Roscoe and Huxley bore witness, was for university education for working men. The other was for university help in the higher education of women. This latter was in itself part of a much wider demand for a thoroughgoing reform of English secondary education—a demand reflected in the appointment, in 1861, of the Clarendon Commission to inquire into the public schools, and in 1864 of the Taunton Commission to inquire into other forms of secondary education. The opening of the Cambridge Local Examinations to girls in 1865 encouraged the hope that in the general reconstruction secondary education for girls, so long neglected, would at last find its due place.

Some steps had already been taken towards improving the standard of teaching in girls' schools, but there was still a desperate need to improve the training and qualifications of women teachers. With this object principally in view there was formed in November 1867 the North of England Council for Promoting the Higher Education of Women, which brought together ladies' groups from a number of northern towns. Mrs. Josephine Butler, afterwards well-known for her fight against organised prostitution, was its first President, Miss Anne J. Clough, afterwards first Principal of Newnham, its Secretary.

It was at the invitation of some of the ladies' groups afterwards associated in this Council that James Stuart, a young fellow of Trinity College, Cambridge, delivered in the autumn of 1867 the four lecture-courses which are usually regarded as the beginning of University Extension.[2] They were given in Leeds, Liverpool,

[1] I am indebted for these details regarding Roscoe to an unpublished paper by Professor R. D. Waller of the University of Manchester. For Huxley see C. Bibby, *T. H. Huxley* (1959), Ch. v.
[2] Stuart was a Scot, from Balgonie in Fifeshire, and graduated at St. Andrews before taking the mathematical tripos at Cambridge. He afterwards became Professor of Mechanism there (1875–89) and Lord Rector of St. Andrews (1898–1901). Between 1884 and 1910 he several times sat as Liberal M.P. for various constituencies.

Sheffield, and Manchester, to audiences consisting mainly of women teachers, and comprised in each case eight lectures.

The original request was for courses on the theory and methods of education, but this request Stuart declined, offering instead The History of Science. It was, one might have thought, a difficult subject for audiences of women, ignorant, as Stuart tells us, of geometry and algebra, and but imperfectly acquainted with arithmetic, but such was the hunger for knowledge that the lectures were enthusiastically received, and each week about 300 women—over half the total attending—gave in written answers to questions set by the lecturer.[1]

Within four or five years similar courses were being arranged in many parts of England, and even in Scotland. Other lecturers had of course to be brought in, amongst them Henry Roscoe and J. R. Seeley the historian. At the same time a parallel demand was coming forward from working men. Already in 1867–8 Stuart was lecturing to railwaymen at Crewe under the auspices of the Mechanics' Institute; and this was followed by a course at Rochdale at the invitation of the Equitable Pioneers' Co-operative Society.

It was during this period of missionary endeavour that Stuart was led to develop, almost accidentally, three features which afterwards became characteristic of University Extension teaching—the printed syllabus, the written work, and the discussion period. The syllabus began as a series of notes distributed at the end of his first lecture, to assist the women students in making notes, but he afterwards found it more useful to distribute it in advance as an aid to the understanding of the lecture. In later University Extension practice the syllabus grew into a very elaborate document, for example a syllabus for a course of eleven lectures on Elizabethan literature by R. G. Moulton[2] extends to 40 pages, followed by a 16-page syllabus for an extra class, and 7 pages of instructions for students' reading and written work.

Written work had its origin in the fact that it was considered improper for a young man such as Stuart to exchange oral question and answer with an audience of young ladies: to avoid this, written questions were circulated in advance and written answers were

---

[1] J. Stuart, 'The Teaching of Science', in J. E. Butler (ed.), *Woman's Work and Woman's Culture* (1869), pp. 128–30. Stuart here gives the subject of his course as Physical Astronomy; in his *Reminiscences* (privately published 1911), p. 158, he gives it as The History of Astronomy, but the course was advertised as on The History of Science, and a report on his first lecture (*Manchester Guardian*, 11 Oct. 1867) shows that it was intended to include astronomy, light, electricity, magnetism, and related subjects. This is one of a number of details on which Stuart's *Reminiscences* are not entirely accurate.
[2] Printed at Nottingham 1879.

required. The discussion class accompanying the lecture arose out of Stuart's experience at Rochdale:

One day I was in some hurry to get away as soon as the lecture was over, and I asked the hall-keeper to allow my diagrams to remain hanging till my return next week. When I came back he said to me, 'It was one of the best things you ever did leaving up these diagrams. We had a meeting of our members last week, and a number of them who are attending your lectures were discussing these diagrams, and they have a number of questions they want to ask you, and they are coming to-night a little before the lecture begins.' About twenty or thirty intelligent artisans met me about half-an-hour before the lecture began, and I found it so useful a half-hour that during the remainder of the course I always had such a meeting.

The idea of a discussion following a lecture was not, of course, new: it had long been common practice in mutual improvement societies and similar bodies; and Roscoe had held a class after each lecture in his first series of Penny Science Lectures. In later Extension work the class always followed the lecture, after a brief interval for the withdrawal of those who did not wish to participate.[1]

As early as 1866 Stuart had in mind the idea of 'a sort of peripatetic university the professors of which would circulate among the big towns'.[2] In 1871 he determined to put the matter to the test, and appealed to the University of Cambridge to take in hand officially the work so successfully begun by voluntary effort. The demand for education existed, he declared. 'I believe that it is incumbent on us to supply it, . . . and I believe that some such system which will carry the benefits of the University through the country is necessary in order to retain the University in that position with respect to the education of the country that it has hitherto held, and to continue in its hands that permeating influence which it is desirable that it should possess.'[3]

Stuart's appeal was supported by memorials from the North of England Council, the Crewe Mechanics' Institute, the Rochdale Pioneers, the Mayor and inhabitants of Leeds, and subsequently from other organisations. D. J. Vaughan of the Leicester Working Men's College, Richard Enfield of the Nottingham Mechanics' Institute, and Dr. J. B. Paton, Principal of the Congregational

---

[1] For these missionary years, see Stuart, *Reminiscences*, pp. 154–68; B. A. Clough, *Memoir of Anne Jemima Clough* (1897), pp. 116–24; and for the Leeds background N. A. Jepson, *Leeds and the Beginning of University Adult Education* (reprinted from Leeds Philosophical Society, *Proceedings*, Vol. VIII, Part III, Leeds, Nov. 1957).
[2] *Reminiscences*, p. 155.
[3] J. Stuart, *A Letter on University Extension* (Cambridge 1871), p. 7.

Institute at Nottingham and a leading figure in many educational movements of the time, are among those mentioned by Stuart as particularly helpful.[1]

The upshot was that the University agreed, in 1873, to the organisation of local lectures for a trial period, and in the autumn of that year the first courses were begun in Nottingham, Leicester, and Derby—three courses in each town. A further series of courses was arranged, in other centres, in the spring of 1874, and in the light of the success of these courses, which drew attendances averaging over 100 per lecture, the scheme was put on a permanent footing for the following session. Stuart acted as Secretary until 1875, when he was appointed Professor of Mechanism. From 1878 onwards the Local Lectures Committee operated under the aegis of a combined Syndicate for Local Examinations and Lectures.

The Growth of Extension Teaching

It is a great pity that so far we have no adequate history of the early phases of University Extension, which threw up problems still of vital interest to workers in this field to-day. The main outlines, however, are clear.[2] Cambridge, in 1875–6, had something like 100 courses at centres up and down England, with an average attendance exceeding 10,000, but after this initial burst of enthusiasm the work ran into difficulties, and it was not until 1886–7 that the number of courses again reached the 100 mark. In the meantime a beginning had been made in 1876 in London, where until the reorganisation of the University in 1901 the work was carried on by the Society for the Extension of University Teaching, with academic advisers from Oxford and Cambridge as well as London. At Oxford a tentative beginning was made, on the initiative of Benjamin Jowett, Master of Balliol, in 1878, with A. H. D. Acland (afterwards Sir Arthur Acland) as first secretary.[3] It was not, however, until M. E. Sadler became secretary in 1885 that the task was taken up in earnest. A separate Delegacy for Extension work was created in 1892. In the

[1] *Reminiscences*, pp. 171–2. For the memorials see R. D. Roberts, *Eighteen Years of University Extension* (Cambridge 1891), Ch. vii.

[2] From the Cambridge angle the story has been told in Roberts, *op. cit.*, and W. H. Draper, *University Extension* (Cambridge 1923); from the Oxford angle in Mackinder and Sadler, *op. cit.* See also *Quarterly Review*, Vol. CLXXII (1891), pp. 399–430; Roberts, *University Extension under the Old and the New Conditions;* R. St. John Parry (ed.), *Cambridge Essays on Adult Education* (Cambridge 1920), Ch. viii; and for Victoria University, T. Kelly, *Outside the Walls* (Manchester 1950). For Scotland see R. M. Wenley, *The University Extension Movement in Scotland* (Glasgow 1895); and W. H. Marwick, 'The University Extension Movement in Scotland', in *University of Edinburgh Journal*, Vol. VIII, No. 3 (1937).

[3] On the contribution of Jowett and the Balliol group see H. P. Smith, *Labour and Learning* (Oxford 1956), pp. 26–36.

North of England the Victoria University began to operate in a modest way in 1886, and Durham was brought into co-operation with Cambridge.

In 1890 the work in England was in full swing. The London Society was active in the capital and a few outlying centres in the home counties, and Oxford and Cambridge exercised a roving commission throughout the rest of the country, with Cambridge on the whole tending towards the east, and Oxford towards the west. Victoria confined its activities to Lancashire, Cheshire, and Yorkshire, and Cambridge gracefully withdrew from some of its major centres in that area. In 1893-4 there were said to be over 60,000 students attending Extension courses in various parts of the country,[1] and though there was afterwards some falling off the number ranged around the 50,000 mark for the next fifteen years.

In Wales and Scotland a less successful story was enacted. In Wales Aberystwyth was engaged in extra-mural teaching as early as 1876, and Cardiff and Bangor began to organise Extension courses in 1883. But the methods and perhaps the subjects of Extension lectures were alien to a people steeped in the Sunday school tradition, and the movement quickly faded out.[2]

In Scotland, as in England, the universities were drawn into the movement for women's education. Women's associations in Edinburgh (1868) and Glasgow (1877), both arranged diploma courses by members of the university staff, and St. Andrews, from 1877, organised special women's courses leading to the L.L.A. (Lady Licentiate in Arts). Some courses of a more general character were also arranged, at Dundee by St. Andrews University, and at Glasgow by William Smart, afterwards Professor of Political Economy. In 1888 Edinburgh, Glasgow, and St. Andrews all set up official machinery for the provision of Extension courses; and Aberdeen followed suit in 1890.

Unfortunately, in spite of some initial enthusiasm, Extension work failed to take root in Scotland, and by 1893-4 it was virtually extinct—at Aberdeen it never got going at all. The historian of the movement has advanced various reasons for this, amongst these the greater accessibility of the Scottish universities (there was no entrance examination before 1893); the extensive provision of lectures by local societies, the Combe and Gilchrist Trusts, etc.; the scattered

---

[1] Royal Commission on Secondary Education, *Report*, Vol. I (1895), p. 55. These figures exclude courses conducted under the auspices of local colleges, of which more later.
[2] University of Wales Extension Board, *Survey of Adult Education in Wales* (privately published, Cardiff 1940), pp. 14–15.

nature of the population; and 'the Scotsman's well-known failing, or virtue, in matters financial'.[1]

Types of Courses

The range of subjects covered by Extension courses was very wide. In 1890–1, out of 457 courses arranged by Oxford, Cambridge, and London, 159 were on history or political economy, 104 on literature, art, or architecture, 191 on natural science, and 3 on philosophy.[2] The courses ranged in length from 6 to 12 lectures. Cambridge preferred 12, but Oxford found it convenient to organise 6-lecture courses to meet the needs of the smaller centres. Though short, however, the courses were intensive: each lecture was followed by a class for questions and discussion; reading and written work were regularly prescribed (Oxford introduced book-boxes in 1885); and at the end of each course there was an examination, with a university certificate for the successful candidates.[3] Cambridge, according to the statistics compiled by its Extension Secretary, R. D. Roberts, had in 1890–1 125 courses with an average attendance of 93 students per course, of whom 43 stayed for class instruction after the lectures, and 14 took the examination; on the average 20 papers were submitted weekly.[4]

The examinations were no walk-over. At Oxford, in this same year, it was reported that they were conducted by examiners in the Final Honour Schools of the University, and that the minimum pass standard required was that of the Oxford Pass School. A mark of distinction, which was awarded to more than one-third of the 927 students taking certificates in this session, was equated with the Oxford Honours standard.[5]

In most centres Extension students were predominantly middle-class. 'In the case of afternoon lectures, probably 70 per cent of the audiences are ladies of leisure and older schoolgirls . . . the great majority of courses are delivered in the evening to audiences composed, in the main, of the professional classes, of tradesmen and their families, and of artisans.'[6] Elementary schoolteachers were regular

---

[1] Wenley, *op. cit.*, pp. 43–50. W. H. Marwick, 'Adult Education in Scotland', in World Association for Adult Education, *Bulletin*, 2nd Ser., No. XL (Feb. 1945), p. 2, thinks the main reason was the opening of university courses to women.

[2] Mackinder and Sadler, *op. cit.*, p. 62.

[3] In 1890 Oxford and Cambridge agreed not to award a certificate for a course of less than 12 lectures.

[4] Roberts, *Eighteen Years*, p. 131.

[5] Mackinder and Sadler, *op. cit.*, p. 63. See for the figures Roberts, *op. cit.*, p. 133. The average attendance at the Oxford courses in this year was 17,904.

[6] Mackinder and Sadler, *op. cit.*, pp. 68–9. Courses for ladies were also held in the mornings.

attenders, being often admitted at reduced prices;[1] and older school-boys and schoolgirls are said to have constituted 10–12 per cent of the total attendance in 1893–4.[2] The mixture of social classes in the courses was regarded with satisfaction by the organisers, and Roberts cites a Tyneside course on Political Economy in 1879 in which the first place in the examination was taken by a miner and the second by the daughter of a wealthy manufacturer.[3]

This instance brings up the general question of the attendance of working men at Extension courses, which is worth a little examination because of the persistent legend that University Extension failed to attract the working classes. The workers did not, of course, attend morning or afternoon courses, and at the average evening course they were not present in large numbers. They were prevented from attending partly by lack of education, partly by lack of time, but mainly by lack of money. The students in these courses had to pay the entire cost, and consequently fees were high—a guinea for a morning or afternoon course, and 7s. 6d. for an evening course, were common charges, and such fees were prohibitive to men who might be earning little more than £1 a week. Where the course could be offered at a low fee, say 1s., the response was enthusiastic.

This happened in a number of places—on Tyneside, where the colliery-owners came to the rescue; in the industrial centres of Lancashire and Yorkshire, where the local co-operative society often took financial responsibility; and in the working-class suburbs of London, where the London Society helped.[4] Science and political economy seem to have been the most popular subjects amongst these working-class audiences, but popular lecturers such as G. W. Hudson Shaw and R. G. Moulton could attract audiences of hundreds to the study of history and literature. Albert Mansbridge wrote:

> University men of the highest quality readily went to industrial towns in the north, and not only lectured but made friends with their audiences, and so entered into understanding of the conditions of working-class life . . . It was even as though the lecturers poured out streams of light and learning, playing upon places where thoughtful working people of the time foregathered.[5]

R. D. Roberts has left us a vivid description of some of the working-class centres in London and the North-East, and in particular of the

[1] Op. cit., pp. 69–70.
[2] Royal Commission on Secondary Education, Report, Vol. I, p. 55.
[3] Roberts, op. cit., p. 21.
[4] Op. cit., pp. 59–60.
[5] A. Mansbridge, The Trodden Road (1940), pp. 52–3.

heroic efforts of the Northumberland miners, who often travelled long distances in order to hear the lectures:

Two pitmen, living in a village five miles from one of the centres, were able to get in to the lectures by train, but the return service was inconvenient and they were compelled to walk home. This they did weekly for three months, on dark nights, over wretchedly bad roads and in all kinds of weather. On one occasion they returned in a severe storm, when the roads were so flooded that they lost their way and got up to their waists in water. It is not surprising that they distinguished themselves in the examination and eventually succeeded in making their own village a lecture-centre. This missionary spirit is thoroughly characteristic of the movement . . .[1]

Roberts also tells the story of the Backworth Students' Association, a mutual improvement group formed about 1880 in a mining village north of Newcastle which met week by week to study the subjects which were being dealt with in their local Extension courses. On one occasion when there was no course in Backworth two of the members travelled on foot each week to the nearest Extension centre, which was four or five miles away, and subsequently repeated the substance of the lectures to a class in their own village. The first Extension course in Backworth was on Mining, but over the years the members of the group studied also Ancient Comedy, Shakespeare, Physiology, Plant Life, and Chemistry.[2] R. G. Moulton was one of those who lectured there, and in 1890 he established there a Classical Novel-Reading Union, whose members undertook to read one novel a month. During their first four years they read their way through a variety of works by well-known novelists of the nineteenth century, from Jane Austen to Meredith.[3]

Unfortunately the work in this north-eastern area was badly hit by the great colliery strike of 1887, and although it recovered in some centres, such as Backworth, it never reached quite the same level again.

Some Extension courses were arranged specifically for vocational groups. From 1891 onwards the universities for some years gave extensive assistance to the county and county borough councils in fulfilling their new duty of providing technical instruction, especially in the rural areas, where courses were delivered on such surprising subjects as Dairy-making, Manures and Soils, and Veterinary Science.[4] A little later, and especially between 1894 and 1905,

[1] Roberts, op. cit., pp. 25–6.
[2] Op. cit., pp. 38–47, 67–9.
[3] W. F. Moulton, Richard Green Moulton (1926), pp. 43–5.
[4] Kelly, Outside the Walls, p. 17.

numerous courses were provided for pupil-teachers, the Board of Education having agreed to recognise a sessional Extension certificate as a part qualification for the Queen's Scholarship examination.[1]

The technical courses, though useful in their time, were something of an aberration from the main line of development, for they were not easily susceptible of the liberal approach that characterised the work as a whole. R. D. Roberts, indeed, was rather worried by them. He thought it would be disastrous if the universities came to be regarded as agents of technical education, though he was prepared to concede that there was a strong case for courses for advanced students, by university specialists 'able to give at first-hand the very latest results of the most advanced investigations, which could not be obtained through any other channel'.[2]

The courses for pupil-teachers, on the other hand, were a great liberalising influence. Stuart, in his first lecture to the ladies of Manchester in 1867, had laid down that his purpose was not so much 'to give detailed information as to rouse in his hearers a desire to learn something about science, and to enable them to grasp the true spirit that should pervade the study of science',[3] and this principle was widely adopted in Extension work. One pupil-teacher in the Manchester area afterwards wrote:

> I experienced for the first time the gain that accrues from contact with lecturers of first-rate ability and vision. We P.T.s had never previously had such a privilege, and the encouragement we received to read widely, to search and sift information for ourselves, was of the utmost value in our self-development . . . I feel that the extra-mural lectures were a turning-point in my life.[4]

One of the most valuable features of Extension work was the attention paid to the needs of women. Hitherto adult education had been, broadly speaking, a man's world. There had been exceptions, for example the women's adult schools, and the lyceums, in which the membership of women had been encouraged, but in general women had been either firmly excluded, as they were from the London Working Men's College, or admitted with reluctance, as was the case in many mechanics' institutes. Now for the first time a major adult education organisation had arisen which placed the needs of women in the forefront of its programme. It is difficult for us nowadays to realise just how important this was. 'University Extension came', wrote one early woman student, 'as a gift from heaven.'[5]

---

[1] *Op. cit.*, pp. 24–6.   [2] Roberts, *op. cit.*, pp. 120–1.
[3] *Manchester Guardian*, 11 Oct. 1867.   [4] Kelly, *op. cit.*, p. 26.
[5] *University Extension Bulletin*, Lent 1909, pp. 10–11.

It was a gift all the more remarkable in that the institutions that bestowed it were themselves strongholds of masculine privilege.

Summer Meetings

A development which brought a great accession of strength to the Extension movement was the inauguration of summer schools. At Cambridge, in 1885 and 1887, scholarships were provided to enable small groups of students from the mining areas to continue their studies at the University during the summer vacation; but the first large-scale Summer Meeting was organised by Oxford in 1888, and was attended by some 900 students. Cambridge made a cautious beginning in 1890, but an Extension Vacation meeting organised at Edinburgh in 1889 proved a disastrous failure.[1]

In its Oxford form the idea of the summer meeting derived from the American 'chautauqua', an institution which had its origins in a Methodist camp-meeting on the shores of Chautauqua Lake in New York State. From 1874 provision began to be made for systematic study, first in religious subjects for Sunday school teachers, and later in a wide range of secular subjects; and for a time (1883–92) there was actually a Chautauqua University, awarding degrees. The idea was widely imitated, so that 'chautauqua' became synonymous with 'summer school'.[2]

J. B. Paton, who as we have seen had taken a prominent part in the establishment of University Extension in Nottingham, was particularly interested in the home-reading circles which were run in association with the Chautauqua meetings, and in 1887 he formed a small committee, with John Percival, Headmaster of Rugby, as chairman and M. E. Sadler, the Oxford Extension secretary, as one of the members, to consider the possibility of creating such a system in Britain. It was at one of these meetings that Charles Rowley, of Manchester, suggested the idea of summer meetings at the English universities, an idea which Sadler at once seized upon and put into practice.[3]

[1] Edinburgh, however, already had a Summer School of Art and Science, organised very successfully by Patrick Geddes, Professor of Botany at Dundee. The School began in 1887, and was designed particularly for teachers. It continued into the present century, and acquired an international reputation—Wenley, op. cit., p. 37.

[2] J. S. Noffsinger, Correspondence Schools, Lyceums, Chautauquas (New York 1926), pp. 7–11, 107–12; C. H. Grattan, In Quest of Knowledge (New York 1955), Ch. xiv.

[3] J. L. Paton, John Brown Paton (1914), pp. 271–5; C. Rowley, Fifty Years of Work without Wages [1911], pp. 215–16; W. Temple, Life of Bishop Percival (1921), p. 266; L. Grier, Achievement in Education: the Work of Michael Ernest Sadler (1952), pp. 14–15; M. Sadleir, Sir Michael Sadler (1949), pp. 102–3. For the reading circles see further below, p. 238. Percival, who had previously been Headmaster of Clifton and President of Trinity College, Oxford, and was later Bishop of Hereford, was an enthusiastic supporter of University Extension.

From 1893 onwards the Oxford and Cambridge Summer Meetings were normally held in alternate years,[1] and for a generation they were a central feature of the Extension scene, attracting gatherings of many hundreds of students for lectures and classes related to those of the winter courses. They not only gave the students an opportunity of residing for a short period in a university, and meeting and hearing some of the most distinguished scholars of the day; they also demonstrated the national character of the movement and thus helped to bind isolated centres together.[2] J. A. R. Marriott, Sadler's successor as Oxford Extension secretary, wrote:

What it meant to an elementary teacher from a country school, or to a Lancashire mill-hand, or a collier from South-Wales, to come even for a month under the magic spell of Oxford's beauty, to listen to some of the greatest authorities on history, science, or art, come into daily contact with men and women inspired by similar zeal for higher education, and to exchange ideas with them can be understood only by those who, like myself, were privileged to be their confidants, and to see the leaven visibly working.[3]

Extension Colleges

Not the least of the ways in which this phase of University Extension left its imprint on the intellectual life of the nation was through its contribution to the growth of local colleges, many of which afterwards became universities. We have already noted the foundation of a number of such colleges during the years 1850–80. There were others before the end of the century: Nottingham in 1881, Reading in 1892, and Exeter in 1893, besides new Welsh colleges at Cardiff (1883) and Bangor (1884), and a college at Dundee (1883), which was later affiliated to St. Andrews.

These colleges sprang out of a variety of local needs—for medical training, for instruction in science and art, for the training of teachers—but in many cases the effective impulse came from University Extension. Particularly was this so at Sheffield, Nottingham, and Exeter, which began as Cambridge Extension colleges; and at Reading, which was originally an Oxford Extension college. At Leeds the work of the 'Cambridge missionaries' led Yorkshire College, originally founded for the teaching of science, to enlarge its scope and provide also for the teaching of the arts. At Dundee, also, Extension lectures prepared the way for the creation of the College.

---

[1] In 1898 Cambridge forbore in favour of London.
[2] Mackinder and Sadler, *op. cit.*, p. 37.
[3] Sir John Marriott, *Memories of Four Score Years* (1946), p. 106. For a general account of the summer meetings see Draper, *op. cit.*, Ch. v and App. I.

Bristol University College, which in its early years received financial assistance from Balliol and New College, was an example of University Extension in the older sense of the phrase, and in its origins was closely connected with the local movement for the higher education of women, in which John Percival, at this time Headmaster of Clifton, was the leading figure. Jowett, Master of Balliol, insisted that if help were to be given the College must provide not only, as originally planned, for teaching in science, but also for literary studies and adult education.[1]

The Extension colleges, once established, naturally became preoccupied with the needs of their full-time students, and the connection with the parent university became increasingly tenuous as time went on. Schemes for the affiliation of local colleges were announced by Cambridge in 1879, and Oxford in 1880, but there was little disposition to take advantage of these.[2] None the less, the local colleges did feel an obligation to continue Extension teaching under their own auspices, and this work formed a useful and often substantial addition to what was officially recognised as Extension work.

Some Leading Figures

Much of the success of University Extension at this period was due to the fact that it enjoyed the services of a first-class team of administrators and lecturers. The leading figure on the administrative side was Dr. R. D. Roberts, a fervent though rather humourless Welshman who gave the services of a lifetime to Extension work at Cambridge and London.[3] He was appointed as Assistant Secretary at Cambridge in 1885, and from 1891 to 1894 served also as Secretary for the London Society. He returned to Cambridge as Secretary in 1895, and finally went back to London in 1902 as Registrar for the new Board for University Extension. There were others who in later life won fame in other spheres. Among these were M. E. Sadler, Secretary at Oxford from 1885 to 1895; J. A. R. Marriott, who succeeded him and held office till 1920; H. J. Mackinder, first Principal of the Extension College at Reading (1892–1905); and P. J. Hartog, Secretary at Manchester 1895–1903.[4]

[1] The details of these developments must be sought in the various university histories, but J. Simmons, *New University* (Leicester 1958), Ch. i, provides an admirable summary. Cf. Draper, *op. cit.*, Ch. iii; and W. H. G. Armytage, *Civic Universities* (1955), Chs. viii–x. An Extension College founded at Colchester in 1896 developed into a technical college.

[2] Mackinder and Sadler, *op. cit.*, pp. 72–3; Draper, *op. cit.*, pp. 29–31. Nottingham and Sheffield became affiliated, not, surprisingly, to Cambridge, but to Oxford.

[3] There is an admirable essay on Roberts's life and work by B. B. Thomas in the volume edited by him, *Harlech Studies: Essays presented to Dr. Thomas Jones* (Cardiff 1938).

[4] All these were later knighted. Sir Michael Sadler was Vice-Chancellor of Leeds University and Master of University College, Oxford; Sir John Marriott became an

The lecturers, many of them men of considerable intellectual distinction, were carefully selected not only for their scholarship but also for their ability to present their subject to a mixed popular audience, and many of them were very fine speakers indeed.[1] The Oxford team included C. G. Lang (afterwards Archbishop of Canterbury), F. E. Smith (afterwards Lord Birkenhead), J. C. Powys, and Hilaire Belloc; the Cambridge list was strong in historians— William Cunningham, G. W. Prothero, A. Hamilton Thompson, A. J. Grant, and J. Holland Rose; and Victoria enlisted the services of T. F. Tout in history, W. A. Raleigh and Oliver Elton in literature, and W. Boyd Dawkins in geology.[2]

By common acclaim the greatest of the Extension lecturers, in their power to interest and stimulate a popular audience, were G. W. Hudson Shaw of Oxford and R. G. Moulton of Cambridge. Of Hudson Shaw, a historian, Mansbridge wrote in 1948 that his name 'still rings in the cities of the north and midlands'. A Church of England parson, he was enlisted by Sadler in 1886, and during the next twenty-six years delivered courses in about 150 different centres. Sadler said of him that he had been 'for more than twenty years . . . one of the great moving forces for good in English life'.

Shaw's programme of work was prodigious: for example his opening week in the Autumn Term of 1889 took him to Rhyl, Chester, Manchester, Nantwich (afternoon and evening), Runcorn, and Altrincham; and when he returned home at the week-end he had his parish work to do. At Oldham he lectured for nine successive years, with an average weekly attendance of 650 and a final attendance in 1895 of over 1,000.

Shaw took enormous pains with his lectures. Dr. Maude Royden, his third wife, says his syllabuses were 'masterpieces of research and in themselves works of art'. Of his lecturing Mansbridge says that he 'relied greatly upon a script, but he simply used it as a tool. The man was above it all . . . In the subsequent discussions, he watched

M.P. and was a prolific writer on historical subjects; Sir Halford Mackinder was Professor of Geography at London and Director of the London School of Economics; and Sir Philip Hartog was Vice-Chancellor of Dacca University, Bengal. See for their work in University Extension Sadleir, *op. cit.*, Chs. v–vii; Grier, *op. cit.*, Ch. i; Marriott, *op. cit.*, Chs. ix–x; and M. Hartog, *P. J. Hartog* (1949), Ch. ii.

[1] D. H. S. Cranage, who succeeded Roberts as Secretary at Cambridge in 1902, and was afterwards Dean of Norwich, describes the 'severe ordeal', involving three lectures to the ladies of the Cambridge Training College, which he had to undergo before he was accepted as a lecturer in 1891 (*Not Only a Dean*, 1952, p. 45); and J. C. Powys describes a similar trial at Oxford in Marriott's day (*Autobiography*, 1934, pp. 284–5).

[2] Interesting descriptions of lecturing experiences are to be found in Cranage, *op. cit.*, Ch. iv, and Marriott, *op. cit.*, Ch. ix; and Powys, who lectured for Cambridge and London as well as Oxford, has also left his impressions (*op. cit.*, pp. 234–8).

for interest and ability even as a gardener for germinations, and tended them as eagerly.'[1]

R. G. Moulton lectured on literature for Cambridge for twenty years before leaving in 1894 to become Professor of Literature at Chicago. Everywhere he went he attracted fabulous audiences. 'Secretaries who traced a curve to show the fluctuation in their audiences', wrote A. J. Grant, 'pointed to the high peak which indicated a visit from Moulton, as they showed in Phæacia the marks which proclaimed to what incredible distances the Gods and heroes of old had hurled the quoit.' Of his lecturing Grant wrote:

His lectures, I believe, practically always took the form of recitals of literature, and it was amazing to note how he won in this way an interested and eager audience for the masterpieces of Greek tragedy and comedy, and for the books of the Bible, as well as for the more popular works of dramatic literature . . . He carried his audience to the heart of great literature, and made them eager to study it for themselves . . . He spoke, I believe, nearly always without notes . . . He recognised that lecturing was his business in life, and he considered with care every detail of gesture and voice management. There was one small point in which, I think, his lectures had an almost solitary pre-eminence. They always ended exactly at the appointed moment. Audiences used to cheer as his last words were mingled with the striking of a neighbouring clock.[2]

Financial and Other Difficulties

In spite of its successes, the Extension movement had certain serious weaknesses. In the first place it suffered from a fundamental ambivalence of purpose. It was, in fact, trying to do two distinct things. In pursuance of the older ideal of University Extension it was seeking to provide university teaching (or the best substitute available) for people unable to attend a university. At the same time, in response to the actual needs of many of its students, it was attempting to provide general cultural courses by which the knowledge and values of the universities should be more widely spread through the community. R. D. Roberts wrote, in an early report:

It is clear from experience that two elements are inevitably present in the audiences. The one consisting of earnest students willing to give time

---

[1] For Hudson Shaw see A. Mansbridge, *Fellow Men* (1948), pp. 76–7; M. Royden, *A Threefold Cord* (1948), Chs. i–iii; N. A. Jepson, *University Extension Lecturers* (Univ. of Leeds, Dept. of Extra-Mural Studies, *Adult Education Papers*, Vol. III, No. 2, May 1952), pp. 13, 22, 32. Dr. Royden's book is the story of her life with Shaw and his first wife The quotation from Sadler is at p. 33.

[2] *University Extension Bulletin*, Oct. 1924, quoted W. F. Moulton, *op. cit.*, pp. 30–1.

to private reading and home study, and the other of busy people anxious mainly to be interested and to find in the lectures a recreation.[1]

Roberts thought the needs of both groups should be catered for, but had no hesitation in awarding primacy to the former. Mackinder and Sadler saw the position a little differently:

The aim of the great majority of these students is not to make themselves professional scholars, but by self-culture to widen and deepen their ideals of life . . . While furnishing men and women, of all ranks and ages, with stimulus and guidance in elevating studies, University Extension must not seek to inspire unsuitable persons with an ambition for callings for which they are not intellectually fitted.[2]

Tout of Manchester, in 1894, placed the main stress on general cultural education:

It is not our object to increase the number of pure students . . . It is the stimulating of intellectual interest which is the main object of the movement.[3]

This problem is still with us in the Extension field. At this period it was solved, more or less satisfactorily, by the device of the lecture and the class, with optional written work and examinations; and by 1895 Moulton, after the fashion of adult educators, had succeeded in rationalising the difficulty into a positive advantage:

The combination of these two kinds of people is found to be for the advantage of both: the presence of students raises the educational character of the Lectures, and the association of students with a popular Audience gives to the teaching an impressiveness that mere class-teaching could never attain.[4]

Apart from this uncertainty as to its educational purpose, the Extension movement suffered, by comparison for example with the W.E.A. at a later stage, from the lack of any clear social dynamic. The movement for the higher education of women, which provided such a dynamic in the early days, inevitably weakened as time went on, and this was one of the factors that made it difficult to maintain a stable local organisation.

Undoubtedly, however, the principal weakness in organisation was lack of money, and this affected the success of the work in a variety of ways. The fee paid to the lecturers was customarily £3 to

[1] Quoted Draper, *op. cit.*, p. 26. Cf. Roberts, *University Extension under the Old and the New Conditions*, pp. 16–17.
[2] Mackinder and Sadler, *op. cit.*, pp. 73–4.
[3] Kelly, *op. cit.*, pp. 21–2.
[4] R. G. Moulton, *University Extension Movement* [1885], p. 7.

£4 per lecture, and when the cost of accommodation and advertising was added this meant that the total cost of a twelve-lecture course was of the order of £60 to £70. Except in the case of the technical courses supported by the local authority, the whole of this sum had to be met by the local centre, so that even with a fee of 10s. 6d. it was necessary to have an audience of well over 100. Several evil consequences followed: working-class students were discouraged from attending; subjects had to be selected on the grounds of popularity rather than educational value, so that any planned sequence of courses was very difficult; the numbers in attendance, even at the classes, were larger than was desirable if effective teaching work was to be done; and the risk of financial loss was so great that after a year or two in a centre it was often difficult to find a local committee willing to accept responsibility.

'A small but recurring deficit', wrote Hartog of Manchester in 1899, 'has proved fatal to many centres . . . Again, popularity of subject being in too many centres essential to financial success, educational continuity is neglected, and we find six lectures on Astronomy sandwiched between six on Literature and six on Architecture in successive terms or sessions.'[1]

This is typical of many contemporary criticisms.

Financial difficulties also adversely affected the recruitment of lecturers, for though the fees were relatively high the work was too irregular and uncertain to offer an attractive career. To earn £450 a year a lecturer had to undertake seven lectures a week during the winter season, involving endless journeys in ill-heated trains, and the marking of scores of scripts every week.[2] Extension lecturing thus tended to be a young man's job, and it was difficult for the universities to retain the core of experienced practitioners which they felt to be essential to the success of the work.

All these difficulties were very clearly seen at the time, and both the local centres and the university authorities made strenuous and not entirely unsuccessful attempts to meet them. Many local centres adopted the device of differential fees to encourage the attendance of the poorer sections of the community: for example they would run a course in the afternoons at a guinea, and repeat it in the evenings at five shillings. Other centres were able to supplement their resources by grants from co-operative societies, employers, and wealthy private individuals. The London Society drew much help from the Gilchrist Trust and the City Companies,[3] and the Gilchrist Trust

---

[1] Kelly, op. cit., pp. 28–9.
[2] On the quantity and quality of written work see Jepson, op. cit., pp. 31–6.
[3] Mackinder and Sadler, op. cit., p. 126.

also assisted centres elsewhere, e.g. in Northumberland.[1] Here local centres combined, in 1883–6, in an effort to secure assistance from the Miners' Union, but they were unable to secure the necessary alteration in union rules.[2]

The efforts of the universities to secure additional funds met with little success. They themselves were unable to do more than support the central administration. Stuart had a scheme for using university fellowships to provide an endowment for Extension lecturers,[3] but the only practical step taken in this direction was the election of Hudson Shaw to a fellowship of Balliol in 1890. A campaign to secure state aid, which was launched in 1889 and culminated in 1895 in a petition to Parliament for an annual grant of £6,000 in aid of University Extension, proved abortive in spite of the fact that it was supported by a distinguished array of peers, bishops, members of Parliament and other notables.[4]

Oxford and Cambridge did succeed in creating, however, mainly from private sources, small reserve funds from which it was possible to make grants to full-time lecturers in the event of illness or the breakdown of a class programme. In 1886 Oxford appointed Hudson Shaw as an 'endowed lecturer', with a guaranteed minimum income of £350 per annum.[5]

The universities were much more successful in dealing with administrative and academic problems. The local organisation was strengthened and encouraged in a variety of ways: by the formation of local students' associations to keep the course-members together, and promote continued study between courses; by the formation of district associations of local centres, bringing together centres attached to the various universities for consultation and for co-operation in the planning of programmes[6]; by the summer meetings;

---

[1] The Gilchrist Educational Trust was founded under the will of Dr. J. B. Gilchrist (d. 1841), and from 1878 onwards was active in promoting short courses of popular lectures, usually on science, in various parts of Great Britain. The trustees were sympathetic towards Extension work, and their courses sometimes prepared the way for Extension centres. See Lord Shuttleworth and D. H. S. Cranage, *Pioneering Work in Education* (Cambridge 1930).

[2] Roberts, *Eighteen Years*, pp. 61–5.

[3] Expounded in *University Extension*, an address to the Leeds Ladies' Educational Association (Leeds 1871), and in Stuart's *Letter on University Extension* in the same year. R. S. Watson, Secretary of the Newcastle Literary and Philosophical Society, had made a similar suggestion at the meeting of the National Association for the Promotion of Social Science at Newcastle in 1870—see the Association's *Transactions* for that year, pp. 361–6.

[4] Mackinder and Sadler, *op. cit.*, pp. 131–44; Kelly, *op. cit.*, p. 29.

[5] For the reserve funds see Mackinder and Sadler, *op. cit.*, p. 126; and for details regarding the status and remuneration of tutors at Oxford, Jepson, *op. cit.*, pp. 37 sqq.

[6] In 1891 there were District Associations for the South-Eastern Counties, the South-Western Counties, the North Midlands, Yorkshire, Lancashire and Cheshire, and Northumberland—Mackinder and Sadler, *op. cit.*, p. 51; Moulton, *University Extension Movement*, pp. 47–8.

by periodical national conferences of local secretaries; and by the publication of a *University Extension Journal* giving news of the movement throughout the country.[1]

Oxford, Cambridge, and London also took special measures to encourage continuity of study. Cambridge in 1886, and Oxford in 1893, made arrangements for the affiliation to the university of Extension centres which were prepared to undertake a systematic sequence of courses over a three-year period. A student who secured certificates for eight approved terminal courses, and passed an examination in elementary mathematics, Latin, and another language, was entitled to exemption from the first year of the B.A. course at the parent university.[2] Cambridge and London also introduced additional certificates. London was first in the field with the Certificate of Continuous Study (1883), covering three years' work. A Sessional Certificate was established in 1889, and a Vice-Chancellor's Certificate, for four years' work, in 1904. Cambridge introduced the Sessional Certificate and the Vice-Chancellor's Certificate in 1895. Victoria University disapproved of this emphasis on certificates, and declined to follow suit.[3]

The net result of these various measures seems to have been a considerable improvement in the duration and continuity of the courses, and many centres established such a strong tradition that the work went on well into the twentieth century. Cambridge, for example, had more than a score of centres (including a strong group in the North-East) which were founded in the 1870s and 1880s and were still flourishing in the 1920s and 1930s, and some of these early centres still exist to this day.[4]

Significance of the Movement

It has seemed worth while to treat this early Extension movement at considerable length because of its great significance for adult

---

[1] This *Journal*, launched in 1895 under the joint auspices of Oxford, Cambridge, London, and Victoria, took the place of the *Oxford University Gazette* and a *University Extension Journal* sponsored by London, both established in 1890. After the withdrawal of Victoria the *Journal* was continued as *University Extension* (1904–7), and finally as *University Extension Bulletin* (1907–26).

[2] Roberts, *op. cit.*, pp. 82–5; Mackinder and Sadler, *op. cit.*, pp. 71–2. Six of the subjects had to be from the sciences, and two from the arts, or *vice versa*. Newcastle, Sunderland, Scarborough, Hull, Derby, Exeter, and Plymouth were the first centres to affiliate to Cambridge under this scheme.

[3] Kelly, *op. cit.*, pp. 21–3. Oxford also, in spite of frequent statements to the contrary, does not appear to have offered any long-term certificate other than the affiliation certificate.

[4] E.g. Derby (founded 1873, continuous since 1881), Southport (from 1874), and Colchester (from 1889). Some other notable centres, e.g. Norwich and Grantham, have ceased operations only within the last few years. The earliest Oxford centre still existing is Heaton Chapel (since 1897–8).

education, for the universities themselves, and for the nation at large. Its significance for adult education lay partly in the attention it paid to the needs of women—a point that has been touched on above— and partly in the character of the university approach to the work. At a time when many adult education movements were tending to drift in the direction of technical and vocational education, when even the working men's colleges were finding it difficult to resist the general trend, the universities clearly restated the concept of liberal study. In doing so they did not neglect the vocational needs of the students, but they insisted that even studies directed to vocational ends should be undertaken in a broad humane spirit, and that the fundamental values and purposes of human life should be kept steadily in view. Thereby the universities established a tradition of liberal study which has ever since been the distinctive mark and special pride of English adult education.

For the universities the significance of the Extension movement was immense. In 1850 the universities were little known and little understood. 'There was little communication between them and important sections of the population, and in consequence they were often viewed with envy and jealousy, one sign of which was a demand for the decentralisation of their endowments.'[1] Extension lecturing brought missionaries from the universities—many of them men destined to eminence in the life of the nation—into contact with men and women of all social classes in every corner of the country; and Extension summer meetings annually brought hundreds of ordinary people face to face with leading figures in the internal life of the universities. Out of this personal contact came mutual respect and understanding. The ordinary men and women learned something of the patient, unending search for truth that characterised university scholarship; the scholar learned that life has lessons which books cannot teach. The universities became familiar, even popular, institutions, so that students might be heard to speak of 'the grand old university of Cambridge'. 'All at once', wrote a Northumberland miner, 'Cambridge and everything pertaining to it becomes interesting, and the class to which the lecturer belongs is regarded with generous feelings.'[2]

Thus at the very time when the universities, as a result of internal reforms, were resuming their rightful place as the intellectual leaders of the nation, they were drawn out of their isolation and brought

---

[1] Roach, 'Victorian Universities and the National Intelligentsia' (*Victorian Studies*, Vol. II), pp. 142–3.
[2] Roberts, *op. cit.*, pp. 36–7.

into friendly and fruitful contact with the world outside. Here was a change of tremendous import, of which the full consequences for the social and political life of the country were to be seen in the twentieth century.

The National Home Reading Union

A movement closely associated with University Extension, at least in its origins, was the National Home Reading Union, in which the leading figure was J. B. Paton of Nottingham. We have seen that the idea of home-reading circles, like that of summer meetings, was inspired by the American Chautauqua, and that Paton formed a committee in 1887 to consider the matter.[1] Sadler of Oxford was a warm supporter, and was anxious to develop the movement as a supplement to University Extension, in order particularly to meet the needs of those centres where it was not possible to arrange regular courses of lectures. Paton, however, had in mind a wider audience, and in particular the needs of the generation of new literates emerging as a result of the 1870 Education Act, for whom he feared that the gift of literacy, without sound guidance, might merely open up new paths of wickedness. He therefore wished to bring into the scheme senior elementary schools, Sunday schools, Y.M.C.A.s, co-operative societies, trade unions, technical schools, mutual improvement societies, and other organisations.

On this difference of opinion the committee split. Sadler attempted to establish reading circles in connection with University Extension, but had to abandon the scheme because of the enormous labour involved. Paton, meanwhile, went ahead and founded, in 1889, the National Home Reading Union. The Union's main activity lay in the publication of courses of guided reading at various levels: Young People's Courses, General Courses, and Special Courses. It also issued booklists, encouraged the formation of reading and discussion circles among people undertaking the courses, offered tutorial help and correspondence to individual readers, and arranged summer assemblies at Blackpool and other holiday resorts. In spite of constant financial difficulty, the work of the Union was carried on for more than forty years, and as time went on relied increasingly on the collaboration of public libraries and local education authorities. In consequence the emphasis came to be more and more on work with young people. Over 6,000 members were enrolled in the first year: in 1914 there were over 76,000 members, but about 70,000 of these were school children. After the first World War the development of

---

[1] See above, p. 228, and authorities there cited.

other forms of adult education made the work of the Union less necessary, and publication of the reading courses ceased in 1930.[1]

The First University Settlements

The missionary aspect of University Extension has several times been referred to, and in this sense it links with the settlement movement which was such a notable feature of the closing years of the nineteenth century. It was primarily a desire to establish a common brotherhood which sent men and women from the universities to dwell among the poor in London, Manchester, Liverpool, and other great cities. As Sir John Gorst put it:

> The first object, to which every other is subsidiary, is to make friends with the neighbourhood—to become part of its common life; to associate with people on equal terms, without either patronage on the one side or subserviency on the other; to share in the joys and sorrows, the occupations and amusements of the people; to bring them to regard the members of the Settlements as their friends.[2]

Out of such activities, however, efforts in the direction of adult education arose very easily and naturally, and in some settlements became an important part of the work.

The debt of the settlement movement to the ideas of F. D. Maurice and his friends is very obvious. Indeed we may well regard University Extension and the settlements as the twin offspring of Christian Socialism, the one being a development mainly in the direction of education, the other mainly in the direction of social work. The settlement movement was also greatly influenced by the ideas of John Ruskin, whose *Unto This Last* (1862) was the first of a series of trenchant and lucidly written attacks on the social and economic system of the time.

In its immediate origins the movement derived from the missionary work of men such as Edward Denison, Rev. J. R. Green (the historian of the English people), and Rev. Samuel Barnett, in the east end of London. When Barnett was appointed Vicar of St. Jude's, Whitechapel, in 1872, he and his wife at once embarked on a vigorous programme of social and educational work among the inhabitants of this depressed area, and began to gather round them a band of resident and non-resident helpers, many of them young men recruited from Oxford. Barnett himself paid many visits to Oxford,

---

[1] See, in addition to the works cited above, M. E. Sadler (ed.), *Continuation Schools in England and Elsewhere* (Manchester 1907, 2nd edn. 1908), pp. 80–4; J. Marchant, *J. B. Paton* (1909), pp. 247–59.
[2] W. Reason (ed.), *University and Social Settlements* (1898), p. 45.

and the presence of Ruskin there, as Slade Professor of Art, was an influence in the same direction. One of those attracted was the young Arnold Toynbee, who gave much to the work until his premature death in 1883.

In that year the conscience of England was powerfully stirred by the revelations in an anonymous pamphlet called *The Bitter Cry of Outcast London*, which recorded the terrible results of an inquiry by the London Congregational Union into the condition of the poorer quarters of the city. A year later Barnett was able to establish in Whitechapel, with powerful support from Oxford and later from Cambridge, a permanent residential settlement under the name Toynbee Hall. Among those who gave their support were R. D. Roberts (an early resident), M. E. Sadler, William Cunningham, C. G. Lang, James Stuart, and others associated with the Extension movement.[1]

Toynbee Hall was officially opened in 1885, with Barnett as its first Warden, and a group of fourteen resident helpers. In the same year another Oxford group opened Oxford House, Bethnal Green, and in 1889 a group from Cambridge established Trinity Court, afterwards Cambridge House. By 1898 there were more than a score of such settlements, not only in London, but also in Bristol, Ipswich, Liverpool, Manchester, Edinburgh, and Glasgow, about half of them being associated with universities. Some were organised by women, the first being the Women's University Settlement in Southwark, established in 1887 by women students of Oxford and Cambridge.[2]

The Educational Work of the Settlements

The extent of the educational work of the settlements varied. Barnett regarded education not merely as a form of training but as a means of life, and one of his first steps when he became Vicar of St. Jude's was to launch adult classes in arithmetic, composition, drawing, and languages. Later, in 1877, he helped to establish the East London branch of the University Extension Society. In 1881 he organised the first of a series of annual art exhibitions. Toynbee Hall, in consequence, was always outstanding among the settlements for its educational work. Indeed Barnett always regarded it as the nucleus of an East London University, and this idea was emphasised by the opening in 1887 and 1890 of two students' hostels, Wadham House and Balliol House.

[1] For the general background of the Settlements see J. A. R. Pimlott, *Toynbee Hall* (1935), Chs. i–ii.
[2] Reason, *op. cit.*, pp. 179–90, gives a directory of settlements in 1898.

The programme for the autumn term, 1897, included elementary classes for men in arithmetic, writing, composition, citizenship, and chemistry; a variety of afternoon classes for girls; classes in practical subjects such as first aid, nursing, ambulance work, life-saving, and photography; and a whole range of classes on more academic subjects—Latin, Greek and Hebrew, Italian literature, German literature, French literature, English literature (various aspects), history, music, geology, botany, anatomy. Among the six Extension courses were European History, 1852–97, by S. R. Gardiner, The Making of Modern England, by Edward Jenks, and Sir Walter Scott, by F. S. Boas.

All this was in addition to popular lectures, discussion-groups, Sunday afternoon concerts, and other activities too numerous to mention. The art exhibitions were held each Easter: by this time they were attracting attendances of over 60,000, and had become a great event in the life of East London. Very shortly, thanks largely to the generosity of Passmore Edwards, they were provided with a permanent home in the Whitechapel Art Gallery, opened in 1901. Earlier Toynbee Hall had been instrumental in securing the establishment of the Whitechapel Public Library, opened in 1892. The Hall had, of course, its own library from the beginning.[1]

Though every effort was made to maintain a range of popular activities, a programme of this order naturally tended to attract an *élite* rather than the masses. A discussion group on 'the Connection between Morality and Metaphysics', for example, could hardly be expected to appeal to the average inhabitant of Whitechapel. In fact we find that many of the students were lower middle-class rather than working-class, and nearly half of them came from other parts of the city.[2] Barnett himself early perceived the weakness of University Extension for the working-class student, namely that it did not provide sufficiently for the needs of individuals. 'The students', he said in 1887, 'must have not only the direction of the professor, but the constant care of the tutor.'[3]

Towards the close of the century, when Extension courses were beginning to wane a little in popularity, Barnett was experimenting in new forms of teaching. In 1898 a 'History School' was established, with R. E. S. Hart as tutor, to provide a course of guided study extending over two years. The students were pledged to spend three

<hr />

[1] For the early educational work at Toynbee see Reason, *op. cit.*, pp. 170–3; Pimlott, *op. cit.*, Chs. iv, ix and x; and *Canon Barnett: his Life, Work and Friends*, by his wife [Dame Henrietta Barnett] (2 vols. 1919), Chs. xxvi–xxix and xl.

[2] Pimlott, *op. cit.*, p. 60.

[3] Barnett, *op. cit.*, Vol. I, p. 335.

or four hours a week in study and to produce written papers from time to time.[1] In 1900–1 the Extension Society agreed to provide three 'tutorial classes'—in Literature, History, and Chemistry—which were to be limited in the number of students, and were to provide 'far more thorough and systematic teaching than is possible in a course of lectures'.[2] In these experiments Toynbee Hall anticipated the later work of the Workers' Educational Association.

No other settlement devoted the same attention to adult education as Toynbee Hall, but most of them organised educational activities of one kind or another—lectures, debates, concerts, and the like.[3] The University Settlement at Ancoats, Manchester, which was founded in 1895, and was closely associated with Owens College, ran a considerable educational programme, its lecturers in the early years including men of the calibre of Samuel Alexander, T. F. Tout, Ramsay Muir, and G. M. Trevelyan.[4] Some London settlements copied the Toynbee plan of periodical art exhibitions, and Mansfield House in Canning Town (established by the students of Mansfield College in 1890) went further and established a loan collection of pictures and prints.[5]

At the very end of the century, in 1899, came a new portent in university adult education, the foundation of Ruskin College, Oxford. This, however, can be most conveniently dealt with in a later chapter.

[1] Pimlott, op, cit., p. 146.
[2] Barnett, op. cit., Vol. I, p. 338.
[3] Reason, op. cit., pp. 45–62.
[4] M. D. Stocks, *Fifty Years in Every Street* (Manchester 1945, 2nd edn. 1956), Ch. iii; Kelly, op. cit., pp. 34–5.
[5] Reason, op. cit., p. 88.

15

The Twentieth Century

THE UNIVERSITIES AND WORKING-CLASS ORGANISATIONS

IN the closing decades of the nineteenth century the apparently solid structure of Victorian society was already being undermined. Socialism in its various forms was questioning the basic concepts of *laissez faire* capitalism; Darwinism and the higher criticism were weakening the accepted religious faith; household suffrage and universal education were creating among the working classes a sharper awareness of their rights and capabilities. The turn of the century brought new and forceful critics of the established order—Bernard Shaw, Sidney and Beatrice Webb, H. G. Wells.

The formation of the Labour Representation Committee in 1900, and the election of two of its candidates to Parliament—Keir Hardie at Merthyr Tydfil and Richard Bell at Derby—demonstrated that labour was at last on the march to political power. Three years later the foundation by Mrs. Pankhurst of the Women's Social and Political Union showed that women, too, were on the march. The election of 1906 brought a Liberal government to power in a Parliament that included over forty representatives of labour, and the six years that followed were marked by new and important steps towards a more democratic and egalitarian society: old age pensions, national health insurance, salaries for M.P.s, and a limitation on the power of veto of the House of Lords. The ramparts of Victorianism were crumbling on all sides.

Ruskin College

A feature of the period was a renewed and powerful demand for adult education for working people, especially in such subjects as politics, economics, and industrial history. This demand reflected at once the political evolution of the working class and the inadequacies of the state system of schooling as clarified and codified by the Board of Education Act of 1899 and the Education Act of 1902. The first of these Acts established a single central education authority; the second brought the local education authorities into being to take over the functions of school boards, technical instruction committees, and other *ad hoc* bodies. But the system thus codified was one that was efficient only for elementary and technical education: the Act of 1902 opened up the possibility of a state system of secondary education, but the actual achievement of such a system was still in the future. For the intelligent working man who had received an elementary schooling, and wished to pursue his general education, adult education was still the only way of advance.

The new movement was particularly marked in university adult education. In this field its beginning is signalised by two events: the opening in 1899 of Ruskin Hall (from 1907 Ruskin College) and the foundation in 1903 of the Association for the Higher Education of Working Men (from 1905 the Workers' Educational Association, or more familiarly the W.E.A.).

The origin of the former institution was rather unusual. It was established on the initiative of two visiting American students at Oxford, Walter Vrooman and Charles Beard, and the former's wife Mrs. A. L. Vrooman. All three were admirers of Ruskin and interested in the labour movement. Vrooman believed that this movement would become increasingly powerful in Britain and the United States, and that its leaders 'should go beyond trade union interests and equip themselves for statesmanship'. He hoped that a residential working men's college at Oxford would be the centre of a national movement, and that similar institutions could be established in the United States.[1]

Ruskin Hall began its career in a house in St. Giles Street leased from Balliol College. It was not until 1903 that it moved to its present site in Walton Street, where a new college was built ten years later. At its inception it aimed to provide a training in 'subjects which are essential for working-class leadership, and which are not a direct avenue to anything beyond'.[2] In practice this meant mainly history, economics, and political science, with supplementary classes in such subjects as grammar, logic, and public speaking. The teaching was done for the most part by a small full-time staff, Vrooman himself acting as Principal in the early days. The fees were very low (£52 for a full year's residence), the accommodation was very simple, and the students were expected to do most of their own domestic work.[3]

---

[1] *The Story of Ruskin College* (Oxford 1949, 2nd edn. 1955), p. 5.

[2] Ministry of Reconstruction, Adult Education Committee, *Final Report* (1919), p. 31.

[3] 'Vrooman had peculiar ideas about food. He thought that people should eat only when they were hungry, and he had bags of oatmeal and apples, loaves of bread, pieces of cheese, etc., put about the house so that anybody could help himself when he felt

Constitutionally the college was (and remains to this day) independent of the University, but it had the support of a number of university people, notably Professor York Powell, the historian. It also won widespread support from working-class organisations: its governing council on its incorporation included representatives of the Trades Union Congress, the Amalgamated Society of Engineers, and the Co-operative Union. This support was vital, for many students attended with the help of trade union or co-operative scholarships. The twenty students in residence in 1903 included 'four miners, two compositors, a brushmaker, a joiner, an engineer, a warp-dresser, a weaver, a docker, a billposter, a clerk, a tailor, a shop assistant, a postal worker, a farmer, and two trade union officials'.[1]

Before the close of 1902 Beard and the Vroomans were back in America, the latter having lost a great deal of money. The college was now left to its own resources, and the support of working-class organisations became more important than ever. In 1907 the T.U.C. issued an appeal to its constituent unions, urging that the time had now come for the labour movement to take the college in hand and make it an assured success. Just at this time, however, the college began to run into serious internal difficulties.

A substantial group of left-wing students complained that the college was too much under the domination of the university members of the council, and that the teaching was bourgeois and reactionary. In this attitude they were supported by the Principal, Dennis Hird, who wished to make the college a centre for Socialist education. In 1909 the college executive, after inquiry, decided to dismiss Hird, whereupon the majority of the students went on strike, and ultimately a group of them seceded to form, with other ex-Ruskin students, a new institution known as the Central Labour College, with Hird as Principal.[2]

The serious consequences of this split in the working-class educational movement will have to be examined later. In the meantime it is significant that before the end of the year one of the main points of the malcontents was in fact conceded. In October 1909 the

---

inclined, and prepare what he liked.' This arrangement, however, was not popular with the students, and in the end a professional cook had to be engaged—H. S. Furniss (Lord Sanderson), *Memories of Sixty Years* (1931), p. 87.

[1] *Story of Ruskin College*, p. 12.

[2] For accounts of this dispute from the opposing sides see Furniss, *op. cit.*, Chs. vii–viii; and *The Burning Question of Education* (Plebs League, Oxford 1909, 2nd edn. 1909). Furniss was one of the lecturers to whose teaching the rebels objected. Though almost blind, he served as Principal of the College from 1916 to 1925, and was afterwards, as Lord Sanderson, a Labour peer.

government of Ruskin College was transferred to a council representing the T.U.C., the General Federation of Trade Unions, the
Co-operative Union, the Working Men's Club and Institute Union,
and other working-class contributory bodies. Under the new régime
relationships with the University were placed on a much more
satisfactory footing, and from 1910 Ruskin students were permitted
to take the University Diploma in Economics and Political Science.[1]
By 1913 the College was established in new buildings, with an
average of 34 students a year, many of them in residence for two
years.[2]

Ruskin College did not become, as its founders had hoped, the
centre for a nation-wide system of working-class colleges. It did
indeed develop a flourishing scheme of correspondence courses, and
in the early years classes developed in connection with some of these
courses, for example at Rochdale.[3] The only attempt to create
another permanent institution, however, was at Manchester, where
Beard established a Ruskin Hall in connection with the University
Settlement in 1899. It was intended to provide residential facilities
and evening study courses for men at work during the day, and for
a year or two it flourished, but it did not long survive the return of
Beard to America in 1902.[4]

The Progress of University Extension

The task of organising on a national scale the new working-class
demand for adult education was taken over from 1903 onwards by
the W.E.A., which used the medium of evening classes and attached
itself firmly to the existing tradition of University Extension. This
tradition, contrary to common belief, was still alive and vigorous,
and it will be useful to say something of it before describing the
development of the W.E.A.

Throughout the first decade of the new century University Extension continued to flourish, with about 50,000 students in average
attendance. Most of them were in courses arranged by Oxford,
Cambridge, and London, but the newer universities also made some
contribution, especially in the earlier years of the century—Liverpool, which had a University Extension Society founded in 1899
under the energetic leadership of Ramsay Muir, was particularly

[1] Story of Ruskin College, p. 18.
[2] W.E.A. Education Year Book, 1918, p. 388.
[3] T. W. Price, The Story of the Workers' Educational Association (1924), p. 22.
[4] T. Kelly, Outside the Walls (Manchester 1950), pp. 35–7.

active at this time.[1] It is true that there was during this period a falling-off in the number of Extension students who presented themselves for examination, but this does not necessarily imply any waning of enthusiasm: it was probably due in the main to developments in secondary education and in teacher training.[2] In 1908, in order to encourage continuity of study, London successfully launched a scheme for diplomas in the humanities, involving four years' study in literature, history, economics, or social science, with an examination in each year.

Only Wales and Scotland were still unresponsive. In Wales a new attempt at University Extension was launched from Cardiff in 1902, but the tight chapel-centred circle of traditional Welsh culture was still difficult to penetrate, and after a few years the movement dwindled to very small proportions.[3]

As in the nineteenth century the courses were either for the general public or for teachers and other specialist groups. In the former the students were predominantly middle-class, but there were centres in the North and Midlands where working people were in a majority. The report of the Cambridge Syndicate for 1902–3 records attendances of from 300 to over 600 at working-class centres at Leicester, Middlesbrough, Cleator Moor (a small iron-mining town in Cumberland), and South Normanton (a coal-mining village in Derbyshire).

It was only from 1909–10 onwards that Extension work began to take a marked downward turn, the decline being at least partly due to the increasing preoccupation of the universities with W.E.A. tutorial classes. By 1913–14 the average attendance at Oxford, Cambridge, and London had fallen to about 30,000, and no other university was organising more than a handful of courses. Then came the First World War, which disrupted the local centre organisation and in many cases put an end to the older type of Extension work altogether.

---

[1] From statistics in the annual reports it appears that the peak years for attendance were 1905–6 at Cambridge, 1907–8 at Oxford, and 1908–9 at London. The statistics are not, however, strictly comparable: Oxford and Cambridge recorded average attendances, London terminal enrolments. For other universities no comprehensive figures are available, but some information is given in W. H. Draper, *University Extension, 1873–1923* (Cambridge 1923), pp. 140–6. For Manchester see also Kelly, *Outside the Walls*, pp. 41–4 and App. III; and for Liverpool T. Kelly, *Adult Education in Liverpool* (Liverpool 1960), pp. 33–40. The best general review is in W. Picht, *Toynbee Hall and the Settlement Movement* (Tübingen 1913, transl. L. A. Cowell, London 1914, new edn. 1916), pp. 136–71.

[2] In 1905 the Board of Education terminated the arrangement which had operated since 1894 under which a certificate for a University Extension sessional course had counted as a part qualification towards the King's Scholarship examination for pupil-teachers.

[3] University of Wales, Extension Board, *Survey of Adult Education in Wales* (privately published, Cardiff 1940), pp. 16–17.

The Workers' Educational Association

The W.E.A. was founded by Albert Mansbridge, one of the great prophets of English adult education. The son of a Gloucester carpenter, he was born in 1876, had a board school and grammar school education in London, and left at fourteen to become eventually a clerk in the C.W.S. at Whitechapel. His mother, an ardent co-operative worker and a friend of the Barnetts, introduced him to Toynbee Hall and from his experiences there, and from attendance at evening classes and Extension lectures, he caught a vision of what he called 'the glory of education', and a belief that somehow his fellow-men, however humble, must be made partakers of this vision.[1]

It was a vision shot through with deep religious feeling. Mansbridge was from his early manhood a lay preacher in the Church of England, and to him the gospel of education was an integral part of the gospel of Christianity. He preached adult education with an evangelical fervour and a passionate conviction that won him the enthusiastic support of gatherings of working people and the intimate friendship of men influential in Church and university— men such as Charles Gore, William Temple, Michael Sadler, J. A. R. Marriott, R. D. Roberts, A. E. Zimmern, A. L. Smith, and R. H. Tawney.

At co-operative gatherings in 1898 and 1899, and subsequently in three articles in the *University Extension Journal* in 1903,[2] Mansbridge argued the case for true education as the basis of working-class representation in a democratic state, and pleaded for an alliance of co-operation, trade unionism, and the universities to this end.

Co-operation and trade unionism are the chief movements of democracy. University Extension, of all educational movements, promises most to be capable of infusing them with a wise and free education.

The appeal of the hour to trade unionists and co-operators is that they make political strokes, promote Bills, register protests, and send deputations to responsible ministers. The true appeal is that they lift themselves up through higher knowledge to higher works and higher pleasures, which, if responded to, will inevitably bring about right and sound action upon municipal, national, and imperial affairs; action brought about without conscious effort—the only effectual action. It will be promoted by wise and free education and sustained by it. That is my interpretation of

[1] For Mansbridge's Toynbee contacts see J. A. R. Pimlott, *Toynbee Hall* (1935), p. 147. Oddly enough, Mansbridge himself says he first knew Canon Barnett in 1903 (*Fellow Men*, 1948, p. 60).
[2] Reprinted in A. Mansbridge, *The Kingdom of the Mind* (1944), pp. 1–11.

the message of University Extension to the two great movements of democracy.[1]

In his third article he proposed a joint university and working-class association 'to make ready and prepare the democratic mind for the ordinary operations of University Extension'. In May 1903 he and his wife became the first members of An Association to promote the Higher Education of Working Men. 'In a completely democratic meeting', he records, 'she appointed me honorary secretary, *pro tem.*, contributed half a crown out of her housekeeping funds, and the movement was on foot.'[2]

Mansbridge's enthusiasm met with a ready response from universities and working-class organisations in many parts of the country. Co-operative societies, trade unions, and other bodies began to affiliate to the Association in considerable numbers, and local branches came into existence—the first four were formed at Reading in 1904, and at Derby, Rochdale, and Ilford in the early months of 1905. In this latter year Mansbridge became full-time General Secretary at a salary of £50 a year, and his little office in his home at Ilford became the centre of a far-reaching network of organisation and propaganda. Within five years of the establishment of the Association it had 50 branches, over 900 affiliated organisations, and over 5,000 members.

The first three branches, Reading, Derby, and Rochdale, all inherited a flourishing tradition of University Extension, and most branches, in these early years, considered the organisation of Extension courses as one of their primary objectives. Their enthusiasm, however, did not limit itself to this. The record of the first year of the Rochdale branch, which called itself the Rochdale Education Guild, was particularly impressive. T. W. Price summarises it as follows:

There were two courses of Extension lectures, with average audiences of over 500, and classes were run in connection with each. A course of six lectures on 'The Care of the Horse' was arranged at the suggestion of the Carters' Union, and was attended by over 100 carters. Reading circles were held in various parts of the town, and members of the Guild gave a course of six lectures on 'English History' in three of the outlying districts. Four 'Talks' on 'Botany' and four on 'Geology' were given in the Museum, and three on 'Pictures' in the Art Gallery. Two courses of afternoon lectures on 'The Home and the Children' were arranged for women, and at the request of the Guild the Local Education Authority provided classes

---

[1] *Op. cit.*, p. 2.
[2] A. Mansbridge, *The Trodden Road* (1940), p. 60.

on Elementary and Advanced English, and on Citizenship and Economics, and also special classes for adults at the Evening Schools, at which elementary subjects, such as Arithmetic and Composition, were taught. Finally, particulars of the various educational activities carried on in the town were compiled and published as an *Educational Calendar*.[1]

An important point here is the emergence of the local education authority as a factor in adult education. Hitherto the only assistance to adult education from local authority funds had been the grants occasionally made by technical instruction committees towards Extension courses in science. Under the Education Act of 1902, however, the authorities responsible for higher education, i.e. the county and county borough councils, were permitted to organise or assist evening courses for adults without limitation as to subject.[2] This opened up much wider possibilities of co-operation.

The Act came into force in March 1903. By that time it was also possible for adult courses, under certain circumstances, to earn grant from the central government under the Board of Education's regulations for evening schools.[3] From 1903 onwards the combination of government grant and local authority aid was a powerful factor in stimulating the development of adult education, and especially the work of the W.E.A. The growth of the tutorial class movement, in particular, would hardly have been possible without it.

It will be seen from the example of Rochdale that the W.E.A. quickly developed a life of its own independently of its university connection. It ran its own courses and other activities, and also carried on a vigorous propaganda on more general educational issues. As time went on it began to demand university teaching of a new kind—teaching at the highest level for small groups of students. This, as we have seen, had long been desired by the Extension authorities, and in the tutorial classes at Toynbee Hall something of the kind had been achieved.[4] Generally, however, the financial obstacles had proved insuperable.

---

[1] Price, *Story of the W.E.A.*, pp. 25–6. For the range of W.E.A. branch activities see also M. D. Stocks, *The Workers' Educational Association: the First Fifty Years* (1953), p. 35. The full record of the first year of the Rochdale Guild is printed in Mansbridge, *Adventure in Working-Class Education* (1920), App. II.

[2] The relevant passage of the Act (Part II, Section 2) is reprinted in the report on *Oxford and Working-Class Education* (see below, p. 252), p. 99.

[3] The revised regulations of 1902 permitted a higher rate of grant in respect of a wide range of subjects where the instruction was at an advanced level. The Oxford Extension centre at Littleborough (Lancs.) and the London Extension centre at Toynbee Hall, claimed grant under these regulations in the session 1902–3. See Oxford Extension Delegacy, *Annual Report*, 1902–3; and [H. O. Barnett], *Canon Barnett* (1919), Vol. I, pp. 338–9.

[4] See above, pp. 241–2.

Tutorial Classes

The new movement for tutorial classes for working people had its origins in a conference held at London University in 1906. A committee appointed by the conference recommended the formation of such classes, and in the autumn of 1907 Professor Patrick Geddes conducted a ten-week course on Civics, on tutorial lines but without written work, for the newly formed W.E.A. Branch at Battersea.[1]

The demand which actually launched the movement, however, came in 1907 from a group of W.E.A. students who had been attending an Oxford Extension course at Rochdale. They consulted Mansbridge, who in turn consulted the University authorities, and the ultimate outcome was the opening at Rochdale, in January 1908, of a three-year tutorial class in Economic History, with R. H. Tawney of Balliol as tutor. There were forty students, all pledged to regular attendance and the writing of fortnightly essays. A parallel class was arranged at Longton, Staffordshire, at the request of the Oxford Extension centre there, and actually began one day before the Rochdale class. New College made a grant of £300 towards the cost.[2]

This was a crucial experiment, and thanks to Tawney it succeeded. He was at this time a part-time assistant lecturer at Glasgow University, and he travelled down weekly to take the Longton class on Friday evenings and the Rochdale class on Saturday afternoons. Though a public school man, he was already familiar with the needs of working-class students through his contacts with Toynbee Hall and the W.E.A. 'He talked to them', says Mrs. Stocks, 'as man to man, neither claiming authority nor asking for unquestioned agreement. But as he talked, the breadth and quality of his mind and the meticulous accuracy of his scholarship reflected itself in the work of his students and established the standard of their thought.'[3] It was in these early classes that the distinctive tradition of tutorial class teaching was shaped.

The great battle that was raging at Ruskin College just about this time inevitably had its echoes in the W.E.A., for the W.E.A., too, had its militant trade union wing. Thanks to Mansbridge, however, these discordant elements were brought into harmony. In 1907, in connection with the Oxford Summer Meeting, a special conference of university and W.E.A. representatives was arranged, under the

---

[1] A. Mansbridge, *University Tutorial Classes* (1913), pp. 16–17; B. B. Thomas (ed.), *Harlech Studies* (Cardiff 1938), pp. 27–8. On Geddes see above, p. 228 note.

[2] Mansbridge, *op. cit.*, pp. 17–20.

[3] Stocks, *op. cit.*, p. 39.

chairmanship of Charles Gore, Bishop of Birmingham, to consider 'What Oxford can do for Workpeople'. There was much forthright speaking. J. M. Mactavish, a Portsmouth shipwright, declared:

> I am not here as a suppliant for my class. I decline to sit at the rich man's gate praying for crumbs. I claim for my class all the best of all that Oxford has to give.[1]

He went on, moreover, to warn the conference that in those things which concerned the workers most intimately they would not be satisfied with what Oxford had been accustomed to offer. The upshot of the conference, however, was the appointment of a joint committee—seven working-class representatives nominated by the W.E.A., and seven university representatives, to prepare a report on the provision of tutorial teaching for working people and their admission as full-time students of the University.[2] Out of its deliberations there arose in October 1908 a permanent joint committee, again equally representative of the University and working people, to be responsible under the Extension Delegacy for the conduct of tutorial classes.

The example of Oxford in this matter was of vital importance, for it was quickly followed by other universities embarking on tutorial class teaching. Although the original joint committee had strongly emphasised the importance of working-class control,[3] the decision of the University to accord equal representation to working people on a permanent committee was none the less remarkable. J. A. R. Marriott, the Oxford Extension Secretary at this time, clearly did not like it: he approved of the educational proposals put forward in the *Report*, but declined to concur in the proposed administrative changes.[4] He distrusted the demand from the left wing among the workers for some special kind of proletarian economics, and disliked the separation of working-class education from the main body of University Extension, which 'catered for all classes and in its summer schools brought all classes together'.[5]

Such was the beginning of the tutorial class movement, one of the great English contributions to the practice of adult education. The idea quickly caught the imagination alike of the universities and of

[1] Mansbridge, *op. cit.*, p. 194.

[2] *Oxford and Working-class Education, being the Report of a Joint Committee of University and Working-class Representatives on the Relation of the University to the Higher Education of Workpeople* (Oxford 1908, 2nd edn. 1909, reprinted 1951).

[3] *Op. cit.*, p. 51.

[4] *Op. cit.*, p. 90 note.

[5] Sir John Marriott, *Memories of Four Score Years* (1946), pp. 139–40.

working-class students, and by 1913–14 tutorial classes were being organised in association with every university and university college in England and Wales except Exeter and Southampton. Of the total of 142 classes (embracing over 3,000 students) 30 were organised by London, 18 by Oxford, 17 by Manchester, and 16 by Liverpool. The three Welsh colleges were responsible in all only for 11 classes, and the movement in Scotland was only just beginning to get under way.[1]

It should be remembered that all this was achieved at a time of great economic and political excitement. These years saw the struggle for the Parliament Act, the struggle for Irish Home Rule, the militant suffrage movement, the railway strike of 1911, and the miners' strike of 1912. Only Mansbridge, with his firm belief in objective education, could have piloted the W.E.A. through such a storm. Only he could have established and maintained the thin line of distinction between the educational aspect of the working-class movement, as represented by the W.E.A., and its political and economic aspects, as represented by the Labour Party, the trade unions, and the co-operative societies.

Most, though not all, tutorial classes were arranged in association with the W.E.A., and in the majority of cases the work was under the control of a university joint committee on the Oxford model.[2] In 1910 the universities formed a Central Joint Advisory Committee on Tutorial Classes, for the discussion of common problems: it was, it seems, the first time the universities had been persuaded to form any kind of joint committee.

Of the teaching costs the universities contributed nearly one-half, the Board of Education nearly one-third, and the balance was made up by grants from local education authorities and other sources (notably the Gilchrist Trust).[3] The Board's attitude was particularly helpful. 'We believe,' said the Permanent Secretary, Sir Robert Morant, at the Oxford conference in 1907, 'it is to small classes and solid, earnest work that we can give increasingly of the golden stream.' In the following year the Board's regulations for further education were amended to permit of a higher grant to tutorial classes, and in 1913 the Board issued special *Regulations for Tutorial*

---

[1] For a summary of the statistics see Adult Education Committee, *Final Report*, pp. 190–204. Interesting details regarding developments at individual universities are to be found in *W.E.A. Education Year Book, 1918*, pp. 286 sqq.

[2] Leeds and Sheffield had tripartite committees on which the West Riding County Council was also represented. The L.E.A.s also had substantial representation at Aberystwyth and Cardiff.

[3] Adult Education Committee, *Final Report*, p. 197; *Oxford and Working-class Education* pp. 103–4.

Classes, in which it undertook, under certain conditions, to meet half the tutor's fee up to a maximum of £30 per class.[1]

Characteristics of the Work

These years before the first World War were the heroic age of the tutorial class movement, and its admirers, not excluding Mansbridge himself, have at times been guilty of a certain romantic exaggeration in describing its achievements. The facts, however, as attested by official documents and statistics, are sufficiently remarkable.

A tutorial class comprised (as it still does) twenty-four two-hour meetings in each of three successive years. There were usually about 30 students,[2] mainly though not exclusively men, and mainly but not exclusively manual workers.[3] They came in search of knowledge, not certificates,[4] and their interest was principally in political and social subjects. Economics and economic history still accounted for more than half the classes in 1913–14, though almost from the beginning there were classes in literature (17 in 1913–14) and an occasional class in biology or natural history.[5] The enthusiasm and determination of the students was tremendous. In spite of overtime and changes of employment, attendance in each year generally exceeded 80 per cent, and often 90 per cent,[6] and about half the original students completed the three-year course.

The students of the first Longton tutorial class, not content with the burden of normal class work, organised and conducted at various times a weekly discussion class; a preparatory class for potential new students; and an essay-writing class. The students of the second class, which began in 1911, embarked on an ambitious scheme to carry liberal education to the mining villages of North Staffordshire, and quickly established ten village centres with classes conducted by tutorial class students. The same kind of missionary work was under-

[1] The relevant documents are reprinted in Mansbridge, *Tutorial Classes*, App. II.
[2] The Board, in its 1913 regulations, prescribed a maximum of 32, afterwards (1924) reduced to 24.
[3] Mansbridge sometimes claimed that the students were almost entirely manual workers, but in his *University Tutorial Classes*, pp. 54–5, he is much more cautious, and the statistics for the session 1911–12 which he prints in Appendix VII to this work (from the *Report* of the Central Joint Advisory Committee on Tutorial Classes), show that of the students whose occupations were known 20 per cent were 'clerical workers, telegraphists, etc.', 7 per cent teachers, and 4 per cent housewives. About 15 per cent of the total in that year were women.
[4] Certificates were offered or issued in a few instances, but met with little response—see Mansbridge, *Tutorial Classes*, p. 56; Kelly, *Outside the Walls*, pp. 57–8.
[5] Adult Education Committee, *Final Report*, p. 195.
[6] *Op. cit.*, p. 196.

taken by the tutorial class students of Rochdale, Battersea, Swindon, Leicester, and other centres.[1] Naturally working-class students, who had left school at 10–14 years of age, found difficulty in the reading of academic textbooks and in the writing of essays, especially as their home background seldom gave much opportunity for quiet study. It is not surprising, therefore, that the ideal of twelve essays per year from each student was one rarely achieved. But a tremendous amount of reading and writing *was* done,[2] and the quality of the best work was astonishingly high. Mansbridge liked to compare the work of tutorial classes with the work of university honours schools, and this standard was officially adopted by the Board of Education both in its 1908 regulations and in the special regulations of 1913.[3]

The comparison was not altogether extravagant, for many of these students were men and women of outstanding ability who in later times would have found their way to a grammar school or university.[4] A. L. Smith of Balliol, a great friend of the W.E.A., reported that

Twenty-five per cent of the essays examined by him after second year's work in two classes, and first year's work in six classes, were equal to the work done by students who gained first classes in the Final Schools of Modern History. He was astonished, not so much at the quality as at the quantity of the quality of the work done.[5]

A more sober, and probably a more just assessment, is to be found in a special report on tutorial classes prepared for the Board of Education by J. W. Headlam, H.M.I., and L. T. Hobhouse, Professor of Sociology in the University of London (1910). The report points out that it is 'a method of doubtful value' to compare work accomplished within the limits of a single subject, and in the scanty leisure of hard-worked men, with the work of undergraduates, which involves full-time study in a number of subjects, and presupposes an extensive preliminary education.

[1] Mansbridge, *Tutorial Classes*, Chs. vii–viii; Adult Education Committee, *Final Report*, pp. 296–309; J. A. Mack (ed.), *The History of Tunstall II Tutorial Class* (Tunstall 1935), Ch. ii. The Longton class still continues, and recently celebrated its fiftieth year.

[2] The early reports of the Central Joint Advisory Committee print details of the number of essays written. Of 31 classes of which particulars are recorded for 1909–10, 16 produced more than 200 essays each. A class on Economic History conducted by Henry Clay at Rochdale achieved the record total of 356 essays!

[3] The 1908 regulations prescribed that the course should be 'of a standard corresponding with that required for an Honours degree'. The 1913 regulations prescribed that 'The instruction must aim at reaching, within the limits of the subject covered, the standard of University work in Honours.'

[4] The first Rochdale and Longton classes contained several students who afterwards distinguished themselves in adult education or public affairs, the most notable example being A. P. Wadsworth, who became editor of the *Manchester Guardian*.

[5] Mansbridge, *Tutorial Classes*, p. 178.

The conditions differ, and the product is in some respects better and in others not so good. There is more maturity of mind and more grip of reality behind many of these papers. There is as a rule, naturally, less of the qualities arising out of a general literary education. If, however, the question be put whether, so far as they go, and within the limits of time and available energy the classes are conducted in the spirit which we have described, and tend to accustom the student to the ideal of work familiar at a University, we can answer with an unhesitating affirmative; and in particular, the treatment both of History and Economics is scientific and detached in character. As regards the standard reached, there are students whose essays compare favourably with the best academic work.[1]

One of the great difficulties facing tutorial classes was to secure an adequate supply of textbooks. To help meet this difficulty the W.E.A., in collaboration with Toynbee Hall, established in 1912 a small Central Library for Tutorial Classes. With generous help from the Carnegie Trust, this later became (1916) the Central Library for Students, reconstituted in 1930 as the National Central Library.[2]

The work of tutorial classes was also greatly strengthened by the opportunity of further study during the summer months. The first summer school for tutorial class students was arranged at Oxford, on the suggestion of A. L. Smith, in 1910, and the idea quickly spread to other universities. From 1919 Holybrook House, Reading, which had been placed at the disposal of the W.E.A. and was used during the winter as a centre for various adult education activities, arranged special summer courses to train tutorial class students for teaching work.[3]

One of the most striking features of the whole movement, indeed, was the alacrity with which it was taken up by the universities. This alacrity arose from a genuine desire to assist in the task of working-class education, but in the event the universities gained as much as they gave; for to those social and economic studies with which they were particularly concerned the experience of working men brought new ideas, new values, a new sense of realism, which in turn gave a new direction to university studies.

War-Time Developments

In 1915 Mansbridge was compelled by ill-health to resign the General Secretaryship of the W.E.A. By this time, fortunately, the

[1] Board of Education, *Special Report on Certain Tutorial Classes in Connection with the Workers' Educational Association* [1910], p. 2; Mansbridge, *Tutorial Classes*, App. III, p. 146. For further discussion of this point see Adult Education Committee, *Final Report*, pp. 62–8; S. G. Raybould, *University Standards in W.E.A. Work* (W.E.A., 1948); Kelly, *Outside the Walls*, Ch. 13.
[2] Mansbridge, *Trodden Road*, pp. 94–6.   [3] Price, *Story of the W.E.A.*, pp. 75–6.

foundations of the Association's work were solidly laid. It had, in 1914, 179 branches, 11,430 individual members, and 2,555 affiliated organisations—trade unions, co-operative societies, adult schools, working men's clubs, and a variety of other bodies. It had its own journal, *The Highway*, established in 1908, and a wide range of tutorial classes and other activities was being carried on under its auspices or on its initiative. Constitutionally it was developing along federal lines, and its branches were now grouped into nine districts (most of them with full-time secretaries), covering all England and Wales except the Cornish peninsula.[1]

Mansbridge was replaced as General Secretary by J. M. Mactavish, the radical trade unionist who had first made his mark at Oxford in 1907. The tradition of Christian democracy for which Mansbridge had stood, however, was still represented in the counsels of the W.E.A. in the rotund person of William Temple, who was elected as first President in 1908 and, though appointed Bishop of Manchester in 1921, continued in office until 1924. Mansbridge himself, when he recovered his health, turned his energies to other adult educational projects. In 1918 he founded the World Association for Adult Education, out of which sprang in turn, in 1921, the British Institute of Adult Education. Both these bodies were active throughout the inter-war years in promoting conferences and collecting and publishing information about various aspects of adult education. Another of his enterprises, of which more will be said in a later chapter, was the Seafarers' Education Service, founded in 1919.

The W.E.A., with its widespread national organisation, did not suffer nearly as much from the First World War as did University Extension. 'This crisis proves the need for our work as it has never been proved before', declared Temple in the autumn of 1914; 'let us then be up and doing.'[2] There was, of course, a setback in the work during the early years of the war, as tutors and students went off to war work or the armed forces, but by 1917 there was already a recovery. In 1918–19 the Association, with 219 branches, 557 classes (including 153 tutorial classes), and 12,438 students, was in every way stronger than it had been in 1913–14.[3] The most significant change was the increase in the proportion of women students. This was due, of course, in the first instance to the war, but it proved to be a

---

[1] In Scotland, where all classes, even tutorial classes, had to be under the control of the local School Boards, progress was very slow, but a beginning had been made in Edinburgh and Aberdeen—*W.E.A. Education Year Book, 1918*, pp. 314–16.

[2] Stocks, *op. cit.*, p. 65.

[3] These figures include a small body of work in Northern Ireland. Separate figures for Ireland are not available, but there were three tutorial classes under the auspices of Queen's University.

permanent trend. By the end of the war the W.E.A. had ceased to be predominantly a men's movement.[1]

The Labour College

By this time, too, the W.E.A. had a rival. The Labour College formed at Oxford by the Ruskin secessionists in 1909 had a hard struggle. After two years it moved to London, and there at length it succeeded in establishing itself with the help of certain trade unions, notably the South Wales Miners' Federation and the National Union of Railwaymen. In 1916 these two unions combined to take over full control and financial responsibility. The residential work of the College was suspended during the war, but correspondence courses continued, and a considerable number of classes were organised in the industrial areas of South Wales, Northern England, and the Clyde Valley. By 1918 there were said to be 5,000 students in attendance,[2] and in that year a Scottish Labour College was established at Glasgow. Ex-students and supporters were organised nationally in the Plebs League, which had a monthly journal, *The Plebs*. The teaching work was carried on without assistance from public funds, mainly by voluntary teachers.[3]

The trade unions were thus faced with competing philosophies of adult education. The work of the W.E.A. was rooted in the liberal, humane philosophy of the universities: it believed that truth was one, and that differences could be resolved by impartial study and discussion. The Labour College, on the other hand, based its work on the Marxian analysis of the class struggle, and offered an education 'designed to equip the workers for their struggle against capitalism and capitalist ideology'. It did not believe that impartiality was possible.[4] The W.E.A., being politically neutral, had the advantage in being able to draw on public funds, but the Labour College was able to claim support as the champion of independent working-class education. Most of the unions, confronted with these rival claims, declined to commit themselves wholeheartedly to either.

The Co-operative Movement

Although the advent of the W.E.A. and the development of the tutorial class inevitably steal the limelight in any presentation of the

---

[1] The percentage of women in tutorial classes rose from 16·5 per cent in 1912–13 to 39 per cent in 1917–18.

[2] Adult Education Committee, *Final Report*, p. 333.

[3] *Op. cit.*, pp. 222–4; *W.E.A. Education Year Book, 1918*, pp. 390–1; J. F. and W. Horrabin, *Working Class Education* (1924), pp. 46–53.

[4] J. F. Horrabin in *W.E.A. Education Year Book, 1918*, p. 391. In another article in this volume (pp. 370–3), G. D. H. Cole tries in vain to reconcile the two philosophies.

story of adult education at this period, it should be recognised that they are merely one facet of a general resurgence of working-class adult education during the first quarter of the century. The same spirit may be seen in the educational work of the co-operative movement. Much of this work, of course, was carried out through other organisations. In the nineteenth century the movement had supported University Extension. Now in the twentieth century it gave active assistance to the W.E.A., Ruskin College, the London Working Men's College, and other working-class educational enterprises, and many of its members participated in the work of these bodies. It also undertook, however, a small but significant amount of adult education on its own behalf.

We have seen that in the 'eighties and 'nineties much of the educational work of the co-operative societies was taken over by the local authorities, and that a beginning was made in developing new forms of education directed specifically to the needs of co-operators. When the First World War came the new model was firmly established. The number of students in classes organised by the Central Education Committee of the Co-operative Union increased from 2,416 in 1899–1900 to 21,953 in 1913–14, and although most of these classes were vocational in character, and designed for juniors, some 1,500 adults were attending classes not dissimilar in character to the elementary classes of the W.E.A. Of these 682 were attending special courses for women in co-operation and citizenship (a recent development); 463 were studying co-operation and 211 industrial history; and the remainder were taking classes in citizenship, economics, or elocution.

These figures are small beside those of the W.E.A., but a good deal of less formal educative work was also undertaken, especially through the meetings of the Women's Co-operative Guild. A Co-operative Men's Guild was founded in 1911, but did not really get going until after the war.

In all this work the Central Education Committee played an important part. It advised local societies, prepared programmes of studies and syllabuses of instruction, and organised a variety of week-end and summer schools. In 1915 an Adviser of Studies was appointed to co-ordinate the educational activities of the Committee, and in 1919 a Co-operative College was established, on a small scale, at Holyoake House, Manchester, the headquarters of the Co-operative Union.[1]

[1] Adult Education Committee, *Final Report*, pp. 236–9; H. J. Twigg, *Outline History of Co-operative Education* (Manchester 1924), Chs. v–vi and App. XIII.

Adult Schools

The general revival in working-class adult education is nowhere more strikingly illustrated than in the oldest movement of all—the adult school movement, which since its beginnings had always been concerned first and foremost with working people, often very humble people indeed. We have seen how in the last quarter of the nineteenth century the adult schools had adapted themselves to the new conditions of growing adult literacy, with the result that by 1899, when the National Council of Adult School Associations was created, there were 350 schools with 45,000 members. In the next few years the growth was phenomenal, and by 1909–10 the movement had reached a peak figure of over 1,900 schools and over 100,000 students. In 1914 there were still nearly 1,900 schools and over 80,000 students (42 per cent of them women).[1]

This growth was not, it should be said, evenly spread through the country. Yorkshire and the Midlands continued to be the main strongholds; Wales still had very few schools, and Scotland remained almost completely untouched. By 1909, however, the task of mapping England out into local Adult School Unions was virtually complete. This development was greatly aided by the decision of the Friends' First-Day School Association, in 1906, to dissolve its district organisation for adult schools, so that the Friends' schools might be free to join the non-denominational unions under the National Council. In 1914 the national body adopted its present title, the National Adult School Union.

Many of the traditional features of the adult schools survived into the new era. Bible study was still the central feature of the work, and the main classes still customarily met on Sundays, the men before morning service, the women in the afternoon (there were some mixed classes, but they were in a minority). These modern adult schools were, however, keenly interested in social problems, and more generally in the relation of religion to the changing currents of thought of the day; and these wider interests were reflected in a variety of subsidiary activities—lectures, classes, discussions, and study-circles on week-day evenings, and lecture schools at the week-end. A great many adult schools, indeed, were affiliated to local W.E.A. branches, and the central organisation became affiliated nationally in 1919. In 1911 the National Council inaugurated an annual *Adult School Lesson Handbook*, in order to assist local

[1] For the figures see *Adult School Year-Book and Directory* (N.A.S.U., 1901, 1903, and annually 1905–15).

schools to undertake more systematic educational work. The early *Handbooks* suggested schemes for Bible study, and listed allied subjects suitable for lectures and discussions, e.g. the story of Joseph in prison is linked with a study of prison reform, and Christ's words about our duty to our neighbours with a study of Mazzini's *Duties of Man*.[1] In 1917 correspondence courses were also inaugurated to encourage home study.[2]

Educational Settlements: Woodbrooke and Fircroft

Out of the alliance of the adult schools and the Quakers there came in the early years of the century a new development in English adult education—the educational settlement. The name settlement indicates the ancestry of the movement, and bears witness to the concern felt for social problems, but in organisation and methods the educational settlements were quite different from the settlements established in the late nineteenth century. These, with their characteristic mixture of education and social reclamation, still carried on their battle against poverty and squalor in the industrial towns, and quite a number of new settlements came into existence before and during the First World War, for example the University Settlements at Edinburgh (1905), Liverpool (1906), and Bristol (1911).[3]

The educational settlements, of which ten were founded (all in the Midlands or the North of England) between 1903 and 1918, were of two main types. The two earliest, Woodbrooke and Fircroft, were residential—after Ruskin the first residential colleges for adult education in Great Britain. The remaining eight were what we should now call non-residential centres. The two groups of institutions had, however, certain ideals in common: they held their primary purpose to be education, not social missionary work; they believed that adult education was fundamentally spiritual in character; and they believed that such education could only be effectively carried on in an atmosphere of fellowship.

Woodbrooke owed its origin to discussions at Quaker summer schools, in the closing years of the nineteenth century, on ways and means of bringing the traditional faith into line with modern discoveries in science and Biblical studies. It was about this time, it will be remembered, that Mansbridge was first expounding to the

---

[1] *Adult School Lesson Handbook* (1912).
[2] For this phase of the adult school movement see Adult Education Committee, *Final Report*, pp. 211–14; G. C. Martin, *The Adult School Movement* (1924), pp. 139–64 and Chs. vi, vii and x. E. Champness, *Adult Schools* (1941), is also of value.
[3] Others were at Chesterfield (1902), Red House, Leeds (1913), John Woolman House, Islington (1917), and Sheffield (1918). See *Handbook of Settlements in Great Britain* (c. 1922).

co-operative movement his plans for an alliance between labour and learning. In 1899 John Wilhelm Rowntree of York, a leading figure in the adult school movement, outlined in *Present Day Papers* a scheme for a kind of permanent summer school for the study and discussion of these problems. He did not want a theological college, but rather 'a Way-side Inn, a place where the dusty traveller, stepping aside for a moment from the thronged highway, shall find refreshment and repose'. George Cadbury generously offered Woodbrooke, his former family home at Selly Oak, near Birmingham, and in 1903 the Wood-brooke Settlement came into being, with J. Rendel Harris, the well-known Biblical scholar, as its first Director of Studies.

This new institution, conducted by a private trust, was not origin-ally envisaged as a long-term residential college, but as a community to which men and women of all ages and all religious denominations might come, for longer or shorter periods according to their circum-stances, to equip themselves by study and fellowship for some form of Christian service. As the years went by, however, Woodbrooke found itself the centre of a group of satellite colleges founded under various religious auspices, mostly to provide training for missionary work and other forms of religious service. Partly to meet the needs of these colleges, and partly to meet those of its own students, Wood-brooke was thus led to develop long and systematic courses for missionaries, teachers, Sunday school teachers, and social workers. Short courses continued to be provided, and the idea of a wayside inn was not entirely abandoned, but a year's residence came to be the norm.

An interesting feature of Woodbrooke's history is that almost from the first it had an Extension department, arranging lectures, con-ferences, week-end schools and summer schools for Friends' Meetings, adult schools, and others interested in religious and social questions.[1]

Fircroft, the second of the residential educational settlements, was one of the Selly Oak group. Founded by George Cadbury, junior, in 1909, in response to a demand from the adult school movement, it was designed as a centre to which working men 'might go for a week, a month, a term, or a year to study seriously, with a view to equipping themselves better as citizens, adult scholars or teachers'.[2] The fees were very low (£1 a week or £10 a term) and a number of

---

[1] A. S. Rowntree, *Woodbrooke: its History and Aims* (Birmingham 1923); A. G. Gardiner, *Life of George Cadbury* (1923), Ch. xi; R. Davis, *Woodbrooke, 1903–1953* (London 1953). In 1919 a Central Council was established for Woodbrooke and the four other Selly Oak colleges, and eventually central premises and staff were established to provide the basic courses formerly undertaken by Woodbrooke. The group now includes eleven colleges.

[2] H. G. Wood and A. E. Ball, *Tom Bryan, First Warden of Fircroft* (1922), p. 52.

bursaries were made available by adult schools and from private sources.

Like Woodbrooke, with which it was from the first closely associated, Fircroft quickly assumed the character of a long-term residential college, while continuing to meet the needs of a certain number of short-term students. By 1912 ninety long-term students had been in residence. Fircroft also resembled Woodbrooke in developing a considerable range of extension activities, including, in the early years, correspondence courses.

The direction of Fircroft was placed in the hands of a committee representing Woodbrooke, the National Council of Adult School Associations, and the W.E.A., but the principal factor in shaping the early tradition of the college was the character and personality of the first Warden, Tom Bryan. Bryan began his working life as a hosiery packer in Leicester, but afterwards graduated at Glasgow and trained as a Congregational minister. On the completion of his training, however, he turned to social and educational work, and he served for eight years at the Browning Settlement in Walworth before joining the staff at Woodbrooke in 1903. He was a keen adult school worker, and he was also tremendously impressed by the achievements of the Danish Folk High Schools, which he first visited in 1905.

The characteristic features of the college under his leadership were, first, its wide-ranging curriculum, embracing not only history, economics, literature, and Bible studies but also natural science, gardening, and physical training; and second, a strong emphasis on community living. In a last message written shortly before his early death in 1917, at a time when Fircroft was closed as a result of the war, he described the college as not only 'a school for the education in the humanities of working men', but also 'a Koinonia, a community, in English, a fellowship'. 'Fircroft', he declared, 'was fashioned with the Danish High School as its model, adapted, of course, and altered to suit English conditions and English life.'[1]

Non-Residential Settlements

The first of the non-residential educational settlements was Swarthmore, at Leeds, established in 1909. It was a Quaker foundation and included a considerable proportion of adult school students among its members. It was concerned especially with equipping

[1] M. E. Pumphrey, *Recollections of Fircroft* (1952), p. 20. The first four chapters of this work are valuable on the early history of Fircroft. See also Wood and Ball, *op. cit.*, and W. H. Leighton, *Fircroft 1909–1959* (Fircroft 1959), Ch. i.

men and women for religious and educational work, e.g. in adult schools, Sunday schools, and the Quaker ministry. St. Mary's Settlement, York, founded later in the same year by Arnold S. Rowntree, sought to attract thoughtful working men and women, and emphasised the importance of connecting 'all our education with our social life, with our fellowship as human beings'. Both of these offered instruction in religious subjects, and also in secular subjects such as history, economics, and literature, and both undertook Extension work at other centres. In each case the programme included a W.E.A. tutorial class.

The Settlement at Lemington-on-Tyne, near Newcastle, and the Homestead at Wakefield, were both founded in 1913, and were alike in centring their activities on adult school work. Beechcroft, Birkenhead, opened in 1914, broke new ground. The aim of its founder and first warden, Horace Fleming, was to provide a meeting-ground for all local organisations engaged in adult education, to create 'a fellowship of all who are anxious for the betterment of society'.[1]

In two addresses delivered in 1922 Fleming admirably expounded the aims of the educational settlement movement as a whole:

We believe that man is a spiritual being, and that the universe has a spiritual basis, and that it is only when man is able to dwell on the plane of admiration, hope and love, that he will find his life worth while.[2]

The aim is to help men and women to enter fully into life, to be of service to the world in which they find themselves, to have wide interests and large views: to recognise the substance of the spirit rather than the shadow of the label. In other words, it is to lead men out of the insular, the sectarian and the personal into the wide expansiveness of the Kingdom of God, and to teach them to judge their lives, their interests and their politics by its standards.[3]

The environment which a Settlement seeks to provide is that of fellowship. In its warmth, many a dwarfed and sullen spirit has budded and flowered into a valued personality. It is something more than the college atmosphere, though that is part of it. It is a thing of the spirit, and in its glow men are freed, for the time, from their bondage to sect, party or class, and become members of a family.[4]

In spite of the war Beechcroft quickly achieved a remarkable measure of success. It had its origins in W.E.A. and adult school

---

[1] F. J. Gillman, *The Workers and Education* [1916], p. 20.

[2] H. Fleming, *The Philosophy of Settlements* (Beechcroft Bulletin No. 4, Birkenhead 1922), p. 6.

[3] H. Fleming, *Education Through Settlements* (Beechcroft Bulletin No. 2, Birkenhead 1922), p. 5.

[4] *Op. cit.*, p. 3.

work, and these organisations at once made their home there. Provision was also made for classes for the local Trades Council and two railwaymen's unions, women's study circles, a youth club, a Sunday morning meeting, and a variety of other activities. The University of Liverpool interested itself keenly in the work, and was strongly represented on the governing council formed in 1917.

At least one further educational settlement came into existence before the end of the war. This was Rowancroft at Scarborough, founded in 1918 and described as 'open to all who wish to unite in studying the vital questions of the day'. It was not, however, until after the war that the emergence of this new type of adult education organisation was recognised by the establishment in 1920 of the Educational Settlements Association.[1]

The importance of the non-residential educational settlements has, I think, been underestimated. They never became very numerous or very strong, but they represented a re-statement in the twentieth century of the belief that had led fifty years before to the foundation of the working men's colleges, namely that adult education, to be successful, must have both a home and a spirit.

Other Organisations

Of the original working men's colleges only those at London and Leicester still survived, but the London Working Women's College and Morley College ('for working men and women') were carrying on similar work. All these were adapting themselves in various ways to changing conditions. The London Working Men's College and Morley College became from 1909 centres for W.E.A. tutorial classes, and at Morley there was an astonishing growth of musical activities under the inspired guidance of the musical director, Gustav Holst.[2]

Closely allied to the work of the adult schools and educational settlements was the adult educational work carried out under the auspices of the churches. This was very considerable, though its precise extent cannot be statistically computed. The Congregationalists, Wesleyan Methodists, and Unitarians all had social service

---

[1] For the educational settlements of this period see Gillman, *op. cit.*, pp. 13–33; Adult Education Committee, *Final Report*, pp. 233–5; *Handbook of Settlements*; H. Fleming, *Beechcroft: the Story of the Birkenhead Settlement 1914–1924* (1938); Swarthmore Centre, *An Experiment in Adult Education in the City of Leeds, 1909–1949* (Leeds, 1949); A. J. Allaway *The Educational Centres Movement* (1961). The date of the foundation of the E.S.A. is sometimes wrongly given as 1914.

Ch. ii of Gillman's book also gives an account of the various adult school guest-houses and holiday homes, which frequently provided accommodation for week-end schools and other educational activities.

[2] J. F. C. Harrison, *History of the Working Men's College, 1854–1954* (1954), Ch. vi; D. Richards, *Offspring of the Vic: a History of Morley College* (1958), Ch. viii.

organisations which promoted lantern lectures, classes, and study circles for the study of social and economic problems. The Friends undertook similar work through their Central Study Committee and their Committee on War and the Social Order. The Catholic Social Guild, founded in 1909, had 100 study clubs by 1914: it supplied books and pamphlets, produced outline courses of study, conducted correspondence courses, and organised examinations on the results of which certificates and diplomas were awarded. The Church of England had the Church Tutorial Classes Association, founded by Mansbridge in 1917 for the study on tutorial class lines 'of the Christian faith, its origins, history and teaching, and of its application to modern life and problems'. All this work was in addition to the specifically religious teaching given through Bible classes and the like, and illustrates once more the great stirring of social conscience that lay behind so many of the adult educational movements of this period.[1]

[1] Adult Education Committee, *Final Report*, pp. 251–5. B. A. Yeaxlee, *Spiritual Values in Adult Education* (1924–5), Vol. II, pp. 62–92, 225–350, is also of value, though referring for the most part to a later period. For the Church Tutorial Classes see Mansbridge, *Kingdom of the Mind*, pp. 38–44, and *The Trodden Road*, p. 103.

16

The Twentieth Century

LIBERAL ADULT EDUCATION BETWEEN
THE WARS

The Adult Education Committee

IN 1917 the Reconstruction Committee presided over by Lloyd
George appointed a special committee to report on adult education.
Its Chairman was A. L. Smith, and its Secretaries were Arthur
Greenwood, afterwards Minister of Health in the first Labour
Government, and E. S. Cartwright, a former Longton student who
had become first organising secretary to the Oxford Tutorial
Classes Committee.[1] Mansbridge and Tawney were inevitably among
the members. The *Final Report* of this committee, published in 1919,
was the first and is still the most comprehensive survey of the history
and organisation of adult education in this country. It recommended,
in general, a much larger expenditure of public funds on adult
education, and it also made a number of specific recommendations.
Amongst these were:

That 'adult education should cater for the varied needs and tastes of
the people'. It should therefore include not only citizenship studies but
science, music and languages, literature and drama, and craftsmanship.

That 'the provision of a liberal education for adults should be regarded
by universities as a normal and necessary part of their functions'.

That each university should establish a department of extra-mural
adult education, with an academic head and adequate teaching and
administrative staff, to develop and co-ordinate the various branches of the
work.

That University Extension courses should be eligible for government
grant.

That joint committees of education authorities, universities and
voluntary bodies should be established to do for non-university adult
education what the university joint committees had done for tutorial
classes.

That local education authorities should establish evening institutes for

---

[1] On Cartwright see H. P. Smith, 'Edward Stuart Cartwright', in *Rewley House Papers*,
Vol. III, No. 1 (1949–50), pp. 8–24.

social, recreational and educational activities, especially for young people.

That generous help should be given to the establishment of village institutes, and that experiments should be made in the establishment of residential colleges in rural areas.

These recommendations, most of which, as we shall see, were eventually implemented, were a powerful factor in the development of adult education between the wars.[1]

In liberal adult education during this period the alliance of the universities and the W.E.A. was still the dominant feature, and in spite of setbacks due to the post-war depression, the great slump of 1931, and the consequent economy campaigns, the two partners steadily expanded both their own work and the work they had in common. In describing this development it will be convenient to deal first with England and Wales, since the position in Scotland was rather different.

The expansion of the work was greatly assisted by more liberal grants from the Board of Education. New and more comprehensive regulations for adult education issued in 1924 enabled the universities to claim grant not only on tutorial classes and classes preparatory or supplementary thereto, but also, for the first time, on Extension courses; and the same regulations established a category of 'approved associations', of which the W.E.A. was the most important, which might claim grant on one-year and terminal courses. The universities and approved associations were designated as 'Responsible Bodies'. Under amended regulations of 1931 designed particularly to encourage the development of work in the rural areas, the Board agreed to contribute to the salaries of full-time organising tutors appointed by the universities; and at the same time both the universities and the W.E.A. were enabled to claim grant on short pioneer courses of six lectures and upwards. The development of this more elementary work was further facilitated by the amended regulations of 1938.[2]

The Development of University Extra-Mural Departments

The universities, for their part, undertook a fairly comprehensive reorganisation of their extra-mural machinery. Many of the English universities, following the advice of the Adult Education Committee, and the example set by Nottingham in 1920, replaced the *ad hoc* and

---

[1] For the significance and influence of the Report see Professor R. D. Waller's Introduction to the abridged reprint published in 1956 under the title *Design for Democracy*.

[2] The Board's regulations and their effects are analysed in detail in S. G. Raybould *The English Universities and Adult Education* (1951), Apps. I and II.

often ill co-ordinated committees which had done duty in the past by a special Department of Extra-Mural Studies, with a full-time head of senior academic standing. Others, without creating a special department, none the less appointed a full-time director or similar official to co-ordinate the work. By 1939 the only English universities which had not either an extra-mural department or a director were Leeds and Sheffield, which still limited their provision almost entirely to tutorial classes, and Reading, which operated only within the borough boundaries. In Wales Aberystwyth appointed a director as early as 1920, and in 1922 a central University Extension Board was established at Cardiff to assist and co-ordinate the work of the four colleges.

As time went on the universities gradually defined their extra-mural areas, limiting themselves for the most part to the region immediately contiguous to the university centre.[1] The W.E.A. elaborated its district organisation on similar lines, so that by 1939 the whole country was covered by a network of 23 extra-mural areas (3 of them attached to Oxford), in each of which there was machinery for collaboration with the appropriate W.E.A. district.[2] From 1923 the operations of the Central Joint Advisory Committee on Tutorial Classes were supplemented by periodical meetings of extra-mural officers, which took formal shape in 1926 as the Universities Extra-Mural Consultative Committee.

The universities also expanded their teaching staffs, especially in the 'thirties when government assistance became available. In 1924-5 there were already a score of full-time tutors at work; by 1939 there were 84, more than one-third of them organising tutors grant-aided by the Board.[3]

Extra-mural teaching programmes expanded between the wars both in numbers and in scope. The largest increase was in tutorial and allied classes arranged in collaboration with the W.E.A., which grew in numbers from 147, with 3,404 students, in 1918-19, to 882, with 14,953 students, in 1937-8.[4] Basically these courses remained

[1] For historical reasons Oxford took responsibility not only for its own home territory but also for two outlying areas—Kent and East Sussex, and North Staffordshire; and both Oxford and Cambridge retained extra-territorial rights in certain centres, e.g. Oxford in Lincoln, and Cambridge in Southport.

[2] In some cases a W.E.A. district covers more than one extra-mural area, e.g. the Northern District includes both Durham and Newcastle. In Wales the boundary between the two W.E.A. districts bisects the Aberystwyth extra-mural area. See the map in R. Peers, *Adult Education: a Comparative Study* (1958), p. 105.

[3] Wales had 14, Oxford 11, Leeds 8, Bristol, Hull, and Nottingham 7, Birmingham and Cambridge 6—Universities Extra-Mural Consultative Committee, *Report on the War Years, 1939-40 to 1944-45* (1947), p. 34.

[4] Board of Education, *Statistics of Public Education*, 1919-20, *Report*, 1938.

what they had always been—small, intimate groups of earnest students engaged in systematic study over a long period under the guidance of a university tutor. But thirty years inevitably brought changes, and in particular a great widening of the range of subjects studied. Classes in economics and other social sciences, which had formed more than four-fifths of the total in 1913–14, continued to increase in numbers but formed an ever-dwindling proportion of the whole. There was, in fact, a swing away from the social sciences in the direction of philosophy and psychology, literature and music, and to a lesser extent science. Art, as a subject for tutorial classes, first makes its appearance in the 'thirties.[1]

The students remained, as we shall see, substantially working-class,[2] but working-class with a difference. The development of secondary education, linked with the scholarship system, meant that many working men who in the old days would have been leading members of tutorial classes were selected for secondary education, perhaps even university education; while others, thanks to improvements in primary education, entered the classes with a better educational background than was formerly the case.

It was perhaps for this reason that tutorial class students showed themselves less willing than formerly to undertake the discipline of written work. In the Manchester area, where in 1921–2 the classes were producing essays at the rate of about 200 a year, the number by 1929–30 seldom exceeded 20–30 per class.[3] Experience in other areas seems to have been similar.[4] Whether this reduction in the quantity of written work necessarily implies a general falling-off in standards is a debatable point, but certainly in other respects—in students' reading and discussion, in the quality of the teaching, and in the relationship between tutor and student, the standard seems to have remained as high as ever.

For University Extension work there are no comprehensive figures available until 1924–5, but between that year and 1937–8 the total programme increased from 360 to 537 courses. Since the increase was mainly in the longer courses, i.e. courses of terminal

---

[1] C.J.A.C., *Annual Reports*, 1913–14 sqq. The subject groupings here are, of course, open to question, but even if we count philosophy and psychology with the social sciences these still form a smaller proportion of the total in 1937–8.

[2] See below, p. 275.

[3] T. Kelly, *Outside the Walls* (Manchester 1950), p. 74.

[4] Cf. Board of Education, *Adult Education in Yorkshire* (1928), p. 24: 'there is some evidence to show that whilst the present generation have had a better educational preparation, they are not quite so willing as their predecessors to make sacrifices for their tutorial class. With some of the older students also the novelty has to some extent worn off, and, owing to long familiarity with tutors and fellow students, they are apt to be too much at ease in Zion.'

length and over, these figures really understate the extent of the development. The provision of shorter courses, in spite of the encouragement offered by the 1931 regulations, steadily declined in number: in 1924–5 they accounted for nearly half the total, in 1937–8 for less than one-seventh.[1]

It is of interest also to note that as the work expanded, so did the participation of the newer universities, and especially some of the university colleges—Hull, Leicester, Newcastle, Nottingham, and Southampton. In the years before the first World War, University Extension was almost a monopoly of Oxford, Cambridge, and London; by 1937–8 these universities were responsible for only about two-fifths of the total provision, the remainder being shared among 17 universities and colleges.[2]

Throughout the inter-war years Oxford, Cambridge, and London continued to organise a considerable number of courses of the older type, in which the lecture, attended by a fairly large audience, was followed by a class for a smaller group of students who were prepared to undertake reading and written work, and might sit for an examination. Elsewhere, however, there was a tendency for the special characteristics of this type of course to be lost, and for the lecture audience to become identical with the class.[3]

Certain universities and colleges, not content with tutorial classes and Extension courses, undertook also classes of a more elementary type, of the kind usually provided only by the approved associations. The lead in this development came from Nottingham. Here the Department of Adult Education, under the vigorous direction of Robert Peers (from 1923 the country's first Professor of Adult Education), set out to provide a complete and comprehensive scheme of adult education for the whole East Midlands area. Under an arrangement antedating the establishment of the Department, the Joint Committee for Tutorial Classes was already responsible not only for tutorial and allied classes but also for W.E.A. one-year and terminal classes. In the early 'twenties the Department extended its field of activities to embrace classes conducted in collaboration with the miners' welfare organisations, and the newly established Rural Community Councils. The result was a really remarkable expansion of adult educational activities among the small towns and villages of the East Midlands. For the conduct of this elementary work with the W.E.A. and other bodies the Joint Committee

[1] U.E.M.C.C., *Annual Report*, 1937–8, p. 20.
[2] U.E.M.C.C., *Annual Report*, 1937–8.
[3] Raybould, *op. cit.*, pp. 78, 121–2, 126.

was specially recognised by the Board as an approved association.[1]

Cambridge and Leicester, which also had considerable rural areas to provide for, followed a similar policy in the 'thirties, though not on so extensive a scale as Nottingham.[2] Bristol, by contrast, developed a comprehensive scheme under which in each county a university resident tutor collaborated with an adult education committee through which courses were allocated to the local authority, the W.E.A., or the university as might be appropriate. Even under this scheme, however, the university tutors were responsible for a certain amount of pioneer work.[3]

As a result of these developments, and the changes noted above in the character of Extension courses, there was undoubtedly a tendency by the late 'thirties for the line between extra-mural work and the work of the approved associations to become increasingly blurred. The 1938 regulations attempted to clarify the position by introducing a new category, the 'university sessional class', which was intended to be at first-year tutorial class level, and took the place of the former preparatory tutorial classes and also of many university one-year classes. Some critics, however, have taken the view that the expansion of the universities into the field of pioneer courses was fundamentally a mistake, and that they should have limited themselves strictly to advanced work.[4]

A notable feature of extra-mural work between the wars is that for the first time English developments found an effective parallel in Wales. The native forms of Welsh culture were still flourishing at the close of the first World War,[5] but the W.E.A. tutorial class, perhaps because it was so closely akin to the traditional forms, had at last succeeded in making a lodgment. In the post-war years the number of these classes rapidly increased, until by 1933 there were over 100, besides a considerable number of preparatory classes. In the mean-

---

[1] R. Peers, 'The Nottingham Experiment in Adult Education, 1920–1935', in World Association for Adult Education, *Bulletin*, 2nd Ser., No. II (Aug. 1935); H. L. Featherstone, 'The Cultural Education of Miners', *ibid.*, No. XVIII (Aug. 1939). An excellent account of what is described as 'one of the most complete schemes yet launched in this country' is given in Board of Education, Adult Education Committee, *Adult Education and the Local Authority* (1933), pp. 28–34.

[2] Raybould, *op. cit.*, App. II. Nottingham shared responsibility for work in the county of Leicester, and from the early 'twenties tutorial classes and W.E.A. one-year and terminal classes there were administered through a joint Committee for Adult Education centred on Loughborough College. For details of this unusual arrangement see Board of Education, Adult Education Committee, *op. cit.*, App. II.

[3] Board of Education, Adult Education Committee, *op. cit.*, pp. 41–4.

[4] This is the viewpoint of Professor Raybould in the work already cited. For the opposing point of view, and for a valuable first-hand account of extra-mural development during this period, see Peers, *Adult Education*, Ch. iv.

[5] See the enthusiastic description in Ministry of Reconstruction, Adult Education Committee, *Final Report*, pp. 276 sqq.

time, from 1926–7 onwards, there had again been cautious experiments in the way of Extension courses. These courses were used particularly for pioneering work in the country districts, and proved so successful that provision continued to expand until the eve of the second World War.[1]

The Growth of the W.E.A.

Besides collaborating with the universities in the development of tutorial classes, the W.E.A. steadily increased its own provision of more elementary classes. Its one-year, terminal, and shorter courses numbered, in 1924–5, 682, with 17,131 students; by 1938–9 the total had reached 2,172, with 39,844 students.[2] From 1927 onwards a special effort was made, with the help of grants from the Carnegie and Cassel Trusts, to develop W.E.A. work in the rural areas. By 1931 seven full-time resident tutors were at work, and by 1935, when the Carnegie grant ended, a solid foundation had been laid for future development.[3]

The Association also created special machinery to promote education among trade unionists. The Workers' Educational Trade Union Committee, created in 1919, was originally a partnership between the W.E.A. and the Iron and Steel Trades Confederation, but a dozen other unions affiliated to the scheme during the 'twenties, among them the Post Office Workers, the Railway Clerks, the Engineering and Shipbuilding Draughtsmen, and the Operative Printers. The unions supplied the funds for the education of their members, and the work was carried out through the central and district organisation of the W.E.A., with the help of local W.E.T.U.C committees.[4]

The success of these trade union developments owed much in their early phases to Mactavish, Mansbridge's successor as General Secretary. Unfortunately he had to resign in 1928, and his two immediate successors held office only for short periods, but in 1934 the reins fell into the hands of Ernest Green, whose combination of

---

[1] Board of Education, Welsh Department, *Report on Adult Education in Wales* (1936); University of Wales, Extension Board, *Survey of Adult Education in Wales* (privately published, Cardiff 1940).
[2] *W.E.A.: A Retrospect 1903–1953* (1953), pp. 12–13. These totals include Scotland and Northern Ireland, but the number of classes and students in these areas was small.
[3] M. D. Stocks, *The Workers' Educational Association: the First Fifty Years* (1953), p. 115. For details of the development schemes see Board of Education, Adult Education Committee, *op. cit.*, Ch. ii, *passim*. M. Hansome, *World Workers' Educational Movements* (Columbia Univ. P., Chicago 1931), pp. 314–33, gives an excellent critical account of the W.E.A. as it was about 1928.
[4] Stocks, *Workers' Educational Association*, Ch. vii.

idealism and shrewd realism was to serve the movement well for the next sixteen years.[1]

The Changing Pattern of Relationships

Before we conclude this account of university–W.E.A. work, we must draw attention to certain fundamental changes in the general pattern of the work. In the first place there was a change in the nature of the university–W.E.A. relationship. At the end of the first World War, when the tutorial class was the chief form of extra-mural activity, the relationship was close and intimate, and the W.E.A. was the dominant partner. When, however, the new extra-mural departments came into the field, and began to deploy the resources increasingly made available to them by the universities and the state, the volume of non-W.E.A. work carried on under university auspices grew, and the universities recovered the independence which, under the spell of Albert Mansbridge, they had virtually lost. Since the W.E.A. was also developing its own independent body of work, the partnership between the Association and the universities inevitably became less close, less all-embracing, than it had once been.

A second and consequential change was that the universities began to move away from their former almost exclusive preoccupation with the education of the workers for social emancipation, and began to look at adult education more in terms of the cultural needs of society as a whole. Thus Professor Peers, writing of his work at Nottingham, describes it as an 'attempt at a comprehensive treatment of adult education over the whole area'.[2]

Finally we may note that the W.E.A. itself was becoming less exclusively concerned with working-class students and with the subjects formerly considered most appropriate to such students, i.e. history, politics, and above all economics. This tendency was less marked, at this period, than is often supposed, and can easily be exaggerated.

As far as subjects are concerned, the decline in the proportion of classes in social studies to which attention has been drawn in the case of tutorial classes was not paralleled in the W.E.A.'s more elementary classes. The range of subjects was indeed broadened greatly, but during the 'thirties the proportion of classes in the social sciences, taking the W.E.A. programme as a whole, actually increased.[3]

[1] Op. cit., pp. 97, 114, 152.
[2] Peers, 'The Nottingham Experiment', loc. cit., p. 11.
[3] See the tables in S. G. Raybould, The W.E.A.—The Next Phase (1949), pp. 103–6.

The extent of working-class student participation is impossible to determine with precision, but a careful examination of the annual reports of the Central Joint Advisory Committee suggests that before the war nearly four-fifths of tutorial class students were working-class, and that between the wars the proportion remained fairly steady at about two-thirds, with a slight decline towards the end of the period.[1]

The Position in Scotland

In Scotland the development of extra-mural and W.E.A. work was still, at the close of the inter-war years, rather embryonic. The four universities all had advisory adult education committees which included representatives of the universities, the L.E.A.s (which had replaced the old school boards in 1918), and the W.E.A.; and Aberdeen University used this machinery as a means of promoting a few university courses. Edinburgh and Glasgow also arranged courses, operating through special Extra-Mural Committees. Apart from this limited university provision, however, and a few classes conducted by university settlements, virtually all adult education was controlled by the local education authorities. The W.E.A., though it had established a Scottish district in 1919 and took financial responsibility for a few classes, had no independent providing powers and had to operate for the most part through the local authorities.

A survey of work in the session 1938–9, undertaken by the Scottish Branch of the Institute of Adult Education, shows how inadequate the total provision was.[2] The number of courses in operation in the spring term of 1939 was 271, of which 189 were conducted by local education authorities, 47 by universities, 30 by university settlements, and 5 (in Glasgow) by the W.E.A. The total student enrolment was 9,300. It is notable that 64 per cent of the classes were held in the four large cities—Edinburgh, Glasgow, Aberdeen, and Dundee—and 61 per cent in the West of Scotland. The Highlands were totally unrepresented.

[1] I arrive at these proportions by extracting from the C.J.A.C. figures three broad groups of occupations which seem to me to represent roughly the working-class element—manual trades, clerical and supervisory workers, and shopkeepers and assistants—and by excluding from consideration housewives and domestic workers, whose social status is insufficiently defined. Of the three groups the one that shows the most marked decline is the clerical and supervisory group.

Figures for all W.E.A. classes, given in Raybould, op. cit., pp. 103–6, suggest if treated in the same way a figure of about 70 per cent for working-class students from 1931–2 to 1938–9.

[2] C. Cochrane and D. M. Stewart, Survey of Adult Education in Scotland, 1938–39 (Edinburgh 1944). Cf. W. H. Marwick, 'Adult Education in Scotland', in World Association for Adult Education, Bulletin, 2nd Ser., No. XL (Feb. 1945).

Nearly all the classes were conducted under the Adult Education (Scotland) Regulations of 1934, which were modelled on the English regulations of 1924 and included provision for two-year tutorial classes in which the work 'approximates to a University standard'. In practice classes were normally arranged on a sessional or terminal basis, and only six of the classes under review were described as tutorial, but the report classifies 47 (presumably the 47 university courses) as 'intended to be progressive over a period of years'. The students were drawn, as in England, from a variety of occupational and educational backgrounds, but since only half of them made returns it is not possible to make any valid comparisons.

The Y.M.C.A.

Apart from the W.E.A., the bodies operating as 'approved associations' in England and Wales were, in 1924–5, the National Council of Y.M.C.A.s, the Welsh National Council of Y.M.C.A.s, the National Industrial Alliance, and the Educational Settlements Association. The (Welsh) University Council of Music, and certain residential colleges, were added later.[1] The grant-aided work of these bodies, though small compared with that of the W.E.A., had its own distinctive character, and was often supplemented by a considerable body of less formal work.

The extensive educational work carried out by the Y.M.C.A. among H.M. Forces during the war[2] resulted in a re-formulation of its educational policy. A statement drawn up in 1919 stressed that an adequate educational programme should be a feature of every Y.M.C.A. centre, and that its aim should be 'so to increase acquaintance with facts, strengthen power of thought and judgment, and quicken imagination as to equip for the fullest life and service all members and adherents of the Association'. The emphasis should be on non-vocational subjects, but the centres should avoid trying to duplicate services which could be better provided by L.E.A.s, universities, or the W.E.A. The special educational mission of the Y.M.C.A., it was suggested, lay in informal work with those not sufficiently trained to take advantage of formal academic instruction.[3]

In the early post-war years a serious attempt was made to imple-

[1] The Board of Education's figures for this work include courses arranged by universities active in this field, e.g. Nottingham. In some areas, e.g. Cornwall, the approved association for W.E.A. work was a joint W.E.A.–L.E.A. Adult Education Committee.

[2] See below, pp. 304–7.

[3] *Education in the Y.M.C.A. Programme* (Y.M.C.A., 2nd edn. 1920), pp. 1–5. This handbook is evidently the work of B. A. Yeaxlee, who was at this time Secretary of the Y.M.C.A. Education Committee, and who had been a member of the Adult Education Committee of the Ministry of Reconstruction.

ment this policy. In particular the Y.M.C.A. began to make a contribution to the development of adult education in rural areas, and for some years full-time education officers were at work in Oxfordshire and Wales. In 1926–7 the programme of English and Welsh centres included 3 Extension courses, 5 tutorial classes, and 87 shorter courses, besides much less formal work.[1] Owing to the decentralisation of the Association it is difficult to follow the course of events in later years, but in the 'thirties industrial depression and, according to Edwin Barker, 'moral disillusionment' seem to have led to a certain waning of enthusiasm. The Association still continued, however, to sponsor a considerable amount of educational work, especially work of an informal and pioneer character, such as popular lectures, study circles, discussion groups, and cultural societies.[2]

The Y.W.C.A., though not an approved association, was also in the 'twenties developing an increasing programme of educational work, with classes ranging from Bible study and international affairs to physical culture, singing, and domestic crafts.[3]

The National Industrial Alliance

The National Industrial Alliance was founded in 1916 'to negative the idea that there is an essential antagonism between the interest of employers and employed'. Unlike the W.E.A., it tended to operate mainly through the large industrial and commercial concerns, and in the 'twenties it was active in promoting classes in economics for management and employees. These were organised either independently by the Alliance or through the machinery of University Extension. It had some 1,500 students in classes in 1924–5, and 2,000 in 1926–7, but its work dwindled to very small proportions after the slump of 1931.[4]

Educational Settlements: the Mission to South Wales

The Educational Settlements Association, founded in 1920, steadily expanded its work during the inter-war years. Several new settlements were established in the 'twenties, including such now well-known institutions as the Folk House at Bristol (1920), which

---

[1] There are no comparable figures for Scotland.
[2] Board of Education, Adult Education Committee, *The Development of Adult Education in Rural Areas* (1922), pp. 9–10; B. A. Yeaxlee, *Spiritual Values in Adult Education* (1924–5), Vol. II, pp. 351–64; Z. F. Willis, 'The Y.M.C.A. and Adult Education', in *Journal of Adult Education*, Vol. III (1928–9); E. Barker, 'The Y.M.C.A. and Adult Education', in World Association for Adult Education, *Bulletin*, 2nd Ser., No. XXXII (Feb. 1943).
[3] B. A. Yeaxlee (ed.), *Handbook and Directory of Adult Education, 1928–29*, p. 79.
[4] *Handbook and Directory of Adult Education, 1926–27*, pp. 89–90; *1928–29*, pp. 87–8; T. Kelly, *Adult Education in Liverpool* (Liverpool 1960), p. 43.

was a joint enterprise of a Baptist mission and the Bristol Adult School Union; and the Percival Guildhouse, Rugby (1925), which was founded on the initiative of the W.E.A. and local adult schools.[1] By 1939 there were 27 affiliated or associated settlements and 7 affiliated colleges. The development on the educational side is indicated by the class programme for 1938–9, which, excluding the residential colleges, comprised 34 university tutorial classes, 17 other university courses, 76 W.E.A. classes, 44 Y.M.C.A. short courses, 279 L.E.A. classes, and 317 classes (23 of them grant-earning) organised by the settlements themselves—a total of 767 classes with nearly 15,000 students. The subjects covered the whole gamut of non-vocational studies from philosophy to pewter work.

One has the impression that in their zeal for education some of the settlements were losing something of the social and spiritual impulse which had originally inspired the movement. This was certainly not the case, however, in South Wales, where a group of nine settlements founded between 1927 and 1937 found themselves impelled by the needs of that distressed area to embark on social relief work on a scale comparable with that of the older settlements of the late nineteenth century. They did, of course, provide a considerable range of educational work within their own walls, some of it at a high level; but they also provided advice and specialist instruction for all kinds of groups outside—clubs, drama groups, choirs, discussion groups, craft centres, and the like. Maes-yr-haf, at Trealaw, in the Rhondda valley, which was the first to be founded and had its origin in Quaker relief work, organised clubs and occupational centres for unemployed men, women's clubs, a weaving and handicrafts centre, and a pottery industry.[2]

The formal educational work of these Welsh settlements was carried out, not through the Educational Settlements Association, but through the other approved associations operating in Wales. These included not only the W.E.A. and the Y.M.C.A., but also the University Council of Music—a unique institution founded in 1919

---

[1] The building was provided by old scholars of Rugby School as a memorial to Dr. John Percival, on whom see above, pp. 228, 230.

[2] Educational Settlements Association, *Neighbourhood Education* (1940), gives a good general survey. See also B. A. Yeaxlee (ed.), *Settlements and their Outlook* (International Conference of Settlements, 1922), Ch. iii; Yeaxlee, *Spiritual Values in Adult Education* (1924–5), Vol. II, pp. 381–93; H. Fleming, *Beechcroft* (E.S.A. 1938). For the Welsh settlements see Sir Percy E. Watkins, *Educational Settlements in South Wales and Monmouthshire* (privately published by the Wardens' Group of the South Wales Educational Settlements, 1940), and W. Hazelton, *Maes-yr-haf, 1927–1952* (Maes-yr-haf Settlement 1952). These settlements received much assistance, directly and indirectly, from the South Wales and Monmouthshire Council for Social Service, for which see below. [For Professor Allaway's history see above, p. 265 note.]

to promote a general co-ordination of musical activities and musical education in Wales. In practice the Council organised one-year and terminal classes in music, promoted music-making groups, and arranged lecture-concerts for schools, training colleges, and adult audiences.

In the 'thirties the settlements were associated with these bodies in a comprehensive scheme covering the whole of South Wales and Monmouthshire. In 1929 a joint committee was established to administer funds provided by the Carnegie Trust for the promotion of cultural facilities in the distressed mining areas. Later, when the Carnegie grants ceased, money was provided by the local education authorities and the National Council of Social Service, and in 1934 the work was taken over by the Education Committee of the South Wales and Monmouthshire Council of Social Service. The three approved associations agreed on a delimitation of functions, and thanks to the extra funds available all of them greatly increased their activities. The music classes of the Council of Music were doubled in number, the one-year and terminal classes of the W.E.A. were trebled, the Y.M.C.A.'s short courses were multiplied sixfold.[1]

Other Settlements

Educational work also continued to form part of the programme of many of the older social settlements. In 1926 there were 56 of these (41 of them in London), and they had their own organisation, the Federation of Residential Settlements, which was founded in 1920, and afterwards became the British Association of Residential Settlements. This was not, like the E.S.A., an approved association, but at Toynbee Hall, the Mary Ward Settlement in Tavistock Place, Swarthmore at Leeds, and elsewhere, the help of other organisations was drawn upon to provide a substantial programme of Extension courses, tutorial classes, W.E.A. classes, and L.E.A. classes, and there was also a great deal of informal work, especially in music and drama.[2]

---

[1] Sir P. Watkins, 'Adult Education among the Unemployed of South Wales', in *Year Book of Education, 1935* (eds. Lord Eustace Percy, Sir P. Nunn, and D. Wilson); University of Wales, Extension Board, *Survey of Adult Education in Wales* (privately published 1940), pp. 32–4.
[2] See *Handbook and Directory, 1926–27*, p. 100; *1928–29*, p. 99; Yeaxlee, *Spiritual Values*, Vol. II, pp. 403–8; and for individual settlements J. Rodgers, *Mary Ward Settlement: a History, 1891–1931* (1931); J. A. R. Pimlott, *Toynbee Hall* (1935), Chs. xii–xiv; Swarthmore Centre, *An Experiment in Adult Education in the City of Leeds, 1909–1949* (1949). The word 'residential' in the title of the association refers to the resident settlement workers, not the students. At Swarthmore, from 1929, there were no residents, and the settlement was controlled by the students.

Working Men's and Women's Colleges

In the last chapter we drew attention to the affinity between the work of the educational settlements and that of earlier institutions such as the London Working Men's College and Morley College. The history of these two bodies during the inter-war years provides an interesting contrast. Morley College, divorced at last in 1924 from the Old Vic, was established as a separate institution in Westminster Bridge Road. Accepting in full measure the financial assistance of the L.C.C., it shed its commercial classes (as it had already at an earlier date shed its technical classes), collaborated closely with the W.E.A. and the London Extra-Mural Department, and became a centre for languages, literature, and the arts. Its walls were adorned with some of the finest murals in Britain; its work in English language and literature was outstanding; and its work in music (following in the tradition established by Gustav Holst) was described by the Board of Education in 1928 as 'on a scale quite unique in the whole field of adult education in England'. By 1939 it had 3,300 students, but had ceased to be, in the original sense, a college 'for working men and women'. A majority of its students were now women; most of them were engaged in clerical or administrative work; two-thirds had had a secondary education.[1]

The Working Men's College, on the other hand, by a heroic gesture shook off in 1924 the tutelage of the L.C.C., and raised enough money to re-establish its independence. Turning its back on what it regarded as the too class-conscious teaching of the W.E.A., it reverted to its original ideal of fellowship and self-culture. In 1922 the number of artisan students had fallen to 20 per cent; by 1926–7 about 40 per cent of the students were manual workers, the rest clerical workers, and the College continued to attract over 1,000 such students every year.[2]

Residential Colleges

The institutions affiliated to the Educational Settlements at the time of its foundation included not only non-residential centres but two of the five adult residential colleges—Woodbrooke and Fircroft. Both of these flourished modestly between the wars, drawing their students mainly from Quaker and adult school circles, and

[1] D. Richards, *Offspring of the Vic: a History of Morley College* (1958), Chs. ix–xi. See also D. Hopkinson, *Family Inheritance: a Life of Eva Hubback* (1954), Ch. vii. Mrs. Hubback was Principal from 1927 until her death in 1949.

[2] J. F. C. Harrison, *History of the Working Men's College, 1854–1954* (1954), Ch. vii. The Working Men's College at Leicester, Vaughan College, was transferred in 1924 to the University College as a centre for extra-mural work.

also attracting, through the Quaker connection and the special connection of Fircroft with the Danish folk high schools, a substantial number of students from abroad.

The other three colleges, Ruskin, the Central Labour College, and the Co-operative College, were less fortunate. All these were adversely affected by the strikes, depressions, and industrial unrest of the 'twenties and early 'thirties. The Labour College had to close in 1929, when the South Wales Miners' Federation, hard hit by the General Strike, withdrew its financial support.[1] Ruskin College found it hard to secure students, and survived only with difficulty, in spite of the fact that in 1919 it had agreed to accept women students.[2] The Co-operative College had no serious difficulty in securing students—mainly co-operative employees supported by bursaries from retail societies—but money was lacking to provide adequate premises, and the students in consequence had to reside either in lodgings or, later, in hostels at a considerable distance from the College.[3]

Five other long-term residential colleges were founded in the 'twenties and 'thirties. The first Residential College for Working Women (afterwards better known as Hillcroft), was established at Beckenham, Kent, in 1920, under the sponsorship of the Y.W.C.A., providing a wide range of courses in liberal subjects and domestic crafts. In 1926 it was transferred to Surbiton.[4] In 1921 the Catholic Social Guild established a Catholic Workers' College at Oxford, to provide training in the social sciences for working men and women. Avoncroft College, at Offenham in the Vale of Evesham, was founded by George Cadbury and his associates in 1925 as an agricultural counterpart of Fircroft, its object being 'to prepare rural workers for wider social interests and activities as well as to provide technical instruction in agriculture'. It was removed to Stoke Prior, in Worcestershire, in 1935.[5]

[1] National Council of Labour Colleges, *Education for Emancipation* (1930), p. 9; J. P. M. Millar, 'Forty Years of Independent Working-Class Education', in *Adult Education*, Vol. XXI (1948-9), p. 213. Hansome, *op. cit.*, pp. 283-6, gives an account of the college shortly before its closure.
[2] *The Story of Ruskin College* (Oxford 1949, 2nd edn. 1955), pp. 21 sqq. Cf. Hansome, *op. cit.*, pp. 194-9.
[3] F. Hall, *The Co-operative College and its Work* (Manchester 1928); A. M. Carr-Saunders, P. S. Florence, and R. Peers, *Consumers' Co-operation in Great Britain* (1938), pp. 223-6; G. D. H. Cole, *A Century of Co-operation* (1944), p. 307. The second of these works is severely critical of the standard of teaching provided at the College, especially in the social as distinct from the purely technical subjects.
[4] S. S. McKay, 'Hillcroft College, Surbiton', in World Association for Adult Education, *Bulletin*, 2nd Ser., No. XVII (May 1939).
[5] J. Dudley, 'Avoncroft College for Rural Workers', in World Association for Adult Education, *Bulletin*, 2nd Ser., No. VII (Feb. 1937). '*Avoncroft*', an *Experiment in Rural Education* (Avoncroft College 1944), is a record of the views of the students in the pre-war years.

A residential college for Wales, Coleg Harlech, was established in 1927 under the control of a council representative chiefly of the University and Colleges of Wales, the W.E.A. and the W.E.T.U.C., and the L.E.A.s. The students were drawn from the adult education classes of the country, attending with the help of grants from L.E.A.s and trade unions. Particularly close relationships were established with the adult educational movement in South Wales, and from 1933 onwards, to meet the needs of the unemployed, courses of one month's duration were arranged alongside the normal yearly courses, and the curriculum was enlarged to include art and crafts, music, and the history of science.[1]

Scotland did not secure its first residential college until 1937, when Newbattle Abbey, near Dalkeith, was given for this purpose by Lord Lothian, and was placed under the management of a governing body drawn from the four universities and a variety of other educational institutions. The Carnegie Trust gave a generous grant, and the College made a good start with more than twenty students in each of its first two sessions.[2]

Most of the colleges which have been described received government assistance in some form—Ruskin, Fircroft, Hillcroft, the Catholic Workers' College, and Coleg Harlech from the Board of Education, Avoncroft from the Ministry of Agriculture, Newbattle from the Scottish Education Department. All of them, it will be observed, were long-term colleges, though Woodbrooke and Fircroft had not been originally intended as such. The modern movement for short-term residential colleges had its modest beginning at the Lamb Guildhouse at Bowdon, near Manchester, established in 1938 on the initiative of R. D. Waller, Director of Extra-Mural Studies at Manchester University. It functioned at that time chiefly as a centre for week-end courses, but out of it eventually came the Extra-Mural Department's present residential college at Holly Royde.[3]

Other Voluntary Organisations

There remains to be described the work of a number of voluntary organisations which fall outside the charmed circle of 'approved

---

[1] 'Coleg Harlech', in World Association for Adult Education, *Bulletin*, 2nd Ser., No. VI (Aug. 1936).

[2] J. A. Mack, *Newbattle Abbey College and What it is Accomplishing* (British Institute of Adult Education 1938).

[3] The story is narrated by Ross D. Waller in *Residential College* (Manchester 1954). The idea of the short-term college was popularised by Sir Richard Livingstone's book, *The Future in Education* (1941). Before 1938 the only institutions which catered for residential short courses were the adult school guest-houses (above, p. 265 note).

associations'. Among these were the Labour College movement, the co-operative movement, the working men's clubs, and various religious organisations, notably the adult schools.

Following the establishment of the Workers' Educational Trade Union Committee, the Labour College movement formed itself in 1921 into the National Council of Labour Colleges, so that it might be in a position to offer to trade unions a national scheme. The new organisation, under its General Secretary, J. P. M. Millar, remained as militant as ever, and would have scorned to carry the seal of government approval. Some would deny it a place in a chapter dealing with liberal adult education, but however severely one may judge its propagandist efforts in the teaching of politics, economics, and industrial history, one is bound to recognise the devoted service given by its officials and voluntary teachers, and the solid value of the work done in such non-controversial subjects as English, public speaking, and trade union administration.

The work was supported by contributions from affiliated trade unions, labour organisations, and co-operative societies—by 1937 there were 36 nationally affiliated unions. The local branches, rather grandiosely known as 'colleges', were organised in twelve divisions covering Great Britain and Ireland, and there were in 1938 fifteen full-time organisers. The main strength of the movement, of course, was always in the industrial areas. The period of most rapid advance came in the 'twenties, especially in the years centring on the General Strike of 1926. The number of classes, 529 in 1922–3, jumped to a peak of 1,234 in 1925–6; the number of students in classes reached a peak of 31,635 in the following year. Thereafter class work showed a slow but steady decline: by 1937–8 there were 728 classes and 13,274 students. To some extent, however, this decline was compensated by an increase in the provision of one-day and week-end schools, and by the development of correspondence teaching: by 1937–8 the number of postal students had passed the 10,000 mark.[1]

The educational work of the co-operative movement continued broadly along the lines developed before the war—informal work through the men's and women's guilds, a certain amount of teaching in social subjects—co-operation, history, citizenship, and economics —and a much larger body of work in commercial subjects. The

[1] The figures are from the N.C.L.C.'s annual reports, published under the title *Education for Emancipation*, and from its journal, *Plebs*. For the development of the movement to 1928, see Hansome, *op. cit.*, pp. 286–92; for the position in 1937–8 see especially the survey prepared at the request of the T.U.C. and printed in *Plebs*, Vol. XXXI (Feb. 1939), pp. 37–9. Much interesting historical material is contained in the *Plebs* Jubilee issue of Feb. 1959 (Vol. LI, No. 2).

present Principal of the Co-operative College sums up the work as follows:

A great deal of time and money was devoted to activities for young people, various in scope and organisation . . . With increasing help from the local education authorities local class work was most strongly developed in technical education for adolescents and adult employees. One-day schools and conferences were organised fairly extensively, Societies provided under their auspices a small number of classes for the study of the social significance of Co-operation and the Movement; but for more general social subjects, in spite of the provision of syllabuses by the Union, the tendency was to use the facilities of the Workers' Educational Association, to a much smaller extent those of the National Council of Labour Colleges, and increasingly those of the local education authorities. And very unevenly, but in certain societies very effectively, there was provision for general cultural activities in choirs, drama groups and so on.[1]

Of the working men's clubs it is not necessary to say much. They were now mainly social clubs, and since 1909 they had relied on the W.E.A. and Ruskin College to provide for the small number of members who were interested in adult education. In 1921, of 2,207 clubs, 87 organised classes and 259 popular lectures; 38 had debating societies or study circles; and 14 scholarships were awarded to Ruskin College. The Club and Institute Union had a summer school at Ruskin College, and to this and other summer schools a score or more of scholarships were awarded.[2]

For the adult school movement these years were a period of decline. The number of schools, which had still been nearly 1,900 before the war, fell to 1,409 by 1921, and to 1,096 by 1937. The falling off was particularly marked in the men's schools: the women's schools held their own fairly well, and there was some increase in the number of mixed schools.[3] One may attribute the general decline partly to the competition of other and better-equipped organisations, but the main factor, undoubtedly, was that in an increasingly secular age the religious atmosphere of the schools, and their emphasis on Bible study, were no longer congenial. As a leading figure in the movement put it:

The modern tendency to broaden our religious ideas has been associated with a decrease of conviction, while the reaction from this attitude has

[1] R. L. Marshall, *Co-operative Education* (London Co-operative Society 1948), pp. 6–7 For further detail see Carr-Saunders, Florence, and Peers, *op. cit.*, Ch. xiii.
[2] B. T. Hall, *Our Sixty Years* (1922), Ch. xiv; J. Levitt, 'Adult Education in Working Men's Clubs', in *Adult Education*, Vol. XXVIII (1955–6).
[3] Statistical records are to be found in the *Adult School Year-Book and Directory*, issued periodically by the N.A.S.U.

been in the direction of a Fundamentalism, which it is difficult to harmonise with Adult School ideals of free inquiry.[1]

Of the various organisations connected with the churches it will suffice to mention the Church Tutorial Classes Association and the Catholic Social Guild. The former grew rapidly during the 'twenties, and achieved a total of 234 classes and 3,482 students by 1930. Thereafter, however, financial difficulties and the difficulty of securing qualified voluntary tutors led to a reduction in the work, especially in the three-year classes. In 1931–2 the total of 213 classes included 72 three-year classes; by 1938–9 there were 22 three-year classes only out of a total of 164, and there was a general feeling that the tutorial class was not the most appropriate form of study for the average church member.[2]

The Catholic Social Guild continued to work mainly through study clubs, with a certain amount of correspondence teaching. The number of clubs varied a good deal, but the number of students, apart from a slight falling-off in the years of depression 1929–32, rose steadily to a peak of 3,910 (in 329 clubs), in 1938–9.[3] The clubs were mainly concerned with social studies, and related historical and philosophical themes, and the Guild issued a study handbook for their guidance. The Guild also arranged examinations on which diplomas were awarded, but only a small number of students availed themselves of this opportunity.

General Trends during the Inter-War Period

When we look back over this inter-war period as a whole, we discern in the work of the universities and voluntary bodies two major trends. One, a very obvious one, is an increasing acceptance of state aid; the other, perhaps not entirely unconnected with the first, is a tendency for the various forms of adult education to be assimilated to a common pattern. The pre-war period, with its Extension lectures, its W.E.A. tutorial classes, its adult schools, its educational and other settlements, its residential colleges, its working men's colleges, and so forth, was notable for its rich diversity both of form and of motive. The motives of personal culture and personal advancement were of course to be found among students in every

---

[1] E. Champness, *Adult Schools* (1941), pp. 68–9. For a critical analysis of the situation see the final chapter of this work, and also G. C. Martin, *The Adult School Movement* (1924), Ch. xv.

[2] National Society, *The Church and Adult Education* [1944], App. I.

[3] This information has been kindly supplied by Mr. J. M. Cleary, whose *Catholic Social Action in Britain, 1909–1959* (Oxford 1961), provides a history of the Guild. The figures for 1938–9 include 11 Irish clubs and 19 clubs abroad.

form of organisation, but the tutorial class and the workers' residential colleges arose primarily from the demand for social emancipation; the desire for religious fellowship and religious service dominated the adult schools and their associated colleges, and the Y.M.C.A.; and religion and social reform joined hands in the educational settlements.

In the 'twenties and especially in the 'thirties there was a change. The driving forces of social reform and religious service became noticeably weaker, and the motive of personal culture reasserted itself. The universities and the W.E.A., as they expanded their work within the limits of the Board's regulations, came closer to each other, and found themselves to some extent overlapping in the provision of general cultural courses for general audiences. Many voluntary bodies, such as the settlements, the Y.M.C.A., and the co-operative movement, came under the university–W.E.A. influence and, while continuing to provide for specialised audiences, called upon the universities or the W.E.A. to do part of their work for them. These bodies did not lose their separate identity, but their adult educational activity lost something of its distinctive character. There were, of course, some movements, such as the adult schools, which still clung closely to their original ideals, but the decline of the adult schools illustrates the general trend towards a broad, undifferentiated form of adult education, inspired mainly by the desire for personal culture, and dominated by the humane tradition of the universities.

There was both good and bad in this change. As it happened, however, there were by 1939 new developments outside the orbit of the universities and the traditional voluntary bodies—developments associated particularly with the local education authorities and the new women's organisations. With these we shall deal in our next chapter.

17

The Twentieth Century

THE WIDENING CIRCLE

The Role of the Local Education Authorities

IN the last two chapters there have been several references to the
part played in adult education by the local education authorities,
but these references have done the authorities much less than
justice. They enjoyed, of course, a good deal of local autonomy, so
that policy varied from one part of the country to another, but it is
fair to say that had it not been for the assistance given by local
education authorities much of the work of the universities and
voluntary bodies would have been impossible.

The authorities gave grants in aid, provided accommodation in
their schools and evening institutes, and in many cases actually
provided the classes. Most if not all voluntary bodies took advantage
of local authority classes prior to the adult education regulations of
1924: the W.E.A. had at least 107 such classes in 1922–3, besides
221 grant-aided directly by the Board under the evening institute
regulations.[1] From 1924 onwards the W.E.A. normally provided its
own classes, with financial assistance from the authorities, but other
approved associations, such as the Y.M.C.A. and the E.S.A., continued to rely on the authorities for many of their classes; and the
same was true in even greater degree of non-approved associations
such as the co-operative societies. In the 'twenties and 'thirties the
authorities were also providing numerous classes for the newer
voluntary bodies such as the women's institutes and townswomen's
guilds.[2]

In 1922–3 the Board of Education for the first time made a
survey of assistance rendered to adult education by local education
authorities. The results were summarised as follows:

(i) The London County Council maintained Literary (men's and
women's) Institutes, and the Warwickshire Local Education Authority

---

[1] Board of Education, *Report*, 1922–3, p. 104.
[2] Below, pp. 301–4.

had staff tutors for adult education. A number of Local Education Authorities provided occasional popular lectures.

(ii) Bradford, Huddersfield, Leicestershire and Stoke-on-Trent assumed full responsibility for the University Tutorial Classes in their areas. In addition, sixty-one Local Education Authorities contributed sums amounting to £5,047 in support of Tutorial Classes in their areas.

(iii) Fifteen Local Education Authorities contributed sums amounting to £469 in support of one-year classes under University joint committees, and Warwickshire assumed direction of the classes of this type in its area.

(iv) Blackburn, Buckinghamshire, Durham County, Hampshire, Kingston-upon-Hull, London, Norfolk, Rotherham, York and the North and West Ridings of Yorkshire assumed direction of classes in their area organised by the Workers' Educational Association. In addition, thirty-eight Local Authorities contributed sums amounting to £1,562 in respect of such classes, and three Authorities contributed £150 towards administrative expenses of district organisations.

(v) Twenty-nine Local Education Authorities contributed £1,937 in aid of University Extension Lectures.

(vi) A number of Local Education Authorities assumed direction of classes organised by county federations of Women's Institutes, and some assistance was given in respect of less definitely organised educational activities.

(vii) A few Local Education Authorities assumed direction of, or made financial contributions to, classes promoted by settlements, literary and other societies, and the St. John Ambulance Association.[1]

A survey made by the British Institute of Adult Education a few years later reveals other ways in which local authorities were helping, e.g. by subsidising the appointment of full-time Extension or tutorial class tutors (Dorset and Staffordshire), by awarding bursaries for summer schools (Dorset and West Riding), by awarding scholarships to residential colleges (Kent and West Riding), and by publishing handbooks giving details of adult educational facilities in the local authority area.[2]

This assistance to the work of other bodies continued, on an increasing scale, throughout the inter-war years.[3] The local authorities, however, also made a substantial and growing contribution in their own right: through their evening institutes especially they were

[1] Board of Education, *Report*, 1922–3, pp. 105–6. Cf. Board of Education, Adult Education Committee, *Report on Local Co-operation between Universities, Local Education Authorities, and Voluntary Bodies* (1922), pp. 9 sqq.

[2] B. A. Yeaxlee (ed.) *Handbook and Directory of Adult Education, 1926–27*, pp. 122–7. The survey probably relates to the work of the session 1924–5.

[3] Later surveys are to be found in *Handbook and Directory of Adult Education, 1928–29*, pp. 148–78, 198–201, 217–22; and Board of Education, Adult Education Committee, *Adult Education and the Local Authority* (1933), Ch. ii.

enlarging the concept of adult education and bringing it within reach of an ever-widening circle of people.

By 1904 the evening schools were operating under revised regulations which brought together the work formerly done by evening continuation schools and that done under the auspices of the Science and Art Department. At this stage non-vocational work for adults was restricted in the main to basic education in the three Rs (a diminishing responsibility as the years went by) and education for women in domestic crafts such as needlework, dressmaking, cookery and home nursing. This was still substantially the case twenty years later, though a survey made in 1923–4 pointed out that 'many of the older part-time students in technical and commercial schools are acquiring intellectual or other attainments not likely to be turned to direct account in their present posts . . .'[1] By this date, however, developments in London had begun to point the way to a larger vision of local authority work.

The L.C.C. Institutes

In 1906, two years before the first tutorial class was formed, the L.C.C. was providing evening courses for adults in liberal studies. These were the so-called 'cycle courses' in English literature: six courses, each of 25 lectures, covering the history of literature from Shakespeare to Victorian times, which were delivered in various centres in rotation (at first in evening commercial centres). These courses achieved a considerable reputation, and continued for more than twenty years.

In 1913 the L.C.C. undertook a wholesale reorganisation of its evening institutes, making provision, amongst other things, for special institutes for adults—women's institutes and non-vocational institutes. The women's institutes were intended to provide mainly practical and recreational subjects but also some humane studies. Before the end of the year 40 of them had been established, with 22,000 students. The work of the non-vocational institutes, of which 7 were opened at this time, was almost brought to a standstill by the war, only 2 institutes surviving. After the war the L.C.C., encouraged by the Education Act of 1918, which required authorities to provide for 'the progressive development and comprehensive organisation of education' in their areas,[2] embarked on a bolder plan. In place of the non-vocational institutes it provided, on the one hand men's institutes, for practical and recreational subjects, and on the

---

[1] Board of Education, *Report*, 1924–5, p. 39.
[2] Education Act, 1918, 8 and 9 Geo. 5 c. 39, clause 1.

other hand literary institutes for studies of a cultural character. The first literary institutes were established in 1919, the first men's institutes in 1920.[1]

By the end of the first decade after the war all three types of institute were firmly established, and by 1937–8 the women's institutes numbered 40, with 44,000 students; the men's institutes 13, with 17,000 students; and the literary institutes 12, with 14,000 students. There were also a number of general and mixed institutes.[2]

The subjects studied corresponded to the original plan. In the women's institutes, in 1928, craft subjects (especially domestic crafts) occupied half the time and recreational subjects about 35 per cent; in the men's institutes, a year later, craft subjects accounted for about 45 per cent of the time and recreational subjects (especially physical training) about 29 per cent.[3] In the literary institutes, on the other hand, the curriculum was mainly academic. This is clearly seen in an analysis made in 1933–4 of student-hours at the City Literary Institute, which was by far the largest of the institutes and the only one to have its own independent premises. The analysis shows that 44 per cent of the time was taken up by studies in literature and languages, and that the other subjects were, in order of popularity: speech training and dramatic art; music appreciation; philosophy and psychology; history; art appreciation; physical culture and dancing; science, topography, and travel; and social and political science.[4]

It would, however, be a great mistake to regard these new ventures as merely additional teaching institutes. In all of them great stress was also laid on the social side of the work. The men's and women's institutes aimed at a club atmosphere, and student societies and social activities of all kinds were regarded as essential to the success of the work. So also the literary institutes did their utmost to foster a sense of corporate life. The establishment of the City Literary Institute in separate premises in 1928 was a great step forward in this direction. 'As soon as there was an unrestricted space in which to forgather', wrote the Principal, 'clubs and societies sprang into existence. There was scarcely any department of study which did

[1] T. G. Williams, 'Adult Education under the London County Council', in World Association for Adult Education, *Bulletin*, 2nd Ser., No. I (June 1935). Cf. R. M. Olivey, 'The London Women's Institute', in *Journal of Adult Education*, Vol. IV (1929–30); S. Myers, 'London Men's Institutes', *ibid.*, Vol. VI (1932–4).

[2] Information kindly supplied by the Clerk to the L.C.C.

[3] Board of Education, Adult Education Committee, *Adult Education and the Local Education Authority*, pp. 13, 85.

[4] Williams, *loc. cit.* This order of popularity has remained fairly constant over the years. From 1926–7 the literary institute programmes included a certain number of University Extension courses.

not develop its parallel social activity . . . Those who guide the destinies of the Literary Institutes have before them an ideal of a collegiate community . . .'[1]

The men's institutes were the subject of a special report published by the Board of Education in 1926, which is worth quoting at length:

. . . whatever the type of interest to which appeal has been made, almost all previous enterprise in adult education has aimed at reaching the more intellectual sections of the community . . .

The starting point of the new Men's Institutes was the frank recognition that outside all the existing institutions and organisations there was a mass of men who, except that they had once passed through the elementary schools, had remained untouched by any educational influences. Their whole mode of life, habits, outlook, tastes and prejudices made it unlikely that any of the recognised forms of education would attract them or be of much use to them. All efforts to organise education for adults are necessarily selective; but by appealing to the intellectual, or to the exceptional individual, they leave large numbers unaffected. Setting aside as futile any attempt to stimulate interest in higher education, the problem was to discover any common interests which could serve as a basis, or even as a starting point, for any educational effort. Vast numbers of men in those parts of London occupied exclusively by working people, especially the unskilled, had remained unaffected by any previous appeals. Among them were many who had returned from the war where they had displayed those characteristics which aroused the admiration of the nation but which did not necessarily fit them to become students. Others were younger people who had passed through adolescence during the years of the war. The restraint and discipline involved in any process of education would be peculiarly irksome to the people who stood most in need of it, and there was little incentive of any kind for them to submit to restraint or to make the effort to learn anything. The lack of interest, the absence of any definite objective, even more than the defects of previous education, constituted a serious obstacle.[2]

After describing the difficulties that faced the heads of the institutes in the early years, the report continues:

Hundreds of young men who would otherwise be 'running to seed' are submitting to the healthy discipline of physical training, . . . Hundreds of men of all ages, amongst them many young married men, are practising handicrafts such as home carpentry . . . In every Institute men are

---

[1] Williams, *loc. cit.* For fuller details see T. G. Williams, *The City Literary Institute* (1960), written to celebrate the 21st anniversary of the opening of the Institute's present building in 1939. On social life in the men's institutes see Board of Education, *Work of Men's Institutes in London* (1926), pp. 11–12, and Myers, *op. cit.*; and in the women's institutes R. M. Olivey, *op. cit.*

[2] Board of Education, *Work of Men's Institutes*, pp. 3, 4–5.

learning the possibilities of the rational employment of their leisure. Activity is the key-note. Music appeals to them if they can take part in making music. Hence every Institute has its 'band,' and after the first year or two its orchestra, with subsidiary classes for learners. Hobbies of many kinds are cultivated. Photography is studied under the guidance of an expert, and the chemistry of photography arouses an interest in the wonders of science. Interest in 'wireless' gives an opening for classes in elementary physics. Interest in motors brings groups of young men, some of whom are engaged as drivers in the day time, to classes in 'petrol engines' and kindred branches of the science of engineering, . . . Even Horticulture finds a place in one or two Institutes, and Poultry-keeping and the Care of Animals is supported by large groups who form their own 'societies' for the promotion of scientific breeding and for the discussion of all questions bearing on their hobby. Every Institute has its 'library' with a teacher whose talk about books and whose advice on reading take the place of the more formal lectures on literature familiar in institutions of another type. Interest in certain popular aspects of science has been aroused, and several Institutes support classes in which experienced teachers expound and illustrate the elementary principles of physical science, biology, etc. Classes for the study of economics, or social problems and current events are not, as a rule, a strong feature; although each Institute has one or more of these. The only language for the study of which any spontaneous demand is made is Esperanto . . . A few classes in drawing and painting provide an outlet for the artistic instincts of a number of young men who have not found their way into Art schools . . . In most of the Institutes successful courses in 'First Aid' have been held from year to year since the beginning or from the second year.[1]

These quotations provide an emphatic answer, as far as the men's institutes are concerned, to the question that was frequently asked about this time: were the adult education classes of the L.C.C. overlapping with the work of the voluntary bodies? In the case of the literary institutes the answer was less obvious, for their aim, as defined by H.M. Inspectors in 1923, was 'to provide liberal culture, to combine academic with popular methods, and to meet those demands for education which in the main have hitherto been met by the missionary efforts of voluntary bodies co-operating to some extent with the Universities'.[2] But although there was some overlap, especially with University Extension, the very success of the literary institutes was proof that they were attracting a substantial new body of students. The Adult Education Committee of the Board summed the matter up in 1929 as follows:

[1] *Op. cit.*, pp. 6–7.
[2] Board of Education, *Report of H.M. Inspectors on the Literary Evening Institutes in the Administrative County of London* (1923), p. 1.

The London Literary Institutes and Men's Institutes clearly provide for the needs of a part of the population which has not found its way into adult education through the usual channels. The Workers' Educational Association has attracted students in the main through co-operating with national and local bodies which have already brought together people with certain political or social interests. Other voluntary bodies have brought people together through their common interest in religious questions. But the Literary Institutes provide for the needs of people who have literary and artistic interests, and a desire to keep in touch with modern thought, in fact people who consciously or unconsciously desire further culture for its own sake. This motive, and this type of student, are also found in University Extension Courses, and some evidence which we have received suggests that, although the students are drawn in the main from different occupations, this motive is also dominant in Educational Settlements. The London Men's Institutes on the other hand have attracted a type of student who is not found in the classes at present organised by voluntary bodies.[1]

Alongside this passage we may place another, from the report of H.M. Inspectors already referred to:

There is in London a very large number of men and women between the ages of 20 and 40 who, having received a good elementary education followed by some further general or commercial education, find themselves interested in Literature or Music, or Art, or in what is sometimes called 'modern thought'. They read a great deal, especially the works of living authors. They are not students in the sense that they are pursuing a definite course of academic study, but they are students in the sense that they are cultivating serious intellectual interests.[2]

Before long the group here referred to was reinforced by the rapid development of secondary education as a result of the Education Act of 1918. The Adult Education Committee, returning in 1930 to a consideration of the problem, perceived clearly the significance of the change that was taking place. Two large sections of the community, it remarks, have recently been brought within the scope of adult education. One of these groups is represented by the clientèle of the London men's institutes. The other group, the Committee says,

is made up of people who have already developed literary tastes or other intellectual interests, and who seek opportunities for the employment of their leisure, sometimes in study, sometimes in desultory reading, sometimes in the drama. The last form of interest is now widespread. The

[1] Board of Education, Adult Education Committee, *Pioneer Work and Other Developments in Adult Education* (1929), pp. 27–8.
[2] *Report of H.M. Inspectors*, as above, p. 4.

predominant interest is literary in the widest sense rather than scientific. The influence of an elementary education, which is after all literary in its tendency, and of secondary education which is even more so, upon the mentality of the newer generation cannot be ignored. The literary and artistic influences of the time, which are far more active than the corresponding influences of the last century, provoke a ready response. It is not only in the great cities that people are anxious to read the latest novel or play, or to discuss the latest speculations about art, or morals, or psychology or politics. There is in fact a new society coming into prominence, dependent on daily work for its economic existence, but with considerable leisure, and rapidly acquiring the mental characteristics of the older leisured classes. It may be that they do not take their intellectual interests very seriously; but no leisured class ever did. Such maturity of mind as comes to them comes far less through any systematic intensive effort than through the cumulative effect of a long-continued but somewhat casual process.[1]

The Committee does not hesitate to draw the moral, namely that the traditional forms of adult education are not the only ones, or necessarily the best for all groups of people:

We have seen . . . that the number of persons who are prepared to undertake the strenuous and systematic or intensive studies typified by the University Tutorial class or the continuous University Extension course, is not unlimited. We have seen also that, through efforts of a very different kind, other sections of the community have been reached whose needs are greater or at least as great. It is as if we had hitherto been attempting to grow wheat, regardless of conditions of soil and climate, and had subsequently discovered that many other sorts of crops might be produced.[2]

Of course the L.C.C., with its vast concentration of population, was unique among education authorities. The account already given, indeed, by no means exhausts the record of its non-vocational work for adults: we must also take into the reckoning a certain amount of work of this character carried out in the ordinary technical and commercial institutes, and much more carried out in grant-aided institutions such as Morley College and the polytechnics.

Provision by Other Authorities

No other education authority in the country could hope to make provision on anything like this scale. None the less the example of London, constantly held up to admiration in official documents, set a standard which undoubtedly contributed to that general quickening

---

[1] Board of Education, Adult Education Committee, *The Scope and Practice of Adult Education* (1930), p. 29.
[2] *Op. cit.*, pp. 11-12.

of local authority activity in this field which is observable in the 'twenties and 'thirties.

There were many other factors. One was the pioneering work of the universities and the W.E.A., which, especially in rural areas, helped to awaken the local authorities to their responsibilities, and not infrequently stimulated a demand for their services.[1] Two new voluntary bodies, the women's institutes and the townswomen's guilds, whose work is described more fully below, did much in their respective spheres not only to arouse a demand for instruction in arts and crafts, drama and music, but also to create a cadre of trained teachers in these subjects. The Rural Community Councils, which began in Oxfordshire in 1919, and had become widespread by 1939, were ready to join forces in any educational activities which would help in the development of social life in the villages, and did particularly good work in music and drama.

There were also a number of specialist organisations. The Rural Industries Bureau (established by H.M. Development Commission in 1921) advised on traditional country crafts. The British Drama League, founded by Geoffrey Whitworth in 1919, organised drama schools and festivals, arranged local pageants and touring companies, and assisted in the selection and circulation of plays, costumes and properties. In 1931 it also took over the functions of the Village Drama Society founded by Miss Mary Kelly in 1918. A Scottish Community Drama Association was founded in 1926. The Arts League of Service (1919) interested itself in art as well as drama: it had a travelling theatre which in 1929–30 gave performances in 250 different centres (mostly outside the usual theatre centres), and it also circulated exhibitions of art and crafts. The English Folk Dance Society (1911) amalgamated in 1932 with the Folk Song Society (1898) under the title English Folk Dance and Song Society: it provided instruction and encouraged the formation of local groups for singing and dancing. The Rural Music Schools, of which the first was formed by Miss Mary Ibberson in Hertfordshire in 1929, devoted themselves to the organisation and instruction of village orchestras; and the British Federation of Musical Competition Festivals (1921), operating in both town and country, assisted local music societies and organised annual festivals for choral, orchestral, and chamber music.[2]

[1] Above, pp. 271–3.
[2] Useful short accounts of these organisations are given in Board of Education, Adult Education Committee, *Adult Education and the Local Education Authority*, Ch. iv; and W. E. Williams, *The Auxiliaries of Adult Education* (British Institute of Adult Education [1934], pp. 19–24. See also E. M. Ibberson, 'Rural Music Schools in England', in World Associa-

A report prepared by the Adult Education Committee in 1933[1] provides a convenient survey of the development of local authority provision in adult education in the early 'thirties. In England and Wales 63 county boroughs at this time were providing non-vocational classes for adults. For the most part these were in practical or semi-recreational subjects, and were held in evening institutes or technical colleges, but some authorities had separate adult institutes or adult departments. In Birmingham and Bristol these were for all adult studies, vocational or non-vocational, but in Bradford, Leicester, and Manchester they were for non-vocational studies only. Hull, following the London model, had a men's institute and a literary institute, and a number of authorities had separate institutes for women.

In the county areas the provision for adults was commonly made either in existing evening institutes or, where appropriate, in detached classes, e.g. in an adult school or women's institute. Warwickshire, as we have seen, actually appointed full-time lecturers. Lancashire, in 1928, appointed a full-time organiser to stimulate local adult education groups in the rural northern part of the county: within four years there were 53 centres, 32 courses of ten or more lectures, and a number of musical and dramatic groups.[2] The West Riding, besides taking financial responsibility for courses in academic subjects promoted by the W.E.A., made extensive direct provision of classes in practical and recreational subjects, operating through evening institute committees which served as a channel for demands from local groups or societies. Cumberland, similarly, had a 'further education committee' in almost every parish. Derby, Devon, County Durham, Essex, Gloucestershire, Kent, Leicestershire, Nottinghamshire, Somerset, and Staffordshire also made extensive direct provision for adult education, besides collaborating closely, in many cases, with the universities and voluntary bodies.

In all, in the year 1929–30, the local authorities in England and Wales, outside London, organised 11,142 non-vocational adult classes, of which 29 per cent were in academic subjects (mainly languages, elocution and drama, literature, and natural science), 62 per cent in practical subjects (mainly domestic arts, handicrafts and health

tion for Adult Education, *Bulletin*, 2nd Ser., No. X (Aug. 1937), and 'Music in Adult Education', in *Adult Education*, Vol. XI (1938–9). On the development of dramatic work much interesting information is assembled in the Adult Education Committee's report on *The Drama in Adult Education* (1926).

[1] *Adult Education and the Local Education Authority*, Ch. iii.

[2] Cf. C. James, 'Adult Education in Rural Lancashire', in *Journal of Adult Education*, Vol. V (1930–2); J. H. Higginson, 'Music and the Man in the Street', in *Adult Education*, Vol. XI (1938–9).

subjects), and 9 per cent in recreational subjects (including music, folk-dancing, and physical training). We may compare these figures with the position in London, where of 4,886 courses 33 per cent were academic, 22 per cent practical, and 58 per cent recreational. From the figures in the Board's annual reports it is plain that local authority provision of practical and recreational subjects continued to increase steadily throughout the 'thirties,[1] but the increase in non-vocational studies of the academic type, in so far as it is possible to distinguish them in the statistics, seems to have been quite small. As yet few authorities outside London seemed disposed to embark on the provision of liberal studies for adults on any substantial scale.[2]

Accommodation was always a difficulty. Local authorities rarely found it possible (they rarely find it possible even to-day) to provide separate buildings exclusively for the use of adult education, and as a general rule adult classes had to be content with accommodation in schools or technical institutes—accommodation that offered little in the way of comfort and nothing in the way of social amenities. This was, of course, a problem for most forms of adult education: for the most part only adult schools and settlements had their own premises.

Village Halls and Community Centres

In the rural areas the difficulty was eased a good deal as time went on by the provision of clubs or social centres. Many of these came into existence purely on the initiative and by the efforts of the local inhabitants. Some were specially erected as village war memorials. Others were Y.M.C.A. huts, erected during the war to serve as cultural and recreational centres for the Forces, and afterwards handed over to village organisations to be run as Y.M.C.A. clubs. Others again were miners' institutes—welfare and recreation centres established in the mining areas throughout Great Britain from a special fund which was created under the Mining Industry Act of 1920.[3]

In 1918, at the suggestion of Sir Henry Rew, Chairman of the

---

[1] Enrolments in these subjects in evening institutes and colleges with evening classes increased from 632,000 in 1930–1 to 917,000 in 1937–8.

[2] H. J. Edwards, *The Evening Institute* (1961), studies the history and development of evening institute work to that date.

[3] A special report on *The Educational Possibilities of Village Clubs* (Department of Adult Education, Nottingham University College, 1923) provides a valuable survey of the various types of clubs in the East Midlands area at this date, and the educational work carried on in connection with them. For the miners' institutes see also Ministry of Education, *Community Centres* (1946), p. 31.

Agricultural Club, a Village Clubs Association was founded, in order to stimulate the provision of social, recreational, and educational facilities for both men and women, and thus check the decay of village life. With help from the Treasury, the Association promoted or assisted a considerable number of clubs (460 were affiliated by 1922), but in the end it could not stand up against the competition of the women's institutes, and it was dissolved in 1925.[1]

The greatest impetus towards the creation of village social centres in the inter-war years came from the National Council of Social Service. With financial assistance from H.M. Development Commission and the Carnegie Trust (which invested enormous sums in rural development at this period) the Council was able to offer grants ranging from one-sixth to one-third of the cost of village halls, and loans to cover a further one-third. By 1939 the Council had about 1,000 affiliated village halls and had assisted about 500 local committees with building projects.[2]

By 1925 the N.C.S.S. had become aware of the need for community centres in the large new housing estates which were springing up all over the country. In 1929, acting in conjunction with the Educational Settlements Association and the British Association of Residential Settlements, it established a New Estates Community Committee (known from 1937 as the Community Centres and Associations Committee) to campaign for the formation of community associations and wherever possible the building of community centres. The Carnegie Trust again came forward to help, this time by contributing to the salaries of full-time secretaries. In some cases local education authorities also assisted. By 1939, 92 centres had been provided, by private enterprise or by local authorities or by the two in combination; and several hundred other schemes were under consideration.[3]

Village halls and community centres, of course, are not designed exclusively for education, and experience has shown that where the programme of activities is predominantly social and recreational such centres do not always provide a congenial setting for the more serious forms of adult education. At the more elementary and less formal levels, however, they have undoubtedly been of enormous value.[4]

---

[1] Board of Education, Adult Education Committee, *The Development of Adult Education in Rural Areas* (1922), pp. 13–15; J. W. Robertson Scott, *The Story of the Women's Institute Movement* (Idbury, Oxon., 1925), especially Ch. xv.
[2] Ministry of Education, *Community Centres*, p. 27.
[3] *Op. cit.*, pp. 27–8.
[4] On this point see H. Marks, *Community Associations and Adult Education* (N.C.S.S. 1949), especially p. 5.

Village Colleges

An entirely new approach to educational work in rural areas came in 1924 from Henry Morris, Secretary for Education for Cambridge-shire. In a confidential memorandum submitted to the county education committee, Morris argued that the village was no longer an economical unit for the provision of social and educational services on the scale required by modern conditions, and that if the decline of rural life was to be arrested the only answer was to group the villages into regions, each of which could be provided with a complete range of services. He therefore proposed

to establish in about ten carefully selected centres where Senior Schools are already organised, a system of village colleges which would provide for the co-ordination and development of all forms of education—primary, secondary, further and adult education—together with social and recreational facilities, and at the same time furnish a community centre for the neighbourhood.[1]

Each village college, it was envisaged, would embrace a nursery and primary school for the village, a secondary school for the whole group of villages, a branch of the county library, a village hall, facilities for indoor and outdoor recreation, and rooms for adult classes, which would also share the science and craft rooms of the secondary school.

The village college would change the whole face of the problem of rural education. As the community centre of the neighbourhood it would provide for the whole man, and abolish the duality of education and ordinary life. It would not only be the training ground for the art of living, but the place in which life is lived, the environment of a genuine corporate life. The dismal dispute of vocational and non-vocational would not arise in it. It would be a visible demonstration in stone of the continuity and never ceasingness of education. There would be no 'leaving school'!—the child would enter at three and leave the college only in extreme old age.[2]

Morris's plan was accepted, and four of the eleven projected village colleges were actually opened before the war: at Sawston (1930), Bottisham (1937), Linton (1938), and Impington (1939).[3] Though they may in some respects have fallen short of the high ideal envisaged by Morris, they were unquestionably a tremendous

[1] H. Morris, *The Village College* (Cambridge 1924), p. 9.
[2] *Op. cit.*, p. 18.
[3] H. C. Dent, *The Countryman's College* (British Council 1943), pp. 16–17.

success, and in recent years the idea has been taken up by other county authorities.

In the early 'thirties came a new problem which for some years engaged the attention alike of bodies concerned with social work and of bodies concerned with adult education—the problem of large-scale unemployment. Local education authorities, councils of social service, community centres, settlements, adult schools, women's institutes, townswomen's guilds, the W.E.A., the Y.M.C.A., all found themselves faced with this problem, and all of them, in their various ways, made their contribution. We have seen, in an earlier chapter, how the situation was met in South Wales, by the establishment of special clubs and occupational centres, and similar schemes were adopted in many other areas. Though primarily designed to provide recreation and useful occupation, the centres often developed a considerable range of educational activities—handicrafts and wo-men's classes, gardening, physical training, choral, orchestral and dramatic groups, popular lectures, wireless discussion groups, classes in languages, and so forth. In general the centres were sponsored by voluntary bodies (one in Lincoln was organised by the local W.E.A. branch), but the education authorities often assisted with premises, teachers, and materials. In this way, and through a variety of other special activities, unemployed men and women were helped to pre-serve their self-respect and were at the same time given the oppor-tunity of learning new skills and acquiring new interests.[1]

Scotland

So far we have said little of Scotland. Unfortunately our informa-tion on Scottish developments is very inadequate: the valuable reports of the Adult Education Committee did not cover Scotland, and the statistics provided in official government reports are very scanty. We know that much of the work which in England came within the province of approved associations such as the W.E.A. was in Scotland carried out by the local education authorities, at first under the regulations for continuation schools and later under the adult education regulations of 1934. The volume of work of this type, however, as has been pointed out above, was small,[2] and evening-school provision as a whole was on a smaller scale than in England, even allowing for the difference in population. There was, of course, the usual provision of arts and crafts and similar subjects,

---

[1] A useful account of occupational centres is to be found in *Educational Facilities for the Unemployed* (British Institute of Adult Education 1933).

[2] Above, pp. 275–6.

and a certain amount of non-vocational study was undertaken in the ordinary technical and commercial classes. The Scottish Education Department was, indeed, at pains to point out in its report for 1933 that more than half of the 142,000 students in its continuation schools were adults, and that many of these were pursuing courses of liberal study through technical and commercial classes in such subjects as English and foreign languages, literature, history, economics, natural science, mathematics, art and music.[1]

Women's Institutes

We must now turn to consider in more detail two important new voluntary bodies which have already been several times referred to— the women's institutes and the townswomen's guilds. The growing participation of women is one of the most remarkable features of twentieth century adult education. It is, of course, a reflection of the general movement for the political and social emancipation of women, and dates in the main from the First World War. In a great many instances, it was the women who kept adult education going during the war years, and from this time onwards they played an increasingly important, in some cases a dominating, role.

The idea of special institutes for women in rural areas derived from Canada, where the first women's institute was formed in 1897. In England and Wales the movement developed during the war years, first under the wing of the British Agricultural Organisation Society,[2] and later under the auspices of the Board of Agriculture. It became independent in 1919. The little Anglesey village of Llanfairpwllgwyngyllgogerychwyrndrobwllllandysiliogogogoch, famous for its long name, can claim also the credit for having established, in 1915, the first women's institute in Britain. Within ten years England and Wales were covered by a network of institutes, organised into county federations, and headed by the National Federation of Women's Institutes. By 1927 there were close on 4,000 institutes, with 250,000 members, and the movement had not only ceased to be dependent on government grants but had built up a substantial capital reserve. At the close of 1937 the institutes numbered 5,534.[3]

Unlike most English adult education movements, the institutes also quickly won a foothold in Scotland, where the first institute was

---

[1] *Report of the Committee of Council on Education in Scotland,* 1938, p. 16.
[2] Formed in 1901 to promote co-operation among farmers and smallholders.
[3] For the history of the movement see Robertson Scott, *Story of the Women's Institute Movement;* J. E. Courtney, *Countrywomen in Council* (1933); I. Jenkins, *History of the Women's Institute Movement* (Oxford 1953).

established at Longniddry, near Edinburgh, in 1917. For the first five years of their existence the Scottish Rural Women's Institutes, as they were called, developed under the tutelage of the Scottish Board of Agriculture, but they became administratively independent in 1922, and financially independent five years later. By 1925 there were 460 institutes with 27,500 members; in 1938–9 there were over 1,000 institutes and nearly 50,000 members.[1]

It is difficult to exaggerate the effect of the women's institutes on village life. Hitherto the lives of the womenfolk had been almost entirely circumscribed by the narrow and unceasing round of domestic duties. They had little or no opportunity for social intercourse except through the churches and chapels, and they hardly dreamed of taking part in public affairs, or even pronouncing an opinion on such matters—that was the prerogative of the menfolk. In one English village, when an institute organiser called a meeting to consider the formation of an institute, the audience consisted entirely of men. At the second meeting the room was full of women, the men having in the meantime given their approval for the project.[2]

The monthly meeting of the institute now became for many women the highlight in their otherwise restricted lives—in Scotland women often tramped miles to be present. Here for the first time they learned something about the conduct of public business, about housing, water supplies, sanitation, diet, education, child welfare, about the whole range of government and local government functions as they affected the life of the village. They discovered that they had opinions on these matters, and that their opinions were respected. They learned how to speak in public, how to frame resolutions, perhaps even how to take the chair. Not a few attended special training courses and became voluntary county organisers.

All this was citizenship education at its best and most practical: it brought women out of the home and made them active and influential in public affairs. Of course other factors, at this same time, were helping to revolutionise village life—better education, better transport, improved lighting and sanitation, rural library services, broadcasting. But it was the institutes that fitted women to take full advantage of all these developments, and to help in bringing them about. Robertson Scott records in 1925, for example, 'that in some ten counties [of England and Wales] the adoption of the Libraries Act was the work of the Institutes, and that in ten or fifteen other counties the Act was adopted largely through Institute exertions'.[3]

---

[1] Scott, *op. cit.*, Chs. xix–xx; Courtney, *op. cit.*, Chs. xii–xiv.
[2] Jenkins, *op. cit.*, p. 142.   [3] Scott, *op. cit.*, p. 154.

Lord Ernle, who as R. E. Prothero, President of the Board of Agriculture, had been much concerned in the early phases of the movement, declared: 'The narrowness and hardship of rural life make women pine for the towns. What they want are more casements in their minds through which may pour the warmth and colour of life, and through which they can widen their horizons.'[1] Increasingly as the years went on such casements were opened, not only on to the field of public affairs but on to literature, music, and the arts.

At the outset the institutes were mainly preoccupied with war activities—knitting, fruit bottling, and the like—and the domestic crafts have always occupied a prominent place in institute programmes. From an early stage other crafts became popular—weaving, lace-making, glove-making, basketwork, rug-making, toymaking, and many others. At first there were attempts to place these activities on a commercial basis, to recreate the old rural industries, but it was quickly realised that this was a false path, and that the true aim should be rather to recover the old pride in craftsmanship. With help from H.M. Development Commission schools were organised to train craft teachers, and by 1939 the institutes had thousands of members trained in a great variety of crafts.[2]

Drama and music (especially choral music) became from the early 'twenties onwards important institute activities, and the Carnegie Trust made grants to provide schools and classes for the training of village producers and conductors. Folk-dancing was also popular, and here from the beginning the English Folk Dance and Song Society gave valuable assistance. The range of activities that developed is illustrated by the reports of the county federations in the early 'thirties, which record a drama competition in Lancashire with 19 competing institute teams; a Countryside Musical Festival in Gloucestershire with 40 institute choirs; a Pageant of Women Leaders presented by 600 institute members from Leicestershire and Rutlandshire; and a Combined Gala Day at Scarborough to which institutes from four counties sent teams of actors, singers, and dancers.[3]

The development of the institutes owed much on the organisational side to the skill and devotion of Lady Denman, who was Chairman from the outset until 1946. On the educational side a leading part was played by the Vice-Chairman, Grace Hadow, a distinguished scholar whose rather prim appearance was belied by her warm and affectionate nature and her eager interest in the ideas and activities of others. 'Grace Hadow believed profoundly that

[1] *Op. cit.*, p. 102.　　　[2] Jenkins, *op. cit.*, Ch. vii.　　　[3] *Op. cit.*, Ch. ix.

cultural subjects were accessible in a measure to all men, and she worked untiringly to make them available to Institute members.'[1]

Townswomen's Guilds

In 1918 women were accorded the vote at the age of 30, and the National Union of Women's Suffrage Societies converted itself into the National Union of Societies for Equal Citizenship, under the presidency of Eleanor Rathbone. Ten years later women were granted the vote at 21, and the N.U.S.E.C. wondered in what direction to turn its energies next. Dame Millicent Fawcett, the veteran suffragette, urged that the Union should devote itself to the education of the new women citizens, and it was agreed to launch a movement for townswomen along the lines of the women's institutes, with activities embracing handicrafts, music, drama, and above all civics. The first Town Institute for Women was formed at Haywards Heath in Sussex in Janary 1929—the name was changed to Townswoman's Guild a month later—and others quickly followed. The first Scottish guild was formed at Stonehaven in 1930.

The parent organisation devoted itself to raising funds to enable guilds to be started throughout Britain. In 1932 it abandoned its political propaganda, and in 1933 it was reconstituted as the National Union of Townswomen's Guilds, with over 150 member guilds. One symbol of the militant past was retained however—the colours of the new Union were the old red, white and green of the suffragette movement. Expansion continued throughout the 'thirties, the National Council of Social Service and the Scottish Council of Social Service providing funds to assist the formation of guilds in distressed areas. By 1939 there were 544 guilds, organised, like the women's institutes, into local federations.[2]

Education in H.M. Forces

Two good things in adult education emerged from the first World War. One was the women's institutes: the other was army education. Before the war, education in the army had been concerned mainly with basic education, for which fairly systematic provision was made from about the middle of the nineteenth century, or with instruction for the army certificates in education, which were introduced in

---

[1] H. Deneke, *Grace Hadow* (1946), p. 176. On Miss Hadow and Lady Denman see also Jenkins, *op. cit.*, pp. 39–42.

[2] A history of the guilds is still awaited. See E. H. Smith, 'The National Union of Townswomen's Guilds', in World Association for Adult Education, *Bulletin*, 2nd Ser., No. IV (Feb. 1936); and articles in *The Townswoman*, Vol. XIX (1952), pp. 104–5; Vol. XXV (1958), pp. 100–2.

1860. A certain amount of less formal education was also undertaken, but at a very humble level—by the 'fifties we hear of 'instructive and amusing' lectures illustrated by 'the magic lanthorn'.[1]

This kind of provision was perhaps adequate for a small regular army recruited in the main from the ranks of the poor: it was quite inadequate for the citizen army which enlisted, or was conscripted, for the first World War. When the war broke out, however, the military authorities were occupied with more urgent matters than education, and the lead therefore had to come from the civilian side. At this juncture it was the Y.M.C.A. which stepped into the breach. It was well fitted to do so: it had, as we have seen, long been engaged in the educational field, and since 1890 it had undertaken welfare and educational work at the army's summer training camps.

From an early stage of the war the Y.M.C.A. began to provide lectures and classes for units of the Forces at home and abroad—especially abroad—and in the autumn of 1915 it established a special Educational Committee to develop the work. This ultimately developed, in April 1918, into the Y.M.C.A. Universities Committee, which included representatives of the universities, local education authorities, and voluntary bodies connected with adult education, and became a co-ordinating body for civilian assistance to army education. Dr. Basil Yeaxlee served as Secretary throughout.

It is not possible here to give details of the work undertaken by the Y.M.C.A. and its allies, but the total programme, carried out at a cost to the Y.M.C.A. of over £250,000, was exceedingly impressive. In Britain, France, Italy, Malta, Salonika, Egypt, Mesopotamia, in camps for internees, in munition hostels, provision was made for lectures and wherever possible sustained courses and classes. Distinguished speakers from the universities lectured on history, literature, science, art, and other subjects, often within three miles of the firing line; a considerable staff of teachers was engaged to conduct vocational and non-vocational classes, e.g. in mathematics, foreign languages, commercial subjects, and arts and crafts; and education centres, with libraries of as many as 10,000 books, were established at military bases. In France provision was also made on a large scale for musical and dramatic performances by touring companies. (Percy Scholes became the Committee's chief music organiser, and Gustav Holst acted as organiser for Salonika.)

It was not until the last year of the war that the army developed

---

[1] On the early phases of army education see T. H. Hawkins and L. J. F. Brimble, *Adult Education: the Record of the British Army* (1947), Chs. i–ii.

a complete educational scheme of its own, first in France, and finally, in September 1918, for the army as a whole, under the direction of Lord Gorell. This scheme provided for lectures and a whole range of vocational and non-vocational classes for illiterates. Education officers and instructors were appointed in large numbers, and arrangements were also made for civilian assistance. In France the Y.M.C.A. continued until April 1919 to act as the army's agent on the lines of communication. Hardly had the new scheme got into working order than it was overtaken by the armistice, and had to give way to a much extended programme aimed at preparing 'upwards of 3,000,000 students' for their return to civilian life.

The Adult Education Committee in its *Final Report*, 1919, described army education as 'a triumph of improvisation', and quoted H. A. L. Fisher, President of the Board of Education, as saying that 'Nothing in the shape of adult education has ever been attempted on the same scale in the whole history of the world.' The Committee also noted with satisfaction 'the prominent place taken by non-vocational and humane studies', and rejoiced that the work had arisen 'in response to a spontaneous and growing demand from the soldiers themselves'. As to what was actually achieved the Committee was cautious: 'much of the work was necessarily slight and fugitive; where circumstances were more favourable it was more solid and continuous; while a certain part reached a comparatively high standard'.[1]

One permanent result at least this vast experiment did have. In August 1919 Mr. Winston Churchill, Secretary of State for War, announced to the Commons that 'education is henceforward to be regarded as an integral part of army training'.[2] In 1920 the education branch was accordingly reconstituted as the Army Education Corps. Unfortunately, however, the close co-operation built up during the war between the military and civilian authorities was allowed to lapse, and when the second World War came the whole organisation had to be rebuilt.

In the Royal Air Force and the Royal Navy, because of their special operational requirements, there was greater emphasis than in the army on technical education, and civilian assistance was

---

[1] Adult Education Committee, *Final Report*, pp. 342, 349. Pp. 336–50 of this Report provide a detailed account of these developments, and also of work carried on by the army and other agencies in military hospitals. Cf. the same committee's *Second Interim Report: Education in the Army* (1918). B. A. Yeaxlee, 'The Civilian Contribution to Army Education', in *Army Education*, Vol. XVII (June 1942), is also valuable, and there are useful summaries in Hawkins and Brimble, *op. cit.*, Ch. iii, and S. J. Curtis, *Education in Britain since 1900* (1952), Ch. x.

[2] Hawkins and Brimble, *op. cit.*, p. 66.

possible only on a limited scale. The R.A.F., which had to provide for units varying in size, widely scattered and often out of reach of local educational facilities, devised in August 1918 a comprehensive educational scheme operating through its own service personnel, a scheme which, though directed in the first instance to the special needs of the demobilisation period, was so designed as to form a permanent feature of the peace-time organisation. In the navy education was linked even more closely with service requirements, and was necessarily carried out almost exclusively by service instructors.[1]

The Seafarers' Education Service

To meet the needs of the men of the Merchant Navy, who were of course excluded from official provision, the World Association for Adult Education established in 1919, at Mansbridge's instigation, the Seafarers' Education Service. Its objects were to provide educational facilities, by correspondence or otherwise, for members of the British merchant navy and for fishing fleets, to provide libraries on shore and in ships, and generally to further the education of seafarers; and it was organised by a special commission representing shipowners, seafarers' organisations, and educationists.

The work of the Service developed on two main lines. In the first place it inaugurated a system of ships' libraries—collections ranging from 50 to 300 books and covering a wide variety of subjects, fiction and non-fiction. Wherever possible these libraries were exchanged not less than three or four times a year. Arrangements were made by which exchanges could be effected through the public libraries at Cardiff and Glasgow as well as through the central office in London; and ships abroad could exchange libraries with each other, or through the Mission to Seamen at Fremantle, Australia. Wherever possible books specially requested by seamen were included in new libraries as they were despatched. By 1940 libraries had been established on some 600 ships.

In the second place the Service developed an advisory bureau to deal with individual inquiries on educational matters. From this bureau there developed in 1938 the College of the Sea, to provide guidance, books, and personal tuition to seafarers wishing to undertake systematic study, whether for vocational reasons or simply as a hobby. The tuition was, of course, mainly by correspondence, and

---

[1] Adult Education Committee, *Final Report*, pp. 350–6; C. Lloyd, *British Services Education* (1950), Ch. i.

the College was able to draw for this work on the voluntary services of a large team of university and other teachers.[1]

Prison Education

In all these different ways the circle of adult education was constantly being widened. In the 'twenties it was extended to include even the inmates of His Majesty's prisons. Until after the first World War almost the only instruction available to prisoners was in the form of classes for illiterates, who were at that time fairly numerous—in 1913 they constituted 13 per cent of the total receptions. In 1923, however, at the suggestion of the Adult Education Committee of the Board of Education, a comprehensive adult education scheme was adopted, 'to counteract the mental deterioration inevitably attendant on prison life, and to increase the prisoner's fitness for citizenship, by stimulating his mind and furnishing it with material for healthy activity in confinement, and of continuing value in after life'.[2]

An honorary educational adviser (often the local director of extramural studies, sometimes the director of education) was appointed for each prison, and classes were arranged in a variety of subjects extending from history, literature, and mathematics to shorthand and gardening—almost any subject indeed, in which prisoners were interested and teachers were available. Later, from 1945 onwards, the teaching was provided by the local education authority, but at this time it was carried out entirely by voluntary teachers.

The scheme got under way quickly, and in 1926 there were already about 600 regular classes, attended by 9,300 prisoners. By 1937 the number in classes had risen to 10,753, and 400 voluntary teachers were engaged in the work. Periodical lectures were also arranged, and occasional debates and concerts of music. Partly from government funds, and partly from a special Carnegie Trust grant, provision was made for prison libraries, and suitable prisoners were allowed facilities for study. The older scheme for the education of illiterates was not abandoned—indeed it still continues to-day—but by 1931 the proportion of illiterates received had shrunk to about 2 per cent.

A recent study of educational work in the prisons quotes many

[1] A useful summary is R. Hope, 'Further Education for Merchant Seafarers', in *Further Education*, Vol. I (1948–9), pp. 197–9 and 222–4. See also C. E. Fayle (ed.), *Harold Wright: a Memoir* (1934), Ch. viii; H. T. K. Cook, *In the Watch Below* (1937); and R. R. Ryder, 'The College of the Sea', in World Association for Adult Education, *Bulletin*, 2nd Ser., No. XX (Feb. 1940).

[2] L. W. Fox, *The Modern English Prison* (1934), p. 99.

interesting extracts from the reports of prison governors and chaplains. We have space here only for one example, from the report of the Governor at Shrewsbury in 1931:

The prison visitors and voluntary teachers are doing good work. Classes have been held in Arithmetic, Book-keeping, Shoemaking and Literature. The Literature Class has been a notably good influence. It has come to my notice that those prisoners who dine in association have frequently been absorbed during the whole mealtime with no topic but the Literature Teacher's latest subject. Knowing the tendency for prisoners' conversation to be of a low order, I consider this to be an important and significant fact. It tends to show that character may be strongly influenced by suitable tutors, in classes which might seem to have no practical value.[1]

[1] F. Banks, *Teach Them to Live* (1958), pp. 30–1.

18

The Twentieth Century

THE AUXILIARIES OF ADULT EDUCATION

IN earlier chapters I have described the origin and development of certain agencies—books and newspapers, libraries, museums, and art galleries—which made an important contribution to adult education even though not devised exclusively for that purpose. These agencies I have denominated 'instruments of adult education'. For some people, until at least the middle of the nineteenth century, they were the only instruments available. By the twentieth century, thanks to the development of organised adult education, this was no longer the case. These various agencies, consequently, and others which sprang up alongside them, became from the adult educational point of view auxiliaries rather than primary instruments.

Cheap Books

The provision of books remained, of course, of basic importance. Thanks to the enterprise of some publishers, it was now possible to purchase standard works, reprints of recent works, and even some new books, at very modest cost, so that for a few pounds judiciously laid out even a working man could furnish himself with a substantial library. In 1908, when W.E.A. tutorial classes began, it was possible for a shilling a volume to take one's choice of Nelson's Classics (originally the New Century Library, 1900), the World's Classics (1901), Collins's Pocket Classics (1903), and Dent's Everyman's Library (1906), besides older series by Routledge, Cassell, and others. Nelson and Collins concentrated on fiction, but the World's Classics and Everyman took in a much wider field.[1]

All these series quickly established themselves, and though they increased in price were of enormous value both to the general reader and to the adult student. In 1927 came Benn's Sixpenny Library, not reprints this time but new works—150 slim paper-backed volumes, each a succinct and authoritative survey of some

---

[1] On popular series generally see S. H. Steinberg, *Five Hundred Years of Printing* (1955), pp. 247–58. For the launching of the Everyman series see *Memoirs of J. M. Dent* (1928), Ch. x.

department of history, literature, science, or philosophy. And in 1935 was launched the greatest cheap publishing enterprise of our times—Penguin Books.

Many were the predictions of disaster when Allen Lane, then of the Bodley Head, decided to embark on his sixpenny paperbacks, offering good literature attractively printed for the price of a packet of cigarettes. But Lane had correctly estimated the vast new potential market created by extended secondary and university education. The Penguins, which were at first reprints of fiction and general literature, were an immediate success, and were followed in 1937 by the Pelican series, more specifically educational in purpose, of which the first volume was a new edition of Bernard Shaw's *Intelligent Woman's Guide to Socialism*. Later in the same year came the first of the Penguin 'Specials'—new and specially commissioned works dealing with urgent international issues. When war broke out there were already over 300 separate titles, many of them selling by the hundred thousand, and the little orange-and-white or blue-and-white volumes were already a familiar feature in the book-boxes of adult classes. They assorted oddly with the solemn garb of older volumes, but they were usually the first to be read.[1]

The Public Libraries

Even a plentiful supply of cheap books, however, can never serve as a substitute for an efficient library service, whether the matter be looked at from the angle of the general reader or from the more specialised viewpoint of the adult student. In general, the more books people buy, the more they also borrow. In Britain the public library service has improved enormously during the present century, both in extent and efficiency.

In 1900, though there were 300 library authorities, many parts of the country, including some large towns, were still outside the service.[2] By 1909 the number of authorities had risen to nearly 500, and the coverage of urban areas was fairly complete, but the rural areas were still almost entirely unprovided for. In 1915 it was estimated that 40 per cent of the population was outside the areas covered by library authorities.[3] This grave deficiency was remedied for England and Wales by the Public Libraries Act of 1919, which empowered

[1] *Penguins: A Retrospect* (1951); W. E. Williams, *The Penguin Story* (1956); *Penguins Progress, 1935–1960* (1960).
[2] E.g. the county boroughs of Wakefield, Southend, and Burnley, and several of the London metropolitan boroughs—Board of Education, Public Libraries Committee, *Report on Public Libraries in England and Wales* [Kenyon Report] (1927), pp. 238–9.
[3] W. G. S. Adams, *Report on Library Provision and Policy* (Carnegie U.K. Trust, Edinburgh 1915), p. 7. I have adjusted the figure to exclude Ireland.

county councils to establish public libraries, to be administered by the county education committees. Similar powers had already been granted to the Scottish counties under the Education (Scotland) Act of 1918.

The 1919 Act also eliminated, in England and Wales, the restriction of expenditure to a penny rate, which had so long exercised a crippling effect on library development. In Scotland no limitation was placed on county library expenditure, but the Public Libraries (Scotland) Act of 1920, anomalously, retained a rate limit of three-pence for the burgh libraries.

By 1925 the county library system was getting into its stride. The service was at first inclined to follow nineteenth-century precedents, relying on book-boxes sent out periodically to local centres staffed by voluntary helpers, but before long the book-box began to give place to the library van, and some counties, for example Derbyshire, Durham, Kent, Lancashire, Middlesex, and Nottingham, established full-time branch libraries in the more important centres. By 1935 the more efficient county libraries were providing a service comparable with that of the better urban libraries.

The Carnegie Trust, which had played a leading role in bringing about the reforms of 1919, and which had long taken a particular interest in rural development, did much to assist in the development of the new county libraries. From 1919 onwards the Trust no longer made grants for library buildings, but it gave generous help to the counties in other ways, e.g. by grants in aid of books and equipment. It also made grants to improve the efficiency of many urban libraries, and from 1930 onwards to assist in the organisation of regional library bureaux through which non-fiction works were made inter-available throughout the libraries of the region.

This valuable service was supplemented by the National Central Library, towards which the Trust also made substantial grants. Where a book desired by a borrower was not available in his own region the request was passed to the National Central Library, which was in touch with all the regional bureaux besides a number of specialist libraries outside the public library system. Thus a borrower in any area could draw on the library resources of the whole country. Scotland also had its regional library bureau, and a Scottish Central Library founded at Dunfermline (now in Edinburgh) which was established and maintained by the Carnegie Trust.

By 1939 the only parts of Great Britain still without a public library service were the counties of Rutland and Argyll and about a dozen urban areas which had been excluded from the provision made by their respective counties—the largest of these areas was Swindon, which interestingly enough still relied, until 1942, on the Mechanics' Institute for its library service. Public library stocks at this date totalled, for Great Britain and Northern Ireland, 33 million volumes, and annual book issues were 247 millions, representing 5·3 books per head of the population. Since only just under one-fifth of the population were borrowers, the average annual issue per borrower was 27·2.[1]

These overall figures conceal the fact that the library provision was very unequal both in quantity and in quality. The best urban and county systems were really excellent; the worst were totally inadequate in stock, buildings, and staff. Among these latter were many small libraries run by municipal boroughs, urban districts, and even parishes, which had been established before the 1919 Act and still clung to their independence although the areas they served were quite uneconomic as library units.[2]

In general, however, it remains true that the inter-war years saw a substantial and continuing improvement in the national library service. This improvement was, of course, very much to the advantage of organised adult education, which was now able to draw for supplies of books on the public libraries as well as on the National Central Library. The development of the county libraries was particularly advantageous, since these libraries, operating under the control of the county education committees, in many cases made specific financial provision for books for adult classes: the West Riding, always to the fore in adult education, established in 1923 a special Adult Class Library. Many urban libraries also gave generous help, but in general these libraries, particularly the smaller ones, were less able and less willing to make special provision.[3]

It should not be forgotten, however, that the public libraries were also adult educational organisations in their own right. This comes out very clearly in the statement of the aims of county library policy formulated by the Kenyon Committee in 1927—a statement subsequently accepted in the McColvin Report as a general statement of library objectives:

---

[1] L. R. McColvin, *The Public Library System of Great Britain* (1942), p. 10.

[2] For gruesome examples see McColvin, *op. cit.*, pp. 40 sqq. For general surveys of library development during this period see J. Minto, *History of the Public Library Movement* (1922), Chs. vii–xi and xvi; and especially W. A. Munford, *Penny Rate*, Chs. v–xiv.

[3] Much interesting information on book supplies to adult classes is to be found in Board of Education, Adult Education Committee, *Adult Education and the Local Education Authority* (1933), Ch. vi. The National Library of Wales provided, from 1914, a service for adult classes in Wales; and extra-mural classes in England were able to draw on the increasing stocks of the extra-mural libraries (*op. cit.*, App. VI).

(i) To relieve the tedium of idle hours quite irrespective of intellectual profit or educational gain. It is sufficient to satisfy this purpose that the rural inhabitant should be rendered a happier (and not necessarily a more learned) man by the provision which is made for him.

(ii) To secure that the taste for good English which should be acquired in the elementary school is kept alive and developed by a provision of good literature after school years have ended.

(iii) To enable the rural inhabitant to acquire, without difficulty, that general knowledge which alone can enable him to appreciate to the full what he sees and hears.

(iv) To impart that knowledge of public affairs and of the history of his own neighbourhood which a citizen must possess if he is to perform with intelligence his duties as a member of the community ultimately responsible for the government of the parish, rural district, county and country.

(v) To provide facilities for the study of the arts, trades and professions which constitute the occupation of the inhabitants.

(vi) To remove as far as possible all obstacles from the path of the serious student of any subject.[1]

In recent years some libraries have gone beyond the mere provision of books and embarked on direct adult educational provision in the way of lectures, concerts, and the like, but before the war this was rare, being possible only in those cases where a library operated under a special local act, or in conjunction with a museum or art gallery. Elsewhere public libraries could do no more than offer, where practicable, much appreciated hospitality to the meetings of adult classes and local cultural societies.[2]

Art Galleries and Museums

In comparison with the public library system the provision of art galleries and museums was sporadic and ill-organised—indeed not organised at all. A survey by S. F. Markham, completed in 1938, shows that there were at that time about 800 such institutions in Great Britain. Rather more than half of these were general collections —art, archaeology, botany, zoology, ethnography, and so forth, varying in emphasis from one institution to another, and often with a local bias. Another 165 were historical (archaeological museums, folk museums, naval and military museums, memorial museums,

---

[1] Kenyon Report, p. 95; McColvin, *op. cit.*, p. 2.

[2] C. Thomson, E. Sydney, and M. D. Tompkins, *Adult Education Activities for Public Libraries* (Unesco, Paris 1950), pp. 28–30. The Liverpool Public Library, under the terms of a special act, has provided free public lectures since 1866—T. Kelly, *Adult Education in Liverpool* (Liverpool 1960), p. 32. For pioneer work at Leyton (Essex), in the 'thirties see E. Sydney, 'Adult Education and the Public Library', in *Adult Education*, Vol. XIX (1946–7).

etc.) ; 100 were devoted to natural history, 20 to medicine, and 20 to industry; and about 80 were art galleries. The National institutions, such as the British Museum, the Victoria and Albert Museum, the National Gallery, and the national museums and galleries of Scotland, were under government control; of the rest some 400 were controlled by local authorities, and the others by societies, trusts, universities, colleges, schools, and various private or semi-private organisations.

All this sounds fairly impressive, but in fact these institutions varied enormously in size and efficiency. They ranged from the great national collections, systematically arranged and well displayed, to a jumble of oddments mouldering in a single room under the custody of a caretaker or part-time curator. About 480 of them had to be maintained on an annual income of less than £300. The distribution, moreover, was completely random, depending largely on the incidence of endowments. Central London had 70, Stratford-on-Avon had 6, and there were 250 in centres of less than 10,000 population; but a score of towns with over 40,000 population were without a museum or gallery of any kind. In short, the museum movement was 'one of the most haphazard, one of the most neglected, and one of the least understood of civic services'.[1]

There was, however, one encouraging feature: in the inter-war years, and especially after the issue of an earlier Carnegie Trust report by Sir Henry Miers in 1928,[2] there were in the better-equipped museums notable improvements in methods of conservation and display, and an increasing awareness of their educational responsibilities, both to schoolchildren and to adults. Curators learned to select their material, arrange it attractively, and make it tell a story; and this more effective arrangement was supplemented in many cases by guide lectures, lectures to outside organisations, special exhibitions, and attractive printed guides. But the bad traditions of the past persisted, and these well-meant efforts did not always meet with the public interest they deserved.

The Newspaper Press

We come, in conclusion, to what it is now fashionable to call the mass media—the centuries-old medium of the press, and the new twentieth-century media of the cinema and broadcasting. In the nineteenth century, when 300,000 was a large circulation for a daily

[1] S. F. Markham, *The Museums and Art Galleries of the British Isles* (Edinburgh 1938), p. 11.
[2] Sir Henry Miers, *A Report on the Public Museums of the British Isles* (Edinburgh 1928). Appendix I gives a list of museums, with dates of foundation and other particulars.

paper, the press had not been a mass medium. It was Northcliffe who made it such—Northcliffe and the other press lords who followed in his footsteps: his brother Lord Rothermere, who succeeded to the control of the *Daily Mail* (but not, mercifully, of *The Times*) when Northcliffe died in 1922; Lord Beaverbrook of the *Daily Express*; Lord Camrose of the *Daily Telegraph*, and his brother Lord Kemsley of the *Sunday Times*; Lord Southwood of the *Daily Herald*. Each of these owned not one paper but many, and their operations involved not only the London press but the provincial press also. The local papers, which had contributed so much to the variety and independence of English journalism, found themselves bought, sold, amalgamated, and not infrequently closed down at the whim of the Fleet Street magnates.

By high-pressure journalism and high-pressure salesmanship the sales of the popular national dailies were forced up to undreamt-of levels. By 1937 the *Express* had a circulation of 2,300,000, and the *Herald* was not far behind; while rapidly rising in popularity, and soon to outstrip all the rest, was the *Daily Mirror*, which under the editorial direction of H. G. Bartholomew was aiming at a mass readership below the level so far reached by any daily paper.

Thus on the eve of the second World War there were more newspaper readers in the country than ever before. It cannot be said, however, that most of the newspapers they read were instruments, or even auxiliaries, of adult education. They purveyed, it is true, a certain amount of information, but the emphasis was on the sensational and all too often the salacious, and objective reporting was at a discount. The *Daily Mirror* did not even attempt to cover all the news of the day, believing that most of what passed as important in the quality papers was of little interest to the man in the street. Kingsley Martin, in 1928, described the Northcliffe press as 'an antidote as well as a substitute for adult education'[1]: by the late 'thirties the popular press was an even more powerful antidote.

We must not, however, overlook one very significant fact, and that is, that the circulation of the serious daily papers—*The Times*, the *Manchester Guardian*, and the *Telegraph*—though small in comparison with that of the popular press (it was 6 per cent in 1930) was steadily increasing, and indeed increasing at a proportionately faster rate. It was this sector of the press that continued to serve the cause of adult education. Francis Williams, writing in 1957, comments that taking into account also the continued expansion in the sales of the *Observer*

[1] K. Martin, 'The Press and Adult Education', in *Journal of Adult Education*, Vol. II (1927–8).

and the *Sunday Times*, and of the serious weekly reviews such as the *New Statesman*, the *Spectator*, and the *Economist*, 'the optimism of those who believed that secondary education would eventually produce an increased demand for serious journalism does not seem altogether absurd although it may have been pitched too high'.[1]

The Cinema

Even more dramatic than the rise of the popular press was the advent of the cinema. In 1910 it was still a novelty: ten years later it was the most popular form of entertainment in the country. By 1930 the sound film had arrived, and except in the remoter rural areas cinema-going was an almost universal pastime. At the outbreak of the second World War there were in Great Britain some 5,000 cinemas, catering for an average weekly audience of 20 millions or more.[2] To some extent the cinema displaced the theatre and the music-hall, but it also built up a vast new clientèle of its own. Liverpool, for example, had in 1913 11 theatres and 32 cinemas; in 1931 it had only 6 theatres, but 69 cinemas.[3]

Adult educationists, among others, were quick to appreciate the educational possibilities of the film, and the British Institute of Adult Education took a leading part in securing the establishment, in 1929, of an unofficial Commission on Educational and Cultural Films. The report prepared by this body, *The Film in National Life* (1932), led to the establishment in the following year of the British Film Institute, 'to encourage the use and development of the cinema as a means of entertainment and instruction'. The Scottish Film Council was set up in 1934 with similar functions.

In the meantime Great Britain had begun to make a special and distinctive contribution in this field by the development of the documentary film. The lead was taken by John Grierson, of the Empire Marketing Board, whose film *Drifters*, a study of the Scottish herring fleet produced in 1929, set a pattern and a standard. When the Empire Marketing Board was closed in 1934, the film unit was taken over by the General Post Office, which continued the work. A number of other documentary film units, industrial or commercial, came into existence later in the 'thirties, and by 1939 these various units had made, mainly at the request of industrial concerns or

---

[1] F. Williams, *Dangerous Estate* (1957), p. 209. Chs. x–xv of this book give an admirable account of the development of the press during this period.

[2] The Arts Enquiry, *The Factual Film* (Political and Economic Planning 1947), p. 198. The figures given here, based on an American source, are 5,300 cinemas and 20–23 million average weekly audience. Political and Economic Planning, *The British Film Industry* (1952), estimates the number of cinemas at 4,800.

[3] D. C. Jones (ed.), *Social Survey of Merseyside* (Liverpool 1934), Vol. III, p. 279.

government agencies, some 300 films, providing 'a unique record of British life, its health, education and social services, its industries and communications'.[1] Many of these films were made available free to schools and other educational organisations, and they were also fairly extensively shown by the sponsoring organisations, but it has to be recorded that their use in formal adult education was, up to 1939, almost negligible, chiefly owing to the lack of projectors, screens, and other facilities.

It was, in fact, through the commercial cinema that the film made its biggest adult educational impact. The average adult rarely saw a documentary film, but he saw hundreds of commercial films, and not everything he saw was shoddy and second-rate. He saw, from time to time, films based on some of the masterpieces of world literature; he saw films of current news, of travel, of natural life; he became familiar, by sight, with the world's famous statesmen, and with the ways of life of people in other lands and other ranks of society; his horizons were immeasurably broadened. Much of what he saw, like much of what he read in the newspapers, was bad, but much was genuinely educative.

Broadcasting

Broadcasting, as an instrument of mass communication, dates from the 'twenties. It was in 1920 that the Marconi Company began to broadcast from Chelmsford short daily programmes of news, songs, and music. The British Broadcasting Company took over the service in 1922, and was reconstituted as a public corporation, the British Broadcasting Corporation, in 1927. In 1927 there were already $2\frac{1}{4}$ million licensed receivers; by 1934 there were $6\frac{1}{4}$ million, by 1938, $8\frac{1}{2}$ million (out of a total of some 12 million households).

Though broadcasting was primarily an instrument of entertainment and recreation, the B.B.C. recognised from the beginning that it also had an educational function, and as early as 1924, in co-operation with adult education interests, a regular series of educational talks was included in the evening programme. In 1927 a separate adult education section was formed; short series of twenty-minute talks were arranged regularly on five evenings and one afternoon each week; and the spoken word was supplemented by pamphlets giving detailed notes, illustrations, and guidance on reading.

In 1928 a committee of inquiry set up by the B.B.C. and the British Institute of Adult Education, with Sir Henry Hadow as Chairman, made a number of important recommendations. On the

---

[1] Arts Enquiry, *The Factual Film*, p. 12.

place of broadcasting in adult education they expressed themselves as follows:

The adult education movement, vigorous as it is, touches as yet only a small proportion of the population. Broadcasting, which is the latest agency to place itself at the disposal of this movement, can fill many of the existing gaps; it can widen the field from which students are drawn, by its power to reach and stimulate a large public; it can provide a means of education for those beyond the reach of other agencies; it can put listeners in touch with the leaders of thought and the chief experts in many subjects; and it can lead on to more formal or more intensive study. There is little danger that it will supplant other educational facilities, especially if the educational bodies take their share in its development.[1]

The committee went on to argue, however, that 'contact between mind and mind is a vital part of the educational process', and they therefore recommended that everything should be done to stimulate the formation of discussion groups whose work would be related to broadcast programmes. For this purpose the collaboration of the established adult education agencies was essential, and they therefore recommended the formation of a Central Council for Adult Education, with area councils based on extra-mural areas.[2]

All these recommendations were implemented, and for the next eighteen years a great deal of time, energy, and money were devoted to the promotion of wireless discussion groups.[3] The results were at first very disappointing, and in 1934 the scale of educational broadcasts was reduced. In the immediate pre-war years the B.B.C. enlisted the help of the L.E.A.s, many of whom appointed paid leaders and operated groups under the regulations for further education. As a result the number of groups seems to have increased, but was still under 600 in 1938-9. Eventually in 1946 the scheme was abandoned. Its weakness was, as the North Wales District of the W.E.A. pointed out at an early stage, that 'such groups were only successful where a very well-qualified group leader was present', and 'in these circumstances the need for a wireless lecturer is not great'.[4]

---

[1] B.B.C., *New Ventures in Broadcasting* (1928), p. 87.
[2] *Op. cit.*, pp. 87-90.
[3] The Home Counties, Wales, and Scotland were not included in the area council scheme till 1934-5.
[4] M. D. Stocks, *The Workers' Educational Association: the First Fifty Years* (1953), p. 104. On the listening group movement generally see F. E. Hill and W. E. Williams, *Radio's Listening Groups* (Columbia Univ. P., New York 1941); and articles by G. W. Gibson in World Association for Adult Education, *Bulletin*, 2nd Ser., No. XIX (Nov. 1939), and *Adult Education*, Vol. XI (1938-9), pp. 273 sqq., and Vol. XIII (1940-1), pp. 195 sqq. The figures for the number of groups vary a great deal in different accounts: the figure for 1938-9 given above is based on information kindly supplied to me by the B.B.C.

The one good thing that came out of the movement was the B.B.C.'s weekly journal, *The Listener*.

In spite of the ill success attending group listening, the educational impact of the B.B.C. was enormous. Like the cinema, it did its most effective work through its normal programmes. The regular talks about books, plays, films, music, travel, and current affairs, delivered under the auspices of the Talks Department and not as part of the educational programme, caught the imagination and interest not only of the expert but of people hitherto untouched by the normal adult education agencies, and set a high standard of authoritative and impartial treatment. 'It is undoubtedly', wrote the Hadow Committee, 'in its influence on the general listener that broadcasting is doing its most valuable pioneer work.'[1]

In no branch of its work did the B.B.C. make so big an impact as in music. Mrs. Stocks vividly sums up the changed situation:

The days when the Manchester University Settlement had loaded its piano on to a milk-float and trundled it through the slums in order that the denizens of those mean streets might catch an echo of great music, were gone. From the curtained windows of these same streets would blare the works of the world's finest composers, beautifully performed, if, perhaps, a little over-amplified.[2]

But it was not only the inhabitants of the slums who benefited from the new dispensation. Musical education in the schools was often lamentably inadequate when broadcasting began, and many adults who grew up before or during the 'twenties were indebted almost wholly to the B.B.C. for the opening up of a new world of interest and delight.

[1] *New Ventures in Broadcasting*, p. 8.
[2] Stocks, *op. cit.*, p. 105.

19
The Twentieth Century

THE SECOND WORLD WAR

The Home Front

THE years of the first World War had brought a slump in adult education, followed by a revival. The same happened in the second World War, but this time the slump was less severe and the revival far more dramatic. The difference can be attributed partly to more selective mobilisation of manpower and partly to the fact that women, who were less liable to be mobilised, now formed nearly half the students in university and W.E.A. classes. It also reflects, however, the increased strength and stability of the work following the steady growth of the inter-war years.

That there was some falling off at the outset is not surprising. Mobilisation, evacuation, the black-out, crowded and inadequate transport, overtime and shift working, and in some areas the constant peril of aerial bombardment—all these things were enough, it might have been thought, to deter all but the most fanatical enthusiasts. Everyone seemed to have two jobs to do in the daytime, and another, as fire-watcher or air-raid warden, at night; and everyone was in the front line. In an astonishingly short time, however, people adjusted themselves to these nightmare conditions. Tutors made long and often hazardous journeys across country, in cars with hooded headlights, or in dimly lit trains and buses; students picked their way with shaded torches through the darkened streets; all over the country, in schools, libraries, technical colleges, municipal offices, even private houses, in varying conditions of comfort and discomfort, the work of adult education went on. In some badly hit areas such as Merseyside, classes were transferred to Saturday and Sunday afternoons to allow students to reach their homes before nightfall. Where classes continued to meet in the evenings part of the proceedings might have to be conducted in an air-raid shelter with an accompanying crash of bombs.[1] Attendance was, inevitably, apt to be irregular, and reading and written work was sometimes sketchy.

[1] A. McPhee, *A Short History of Extra-Mural Work at Liverpool University* (Liverpool 1949), p. 10.

The dangers and difficulties of the war-time situation, however, created a comradeship, and a sense of urgency and high seriousness, which had not been matched, one imagines, since the early days of the tutorial class. This was especially so in the last two years of the war, as victory came more and more distinctly into sight, and classes turned their attention increasingly to the problems of reconstruction, the problems of building a new world on the ruins of the old. Some of their hopes were destined to frustration, but not all: the great series of social reforms which followed the war owed much to the favourable climate of public opinion which adult education had helped to create.

By the end of the war the number of Responsible Body courses in England and Wales, which had been 3,040 in 1938–9, and had fallen to 2,656 in 1940–1, had risen to 4,311.[1] It should, however, be remarked that these high figures owed something to a wartime relaxation by the Board of Education of the student numbers required to qualify for grant; and also that the increase in the total masks a decline in the number of three-year and advanced tutorial classes, from 783 in 1937–8 to 579 in 1944–5, and a corresponding increase in the number of one-year and other shorter courses.[2]

An unexpected outcome of the adversities of war was the creation in December, 1939, of C.E.M.A.—the Council for theEncouragement of Music and the Arts.[3] The purpose of this body was to prevent the growing public interest in the practice and appreciation of the arts from being snuffed out by the war. It was founded on the initiative of Lord de la Warr, President of the Board of Education, with the enthusiastic support of Dr. Thomas Jones, Secretary of the Pilgrim Trust, and, among others, W. E. Williams (now Sir William Emrys Williams), Secretary of the British Institute of Adult Education. It was financed, until 1942, partly by the Board of Education and partly by the Pilgrim Trust, but thereafter exclusively by the Board.

C.E.M.A. began by assisting voluntary bodies in music, drama and the arts, but soon moved into the field of direct provision. It organised music concerts in factories, churches, hospitals, air raid shelters, wherever an audience could be found; it assisted professional orchestras such as the Hallé and the Liverpool Philharmonic to visit

---

[1] I take this figure for 1944–5 from Ministry of Education, *The Organisation and Finance of Adult Education in England and Wales* [The Ashby Report] (1954), App. 2, pp. 54–5, which provides a convenient table showing the growth of Responsible Body work from 1907–8 to 1952–3. No comparable figures are available for Scotland, but the Report of the Scottish Education Department for 1947 shows that the number of students enrolled in classes under the Adult Education Regulations was 8,900 in 1938–9 and 10,100 in 1944–5.

[2] Central Joint Advisory Committee on Tutorial Classes, *Annual Report, 1944-5*, p. 6.

[3] Originally 'Committee'—the name was changed in 1940.

small towns which had never before heard a first-class symphony orchestra; it sponsored countrywide tours by three Old Vic companies driven from their London home, and by ballet and opera companies from Sadler's Wells, the Ballet Rambert and the Ballet Jooss; it took over and expanded the 'Art for the People' scheme which had been inaugurated by the British Institute of Adult Education in 1935 in order to provide people remote from the great centres of population with the opportunity to see and appreciate original works of art.

All this activity was so immensely stimulating and successful that when the end of the war came it was inconceivable that it should be abandoned, and in 1946 the Council was reconstituted by royal charter as that now familiar and beneficial institution, the Arts Council of Great Britain. Its first Secretary-General was Miss Mary Glasgow, who had acted in the same capacity to C.E.M.A.: its second, from 1951, was W. E. Williams.[1]

The Civilian Contribution to Forces Education

The greatest achievement of adult education during the war years, however, was in the unpromising field of education for members of H.M. Forces. We have seen that the civilian organisation built up for this purpose during the first World War was quickly allowed to lapse once the war was over,[2] but the lessons arising from this experience were not forgotten. The initiative this time was taken by Ernest Green, General Secretary of the W.E.A., and his colleague George Wigg (now Lord Wigg), District Secretary for North Staffordshire. The support of the universities and the Y.M.C.A. was quickly secured, and by August, 1939, a plan was already agreed for the creation of a central committee and subordinate regional committees to co-ordinate the resources of the civilian bodies for the education of the young 'militiamen' called up under the Military Service Act passed earlier in the year. Within a fortnight, however, war had broken out, and the problem of the militiamen was swallowed up in the greater problem of an army at war.

The civilian bodies, at this critical juncture, boldly demanded not only that a scheme similar to that evolved for the militiamen should be made available to the entire personnel of H.M. Forces, but also that the work should be carried on in strict accord with the

---

[1] A good brief account of all this is given in the *Eleventh Annual Report* of the Arts Council for 1955–6, pp. 5–14. For the origins of 'Art for the People' see *Adult Education*, Vol. VII (1934–5), pp. 183–5.
[2] See above, pp. 304–7.

principles of civilian adult education: voluntary attendance, impartial instruction, free discussion, and as much continuity as possible. By January, 1940, a Central Advisory Council for Education in H.M. Forces was in existence, with Sir Walter Moberly, Chairman of the University Grants Committee, as Chairman, and the sage and experienced Basil Yeaxlee as Secretary. Service representatives attended as observers, and eventually, in August, 1940, satisfactory arrangements were made for the work to be financed from Service funds.[1]

In September, the Army Council issued a memorandum on *Education in the War-time Army*, setting out the recommendations of a special committee under the chairmanship of Lieutenant-General Sir Robert Haining. In their acceptance of the need for education the members of the committee fell short of enthusiasm. They justified it on the same grounds as the welfare service—'not only as a means of satisfying, in the case of many men, a personal want, but also on the ground that it contributes directly to the maintenance of morale and military efficiency'[2]. They did, however, concede that 'whatever is done must be not only on a voluntary basis but related to a genuine demand from the men'[3]. In the circumstances, perhaps it would have been unreasonable to expect more.

At this point I venture to quote a passage from an earlier work concerned with extra-mural work at Manchester University:

It was one of the astonishing things about the late war that, in the midst of the greatest crisis that had ever threatened the British Isles, responsible leaders of the armed forces found time and personnel to expand their educational service. Cromwell's saying about 'the plain russet-coated captain that knows what he fights for, and loves what he knows', was frequently quoted, and an earnest attempt was made to act on it. From the outset, however, it was clear that if adequate provision was made it would be necessary to call in civilian help to supplement the work of the Forces education officers. At Manchester a beginning was made by the Extra-Mural Department in collaboration with the Local Education Authority. Later (1940) on the initiative of the newly formed Central Advisory Council for Education in H.M. Forces, regional committees to organise this work were established in extra-mural areas all over the country. At Manchester the Regional Committee represented the University, the W.E.A., the Local Education Authorities, the Y.M.C.A., the B.B.C., and the Services, and the work was administered throughout from the Extra-

---

[1] The fullest account of this phase is to be found in N. S. Wilson, *Education in the Forces, 1939–46: The Civilian Contribution* (1949), Ch. i.
[2] Army Council, *Education in the War-time Army* (War Office 1940), p. 10.
[3] *Op. cit.*, p. 4.

Mural Department. The Director of Extra-Mural Studies undertook the Honorary Secretaryship. . . .

The Regional Committee served all the armed forces in the area—Army, Anti-Aircraft, Navy, R.A.F. (including the women's services), A.T.S., W.R.N.S., and W.A.A.F. It provided courses and classes, residential and non-residential, for officers and for the rank and file, for audiences of several hundreds in large units, and equally for handfuls of men and women scattered over the countryside at Searchlight and Balloon sites. It taught history, geography, economics and politics, science and psychology, music and literature, carpentry and cookery; no subject asked for was ever refused where resources were available to meet the demand. It instructed the instructors. On one occasion it even provided a course of lectures for the officers of a large army unit on The Strategy of the War.[1]

The same kind of story could be told about any one of the twenty-three Regional Committees in the country, each of which was based on a university area. From the beginning this was a joint enter-prise, in which the Forces and all the appropriate civilian organisations collaborated towards a common end. As the prospect of an early victory receded, and the long, slow build-up towards D-Day began, the provision made was extended and elaborated. The teams of part-time lecturers and teachers recruited by the Regional Committees with the help of the Universities, the W.E.A., and the local education authorities, were supplemented from 1941 onwards by full-time personnel, a few only at first, but increasing to nearly one hundred before the war ended. The programme of lectures and courses arranged under the auspices of the Central Advisory Council steadily built up, until by the winter of 1943–4 the number of meetings arranged totalled more than 4,000 per week.[2]

The Forces, the Regional Committees, and other civilian organisations collaborated in the provision of books for private study, tools and materials for painting, sculpture and handicrafts, instruments and music for bands and orchestras, and records for gramophone clubs; and in promoting concerts, plays and exhibitions. At one stage, Northern, Southern and Western Commands each had a symphony orchestra recruited from among Service men and women. Many units acquired some kind of quiet room, study centre, or craft room, and in towns where there was a considerable concentration of Forces personnel, e.g. Dover, Liverpool, and Glasgow, there was often a 'Quiet Club' or 'Services Centre' open to all three Services.

---

[1] T. Kelly, *Outside the Walls: Sixty Years of University Extension at Manchester, 1886–1946* (Manchester 1950), pp. 83–4.
[2] For detailed statistics see Wilson, *op. cit.*, p. 171.

The Y.M.C.A., which did so much in so many ways to promote Forces education, was particularly generous in making its premises available for purposes of this kind.[1]

If the attendance at Regional Committee lectures was not always as voluntary as the civilian organisers would have liked, if there were more single lectures and fewer courses than could ideally be desired, if the proportion of the work devoted to current affairs was unduly large, these were drawbacks which, under wartime conditions, were accepted philosophically. Indeed heretical spirits were heard to murmur, *sotto voce*, that for some people a measure of compulsion was, in the first instance, no bad thing. The real answer to the problem of those who did not want education, however, was provided by that remarkable pair Dobson and Young, who were nominally attached to the Manchester Regional Committee, but soon became so famous that they were in demand everywhere. Of them I have written elsewhere:

> Walter Dobson and Walter Young came to this work from the world of business. Their gift for the popular exposition of music was discovered early in the war, and in 1941 they were appointed full-time lecturers. Combining as they did a sound knowledge of music and a deep love for it with a manner of presentation which had all the humour and slickness of a music-hall turn, their appeal was irresistible. Even the toughest audiences never failed to respond, and many thousands of men and women were roused, not merely to laughter, but to genuine interest and the beginnings of musical appreciation.[2]

Their formula, Dobson used to say, was 90 per cent entertainment and 10 per cent education. It is a formula worth pondering by·those who are concerned about popular resistance to adult education.

A.B.C.A. and B.W.P.

The Army grasped the nettle of compulsory education firmly when in the autumn of 1941 it directed regimental officers—not the Army Education Corps but the ordinary platoon and company commanders—to talk to their men at least once a week, during training time, about current events and problems, and to allow them full opportunity for questions and discussion. To provide the necessary

---

[1] On all this see Wilson, *op. cit.*, Chs. vi, x: T. H. Hawkins and L. J. F. Brimble, *Adult Education: the Record of the British Army* (1947), Chs. xi–xiii and xxiii; C. Lloyd, *British Services Education* (1950), Ch. i; A. C. T. White, *The Story of Army Education, 1643–1963* (1963), Pt. 2, Ch. i. Lloyds is the only work which deals with all three Services, but a valuable brief conspectus is given in a broadsheet issued by Political and Economic Planning on 'Education in the Services' (*Planning*, No. 234, May 18, 1945).

[2] Kelly, *op. cit.*, p. 85.

teaching material there was established, alongside the Directorate of Army Education, a new organisation known as the Army Bureau of Current Affairs, which from September began to issue expertly written weekly bulletins: a fortnightly series on *War*, to provide general information as to what was happening in the various theatres of action; and an alternating fortnightly series on *Current Affairs*, providing background knowledge on a wide range of problems foreign and domestic. These A.B.C.A. pamphlets were and remained the backbone of the work, but as time went on they were reinforced by other media—films, filmstrips, exhibitions, a fortnightly *Map Review*, 'brains trusts', wall newspapers, radio talks, and even dramatic performances by touring A.B.C.A. Players. Many of the larger units developed attractive Information Rooms where visual material could be displayed.

On the Army side the main impetus for this new scheme came from General Sir Ronald Adam, Adjutant-General and Colonel Commandant of the Army Education Corps; on the civilian side it came from W. E. Williams of the British Institute of Adult Education, who appropriately was appointed Director of the new Bureau. The Central Advisory Council was not consulted in advance, and was only reluctantly brought to consent, but having consented it encouraged the Regional Committees to render the fullest possible assistance, by organising briefing courses to assist officers with background information, and training courses to instruct them in methods of teaching and discussion. The Army Education Corps also played an active part in this work, and when the Army School of Education at Wakefield proved insufficient Coleg Harlech, the Welsh adult education college, was taken over as an A.B.C.A. training centre.[1]

Once A.B.C.A. had broken the ice it was easier for the Regional Committees to accept the British Way and Purpose Scheme, which was announced by the Directorate of Army Education as part of the winter training programme for 1942–3, and continued, like A.B.C.A., until the end of the war. This scheme provided for an hour's compulsory education in citizenship, and was based on a series of monthly briefing bulletins, each dealing with some broad theme such as 'The Family and the Neighbourhood' or 'You and the Empire', and each divided into four chapters suitable for weekly use. In 1944 the bulletins were bound up into volume form. This time it was not insisted that the instruction be given by regimental officers: units were free to find lecturers wherever they were available. The Regional

[1] For A.B.C.A., see especially Hawkins and Brimble, *op. cit.*, Ch. vi; Wilson, *op. cit.*, Ch. iv.

Committees, therefore, were able to assist in this scheme not only by organising briefing courses for officers but also by providing a certain amount of direct teaching.[1]

The Army also organised, from an early·stage of the war, a variety of correspondence courses mainly for professional examinations,[2] and elementary courses in modern languages (textbooks and records)[3]. From 1943 onwards, for both military and educational reasons, a determined effort was made to deal with the illiteracy which still afflicted a small number of recruits—apparently about 2 per cent, though the estimates vary. Fifteen Basic Education Centres were established in various parts of the country, and with the help of sympathetic instruction in small groups many of the men concerned were able to make substantial and encouraging progress. A civilian observer appointed by the War Office to review the work reported:

> The difference between the men beginning a course and the men finishing a course was so great as to be almost incredible. Many men beginning their course were slovenly in appearance, slow, suspicious, shy, afraid, unhappy and obviously feeling inferior. They were emotionally disturbed. Those in the later weeks of a course were clean, smart, alert soldiers. They were happy, friendly, well-mannered, well-poised and confident. They had acquired a self-respect that some had lost and some had never had.

> The progress made in acquiring reading techniques in the short period of six weeks far surpassed my most optimistic hopes. Only total illiterates were selected to attend, yet out of every thirty men attending courses, between ten and twenty reached the stage of being able to read and understand a newspaper. Practically all reached the stage of being able, unaided, to write letters to their families.[4]

Many of the educational activities so far described were provided by the Army. The Royal Navy and the Royal Air Force were till 1943 too heavily engaged operationally to spare much time for education, but thereafter development was rapid, and by the end of the war the facilities available to the personnel of their Services were 'as nearly parallel to those existing in the Army as the conditions peculiar to each Service permit.'[5] Some use was made of A.B.C.A. and B.W.P. material, and the R.A.F. also had its own

---

[1] For the British Way and Purpose Scheme see especially Hawkins and Brimble, *op. cit.*, Ch. vii; Wilson, *op. cit.*, Ch. v.

[2] Hawkins and Brimble, *op. cit.*, Ch. x; White, *op. cit.*, pp. 93–5.

[3] P.E.P. 'Education in the Services', *ut sup.*, p. 11.

[4] Hawkins and Brimble, *op. cit.*, pp. 232–3. On literacy education generally see Ch. xiv of this work, and White, *op. cit.*, pp. 112–15.

[5] P.E.P., *op. cit.*, p. 6.

current affairs journal, *Target*. Some of the R.A.F. Information Rooms and Education Centres were particularly impressive; one station opened in 1945 a 'Community Club' which included a newsroom, a library, a clubroom for lectures, discussions, concerts, films and plays, a handicrafts room, a games room and a canteen.[1]

Even this is not a complete picture of this tremendous and many-sided enterprise. We have to take note also, though we can do no more, of the work done among Allied and Dominion Forces stationed in this country; among the personnel in hospitals, convalescent homes, detention centres and camps for prisoners of war; and by a voluntary extension of the scheme among National Fire Service and Civil Defence personnel, especially in London and North-West England. A Civil Defence Discussion Groups Bureau was established at the beginning of 1944.[2]

Victory and Demobilisation

It might have been supposed that D-Day on 6th June, 1944, would have put a stop to many of these activities, as the camps began to empty and troops poured across the Channel to reinforce the invasion of the Continent, but this was not the case:

The invasion of Normandy in 1944 caused no curtailment of the work of the educational staffs. In fact they shouldered new responsibilities. The dissemination of news, the establishment of education centres, language teaching, and assistance with the rehabilitation of the wounded in hospitals were only four of the tasks which became increasingly the responsibility of the education officer in addition to his other duties. A complement of the Army Educational Corps sailed with the early convoys to the Normandy beaches; instructor-officers were, of course, in the warships which on June 6th stood off the coast of France, while their R.A.F. colleagues had their appropriate rôle with the tactical Air Forces.[3]

By this time planning for eventual demobilisation was already far advanced. This was another immense and carefully thought out operation, covering all three Services at home and abroad. In the Army and R.A.F. it was launched in May, 1945, following the defeat of Germany, but in the Royal Navy it could not become fully effective until the defeat of Japan in the autumn of that year. In all three Services the scheme provided for up to six hours' instruction per week. In the Educational and Vocational Training Schemes of the

---

[1] *Op. cit.*, p. 18.
[2] Hawkins and Brimble, *op. cit.*, pp. 128–32, 405–9; Wilson, *op. cit.*, Ch. viii; White, *op. cit.*, pp. 115–17, 123–5. For the Civil Defence Services see P.E.P., *op. cit.*, pp. 20–2.
[3] C. Lloyd, *British Services Education* (1950), p. 21.

Navy and the Air Force, one hour of the six was to be devoted to compulsory education in citizenship, the rest was available for vocational training in order to fit sailors and airmen better for their return to civilian life. In the Army's Education Scheme for the Release Period two of the six hours were devoted to citizenship and current affairs, the remainder to general or vocational education. Special Formation Colleges, of which there were five in Great Britain and six abroad, provided one-month courses at a more advanced level in science and mathematics, commerce, modern studies, arts and crafts, trades, domestic science and instructor training. Nearly three million carefully selected books were ordered for distribution to command and unit libraries.

For the purpose of these release schemes the teaching resources of the Services were augmented, wherever possible, from within their own ranks, but the Regional Committees also played an important rôle, and the Central Advisory Council was instrumental in securing agreement on the establishment of the Forces Preliminary Examination—an examination at about School Certificate level which was widely accepted by Universities and professional bodies as evidence that a certain standard had been reached.

As events turned out, the sudden collapse of Japan in the autumn of 1945 dramatically foreshortened the time available for the release schemes. Many carefully laid plans, in consequence, were never fully implemented. None the less much good work was done, especially in the Formation Colleges and in the residential centres acquired by certain Regional Committees. One such centre was Holly Royde, Manchester, which was opened for Forces work in November, 1944. An account of one of the general education courses there, conducted for men and women, most of whom had left school at fourteen and had had no experience of adult education in civilian life, shows the traditional techniques being successfully adapted to new tasks. Broadly speaking, these courses were concerned with citizenship—'The Rights of Man' was a common title—but the method used was instructive rather than descriptive:

> While it is true that a knowledge of the machinery of Local Government is useful, real understanding of the nature of citizenship does not necessarily result from it. There is need to delve below the surface to try to discover the significance of concepts like 'democracy', which are used so freely and so vaguely. Therefore at Holly Royde the method adopted was to choose, say, freedom as the central theme and to examine it from a variety of angles, historical, political, literary and economic, in the endeavour to find out how the idea has grown, what it has meant to past generations,

the part It plays or ought to play in modern society, how it has been or can be safeguarded and what the loss of it has involved. Such a subject can, so to speak, be twisted and turned, the light of investigation being directed now on one facet, now on another. By such methods a subject can be brought to life, it can be made stimulating, the study of it an adventure. So handled, it evoked the liveliest interest and response among the students. It gave rise to prolonged discussion and was the means of producing written work of real quality.[1]

It was usually thought that the methods of civilian adult education could not succeed with the rank and file of the Services. This account shows that given the right setting, and the right teachers, they could.

We have quoted H. A. L. Fisher as saying of army education in the first World War that 'Nothing in the shape of adult education has ever been attempted on the same scale in the whole history of the world'.[2] We have also quoted the 1919 Committee's assessment of its quality: 'much of the work was necessarily slight and fugitive; where circumstances were more favourable it was more solid and continuous; while a certain part reached a comparatively high standard.'[3] How can one judge the achievement of Services education in the second World War? Certainly it was on a vastly greater scale than in the first World War. For the first time something approaching the saturation techniques of modern advertising was applied to adult education. Everyone was brought in, willy nilly, even the illiterates. And it was done, of course, by compulsion. The work of the Regional Committees had effected, it was calculated, about twenty per cent of the Forces:[4] it was A.B.C.A. and B.W.P. that brought in the rest. Whether the work at its peak attained a higher level than in the first World War is difficult to say, but certainly the base of the pyramid was broadened.

There were not lacking those who argued that all compulsion was wrong, and that army discipline was incompatible with true adult education. To those involved day by day in the teaching work, however, it often seemed that the element of compulsion was quite irrelevant, and that education was no more incompatible with discipline in the army than it was in a school: everything depended on the way the subject was taught, and the kind of atmosphere the

---

[1] Wilson, *op. cit.*, p. 159. See also for the Release period Ch. xi of this work; Hawkins and Brimble, *op. cit.*, Chs. xix–xxi; White *op. cit.*, Pt. 2, Ch. v; J. H. P. Pafford, *Books and Army Education, 1944–46* (Aslib 1946).
[2] See above, p. 306.
[3] *Ibid.*
[4] See the article by Sir Ronald Adam in *Times Educational Supplement*, 6 Dec. 1941, p. 581.

teacher could create. Perhaps in retrospect we can say that this was one of the most important lessons that war-time education taught.

Something was learned, too, of the techniques which would be needed if a wider interest in adult education was to be aroused and sustained in civilian life: throughout the Forces work there was a new emphasis on discussion, on practical work, on visual aids of all kinds, and on entertainment as an element in popular education. There was recognition, too, that much of the success of the work depended on the community setting that the Forces provided, and the experience of the release period especially emphasised the value of residential centres where adult education could be, for a short time at least, insulated from the distractions of ordinary life.

Something of all this was eventually carried forward into civilian life. It is true that an attempt to convert A.B.C.A. to civilian uses as the Bureau of Current Affairs (still under the directorship of W. E. Williams) met with only indifferent success, and had to be wound up in 1951.[1] But the experience of Forces education did give a fillip to the movement for community centres, an extension of which was high among the priorities of the post-war Ministry of Education; and we shall see that this experience was also an important factor in promoting the development of residential adult education.[2]

[1] B. Ford, *The Bureau of Current Affairs* (1951).
[2] These developments are dealt with in more detail in the next chapter.

20

The Twentieth Century

THE POST-WAR PATTERN

Adult Education and Social Change

THE years that have succeeded the second World War have brought changes of almost unparalleled rapidity in the social, economic and educational setting within which adult education has to operate. The two catch phrases that spring to mind when we contemplate this transformation are 'the welfare state' and 'the affluent society'. Both represent important realities. The foundations of the English welfare state were laid far back in the nineteenth century, but it was the great series of enactments of the years 1944–6 that completed the edifice: the Education Act, the Family Allowances Act, the National Health Act, the National Insurance Act, the National Assistance Act, and the Children's Act. These acts, together with the priceless boon of full employment, brought to the working people of this country not only a much needed measure of security but also a substantial rise in real income.

The results can be seen all round us: better houses, more cars, more television sets, record-players and washing machines, more foreign holidays. Thanks, however, to redistributive taxation, the welfare state, and the better bargaining position created by full employment, the increase in living standards has operated mainly in favour of the lower income groups. It is the comparative affluence of the masses which is the most striking feature of the affluent society. The plumber's mate driving to work in his own car is one aspect of the new dispensation: the obverse is the middle-class householder doing his own home decorating.

From the adult education point of view it is of special interest to consider changes in education and leisure activities. The Education Act of 1944, which raised the minimum school leaving age to 15, and established the principle of free secondary education for all, opened up a period of rapid expansion, in which the growth in numbers at all levels was accentuated by the post-war increase in the birth-rate.[1] Between 1945–6 and 1966–7 the number of primary

[1] The corresponding Scottish Act was passed in 1945, with a consolidating Act in 1946.

school pupils in Great Britain jumped from just under 4 millions to 5 millions; the number of secondary school pupils from 1¾ millions to over 3 millions; the number of university students from 52,000 to 185,000; and the number of full-time and sandwich course students in other forms of further education from 54,000 to 273,000.[1]

It would be a mistake to assume from these figures that the path to higher education was now freely open to every boy and girl of ability. This was certainly not the case when the Crowther Committee reported in 1959. An inquiry made on behalf of the Committee among nearly 6,000 National Service recruits showed that half of the men in the two highest ability groups had left school at 15; for those who were sons of manual workers the proportion was two-thirds.[2] The Committee also noted that at the age of 18, in 1957–8, more than half the boys in England and Wales, and more than three-quarters of the girls, were receiving no education whatever, full-time or part-time. Even at this time, however, the position represented a revolutionary advance from that of twenty years earlier, and there has been a further improvement since. By 1967 the percentage of boys and girls of 15 and over still at school, which was 10·4 in 1950 and 13·0 in 1957, had risen to 21·7.[3]

One inevitable result of this expansion was an immense increase in the cost of education. For England and Wales alone the cost rose in money terms from £120·5 millions in 1944–5 to £1831·7 millions in 1967–8: in real terms, allowing for price inflation, the increase was of the order of 350 per cent. In 1944–5 educational expenditure represented 1·3 per cent of the gross national product, in 1967–8 it was 5·3 per cent. The universities, further education, and teacher training accounted for a large part of this increase, especially after the publication in 1963 of the Robbins Report, recommending a large scale expansion of universities and other forms of full-time higher education.[4] Expenditure by the University Grants Committee on the universities of England and Wales rose from £1·9 millions in 1944–5 to £197·5 millions in 1967–8.[5]

Unfortunately this very rapid expansion of the educational system proved rather more than the country could bear at a time when it

[1] These figures are based on the Annual Reports of the Department of Education and Science and its predecessors, and the Scottish Education Department; and on the quinquennial surveys of the University Grants Committee. The last two figures cited exclude teachers in training.
[2] Ministry of Education, Central Advisory Council (England), *15 to 18* (1959), Vol. I, pp. 8–9, 119, 131–2.
[3] Department of Education and Science, *Statistics of Education, 1967*, Vol. I, p. 23.
[4] *Higher Education: Report of the Committee appointed by the Prime Minister* (1963).
[5] The facts on all this are conveniently and impressively assembled in a pamphlet by S. Maclure, *Learning beyond our Means?* (1968).

was already, for other reasons, under considerable financial strain. The outcome was seen from the 'forties onwards in repeated economy campaigns in which non-vocational adult education came off badly for the simple reason that it was one of the few sectors of education that could be cut without interfering with agreed major developments.

There is a widespread belief that the post-war years brought a great increase in the amount of leisure time. This is in a broad sense true, but certain important qualifications need to be made. For example, office and professional workers benefited substantially from reduced working hours and especially from the five-day week, but manual workers, even though their nominal hours of work were reduced, continued for a long time to work, on the average, almost as long as before the war, taking the benefit in the form of increased overtime pay instead of increased leisure.[1]

Again, earlier marriage, earlier childbearing, and smaller families brought increased leisure in middle age;[2] and the increased expectation of life, coupled with a tendency to earlier retirement, extended the period of leisure in later life.[3] The earlier termination of parental responsibility of course benefited women rather than men, and it was women, too, who benefited most from better housing and household labour-saving devices. One result of these changes, however, was that far more married women were working, especially in the older age-groups.[4]

Whatever happened to the amount of people's leisure, the facilities for using it certainly multiplied. Thanks to the increase in the number of private cars (from under 2 millions in 1947 to over 10 millions in 1968)[5] more people than ever were now spending part of their leisure in travel. Others, having for the first time acquired houses with gardens, devoted much of their spare time to the pleasures and tribulations of gardening. There was also a tremendous upsurge of interest in music and art, both at the popular and at the more serious level.

The really outstanding change in the use of leisure, however, came

[1] According to Ministry of Labour statistics average weekly hours worked by male manual wage-earners of 21 and over were 47·7 in October 1938, 46·0 in October 1966, and 46·2 in April 1968. For women wage-earners of 18 and over the average fell from 43·5 in 1938 to 38·1 in 1966, and rose again to 38·4 in 1968. The position is interestingly analysed by R. Boston, 'What Leisure?', in New Society, 26 Dec. 1968.

[2] W. A. Sanderson, 'The Changing Population Structure', in Adult Education, Vol. XXXII (1959–60).

[3] The expectation of life of a man aged 40 increased from 29·6 years to 31·6 years between 1930/32 and 1964/66; and that of a woman from 32·4 years to 37 years.

[4] Women constituted by 1965 more than one-third of Britain's total working population, and more than half of these women were married—A. Myrdal and V. Klein, Women's Two Rôles (1956, 2nd. edn. 1968), p. 54.

[5] Monthly Digest of Statistics (Nov. 1968), p. 99.

with the advent of television. Before the war it scarcely existed: by 1960 there were television sets in over 11 million homes, and it was estimated that at 8:30 in the evening, every evening, about one-third of the adult population was watching. By 1968 the number of licences had increased to 15 millions.[1] No other medium of mass communication had ever been able to achieve such an impact. For adult education, it clearly had possibilities both good and bad. At its best it was not only in itself a powerful educational force, but also a stimulant to new interests, but just because of its powerful appeal it could exercise a disruptive effect on other leisure-time activities, and in the small household especially it presented a new hazard to the serious student. Adult education increasingly found itself in a situation in which it was not lack of leisure (as it was in the early years of the century) but the multiplicity of opportunities for the use of leisure, which constituted the main obstacle to serious and continuous adult study.

One could mention many other social changes which made themselves evident at this period and were of significance for adult education: for example the changing age-structure of the population and especially the increase in the proportion of older people;[2] the increasing proportion of clerical and administrative workers as a result of technological changes within industry;[3] and the increasing mobility which was reflected not only in people's willingness to travel both for work and for pleasure, but also in their willingness to change their place of residence and occupation.

Partly as a result of the changes that have been described there has been, during these years, a general loosening of social bonds and a blurring of traditional class distinctions. It would be wrong to say that these distinctions, which are based on occupational status, education, speech, place of residence and the like, are not still very real, but the barriers are less rigid than they were, and the fact that working people are increasingly unwilling to accept a position of social inferiority is one of great significance.

Adult education, on the whole, fared remarkably well, and despite the keen competition of other leisure-time activities substantially increased its following. Precise figures are difficult to come by, but the accompanying graphs showing student enrolments in Respon-

---

[1] *Monthly Digest of Statistics* (Oct. 1960), p. 142, (Nov. 1968) p. 145; *Granada Viewership Survey* (Jan.–Mar. 1959), pp. 1–2.

[2] The percentage of people in the United Kingdom over 50 rose from 14·8 in 1901 to 22·6 in 1931 and 30·3 in 1967—*Annual Abstract of Statistics, 1967*, p. 7; *Monthly Digest of Statistics* (Nov. 1968), p. 14.

[3] The percentage of administrative, technical and clerical workers in manufacturing industries rose from 21·3 in 1960 to 24·3 in 1966—*Annual Abstract of Statistics, 1967*, p. 122.

sible Body courses and adult students in evening institutes (both for England and Wales) sufficiently indicate the general trend.[1] It will be seen that Responsible Body students more than doubled, and adult evening institute students actually trebled, in the twenty years following the war. These graphs also reveal, however, that the growth was uneven, with a boom period immediately following the war, a recession from about 1950, and then a much slower growth in the face of increasing competition from other sectors of education. We must now examine some of these developments in greater detail.

Post-War Honeymoon

The Education Act of 1944, which set the pattern for post-war development in England and Wales, placed firmly on the shoulders of L.E.A.s the responsibility of securing adequate provision for further education, including 'leisure-time occupation, and such organised cultural training and recreative activities as are suited to their requirements, for any persons over compulsory school age who are able and willing to profit by the facilities provided for that purpose'.[2] Another clause, however, prescribed that an L.E.A. 'shall, when preparing any scheme of further education, have regard to any facilities for further education provided for their area by universities, educational associations, and other bodies, and shall consult any such bodies as aforesaid . . .'[3]

The position of the Responsible Bodies was thus safeguarded,[4] and in 1946 a new set of grant regulations accorded them a wide discretion in the types of course they might organise, ranging from three-year tutorial classes to terminal courses and (subject to ministerial approval) 'courses of less formal character.' The detailed regulations which had previously governed each type of course were dropped, and apart from the fact that tutorial classes and courses of training for teachers in adult education were restricted to universities and university colleges, the former distinction between university responsible bodies and others disappeared. Within the limits specified all Responsible Bodies might claim from the Ministry of Education (which since 1944 had replaced the old Board of Education) three-quarters of the approved teaching cost of the provision made.[5]

---

[1] Figs. 1, 2 and 9, below, pp. 350–1, 358. [2] 7 and 8 Geo. VI c. 31, section 41.
[3] *Ibid.*, section 42(4).
[4] This applies only to England and Wales: in Scotland grant-aided courses could be arranged only by or in collaboration with a local education authority.
[5] Ministry of Education, *Further Education Grant Regulations, 1946* (S.R.O. 1946, No. 352). The significance of these regulations is analysed by Professor S. G. Raybould in *The English Universities and Adult Education* (W.E.A. 1951), pp. 110–15, and *University Extra-Mural Education in England, 1945–62*, pp. 26–30.

Not only the 1944 Act but a variety of official pronouncements made it plain that the L.E.A.s were expected to assume a much more positive rôle. The White Paper on *Educational Reconstruction* published in 1943, after drawing attention to the special contribution of the universities and the W.E.A., declared: 'Local Authorities will undoubtedly be called upon to play a larger part than heretofore in this field.'[1] A Ministry of Education report on *Community Centres*, prepared in 1944 and published in 1946, recommended a large-scale development of such centres after the war, and placed the main responsibility for their provision and maintenance on the L.E.A.s.[2] And in the following year a pamphlet on *Further Education*, designed to provide guidance to authorities in the preparation of their development schemes, defined further education as 'a community effort in which the authority must play the leading part.'[3] In the chapter in this pamphlet on 'Learning for Leisure', L.E.A.s were specifically enjoined to appoint suitable organising staff and to make urgent provision, even on a temporary basis, for better accommodation. Development plans were called for by 31 March, 1948.[4]

The L.E.A.s accepted the Minister's invitation 'to plan boldly and comprehensively',[5] and some most impressive development schemes were prepared, but by 1949 the country was already in the middle of one of those recurring economic crises which have been such a depressing feature of Britain's post-war history. Proposals for 'county colleges' for the part-time education of young people between 15 and 18 were suspended indefinitely; all building for community centres and institutions for youth and adult welfare was stopped; and L.E.A.s were advised to increase the fees of evening class students. Such funds as were available were devoted to the schools and to technical education. By 1951 the position was even worse, and L.E.A.s were asked to 'consider the possibility of making recreational classes self-supporting'.[6]

So it came about that the Authorities never had a chance to implement the plans they had drawn up for a brave new adult education world. They did indeed play a leading rôle in the movement to establish short-term residential colleges for adult education, of which

[1] Board of Education, *Educational Reconstruction* (1943), p. 23.
[2] Ministry of Education, *Community Centres* (1946), pp. 25–6.
[3] Ministry of Education, Pamphlet No. 8, *Further Education* (1947), p. 32.
[4] Ministry of Education, Circular 133, *Schemes of Further Education and Plans for County Colleges*, 19 Mar. 1947.
[5] Ministry of Education, *Further Education* (1947), p. 8.
[6] Ministry of Education, Circular 242 7 Dec. 1951, quoted H. J. Edwards, *The Evening Institute* (1961), p. 125.

more than a score had come into existence by 1951.[1] Otherwise there remained from the wreckage only a scattering of village halls and community centres, a few adult education centres in converted buildings, and the traditional evening institutes, now because of reorganisation beginning to attract a rather higher proportion of older people. These institutes, probably because they relied so much on young people who were still liable to military service, were slow to recover after the war, and it was not until 1947–8 that attendance was back at its pre-war figure of 910,000. Thereafter it shot up rapidly, to reach 1,260,000 by 1949–50, but at this point the Government squeeze began to take effect, and it was not until the 'sixties that the ground lost at this time was recovered.[2]

The task of providing liberal adult education, therefore, continued to fall almost exclusively to the Responsible Bodies, i.e. principally to the university extra-mural departments and the Workers' Educational Association.[3] These bodies, entitled as they were under the regulations to receive 75 per cent grant automatically on the teaching costs of all approved programmes, were in a specially favourable position, and they seized the opportunity with both hands. The number of grant-aided courses, 4,311 in ·the final year of the war, rose steeply to 7,842 in 1948–9, and thereafter more slowly to a peak of 8,090 in 1950–1.[4] The number of students showed a similar dramatic increase, and so, significantly, did the number of grant-aided full-time tutors and organising tutors, which jumped from 43 in 1944–5 to 260 in 1951–2.

The Ashby Report and After

These years of rapid growth coincided almost exactly with the six years of Labour rule which began when Clement Attlee defeated Winston Churchill in the general election of 1945. In spite of the immense programme of welfare legislation which the Attlee government carried through, these were harsh and uncomfortable years, during which the country recovered only slowly from the severe damage and losses caused by the war. In 1951 taxes were still high; food, clothing and coal were still rationed; furniture was scarce

---

[1] See on this development below, pp. 392–5.
[2] For details of these developments see the graph on p. 358 (fig. 9).
[3] Other Responsible Bodies which have functioned in the years since the Second World War are the Educational Centres Association, the Joint Adult Education Committees for Devon and Cornwall, the University of Wales Council of Music, the Welsh National Council of Y.M.C.A.s, and five long-term residential colleges. By 1967 the Welsh National Council of Y.M.C.A.s was the only survivor: the other bodies either had been dissolved or, as in the case of the residential colleges, were being grant-aided in another way.
[4] For details see the graphs on pp. 350–1 (figs. 1 and 2).

and houses even scarcer. Small as the scale of government expenditure on the work of the Responsible Bodies was (£336,000 in 1951–2) it is not a little surprising that it had up to this time escaped unscathed.

In 1951 a people weary of shortages and controls swept the Labour Party out of office and brought Churchill back to power, at the age of 77, at the head of a Conservative government. This change marked the beginning of a period of Conservative rule which was to last, under the successive leadership of Churchill, Eden, Macmillan, and Douglas-Home, for thirteen years. Churchill's first Minister of Education, Miss Florence Horsbrugh, noting with alarm that expenditure on the Responsible Bodies, though small, had trebled in six years, first imposed a standstill on grant for 1952-3, and then in January, 1953, announced that there might have to be a 10 per cent reduction in the estimates for 1953–4. In the ensuing storm of protest the Trades Union Congress sent to the Prime Minister a resolution demanding the reversal of 'this most reactionary decision'. Churchill responded on 11th March, 1953, with a letter of which the penultimate paragraph, in spite of its rhetorical extravagances, at once took its place as a historic statement of the place of liberal adult education in a technological society:

There is, perhaps no branch of our vast educational system which should more attract within its particular sphere the aid and encouragement of the State than adult education. How many must there be in Britain, after the disturbance of two destructive wars, who thirst in later life to learn about the humanities, the history of their country, the philosophies of the human race, and the arts and letters which sustain and are borne forward by the ever-conquering English language? This ranks in my opinion far above science and technical instruction, which are well sustained and not without their rewards in our present system. The mental and moral outlook of free men studying the past with free minds in order to discern the future demands the highest measures which our hard pressed finances can sustain. I have no doubt myself that a man or woman earnestly seeking in grown-up life to be guided to wide and suggestive knowledge in its largest and most uplifted sphere will make the best of all the pupils in this age of clatter and buzz, of gape and gloat. The appetite of adults to be shown the foundations and processes of thought will never be denied by a British Administration cherishing the continuity of our Island life.[1]

The Ministry of Education covered its confusion by appointing, in June, 1953, a small committee under the chairmanship of Dr. Eric

[1] Ministry of Education, *The Organisation and Finance of Adult Education in England and Wales* [Ashby Report] (1954), pp. 66–7. The T.U.C. resolution and Churchill's letter are here reproduced in full.

Ashby (later Sir Eric Ashby), Vice-Chancellor of Queen's University, Belfast, to inquire into the organisation and finance of adult education in England and Wales, with special reference to the Responsible Bodies. The Committee worked quickly and well, and its report, presented just over a year later, provides a valuable conspectus of the work at this time. The paragraphs describing the administrative complexities of the situation are worth quoting:

Within these Regulations there has developed a pattern of adult education in England and Wales which is remarkable both in its diversity and in its complexity. There are altogether forty-three responsible bodies: twenty-one of these are universities or university colleges, twenty are voluntary associations (seventeen of them being Workers' Educational Association districts), and two are joint bodies . . . By formal and informal consultation most of the responsible bodies agree upon their programmes and their spheres of influence; and thanks largely to the unobtrusive influence of the Ministry of Education, there is on the whole a successful integration of adult education throughout England and Wales.

The variety of pattern is attributable largely to the accidents of history or to the influence of individual personalities. Oxford University continues to provide classes in Stoke-on-Trent because that was one of the early strongholds of the Extension Movement. Aberystwyth University College organises and provides adult education in mid-Wales without the help of the Workers' Educational Association because it is a cherished tradition of the College to keep in direct touch with the folk whose enthusiasm and whose pence made university education in Wales possible. In Kent the Local Education Authority takes a leading part in adult education, and the Workers' Educational Association in this area is not a responsible body. The South Wales Workers' Educational Association District receives support from all local education authorities in its area except Glamorgan: in this one county the Local Education Authority prefers to organise and provide classes directly. Devon and Cornwall each have no less than three responsible bodies: the University College of the South-West of England, the Workers' Educational Association South-Western District, and a joint body composed of these two together with the appropriate education authority. All of these responsible bodies receive grants and organise classes.[1]

In spite of this complexity the Committee felt that the system was working well, and that although the provision made by the Responsible Bodies was reaching only a small minority of the adult population, that minority represented 'in relation to the community at large a social and intellectual asset the loss of which would be deplorable.'[2] Some extra-mural departments, in evidence, argued that university adult education should be financed like other

[1] *Op. cit.*, pp. 12–13.   [2] *Op. cit.*, p. 34.

university work by the University Grants Committee; and one local government organisation (the Association of Education Committees) urged that all other adult education should be, as in Scotland, financed by the L.E.A.s—i.e. that the Responsible Body status of the W.E.A. districts should be abolished. The Committee, however, came down firmly for the maintenance of the existing fourfold partnership of central government, local authorities, universities and voluntary bodies.

Far from suggesting a reduction in Ministry grant, the Committee suggested an easing of the grant regulations to facilitate development in certain directions. To meet the Ministry's fear of uncontrolled escalation, however, it was recommended that the automatic 75 per cent grant should be abolished, and that in its place a grant not exceeding 75 per cent of teaching costs should be fixed annually for each Responsible Body, on the basis of a programme of courses submitted in advance, 'having regard to the quality and standards of work known to be done by the responsible body . . . the needs of the region in which it operates and the activities of other interested bodies in the region.'[1] The net effect of these changes, which the Ministry accepted, was to create a more flexible system and to rid the Responsible Bodies of many irksome detailed controls, while at the same time giving the Ministry a firmer grip on the general level and pattern of expenditure.

From this point the figures for Responsible Body courses and enrolments once more began to climb upwards, but the first fine careless rapture of the post-war years was gone. Progress was now slower and more hesitant, and plans for expansion were inhibited by a sharp sense of what the Ministry was likely to be able to approve. The Labour Government of Harold Wilson which came to power in 1964 was even more beset by economic difficulties than its Conservative predecessors, and the outlook was at one point so bleak that the Joint Consultative Committee of the universities and the W.E.A. felt constrained to publish a manifesto called *Crisis in Adult Education*, in which it was pointed out that the government's annual contribution to the work of the Responsible Bodies (then running at about £700,000) was rather less than the cost of a single mile of motorway. In the end the government did manage to make funds available for a small annual expansion of the work, and in 1965–6 the number of courses for the first time passed the 10,000 mark.[2]

The figures for local authority work, in so far as it can be represented by the work of the evening institutes, are more difficult to

---

[1] *Op. cit.*, p. 44.   [2] See the graph on p. 350 (fig. 1).

interpret. The decline which began in 1950 continued until 1961, by which date the number of evening institute students had fallen from 1,263,000 to 877,000. In part this was certainly due to direct government pressure for economies in adult education, which led to increases in fees and a stiffening of attendance requirements. In part, also, it was because at a time of general financial pressure adult education, having in the eyes of many L.E.A.s still a very low priority, was carrying more than its due share of the burden. To some extent, however, the reduction in student numbers was due to the fact that younger students were staying on at school, or had been transferred to full-time or part-time day courses in colleges of further education. This change is reflected in the accompanying graph,[1] which shows that the fall in the number of students over 18 was less marked than the fall in the overall number. We observe also that when recovery at last began in 1961, it came only among the over 18's: the number of younger students remained in 1967 virtually unchanged.

This belated advance on a limited front was achieved by the local authorities in spite of continuing financial difficulties. Many of them attempted more, but for the most part the ambitious plans of the immediate post-war years remained, twenty years later, still remote from fulfilment.

Some General Factors

One factor in the post-war scene in adult education that must be mentioned in this brief survey of the general pattern is the great predominance of women. This had long been a feature of evening institute work because of the large number of courses in such subjects as dressmaking and cookery: in 1919–20 women accounted for 50 per cent of all students over 18 in the evening institutes of England and Wales, and by 1937–8 the proportion had risen to 67 per cent. In Responsible Body work, however, men were still in the majority in almost every type of course until the outbreak of the second World War. The following figures for England and Wales show the trends in the post-war years.[2]

PERCENTAGE OF WOMEN IN ADULT CLASSES

	Evening Institutes	Responsible Bodies
1946–47	76	55
1950–51	74	50
1965–66	70	54·5

[1] P. 358 (fig. 9). Cf. H. J. Edwards, *The Evening Institute* (1961), pp. 125–88.
[2] There are no comparable figures from Scotland.

It will be observed that the percentage of men in evening institutes has increased slightly, no doubt because of the introduction in recent years of an increasing number of classes in craft and recreational subjects which have a special appeal to men. By and large, however, women have during this period continued to dominate the adult education scene. This is of a piece with the increasingly active part being played by women in social and cultural activities generally. The same trend is seen in the very striking rise in the membership of the national women's organisations. The Women's Institutes, which had some 50,000 members in 1939, had nearly 250,000 in 1968; and membership of the Townswomen's Guilds jumped in the same period from about 50,000 to 460,000.

A word must be said also about a new national consultative organisation for adult education which came into existence soon after the war and grew into increasing strength and influence as the years went by. This was the National Institute of Adult Education, which began in 1946 as the National Foundation for Adult Education and changed its name when in 1949 it merged with the former British Institute of Adult Education. Whereas the British Institute's membership had been purely personal, that of the new Institute was corporate, and its purpose being to bring together for consultation and co-operation all the main partners in the field: the L.E.A.s, the Responsible Bodies, representatives of appropriate government departments, and a great variety of voluntary organisations, among them the Educational Centres Association, the National Federation of Community Associations, the Seafarers' Education Service, the National Adult School Union, the Co-operative Union, the National Federation of Women's Institutes, and the National Union of Townswomen's Guilds. Merely by bringing all these bodies into a single organisation the Institute did much to create among them a sense of engagement in a common enterprise, but it also played a more positive role: its journal *Adult Education* proved to be immensely valuable in the exchange of news and opinions, and the reports of special inquiries such as those on *Accommodation and Staffing* (1963) and *Recruitment and Training of Workers in Adult Education* (1966) have had a considerable influence on policy.[1]

Public Libraries

One of the notable features of the post-war years was the immense increase in reading, an increase which even the advent of television was unable to halt more than momentarily. The increase was no

---

[1] A parallel body for Scotland, the Scottish Institute of Adult Education, was established following the break-up of the British Institute in 1949.

doubt basically due to the great extension of higher education, but it also reflected, and was reflected in, the increasing availability of cheap books and the growing efficiency of the public library service.

The introduction of Penguin paperback books in 1935, referred to above,[1] proved the beginning of a real publishing revolution. Other publishers, even the more staid and sedate of them, were eventually forced to follow suit, and by the 'sixties the potential book purchaser could take his choice from thousands of titles ranging from romantic fiction to scholarly treatises. Owing to wartime inflation, alas, the original price of sixpence was a memory of the past, but prices remained low enough for people to be willing to buy books where they had once bought magazines. For the student this ready availability of a wide variety of texts was especially valuable, and along with the improvement in public library services went far to solve the long-standing problem of securing an adequate supply of books for adult classes. Indeed adult education undoubtedly did much to provide a market for serious paperbacks. It is interesting in this connection to note that the thousandth volume in the Penguin educational series (the Pelican books), published in 1968, was *The Making of the English Working Class* by Dr. E. P. Thompson, formerly extra-mural lecturer at Leeds University.

The public library service was almost completely transformed. Though expenditure on the service was never lavish, as the years went by the old, dark, gloomy Victorian buildings were gradually improved or replaced, and light and spacious new libraries sprang up to meet the new needs. The old-style newspaper room disappeared to make room for more bookstacks or an attractive children's library. Not least, thanks to the invention of plastic covers, the drab old library bindings gave place to an array of gaily coloured jackets. Now at last the lingering nineteenth-century tradition that public libraries were for the working class disappeared, and the libraries became the possession of the community.

It would be wrong, however, to paint too rosy a picture, for as a result of the historical development of the library movement there were still, as at the time of the McColvin Report of 1942, far too many libraries which were too small and too poor to provide a modern and efficient service. In Scotland as late as 1951 an official report commented that 'Much of the library service . . . is hardly beyond the pioneering stage.'[2] The same report came to the conclusion that

---

[1] P. 311.
[2] Scottish Education Department, *Libraries, Museums and Art Galleries* (Edinburgh 1951), p. 115. Cf. Ch. iii of the same Report.

an adequate library service could not be economically provided for a population of less than 30,000,[1] but in England and Wales, in 1957–8, there were 167 out of a total of 484 library authorities with a population below this figure, and 49 with a population of under 10,000.[2]

These details regarding England and Wales are taken from the Report of a committee appointed in 1957, under the chairmanship of Sir Sydney Roberts, to review the present position and make recommendations. The same Report revealed astonishing variations in the annual expenditure of library authorities on books. An expenditure of between 1s. and 2s. per head of population was quite common, but the metropolitan borough of Holborn was spending 8s. 5d., and several parish authorities nothing at all. The Report recommended that the public library service should be placed under the general oversight of the Minister of Education, who should be assisted by advisory councils for England and Wales; that every public library authority should have a statutory duty to provide an efficient service; that parishes should cease to be library authorities; and that urban districts and non-county boroughs not already library authorities should not be eligible for library powers unless they had a population of at least 50,000.

The Report also made certain recommendations regarding the standards by which an efficient library service should be measured, but these were afterwards re-examined and elaborated by a Ministry working party, as also were the proposed arrangements for inter-library co-operation.[3] With the modifications suggested by these further inquiries, the basic recommendations of the Roberts Committee were accepted and embodied in the Public Libraries and Museums Act of 1964. This Act had the immediate effect of eliminating a number of small library authorities which, knowing that they could not measure up to the standards required, surrendered their powers to the appropriate county authorities, but the general upgrading of the library service that ought to have followed was rendered impossible, for the time being, by the severe restriction placed by the government on all forms of public expenditure.

A point of special interest is the sympathetic interest shown in these reports in the relation of public libraries to adult education. Though they did not go so far as the Scottish report of 1951, which concluded that 'the library cannot be regarded as other than an educational

---

[1] *Op. cit.*, pp. 49–50.
[2] Ministry of Education, *The Structure of the Public Library Service in England and Wales* (1959), p. 37.
[3] See Ministry of Education, *Standards of Public Library Service in England and Wales*, and *Inter-Library Co-operation in England and Wales* (both 1962).

service,'[1] they did show themselves fully aware of the educational implications of the work. The report on *Standards*, especially, spelt out the view that 'in many respects public libraries and adult education are complementary services', and that public libraries should therefore do their utmost to assist adult education in the provision of books, premises and equipment.[2] Some libraries, of course, were by this time already doing a great deal not only to assist adult educational organisations but to promote extension activities of their own in the way of lectures, exhibitions, plays, concerts and the like, but here again financial considerations restricted, for most libraries, what would have been a most fruitful development.[3]

Broadcasting and Adult Education

We have noted that early attempts to make broadcasting serve the needs of adult education, through talks broadcast for the use of discussion groups, were abandoned after the war.[4] After a period of further experiment it was at last recognised that radio must be treated 'as a means of education in its own right,'[5] and not as a medium subservient to other purposes. This was the principle followed by the B.B.C. in relation to sound radio from 1952 onwards and subsequently in relation to television. The Independent Television Authority did the same. Adult educationists, on the whole, accepted it thankfully, for experience had demonstrated that broadcast programmes could not conveniently be integrated with ordinary adult education courses, but were best treated as supplementary. Contact between the adult educationists and the broadcasters was ensured by regional consultations and by national advisory committees on which adult education interests were represented.

Throughout the 'sixties adult education provision both on sound radio and on television steadily increased both in range and effectiveness, especially after the opening of a second B.B.C. television channel in 1964. Apart from educational programmes proper, which aimed at systematic and progressive study, and which included science, history, economics, languages, management studies, and a great variety of other subjects, there were many talks, discussions, and feature programmes which had their educative aspect because they awakened

---

[1] *Ut supra*, p. 38.

[2] Ministry of Education, *Standards of Public Library Service in England and Wales* (1962), p. 26.

[3] For a general review see H. Jolliffe, *Public Library Extension Activities* (1962, 2nd. edn, 1968) and for a specific example the same author's *Arts Centre Adventure* (Swinton 1968).

[4] See above, pp. 319–20.

[5] J. Rowntree, 'New Issues in Educational Broadcasting', in S. G. Raybould (ed.), *Trends in English Adult Education* (1959), p. 159.

interests and imparted knowledge. All these the adult educationists welcomed and profited by: if broadcasting times clashed with lecture times that was regarded as an unavoidable hazard, to be dealt with when the problem arose.

The mid 'sixties brought three interesting experiments. One, conducted by the Nottingham extra-mural department under the leadership of Professor Harold Wiltshire in the autumn term 1964, was a small-scale local experiment in the use of television for adult education. A series of thirteen twenty-minute television programmes on *The Standard of Living*, by members of the extra-mural staff, was broadcast by Associated Television weekly on Sunday mornings, with a repeat on Monday mornings. The course was supported not only by the issue of a handbook, which was already standard practice, but also by correspondence teaching and by the opportunity of occasional meetings with the course tutors. Students paid a fee of 10s. on enrolment, and were expected to submit weekly written work on lines set out in the course handbook. Some of the written exercises were in the form of a questionnaire, other called for essay-type answers.

In the event over 3,000 course handbooks were bought, 1,347 people enrolled as individual students, and 549 of these did all the exercises (there were 311 others who enrolled through schools, colleges, etc.). The administration and teaching, which proved a heavy burden, was carried out by members of the extra-mural staff and 38 part-time tutors. This was an interesting attempt at integrating the use of television with other forms of teaching, and seemed to its organisers to show (*a*) that television teaching can reach good students who would not be reached otherwise; (*b*) that television teaching can be effective if it is part of a system that involves students in active learning and in contact with tutors; and (*c*) that the cost need not exceed that of normal class teaching.[1]

The need for further experiment was widely recognised, though some thought that the use of general television channels for programmes aimed at minority groups was wasteful, and that the real answer lay in the use of the closed circuit television systems which by now were being widely developed by universities and local education authorities, and which it was anticipated might number about two hundred by the early 'seventies.[2]

The second experiment of this period was in local radio. The establishment of a local service on sound radio had been recommended

[1] H. Wiltshire and F. Bayliss, *Teaching through Television* (N.I.A.E. 1965), p. 16.
[2] B.B.C., *Educational Television and Radio in Britain* (1966), p. 93.

in the Pilkington Report as early as 1962,[1] but it was not until 1966 that the government authorised the B.B.C. to proceed with nine local stations, broadcasting on the V.H.F. waveband, on an experimental basis. The experiment started about a year later,[2] and was due to conclude in the summer of 1969. This was an enterprise in which adult educationists were deeply interested and often personally involved, but there was a strong feeling that the time allotted for the experiment was too short, and the funds made available too restricted for the rich possibilities of this medium to be fully exploited.

The third and most spectacular experiment was the University of the Air, or as it came to be officially called the Open University. This owed its origin to a speech by Harold Wilson in Glasgow in 1963. When he became prime minister in the following year he entrusted the carrying out of the proposal to Miss Jennie Lee, one of his ministers of state for education. The proposal involved the provision of courses on television and sound radio supported by 'correspondence courses of a quality unsurpassed anywhere in the world', and reinforced by residential courses and meetings with tutors. Students would be able to qualify for an ordinary or an honours degree in about four or five years by the accumulation of credits on the American plan, and it was expected that the courses would also be of value to many who had no intention of proceeding to a degree.[3]

At a time of severe retrenchment in almost every other branch of education this scheme, estimated to cost between £3 millions and £4 millions a year, naturally came under severe criticism, especially as there was no evidence of any substantial research into the potential market. The government, however, went confidently forward, set up a planning committee, appointed a vice-chancellor, and announced that teaching would begin in 1971. It was probably the biggest leap in the dark since the Reform Bill of 1867.

[1] *Report of the Committee on Broadcasting, 1960* (H.M.S.O. 1962), pp. 221–33.
[2] Actually with only eight stations, Manchester having withdrawn from the scheme at the last moment. The eight were: Brighton, Durham, Leeds, Leicester, Merseyside, Nottingham, Sheffield and Stoke-on-Trent. Cf. the Government White Paper on *Broadcasting* (H.M.S.O. 1966).
[3] See the White Paper on *A University of the Air* (H.M.S.O. 1966), and *The Open University: Report of the Planning Committee* (H.M.S.O. 1969).

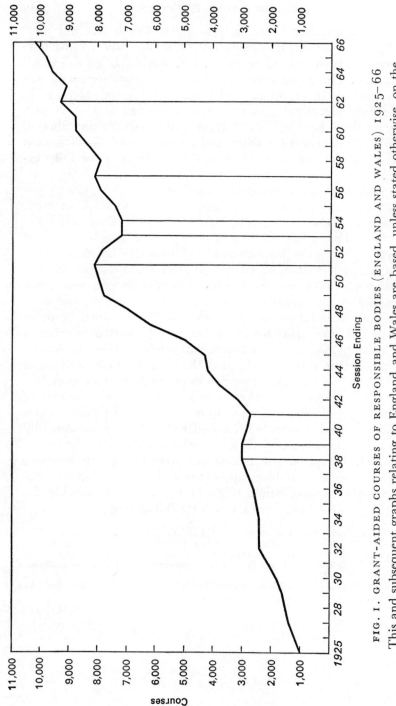

FIG. I. GRANT-AIDED COURSES OF RESPONSIBLE BODIES (ENGLAND AND WALES) 1925–66
This and subsequent graphs relating to England and Wales are based, unless stated otherwise, on the Annual Reports of the Board of Education, the Ministry of Education, and the Department of Education and Science

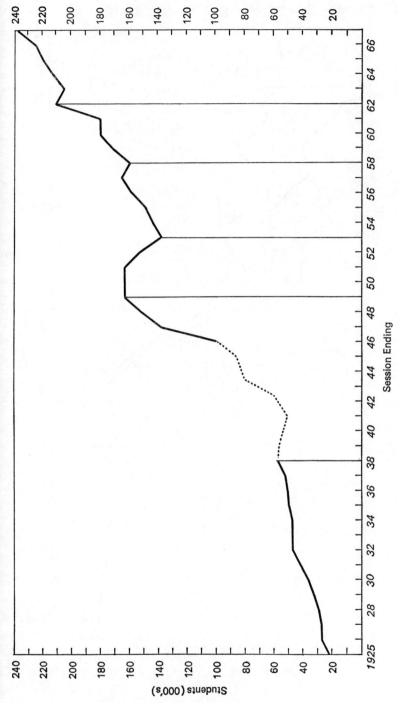

FIG. 2. STUDENTS IN GRANT-AIDED COURSES OF RESPONSIBLE BODIES (ENGLAND AND WALES) 1925–67

The figures for 1939–45 are conjectural

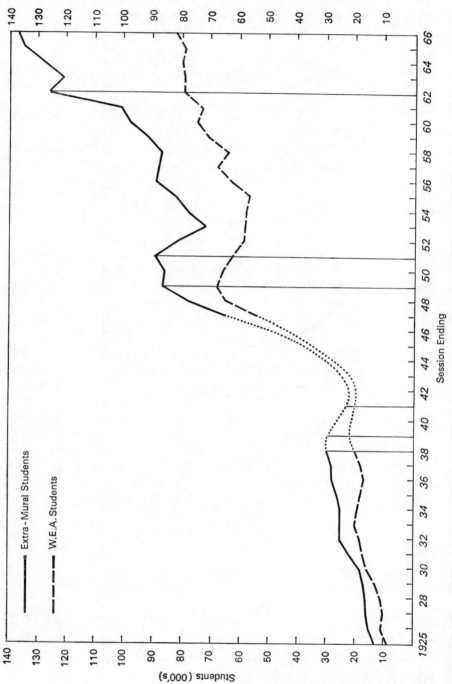

FIG. 3. ENROLLED STUDENTS IN EXTRA-MURAL AND W.E.A. COURSES (ENGLAND AND WALES) 1925–66

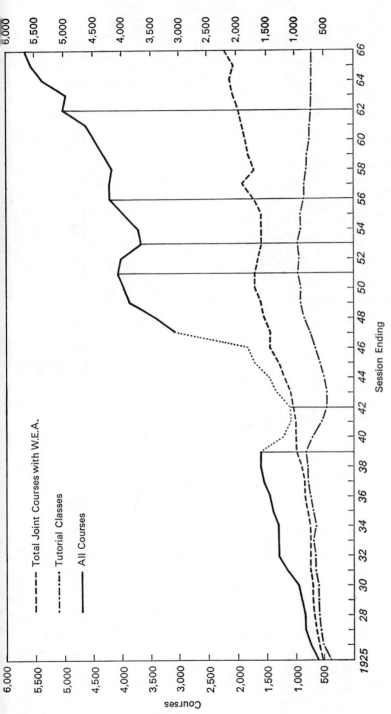

FIG. 4. GRANT-AIDED EXTRA-MURAL COURSES (ENGLAND AND WALES) 1925–66
Figures for 'All Courses' are conjectural 1939–46. Figures for 'Total Joint Courses with W.E.A.' are from
C.J.A.C. Reports to 1955, thereafter from U.C.A.E. Reports

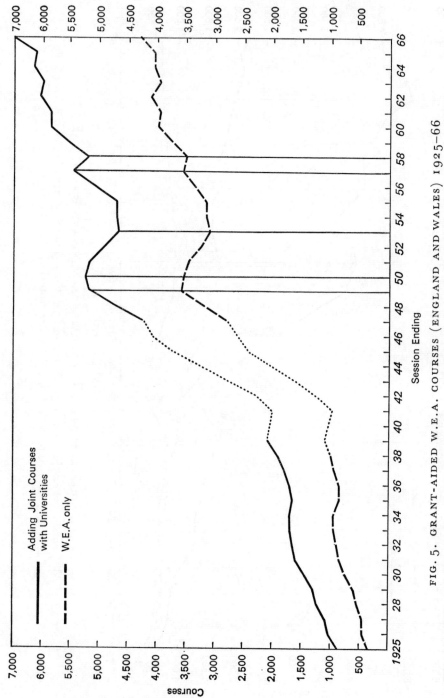

FIG. 5. GRANT-AIDED W.E.A. COURSES (ENGLAND AND WALES) 1925–66

The figures for 'Joint Courses with Universities' are based on C.J.A.C. Reports to 1955, thereafter on U.C.A.E. Reports.
The figures for 1939–46 are based on W.E.A. Reports

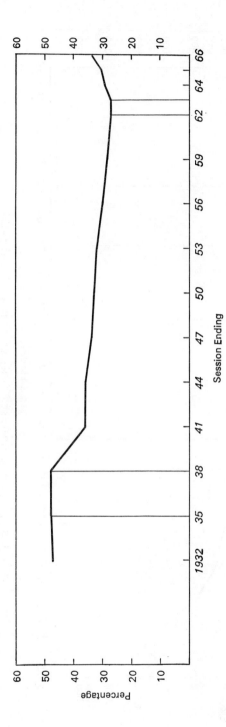

FIG. 6. PERCENTAGE OF MANUAL WORKERS IN W.E.A. CLASSES (UNITED KINGDOM) 1932–66

Calculated from W.E.A. Annual Reports at three-yearly intervals

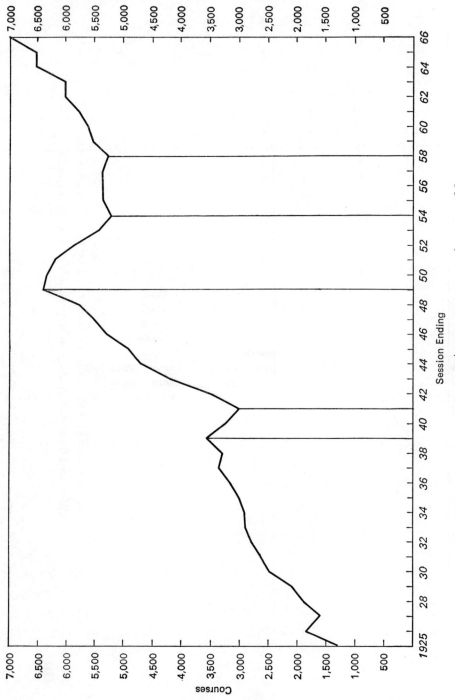

FIG. 7. W.E.A. COURSES (GREAT BRITAIN) 1925–66

Based on W.E.A. Annual Reports. One day and week-end courses and schools are excluded, as are all W.E.T.U.C.

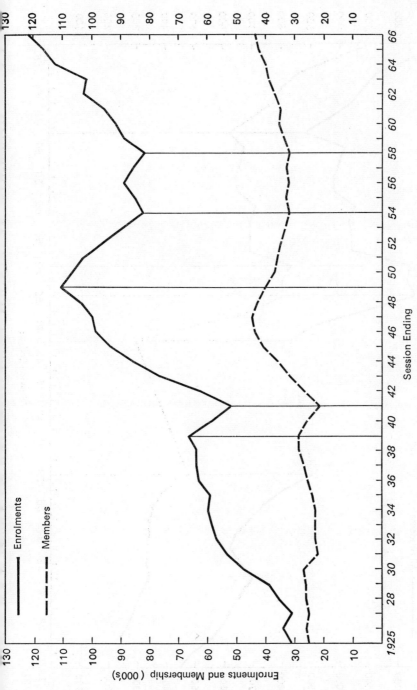

FIG. 8. W.E.A. ENROLMENTS AND MEMBERSHIP (GREAT BRITAIN) 1925–66
Based on W.E.A. Annual Reports. Enrolments in one-day and weekend schools arranged for the W.E.T.U.C. are excluded

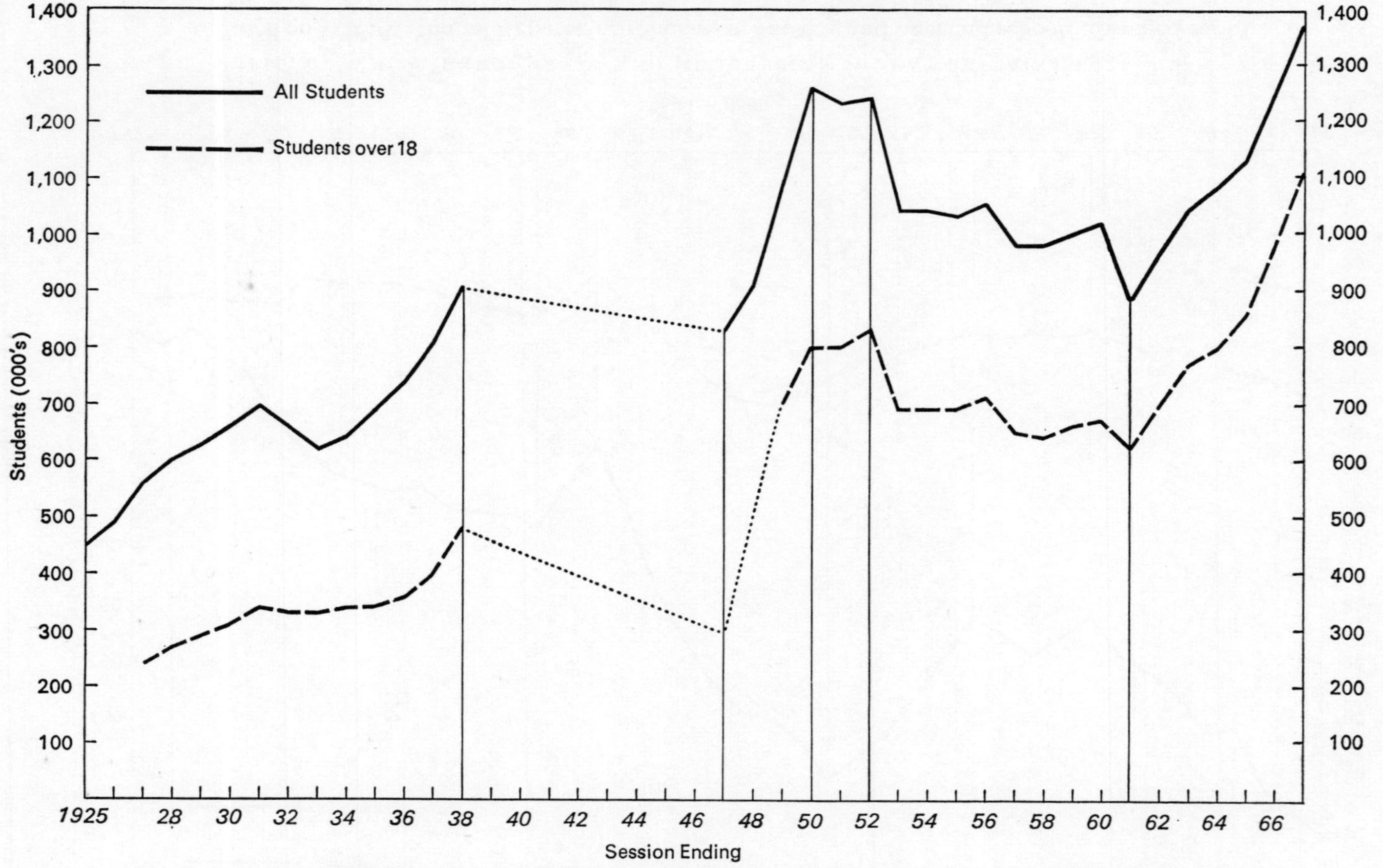

FIG. 9. STUDENTS IN EVENING INSTITUTES (ENGLAND AND WALES) 1925-67

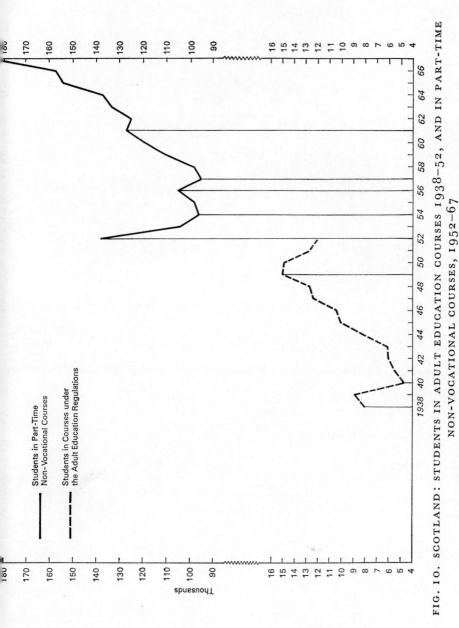

Thousands

Students in Part-Time
Non-Vocational Courses

Students in Courses under
the Adult Education Regulations

FIG. 10. SCOTLAND: STUDENTS IN ADULT EDUCATION COURSES 1938–52, AND IN PART-TIME
NON-VOCATIONAL COURSES, 1952–67

Based on Annual Reports of the Scottish Education Department

21

The Twentieth Century

THE FOURFOLD PARTNERSHIP

THE previous chapter has shown that adult education provision in the post-war years depended on a partnership of the central government with the universities, the voluntary bodies, and the local education authorities. In this final chapter certain aspects of this fourfold partnership will be examined in greater detail.

Extra-Mural Changes

The university extra-mural departments, during the post-war years, grew in strength and rapidly extended the range and variety of their programmes. The creation of departments at Leeds in 1946 and Sheffield in 1947 completed the extra-mural structure of the English and Welsh universities and university colleges with the single exception, for reasons already noted, of Reading.[1] The few remaining boundary problems were now quickly settled, and as the years went by the 'extra-territorial rights' so long exercised by Oxford and Cambridge in such centres as Lincoln and Southport were gradually abandoned in favour of the appropriate local university. In 1951 the anomalous arrangement by which Lough-borough College shared in the responsibility for extra-mural work in Leicestershire was terminated, the county being henceforth divided extra-murally between Nottingham and Leicester.

In May, 1947, the former Universities Extra-Mural Consultative Committee gave way to a more broadly based Universities Council for Adult Education, which included representatives of university senates as well as extra-mural officers, and took within its purview not only extension courses but the whole range of extra-mural teaching. This proved a most significant change, creating among the departments, in spite of their diversity, a new sense of identity and common purpose. Under the chairmanship of successive vice-chancellors the Council became increasingly influential as time went on. From 1950–1 it included representatives from Scotland and Northern

---

[1] Cf. above, p. 269.

Ireland, and a number of Commonwealth universities were from time to time welcomed to associate membership.[1]

These changes were accompanied by a marked rise in the number and status of extra-mural staff. The increase in the number of teaching staff was particularly dramatic, especially in the immediate post-war years: the U.C.A.E. annual reports, which give numbers for all tutors, whether grant-aided or not, record 83 tutors in 1945–6, 244 by 1951–2, and 308 by 1966–7—an average of nearly a dozen per department.[2] The question of status can best be illustrated from a report by Professor S. G. Raybould, first Director of Extra-Mural Studies at Leeds, on the first ten years of the work of his Department. The report comments on the very marginal position which extra-mural activities and extra-mural teachers occupied in the life of the University prior to the creation of the Department in 1946:

... the extra-mural staff constituted a group apart in the University. They were members of no faculty and no department. They might be personally acquainted with other members of the University, but often were not. They had no rooms in the University. The titles of their posts were not those employed for other academic appointments. Their salary scale did not correspond with any existing for intra-mural staff. No provision existed for them to be promoted to posts of higher status and salary.[3]

By the time this report was written all the anomalies here referred to had been swept away. Extra-mural lecturers now enjoyed parity of status and salary with intra-mural staff, and were equally eligible for promotion to senior lectureships and readerships: the first senior lecturer was, in fact, appointed at Leeds in 1953. Similar changes took place, though in some instances rather more tardily, in other universities and university colleges. The status of heads of departments was also upgraded, and by the 'sixties it was common for the director of extra-mural studies to be at least a member of senate, if not a professor.[4]

The increase in the number of full-time staff led to complaints about the 'professionalisation' of the work, and the loss of the voluntary spirit. The use of the word was certainly justified, but the com-

[1] The extra-mural work of Edinburgh, Glasgow, and Belfast went back to the inter-war years. The Aberdeen extra-mural department was created in 1955, that at St. Andrews in 1963. The last-named operated initially from Queen's College, Dundee, which later became a separate university (see below, p. 370, note).

[2] The two later figures include a small number of tutors in Scotland and Northern Ireland. Full-time tutors with H.M. Forces are not included.

[3] *University of Leeds: A Decade of Adult Education, 1946–1956* (Leeds 1956).

[4] Three university colleges, Nottingham, Leicester, and Hull—had professors of adult education before the war, and chairs were created at Manchester in 1948 and at Leeds in 1953, but it was not until the late 'sixties that the title of professor became at all common.

plaints were not, for these full-time tutors proved their worth over and over again. Along with their W.E.A. colleagues they were in the 'forties and 'fifties almost the only full-time teachers in the whole field of non-vocational adult education, and they provided a core of professional skill and experience that could not have been matched by voluntary or part-time workers. Some of them had teaching duties only, others had organising responsibility for an area or a subject, but their influence extended far beyond their immediate teaching or organising duties. The resident tutors especially, i.e., those with an area responsibility, frequently became the focus for a whole range of cultural activities.

The pre-war tendency for the universities to operate more and more independently of the W.E.A. was accelerated by the social and educational changes of the war and post-war years. In 1947 the W.E.A. published a manifesto entitled *The Future in Adult Education: a Programme*, in which it expressed its belief that

the universities have a vital function to perform in the provision of adult education at a level comparable with internal university studies, but adapted to the needs and interests of men and women who bring ability and experience derived from practical affairs rather than trained academic aptitude to their classes. This primary purpose of university adult education should not be displaced by the development of direct university provision of classes of a less specifically university standard.[1]

It can hardly have been an accident that in the following year the U.C.A.E. issued a 'statement of principles' which was, in effect, a declaration of independence:

The services of the University Extra-Mural Department must be made available to any groups or bodies who can provide students prepared to work at a level considered appropriate by the Universities . . .

Universities attach special value and importance to Tutorial Classes and to other forms of their work which they conduct in co-operation with the W.E.A. They cannot, however, regard their services as available exclusively to any one organisation or section of the community.[2]

This declaration inevitably concealed differences of emphasis, for although no extra-mural department was hostile to the W.E.A. the extent of collaboration on the ground varied. Some departments still looked upon the W.E.A. as their major ally, and on the three-year tutorial class as the kind of adult education most worth doing;

[1] W.E.A., *The Future in Adult Education* (1947), p. 13.
[2] *The Universities in Adult Education: A Statement of Principles* (separately published 1948 and also appended to U.C.A.E. *Report on the Years 1945–6 and 1946–7*).

others, while prepared to meet demands from the W.E.A. on request, felt that the remedial function of adult education for which the W.E.A. stood was one of diminishing importance, and that the real future of extra-mural work lay in meeting the great upsurge of demand resulting from the extension of full-time schooling and full-time higher education. As Professor A. J. Allaway of Leicester put it in his evidence to the Ashby Committee in 1953:

Although little has been said about it, university extra-mural work is developing into a public service provided for the benefit not of the 'educationally underprivileged' section of the population, but increasingly for those who have received the advantage of a full-time higher education . . . increasingly the emphasis is on the further education of the products of the grammar schools, technical colleges and universities.[1]

By 1961, however, the need for what a U.C.A.E. statement of that year called 'adult education for the educated' was universally recognised and was increasingly being met.[2] At the end of the war at least 90 per cent of extra-mural work was carried out in collaboration with the W.E.A.; by 1956, when the U.C.A.E. first began to collect statistics on this matter, the proportion had fallen to 40 per cent.[3]

This separatist trend is reflected in various developments. Extra-mural boards and committees were reconstructed in such a way as to provide representation for interests other than the W.E.A., and the Central Joint Advisory Committee on Tutorial Classes, which had so long been the pillar of University–W.E.A. collaboration, gave way in 1958 to a joint consultative committee of the W.E.A. and the U.C.A.E.

Some universities would have liked to go even further in the direction of independence, and more than once there was a move to terminate the connection with the Ministry of Education and seek funds for extra-mural work from the University Grants Committee in the same way as for intra-mural work. On grounds both of principle and expediency, however, these proposals were rejected— fortunately as it turned out, for with the development of local authority work in the 'sixties it became increasingly difficult to see

---

[1] A. J. Allaway, *Thought and Action in Extra-Mural Work, Leicester, 1946–1966* (Leicester 1967), p. 37. Cf. Ashby Report, pp. 25–7, where the opposing points of view are well set forth.

[2] *The Universities and Adult Education* (1961), pp. 16–18.

[3] See the graphs, pp. 352–3 (figs. 3 and 4), and on all this S. G. Raybould, *University Extra-Mural Education in England, 1945–62* (1964), Ch. iii. The local factors are dealt with by J. W. Saunders in Ch. iii of S. G. Raybould (ed.), *Trends in English Adult Education* (1959).

how the extra-mural departments could separate themselves from the public system of education.

Adult Education for the Educated

Statistical evidence for the statement by Professor Allaway quoted above is not lacking. Surveys show that in the early 'sixties a quarter to a half of all extra-mural students had enjoyed full-time education at least to the age of 20. Even in the East Midlands, where the extra-mural work of the University of Nottingham continued to be mainly in collaboration with the Workers' Educational Association, the percentage of such students was 23·4 in 1961-2, and more than 70 per cent of all students fell in the three highest occupational categories, i.e., higher professional, lower professional, and clerical and highly skilled.[1]

The members of this new extra-mural public (which was, we may note in passing, merely an enlargement of the old Extension public), sought either subjects which would contribute to their personal culture and enjoyment, or subjects related to their professional interests. The former demand led to a great increase in courses in the visual arts, in foreign languages, literatures and cultures, and in local studies of various kinds—local history and geography, archaeology, geology, architecture, the study of archives. All these subjects, it will be seen, were directed towards leisure-time pursuits. What may be broadly called 'current affairs', however, whether national or international, attracted little interest, perhaps because it was so extensively covered by the press, radio, and above all television.[2]

These new leisure-time students brought to the work a higher standard of education than had been customary in the past, and a willingness to work at a higher level, but partly for these very reasons, and partly because of the many conflicting claims on their free time, and partly again because they lived in an existentialist post-atom-bomb age in which the here and now was more important than the morrow, they were apt to be impatient of long-drawn out courses such as the three-year tutorial class. For this reason the increase in non-W.E.A. courses tended to be in courses of one session

[1] R. Peers, *Fact and Possibility in English Education* (1963), pp 128-32. Ch. ix of this work gives an excellent conspectus of adult education at this period. For other studies see the same author's *Adult Education: a Comparative Study* (1958), pp. 174-86; University of Hull, Department of Adult Education, *Annual Report, 1963-64*, pp. 29-34; and J. Long, *Universities and the General Public* (Birmingham 1968), pp. 24-33. Unpublished inquiries conducted at Liverpool by Mr B. W. Pashley and Dr J. Lowe gave figures ranging between 36 per cent and 44 per cent for students completing full-time education at the age of 20 or more in classes in the Liverpool extra-mural area and parts of the Bristol and Oxford extra-mural areas.

[2] U.C.A.E., *Annual Report, 1956-57*, p. 7.

or less, and in residential courses which permitted short but intensive periods of study. The following figures for non-W.E.A. provision in England and Wales, extracted from U.C.A.E. Reports, illustrate this tendency:

Type of Course	1955–6 Courses	%	1966–7 Courses	%
Tutorial	242	10·5	265	7·1
Day-release	*	—	82	2·2
One year	601	26·1	897	24·1
Less than one year	1193	51·8	1975	53·0
Residential	267	11·6	510†	13·7
	2303		3729	

* No separate classification for day-release courses in this year.
† Figure for residential courses somewhat inflated owing to change in method of classification.

This trend troubled some observers, notably Professor Raybould at Leeds, who in 1951 and again in 1964 expressed doubts about the value of short courses except where the students had previous training in the actual subject of study, as for example in a post-graduate refresher course.[1] The majority of extra-mural directors, however, were content with the recommendation of the Ashby Committee that an extra-mural department should satisfy itself that any course it offered 'by reason of its nature, of its length, of the competence and experience of the teacher, and of the ability of its students, is one which can properly be given as part of the university contribution to adult education.[2] Many of them agreed with the view forthrightly expressed by D. R. Dudley, first Director of Extra-Mural Studies at Birmingham and one of the leading proponents of the new style extra-mural work, that the sessional class, 'long enough to produce good results in a single session, flexible enough to continue from year to years as the situation allows', was far better adapted than the tutorial class to 'the kind of students who now come to our classes.'[3]

These problems did not arise in the same degree with students who had a strong vocational motivation. For many people, of course, personal and professional interests were difficult to separate, but

[1] S. G. Raybould, *The English Universities and Adult Education*, (1951), pp. 4–12: *University Extra-Mural Education in England, 1945–62* (1964), pp. 89–91.
[2] Ashby Report (1954), p. 38.
[3] D. R. Dudley, *The Department of Extra-Mural Studies of the University of Birmingham: a Survey of New Developments, 1945–1955* (Birmingham 1955), p. 17.

there were some groups, such as teachers, social workers, doctors, lawyers, engineers and industrial research workers, who now looked to the extra-mural departments to provide training or refresher courses related specifically to their professional work. One result of this demand was the provision of technological courses of a type that had not been heard of since the 'nineties. B. W. Pashley comments:

By the early 1950s such esoteric titles as X-ray Crystallography (Manchester), Applied Surface Chemistry (Hull, Sheffield), Automatic Digital Computers (Bristol, Cambridge), Concrete Mixes with Local Aggregates (Newcastle), or Polarisation Microscopy and Optical Crystallographic Methods (Leeds) were not uncommon in Extension programmes.[1]

Liverpool had from 1956 to 1968 a special Standing Committee for Post-Graduate Courses, which provided not only courses of the type just referred to but also refresher courses at various levels for teachers.

It is not clear how far courses of this kind were responsible for the considerable increase during these years in the provision of courses in science—from 6 per cent of the total in 1947–8 to 14 per cent in 1966–7.[2] Many extra-mural departments were at the same time making a drive to popularise science as a cultural study, and although the results of these efforts were somewhat disappointing they certainly contributed something to the increased total. The problem of popular education in science, it may be remarked in passing, is one that still awaits a solution: the technical vocabulary of scientific subjects seems to present an insuperable obstacle to the layman. It may not be irrelevant that in 1966–7 the university with the largest extra-mural programme in science was Bristol, the only university that had a scientist as its extra-mural director.[3]

The major demand for training and refresher courses came from the servants of the new welfare state—the child care officers, health workers, hospital administrators, house-parents, probation officers, police officers, youth leaders, voluntary social workers of all kinds. These were not raw youngsters but people of mature years and often considerable professional experience. They were, in fact, the kind of people whom extra-mural departments were specially fitted to help, and many departments threw themselves into this new task with a real sense of mission.[4]

They were greatly assisted by two recommendations of the Ashby

[1] B. W. Pashley, *University Extension Reconsidered* (Leicester 1968), p. 44.
[2] U.C.A.E., *Report on the Years 1945–6 and 1946–7,* and *Annual Report, 1966–67.*
[3] U.C.A.E., *Annual Report, 1966–67,* p. 15.
[4] See U.C.A.E., *Annual Report, 1961–62: New Developments in University Extra-Mural Work,* pp. 9–11, and later Reports.

Committee in 1954, namely that 'Classes for special groups of students should be acceptable for grant provided that the enrolment of other students is not unreasonably prohibited'; and that 'Courses of high quality should not be excluded from grant on the grounds that they might have a vocational interest for some students'.[1] Where the courses were specifically vocational, however, they were commonly organised without grant-aid from the Ministry of Education. Very often some other government department helped, e.g. the Home Office or the Prison Commissioners. A number of the new courses, e.g. in child care, were full-time and carried some kind of certificate or diploma.

This development on the vocational side was one of the factors that led, in the mid 'sixties, to the re-opening of the whole question of certification in connection with extra-mural courses. In the early days of University Extension, as we have seen, examinations and certificates were regarded as normal, but under the spell of the tutorial class this tradition had been lost everywhere except in London. In the post-war years the London diploma and certificate courses grew and flourished, and cautious experiments were made by a number of other universities, notably Leeds (from 1947) and Leicester (from 1949). In 1966–7, when the U.C.A.E. first took a count, there were in Great Britain 350 extra-mural courses leading to some kind of qualification, 248 of these being provided by London, 36 by Leeds, 17 by Leicester, and the remaining 19 by 12 other universities.[2] It was not, however, until 1966 that, on the initiative of Geoffrey Hickson, Secretary of the Cambridge Extra-Mural Board, the U.C.A.E. began seriously to consider the establishment of a national system of extra-mural awards. By this time some universities were already contemplating the possibility of part-time degree courses—a type of provision long familiar in North America, but quite exceptional in Great Britain.

Thinking on this subject received a powerful stimulus from the report of a committee presided over by Sir Eric Ashby on the future of Birkbeck College, London. Contrary to the expectations of those who suspected that Birkbeck's provision of part-time degree courses was now an anachronism, the committee declared not only that this provision was more necessary than ever but that there was urgent need for a similar institution in every great centre of population.[3]

[1] Ashby Report (1954), p. 49.
[2] U.C.A.E., *Annual Report, 1966–67*, p. 19. For the origin of the London diploma courses see above, p. 247, and for their post-war growth U.C.A.E., *Annual Report, 1958–59*, pp. 20–2.
[3] University of London, *Report of the Academic Advisory Committee on Birkbeck College* (1967), espec. pp. 7–9.

Diversity in Unity

In attempting to generalise about extra-mural departments we must not lose sight of their continuing diversity. The passage quoted above from the Ashby Report[1] draws attention to some of the administrative oddities in England and Wales, and had the Committee been able to look across the border it would have seen in Scotland a completely different system, in which the provision of adult education courses by the universities and the W.E.A. was not grant-aided by the central government, and consequently had to be conducted for the most part through L.E.A.s, which alone were able to pay the tutors' fees. This severely hampered the development of extra-mural work in one way, since it meant that each university had to strike a separate bargain with each L.E.A. in its area of operations: on the other hand it opened up to the universities the possibility of contributing in some sectors of adult education, e.g. language teaching, which in England and Wales were regarded as reserved to the L.E.A.s.[2]

There were, however, many other differences. History, geography and population had a great deal to do with it. London, with its vast population, its metropolitan tradition, and its rich cultural resources, could not be expected to develop in the same way as, say, the rural areas centring on Bangor and Aberystwyth, with their strong native culture rooted in the eisteddfod and the village Sunday school, or the great industrial-agricultural-fishing complex, reaching from the Solway to the Firth of Lorne, which constitutes the extra-mural area of the University of Glasgow. Even within the borders of England one could point to similar though less striking contrasts—between old universities and new universities, between universities in heavily populated industrial areas and those in thinly populated rural areas, and so on. There were differences of policy, too. Just to take one important area of difference, not all universities were willing to accept the principle that extra-mural activities should in future be directed mainly to the educated sector of the population, and many made strenuous efforts, especially through day-release courses, to find new ways of reaching the working masses. Most of this work was done in collaboration with the W.E.A., and it will be described below.

The diversity of the extra-mural scene was greatly increased by the creation, in the 1960s, of a score of new universities. Two of these

[1] Above, p. 341.
[2] For the financial problems resulting from this system see *Scottish Adult Education*, No. 50 (Oct. 1968), which is devoted to the Report by the Working Party on the Finance of Adult Education in Scotland. The Scottish Education Department makes a small contribution to each university for administrative costs only.

were former university colleges,[1] ten more were former colleges of advanced technology;[2] and the remaining eight were completely new universities.[3] The integration of these new institutions into the existing extra-mural fabric was a formidable task. Keele fitted in very easily, taking over in 1962 the former Oxford 'colony' of North Staffordshire; and in one or two other parts of the country it seemed possible for new universities to carve out for themselves separate extra-mural areas, but many new universities, e.g. York and Salford, were too close to existing universities for such an arrangement to be possible.

The U.C.A.E. suggested that adjacent universities might combine to offer a common service; or alternatively that such universities might avoid competition by developing their own extra-mural specialisms.[4] The latter suggestion seemed to appeal more than the former, especially to those universities which had formerly been colleges of technology. By the close of 1968 a number of these, e.g., Bath, Strathclyde, Surrey, and Loughborough, were developing programmes with a scientific and technological bias. The immediate effect of these programmes was to strengthen the vocational, non-grant-aided element in extra-mural work. Those universities which were completely new institutions were not for the most part in a hurry to develop extra-mural work, but it is interesting to note that some of them were disposed to challenge the basic assumptions of extra-mural organisation. Dr. C. F. Carter, Vice-Chancellor of Lancaster, for example, is reported to have expressed the view that universities had 'gone too far in sub-contracting their extra-mural responsibilities to special staff having inadequate contact with the main work of the university.' He added that his university was seeking 'the right form of organisation for encouraging extra-mural work by regular members of university staff.[5]

Theory and Practice

A very important development of the post-war years was the increasing attention paid to the study of the theory and practice of

[1] Keele (1962) and Dundee (1967).
[2] Strathclyde (1964), Aston in Birmingham, Brunel, City, Loughborough, Bath, Bradford, Surrey, and Heriot-Watt (all 1966) and Salford (1967).
[3] Sussex (1961), East Anglia and York (1963), Lancaster and Essex (1964), Stirling, Warwick and Kent at Canterbury (1965).
[4] Universities Council for Adult Education, *Memorandum to the Committee of Vice-Chancellors and Principals* (1962). Some kind of joint arrangement of the kind here outlined might have been particularly appropriate in the St. Andrews–Dundee area, but when Queen's College, Dundee, became a separate university in 1967 it was decided to have separate extra-mural departments.
[5] J. R. Long, *Universities and the General Public* (Birmingham, 1968), p. 37.

further education. It is something of an anomaly that the universities of Great Britain, which were the first in the world to become actively involved in the work of adult education, were among the last to take up the theoretical study of the subject. Adult education was, it was argued, a highly personal relationship between tutor and student, and attempts to draw up rules were not very helpful. In any case, the work was on too small a scale to make training courses worth while. So long as 'adult education' meant mainly extra-mural and W.E.A. courses, this viewpoint had some substance, but the rapid expansion of the post-war years, and the big increase in the number of full-time teachers and organisers, not only in the universities and the W.E.A. but also in the L.E.A.s and a great variety of voluntary organisations, changed the situation completely.

A report on *The Recruitment, Training and Remuneration of Tutors* was produced by the Adult Education Committee of the Board of Education as early as 1922, and a fuller study, entitled *The Tutor in Training*, was published by the Carnegie U.K. Trust in 1928.[1] Nottingham extra-mural department offered a graduate diploma course from 1921, but only a handful of students, mainly from abroad, took advantage of this between the wars, and it was suspended during the second World War.[2] Oxford had more success with a scheme started in 1946 (and in active operation till 1968) under which up to three tutor-trainees a year were each attached to an experienced full-time tutor, but this kind of training was suitable only for extra-mural or W.E.A. work.

The biggest development in this field came at Manchester, where part-time courses began in 1946–7, and a separate Department of Adult Education, distinct from the Extra-Mural Department, was created in 1949. This Department, headed by Professor R. D. Waller, developed a variety of courses in association with the Faculty of Education. Hence arose in 1955 a full-time adult education certificate course and eventually, in 1961, a full-time diploma course. As at Nottingham, overseas students were at first in a majority, but when the special needs of these students had been separately provided for by a diploma in community development the adult education diploma became increasingly useful and attracted an increasing number of British students from a variety of professions. Manchester

[1] British Institute of Adult Education and Tutors' Association, *The Tutor in Adult Education: an Enquiry into the Problems of Supply and Training* (Dunfermline 1928).
[2] See *op. cit.* pp. 174–5. At this stage Nottingham also suffered a certificate course, intended primarily for tutorial class students training for W.E.A. teaching. One cannot resist quoting (without comment) the statement that 'students often obtain their practice at the Nottingham Prison'. Cf. R. Peers, *Adult Education: A Comparative Study* (1958), p. 216.

was also the pioneer in the provision of part-time courses for teachers and administrators outside the extra-mural field, e.g. in evening institutes, townswomen's guilds, and community centres. The great variety of the needs which had to be met was explored in a report by W. E. Styler and R. D. Waller published by the U.C.A.E. in 1954.[1]

Other universities were understandably cautious about following Manchester's example, and most were content to provide as well as they could for the needs of their own part-time tutors. The demand for training, however, steadily built up. A National Institute of Adult Education report of 1966 identified about 500 full-time teachers and organisers in Responsible Bodies, residential colleges, and similar organisations, and about the same number wholly or substantially engaged in L.E.A. teaching institutions such as village colleges and evening institutes.[2]

By 1968 there was a part-time certificate course in adult education under extra-mural auspices in Liverpool; there were part-time diploma courses in Hull and Nottingham and full-time diploma courses in Nottingham, Manchester, and Edinburgh; and a full-time diploma course was about to begin in Liverpool.[3] In spite of what a U.C.A.E. report calls 'the persistent empiricism of the English tradition,'[4] this involvement in training provided, at last, both the opportunity and the need for extra-mural departments to explore the great range of problems, historical, social, philosophical, psychological, and educational, involved in the education of adults.[5]

Forces Education in Peacetime

Another task that fell mainly to the university extra-mural departments was the organisation of civilian assistance to education in H.M. Forces. For some years the Regional Committees set up during the war were kept busy helping with release schemes, and some of them were involved in new tasks: the Liverpool and Edin-

---

[1] W. E. Styler and R. D. Waller, *Tutors and their Training* (1954). Cf. U.C.A.E., *Annual Report, 1955–56*, pp. 21–4.
[2] 'Recruitment and Training of Staff for Adult Education' in *Adult Education*, Vol. XXXVIII (1965–66), pp. 378–90.
[3] The Nottingham course was revived in 1965.
[4] U.C.A.E., *Annual Report, 1955–56*, p. 23.
[5] It is perhaps desirable to add here a word about the confusing nomenclature of extra-mural departments. Before the war the titles 'Department of Adult Education' and 'Department of Extra-Mural Studies' were used almost indiscriminately, with occasional local variants such as 'Delegacy for Extra-Mural Studies' at Oxford. Since the war first Manchester and subsequently Leeds and Liverpool have made a distinction between adult education as a subject of academic study, and extra-mural studies as an administrative provision, but only Manchester has made adult education into a separate department.

burgh committees, for example, were much occupied in the teaching of English to Polish troops who wanted to stay in Britain when hostilities ended.

By 1948, all these clearing up processes had been completed and it was necessary to re-organise the administration on what it was hoped would be a permanent peace-time basis. As far as civilian assistance was concerned the university extra-mural departments were invited to accept responsibility and to set up special committees which were in effect very similar to the war-time Regional Committees. Most universities agreed, and the work, though smaller in volume than during the war and post-war years, went on with very little change. At the centre the old Central Advisory Council was replaced by a Central Committee for Adult Education in H.M. Forces, which included representatives of the universities, the L.E.A.s, and W.E.A. and the Services.[1]

The new machinery worked well and did a good job, reaching the peak of its activity about 1954–6. In the year 1954–5 the programmes arranged by the local committees included over 3,000 single lectures, more than 1,600 part-time lecture-courses averaging about seven lectures apiece, more than 250 full-time residential and non-residential courses, and more than 200 classes. A tutorial scheme, involving interviews and record cards, was also operated in order to meet the special needs of recruits of good educational standard. The Army and the Royal Air Force were the main consumers: the Royal Navy, as during the war, was less well placed to take advantage of civilian assistance. Bristol, Leeds, and Southampton were the university areas principally involved, because of their proximity to important military establishments.

The activities carried on were very varied. In work with the units, current affairs (both domestic and international) occupied first place. Some of the lectures and courses were linked with Army or R.N. current affairs teaching or with the R.A.F.'s General Education Scheme; others were for the benefit of those studying for qualifications such as the Army First-Class Certificate or Staff College Entrance. The full-time courses, which did something to counteract lack of continuity in the units, were also concerned in the main with current affairs, but science was also fairly popular and there was a sprinkling of courses in literature and the arts. In the classes, which were commonly undertaken by teachers provided by the L.E.A.s,

---

[1] London University was unable to accept responsiblity for Forces work, and the London area was accordingly provided for by an *ad hoc* committee responsible to the Central Committee.

the subjects most in demand were handicrafts, commercial subjects, and foreign languages.[1]

In time, however, partly because of the operational commitments of the Forces and partly for reasons of economy, the work began to shrink and to change its character. By 1955–6 the Central Committee was reporting:

Nevertheless the emphasis has altered and there is a perceptible change in some of the purposes for which civilian education is used. In this last year there was, in many areas, a more obvious provision of the kind of education which would be of direct value to the Service concerned or to the individual in his career in the Services or outside it . . . the high place given by many universities to courses for Staff College entrance and Qualifying examinations is typical . . . courses on military history and military law, the technological courses at Bristol and Sheffield, practical science courses at Hull, courses on business administration and, for 'schools liasion officers', on public speaking, are further examples of the trend.[2]

Eventually, following the decision in 1957 to end conscription for national service, a further re-organisation of the work was decided upon. Under a new scheme, which took effect in 1960, the universities were asked to accept responsibilities only for work of an extra-mural character, the various branches of the Forces being left to make their own arrangements with L.E.A.s and other bodies for such other work as they might need. The Central Committee was now replaced by a smaller body known as the Committee for University Assistance to Adult Education in H.M. Forces. At this stage a number of universities with very small numbers of Services personnel in their areas withdrew from the scheme, preferring to deal with such requests as might arise through their normal extra-mural machinery.

From this time forward the emphasis of the work shifted increasingly towards specialist courses for commissioned and non-commissioned officers, in subjects of special value to the men in their Service careers. The report of the new central committee for 1967–8 showed a substantial body of teaching still going on in 264 residential and 362 non-residential courses, mostly in such subjects as current affairs, military history and strategy, and science. At this stage the volume of work seemed fairly stable, and it was a source of satisfaction to both sides that more then twenty years after the ending of hostilities the arrangements for co-operation between the Services and the civilian agencies of education were still in successful operation.

[1] For these details see the *Annual Reports* of the Central Committee for Adult Education in H.M. Forces, especially that for 1954–55. Cf. R. Peers, *Adult Education: A Comparative Study* (1958), Ch. vi.

[2] *Annual Report, 1955–56*, p. 4.

The W.E.A. in Evolution

The general pattern of W.E.A. growth was, as will be seen from the accompanying graphs, not dissimilar to that of the extra-mural departments: if the fluctuations were somewhat more exaggerated, that was no doubt because the W.E.A. was dependent entirely on voluntary subscriptions and annual grants from public funds.[1] The extra-mural departments, because part of their income was drawn from their universities, i.e., from U.G.C. grants on a five-year basis, were able to plan ahead with some degree of confidence, but the W.E.A. was immediately sensitive to every wind of public economy. In studying the graphs, however, one cannot help noting that the period of contraction in the 'fifties was in the case of the W.E.A. particularly severe and prolonged—almost as prolonged as that experienced by the evening institutes. This, too, may be explained partly on financial grounds, but one suspects it was also due to internal doubts and difficulties in the W.E.A. movement. There had been no such doubts in the early post-war years:

The Association felt that it stood on the threshold of greater opportunities for the expansion of its work than ever before. It was preparing to welcome to its classes the young men and women who had come under the influence of discussion groups and more connected forms of study during their military service—'a vast potential of prospective W.E.A. students'— and hoped that those who had first made contact with the W.E.A. as a result of their wartime service in civilian defence units would maintain their contact with the Association and its work.'[2]

Needless to say, the crowds of young men and women from the Forces never materialised: most of them, when their military service ended, were only too glad to put the Forces behind them for ever— and everything connected with the Forces, including adult education. None the less the very rapid build-up of courses and students which had begun during the war continued, to reach a peak only in 1949. Finance was at first a difficulty and at the annual conference of January, 1945, at which the veteran R. H. Tawney occupied the chair for the last time in his sixteen years as president of the Association, it was actually proposed that an approach should be made to the Ministry of Education for a grant in aid of administrative as well as teaching costs. Tawney took the view that independence was more

---

[1] See below, pp. 352, 354–7 (figs. 3, 5–8).
[2] W.E.A., *The Workers' Educational Association, 1946–1952: a Review*, p. 11; cf. *Annual Report, 1945–46*, p. 9.

important than affluence, and his opposition was decisive.[1] For a year
or two the situation was critical, but in 1947–8 an agreement for an
expansion of work with the affiliated trade unions brought a welcome
accession of new income and for the time being financial anxieties
receded into the background.

From 1949, however, the fortunes of the W.E.A. took a sharp
downward turn. The number of courses, the number of class enrolments, the number of members, all fell away, and by 1954, the Association found itself in the trough of a depression which lasted almost
to the end of the 'fifties.[2] It was at this time that the doubts and
self-questionings to which we have referred became particularly
acute. Ernest Green, who retired from the general secretaryship
in 1950, wrote a book called *Adult Education: Why this Apathy?*.
It was published in 1953, the year in which Miss Horsbrugh appointed
the Ashby Committee. The Committee paid a notable tribute to the
achievements of the W.E.A. and to the spirit of 'voluntaryism'
which it represented, but could not resist commenting on the 'fre-
quency and frankness' with which the Association criticised itself,
both at its annual conference and in its journal *The Highway*.[3]

A sharp though not unfriendly critic was S. G. Raybould of Leeds,
who in a volume entitled *The W.E.A.: the Next Phase*, published by
the Association itself in 1949, argued that the movement was losing
sight of its original goal, which was to provide serious study for
working-class students in the subjects relevant to social emancipation.
He admitted that the term 'worker' now needed to be re-defined,
and he accepted for this purpose the proposition that had been
put forward by the Yorkshire North District of the W.E.A. at the
annual conference of 1948 that the main concern of the Association
was with 'workers whose full-time education finished at the minimum
school-leaving age.'[4] He admitted also that the social purpose of the
work might need some re-definition, with more emphasis on 'education for responsibility', and less on 'education for emancipation.'
But he firmly believed that the W.E.A. as originally conceived still
had a big job to do, and that it was not doing it as well as it should:
it was providing the wrong kind of class—too many short courses
and not enough three-year tutorial classes; it was recruiting the wrong
kind of students—too many middle-class students and not enough

---

[1] M. Stocks, *The Workers' Educational Association: the First Fifty Years* (1953), pp. 133–4.
[2] Cf. the rather despondent account of 'The W.E.A. in Scotland' given by W. H.
Marwick in *Scottish Adult Education*, No. 8 (Aug. 1953), pp. 11–13.
[3] Ashby Report (1954) pp. 35–6.
[4] W.E.A., *Annual Report*, 1949, p. 47. As far as I know Raybould's book was the first
to use in print the loaded term 'educationally underprivileged', which was for some years
in current usage to identify this educational group.

manual workers; and it was studying the wrong kind of subjects—
too much music and not enough economics.

On the basis of the facts he adduced, Raybould was certainly
right about the direction in which the W.E.A. was moving. It was
open to those who disagreed with him to argue that the W.E.A. as
originally conceived was no longer either needed or wanted in the
welfare state; that social class was increasingly irrelevant as a basis
for educational provision; and that the most useful thing the W.E.A.
could do in the new social setting was to become a general consumer
organisation promoting a variety of courses for all who were interested
in attending. Unfortunately the debate within the W.E.A. itself was
confused by unlucky pronouncement from no less a person than R. H.
Tawney.

Tawney constantly insisted on the need for high standards: indeed
he provided a foreword to Raybould's book. In an address on the
occasion of the W.E.A. Jubilee in 1953 he declared:

We interpret the word 'Workers' in no narrow sense; but our primary
mission, proclaimed from hundreds of platforms and in scores of pamphlets,
is to the educationally under-privileged majority, who cease their full-
time education at or about fifteen, and who need a humane education
both for their personal happiness and to help to mould the society in
which they live. Our duty to them is equally obvious. It is not to delude
them with the mendacious pretence that an education worth having is a
less exacting alternative to the cinema, dogs, darts or the austerities of the
daily press. It is to put them on their mettle, to pitch our claims high,
and to rely for a response to them, not on the insignificance of the effort
which they demand, but on the magnitude of the reward which effort
will bring, in the discovery of powers previously unrealized and enlarged
capacities for effective action.[1]

This seems clear enough, but it needs to be interpreted in the light
of a passage in an earlier address given by Tawney to the W.E.A.
Annual Conference in 1947:

Our object from the start has not been merely to multiply classes,
irrespective of the type of students in them or of the level of their work.
It has been to provide educational opportunities for a representative
cross-section of the workers of the country, and to do so with sufficient
continuity and for periods sufficiently long to enable education to leave
a real mark upon their minds and characters. We have not interpreted
the work 'worker' in any narrow sense. We have meant it by it all those,
whether in factory, mine, office, or home, who render useful service to
their fellows.[2]

[1] R. H. Tawney, *The W.E.A. and Adult Education* (Athlone Press 1953), pp. 10–11.
Cf. a similar passage in *Jubilee Addresses on Adult Education* (W.E.A. 1953), p. 52.
[2] W.E.A., *The Future in Adult Education: a Programme* (1947), pp. 4–5.

The interpretation here given to the word worker would cover almost anybody, and even if we accept it as limited by the references to 'a representative cross-section' it is still very different from the concept of the 'educationally underprivileged'. Tawney never seems to have realised this contradiction, and this kind of double thinking bedevilled much of the subsequent discussion.[1] Professor G. D. H. Cole, economic historian and veteran W.E.A. tutor, declared roundly, 'The W.E.A. cannot have it both ways. It cannot be a general education provider and at the same time the educational representative of the working-class movement.'[2]

For some years after the publication of *The W.E.A.: the Next Phase* there was no significant change: there was no great increase in the number of tutorial classes, or of classes in economics and related studies; the proportion of middle-class students continued to grow, the proportion of manual workers to decline.[3] Mrs. Stocks commented that 'in some areas, in the Home Counties for example, classes appear to consist largely of the class for which the pioneer University Extension Lectures catered,'[4] and indeed there seemed at times to be a good deal of overlap, if not competition, between the provision made by the W.E.A. and by the universities. At conference after conference delegates from branches rose to move the deletion of the word 'Workers' from the title of the Association, on the ground that it was irrelevant in modern society and a handicap to recruitment.

It was Professor Asa Briggs, who succeeded Harold Clay as president in 1958, who showed the Association a way out of the dilemma in which it found itself. In a policy paper on *Education for a Changing Society: the Rôle of the W.E.A.*, which he wrote shortly after taking up office, he argued that although the W.E.A. still had 'a major responsibility for those who left or leave school early,' modern society had problems demanding 'action based on a general rather than a special sense of responsibility.' There was, indeed, special value in developing forms of adult education which brought together 'men and women of different ages and occupations, with different backgrounds of experience', and the W.E.A. must avoid

---

[1] See for a particularly good example the address by Tawney's successor as president, Harold Clay, in *Annual Report, 1954*, pp. 9–10; and comments on this point by R. Shaw in S. G. Raybould (ed.), *Trends in English Adult Education* (1959), pp. 185–7.

[2] Shaw, *ibid.*, citing Cole, 'What Workers' Education Means', in *Fortnightly* (June 1952).

[3] On this period of W.E.A. history, see Ch. i, by J. F. C. Harrison, in Raybould's *Trends in English Adult Education;* and E. W. F. Malone, 'The W.E.A.—a new Phase,' in *Adult Education*, Vol. XXXIII (1960–1), pp. 78–82, 116–21.

[4] M. Stocks, *The Workers' Educational Association: the First Fifty Years* (1953), p. 154.

'losing its way in barren battles about definitions'. The implication of the whole argument was that there was no necessary contradiction between making provision for people from a wide range of occupations and educational backgrounds and at the same time maintaining a special concern for the 'underprivileged' groups.[1]

It can have been no accident that from this very year the W.E.A. began to gather renewed strength and vigour. Taking *Education for a Changing Society* as its starting-point, a special working party set up in 1958 made far-ranging recommendations regarding the purposes and methods of adult education, and the recruitment and training of tutors.[2] Courses, students, membership of the Association, all began to show a steady increase, and even the proportion of manual workers took in 1964–5 a slight but perceptible upward turn.[3] Only the three-year tutorial class continued its slow but ineluctable decline, and against this could be set, as we shall shortly see, new and increasingly effective work with the trade unions, especially through the medium of day-release and factory courses. It was the W.E.A.'s success in this sphere which made the dual role outlined by Professor Briggs so generally acceptable.

As the 'sixties advanced, indeed, the W.E.A.'s main problem was to find money for all the worthwhile things that needed doing. All too often, from 1956 onwards, the annual accounts of the Association showed a deficit, and when this was not the case it was only through the most stringent economies, e.g. suspending publication of *The Highway*, and holding national conferences biennially instead of annually. A request to the Ashby Committee for additional assistance fell on deaf ears, and an appeal to the Ministry of Education in 1958 produced only a small grant towards the central administration. In 1966 a national conference approved far-reaching proposals for development and reorganisation, including a reduction in the number of districts, but plans such as these cannot be implemented quickly, and in the meantime the Association could go ahead only, as a report of 1964 put it, 'with the brakes on'.[4]

---

[1] The W.E.A. Report for 1964–67, *Action and Advance*, pp. 7–10, pays tribute to the value of Professor Briggs's leadership at this crucial time. He resigned in 1967 on taking up the Vice-Chancellorship of Sussex University.
[2] The working party's report was published as *Aspects of Adult Education* (1960).
[3] See the accompanying graph (p. 355, fig. 6). It should be pointed out here that although much has been made of the proportion of manual workers in W.E.A. classes, this figure in itself is a very imperfect indication of the social composition of the movement.
[4] W.E.A., *The Widening Horizon* [Report for 1962–64] (1964), p. 55. For a review of the Association's financial problems see the Report for 1964–67, published under the title *Action and Advance* (1967). See also *A Report . . . on . . . Structure, Administration, Organisation and Finance* (W.E.A. 1955); and *Working Party on Structure, Organisation, Finance and Staffing* (W.E.A. 1966).

New Approaches to Workers' Education

One of the most striking features of adult education in the 'fifties and 'sixties was the development by the W.E.A. and the universities, together or separately, of new approaches to the education of industrial workers.

The W.E.A.'s work with the trade unions affiliated to the W.E.T.U.C. increased markedly during the war and post-war years, in spite of sharp competition from the N.C.L.C. In 1949 the unions agreed to an annual contribution of 2d. per member per year to provide a central fund for the promotion of this work. At this stage the special W.E.T.U.C. district committees which hitherto operated at the local level gave place to trade union advisory committees attached to each W.E.A. district. During the 'fifties, when W.E.A. work of other kinds was restricted by lack of funds, the trade union work forged ahead, the annual programme including over 500 one-day and week-end schools, besides a variety of summer school courses. Part of this success was due to the establishment, in the Port Talbot area of South Wales, in the Cleveland area of Yorkshire, and on Tyneside, of pilot schemes for the intensive development of trade union work. These schemes, which owed their origin to the recommendations of a working party set up by the W.E.A. in 1951,[1] were in operation from 1954 to 1958. They effectively demonstrated that given sufficient resources in the way of teaching and organising personnel it was possible to attract into adult education many trade union members who would not think of joining an ordinary W.E.A. class. What proved difficult was to provide for sustained work, and to build a permanent bridge between this work and the W.E.A.'s normal teaching. A special report when the experiment was over urged the importance of approaching students of this kind through their own special trade union interests, and suggested the establishment of a 'college of trade union education' to undertake research and prepare teaching material.[2]

The most important advances, however, were not in this traditional field but in day-release and factory courses. The pioneer in this work was the Nottingham extra-mural department, which had a history of day-release courses for miners reaching back to 1922.

---

[1] Workers' Educational Association, *Trade Union Education: a Report from a Working Party* (1953).
[2] H. A. Clegg and R. Adams, *Trade Union Education with special reference to the Pilot Areas* (1959), pp. 82–5; cf. Workers' Educational Association (Northern District), *Trade Union Education 1955–56–57;* and S. G. Raybould (ed.), *Trends in English Adult Education* (1959), pp. 38–41. The proposal for a college of trade union education eventually led to a decision by the W.E.A. in 1968 to establish a Service Centre for Social Studies.

In 1924 the Miners' Welfare Joint Adult Education Committee was set up to encourage recruitment, and with the help of scholarships granted by this Committee some eighty mineworkers attended the University College on day-release before the scheme was suspended on the outbreak of war in 1939. The course called for attendance on two full days in each week for a minimum of one session. The scheme was revived in 1947, but after five years the extra-mural department and the W.E.A. decided to reorganise it on less academic lines with a view to bringing in a much larger number of students. This was a deliberate policy decision, taken in order to counteract the tendency of ordinary extra-mural and W.E.A. classes to recruit increasingly from the better educated sectors of the population.[1]

The new course occupied one day a week for thirty weeks in the year, each day including one period on economics, one period on either politics and society (22 weeks) or the structure of trade unions (8 weeks) and one period for private study. The extra-mural department and the W.E.A. provided the teaching staff, the extra-mural department provided accommodation at its Adult Education Centre; the National Coal Board paid the miners' wages, and other expenses were met by the Coal Industry Social Welfare Organisation. All these bodies, and the National Union of Mineworkers, were represented on the joint committee set up to supervise the work. The initial response was so great that it was necessary to provide two courses instead of one, providing for a total of 64 men, mostly underground workers and mostly under forty years of age. The one-year course, however, was soon felt to be insufficient, and in 1961, after various experiments, a two-year basic course was substituted, with the possibility of a further two years for the best students. By 1965 the normal programme of the extra-mural department included each year four basic courses (two in the first year, two in the second), and two advanced courses (one in the first year and one in the second). The enlarged basic course found room for a valuable addition, namely a specially devised series on 'Studying, Speaking and Writing.'

The success of these courses was undoubted: they produced students of good quality who undertook sustained and progressive work. Alongside them there grew up a variety of residential and non-residential courses, some of them preliminary or supplementary to the day-release courses, others arranged independently in collaboration with various mining trade unions. With the help of a number of large firms in the Nottingham area, arrangements were also made for

---

[1] For the history and development of these courses see A. H. Thornton and F. J. Bayliss, *Adult Education and the Industrial Community* (1965).

day-release courses on similar lines for workers in other industries, so that by 1965–6 there were in all eleven day-release courses (eight in Nottingham, three elsewhere) with a total of some 200 students. In some instances, also, half-day release courses for shop stewards and foremen were organised on the premises of the firm concerned. A welcome by-product of all this activity was the establishment of W.E.A. classes (often on the initiative of former day-release students) on industrial premises, usually at the end of the working day.

In the Sheffield extra-mural area miners' day release courses began in 1952, following discussions between the Director of Extra-Mural Studies and a union official who was a former Nottingham day-release student. In this instance the W.E.A. was not involved, provision being made direct by the University, and the students' wages being paid by the National Union of Mineworkers or the National Coal Board. The courses were on a three-year basis, and were later extended to the steel industry. By 1968 the extra-mural department had eight members of staff mainly engaged in day-release teaching.[1]

It was in the early 'sixties that day-release and other industrially based courses began to form an impressive part of extra-mural and W.E.A. programmes in other parts of the country, and especially in the Birmingham, London and Oxford extra-mural areas. A particular feature of W.E.A. work in some districts was the provision of courses for apprentices, which apart from their immediate value had the great advantage of establishing a contact with the industrial worker at the very outset of his career.[2]

It would, of course, be quite wrong to convey the impression that the W.E.A. and the universities were alone in providing facilities for trade union education. The National Council of Labour Colleges, with more than twice as many unions affiliated to it as the W.E.T.U.C., continued to make extensive provision not only of classes and lecturers but also of correspondence courses; Ruskin College provided full-time residential courses of one or two years' duration; many large unions, such as the Transport and General Workers' Union, the National Union of Municipal and General Workers, the Union of Shop Distributive and Allied Workers,

---

[1] M. Bruce, *The University of Sheffield Department of Extra-Mural Studies, 1947–1968: a Personal Survey* (1968). Cf. U.C.A.E., *Annual Report, 1953–54*, pp. 19–21; and J. E. Williams, 'An Experiment in Trade Union Education', in *Adult Education*, Vol. XXVII (1954–55), pp. 113–24.

[2] On all this see especially W.E.A., *Searchlight on Society . . . Report . . . 1960 to 1962*, pp. 9–16. For some reason courses of this type made little headway in Scotland.

the Electrical Trades Union, and the Amalgamated Engineering Union, had their own educational schemes; and the Trades Union Congress spent substantial sums on training courses for the officers and members of its affiliated unions.

The position was greatly simplified, and the way opened up for what it was hoped would be a substantial expansion, by a decision of the T.U.C. which at last brought to an end the long standing rivalry between the W.E.T.U.C. and the N.C.L.C. From the beginning of 1963 the T.U.C. itself took over financial responsibility for the educational work of both these bodies and made their services available to all members. In 1965 the two organisations were dissolved and the T.U.C. set up its own system of regional committees on which the W.E.A. was represented.

In 1966 the W.E.A. East Midland district, which in collaboration with the Nottingham extra-mural department played a leading part in all these developments, was able to report that '22 per cent of the District's provision was now devoted to work with industry and the trade unions.'[1] Two years earlier a national W.E.A. report commented:

Reports from the field stress the fact that this work has given a new importance to the existence of the voluntary movement . . . As an intermediary between the universities and industry, the W.E.A. has developed new functions, or rather extended old ones. Its prestige and integrity have helped to win the confidence of both management and workers. What the new situation brings out, also, is the continued need for a closer partnership between the W.E.A. and the universities. The notion that the Association has served its purpose and should now hand over to the statutory bodies was never further from the truth than it is seen to be in the light of these new developments.[2]

Adult Education Centres

One of the most encouraging and interesting features of this postwar period was the increasing provision of special centres for adult education, both residential and non-residential. The tradition of the non-residential centre can be traced back to the mechanics' institutes and working men's colleges of the nineteenth century, but few of these survived as educational institutions into the twentieth century.[3] It was the Educational Settlements Association (from 1946 the Educational Centres Association) which took the lead in developing the modern

---

[1] W.E.A., *Action and Advance . . . 1964–1967* (1967), p. 22.
[2] W.E.A., *The Widening Horizon* [Report for 1962–64] (1964), p. 27.
[3] Exceptions are the London Working Men's College, Morley College London, and Vaughan College Leicester. For the earlier history see above, pp. 239–42, 263–5, 277–9.

movement and at the same time provided a link with the historic past.

In the dark days of 1943 the Association published a pamphlet entitled *Citizen Centres for Adult Education*, with a foreword by Sir Richard Livingstone, President of Corpus Christi College, Cambridge, who two years earlier had pleaded the cause of adult education in a widely read little volume, *The Future in Education*. He now once more stressed the need for lifelong education, and continued:

Opportunities for systematic adult study are needed on a wide scale, and these must not be limited to lectures or classes given in any hall or schoolroom that happens to be available. They must have a 'local habitation', a focus in the Latin sense of the word, a hearth where the fire remains continually lit, and where education can be more than isolated individual study and becomes a life shared with others.

The pamphlet itself reinforced and developed the points Livingstone had made. Every building in which adult education was carried on could in a sense be regarded as an adult education centre, but the adult education centre proper was a centre allocated specifically for adult education, a centre moreover in which the students were encouraged to participate in the planning of their studies and the management of the institution.

At this time the Association comprised a very small and miscellaneous group of centres—long-term residential colleges of the type of Ruskin and Fircroft, old-style 'residential settlements' of the Toynbee Hall type,[1] and new style 'educational settlements' of the kind pioneered by Beechcroft. It had very little money, and was dependent for its administrative expenses mainly on grants from the Joseph Rowntree Trust. Though a Responsible body since 1924 it ran very few adult classes itself, preferring to make use of the services of the L.E.A.s, the universities, and the W.E.A. When its president Professor A. J. Allaway wrote its history in 1960 it was still a very small organisation: excluding the long-term colleges it had 25 member-centres, promoting just over 1,000 classes and courses, with just under 18,000 enrolments.[2] An outside observer might have judged the movement a failure, but in fact its ideas were winning increasingly wide acceptance. The L.E.A.s, the extra-mural departments, the W.E.A., the Ministry of Education, were all by now convinced of the value of adult education centres: all that was lacking was the money.

---

[1] For the meaning of 'residential' here seen above, p. 279 n. 2. In the post-war period these settlements have for the most part been more concerned with social work than with education.

[2] A. J. Allaway, *The Educational Centres Movement* (1961), p. 70.

The financial difficulties facing the local authorities and the Responsible Bodies have been sufficiently described in the previous chapter. At no time during the post-war years was there any possibility of expenditure by the authorities on new building solely for the purpose of adult education. Vaughan College, Leicester, rebuilt for the University by the local authority because the old college was demolished for road-widening, stands out as a notable exception. Even in London the City Literary Institute continued to be the only institution of its kind with purpose-built premises.[1]

In spite of all the difficulties, however, some progress was made. Many extra-mural departments managed to acquire teaching centres at least in their own university towns, and a smaller number, either from their own resources or in co-operation with the L.E.A.s, secured centres elsewhere. Nottingham was particularly fortunate in this respect. In addition to its headquarters in the city centre it was able to lease just after the war a beautiful early eighteenth-century mansion at Boston in Lincolnshire, which in addition to providing accommodation for non-residential courses also had limited residential facilities. The Holland L.E.A. gave generous financial assistance, and eventually took over complete responsibility for the maintenance of what was now known as Pilgrim College. In addition, from the late 'fifties onwards, the extra-mural department had the use of centres at Loughborough, Derby, Matlock, Lincoln and Stamford, the premises in all these cases being acquired, adapted, and placed at the disposal of the Responsible Bodies by the respective L.E.A.s.

The Ministry of Education's pamphlet on *Further Education* in 1947 drew attention to the value of centres such as Vaughan College, the London literary institutes, and the Cambridgeshire village colleges, and suggested that 'within the range of experiment and innovation which it is hoped will take place in the next few years, some place should be found in most areas for a college for adults which will provide a wide and varied choice of leisure-time interests and activities.'[2] In the Ministry's pamphlet on *Evening Institutes* (1956), the chapter on 'Organisation' begins: 'Gracious surroundings can help to produce an atmosphere in which learning is a delight.'[3] It goes on to speak of the need for 'roomy and comfortable buildings,

---

[1] By this date the City Literary Institute and the Marylebone Institute (which used school premises) were the only surviving literary institutes. The others, along with the Men's and Women's Institutes (see above pp. 289–94) were replaced in 1958–60 by 33 General Institutes (known from 1966 as Adult Education Institutes).

[2] Pp. 37–8.

[3] P. 42.

furnished in a manner which suggests an adult, cultivated mind,' and contrasts the facilities at that time commonly available for evening institutes, usually in day-school premises. Exhortation and encouragement, however, do not furnish buildings, and the next ten years saw little improvement.

None the less it had to be recorded that over the post-war years as a whole the L.E.A.s did make a valiant effort to change the image of the evening institute in order to make it a real centre for adult education. Imagination and make-do-and-mend can go a long way, and by 1964 the National Institute of Adult Education was able to record, in addition to the voluntary centres, and centres provided by or for the Responsible Bodies, about thirty L.E.A. adult education centres in various parts of England and Wales outside London.[1] Most of them were redundant schools or converted houses: one of the earliest, the Blackburn People's College (1946) was in a former Presbyterian day school.[2] Kent, where the county authority had set out after the war to provide about thirty centres, had by this time seven, in premises varying 'from a luxury hotel and a former boarding school to a residential villa and a seventeenth-century grammar school.'[3] In nearly all these L.E.A. centres there was a real effort to make the surroundings as bright and attractive as possible and to encourage social activities and student participation in·course planning. A very successful centre in a redundant primary school at Whitefield, just outside Manchester, was actually organised on a club basis, with an annual membership fee of 15s. in lieu of all class fees.[4] The club element (but without the composite fee) was also stressed in a number of other Lancashire County centres, for example at Atherton and Tyldesley, where an old technical school and a disused primary school were imaginatively adopted to form a joint adult education institution for the two towns.

Inevitably particular centres developed special interests, sometimes related to the history and character of the building used. The programme of the centre at Bury in Lancashire reflected the fact that it had formerly been a School of Arts and Crafts. At Leicester an adult education centre occupying a converted chapel (known from its

---

[1] 'Accommodation and Staffing—a Report', in *Adult Education*, Vol. XXXV, No. 5 (Jan. 1963), App. 1.
[2] This pioneering venture was closed on grounds of economy in 1968.
[3] R. Reedman, 'Education Centres and University Extension', in *Rewley House Papers*, Vol. III, No. III (1954–55), p. 56. See also on the beginning of the Kent centres F. Jessup, 'Post-war Developments of Adult Education in Kent', in *Adult Education*, Vol. XXIV (1951–2), pp. 91–7.
[4] A. N. Fairbairn, 'The Whitefield Centre', in *Adult Education*, Vol. XXXIII (1960–61), pp. 315–18.

circular shape as the Pork Pie Chapel) acquired an adjoining ware-house which made possible a range of specialist rooms for painting, pottery, sculpture, photography, and language study. At Putney and Eltham redundant schools became art centres for adjoining adult education centres, and in 1969 Morley College, already strong on the musical side, established an art centre in a superannuated public house. On the other hand the tradition of music-making built up at the adult education centre at Almondbury, Huddersfield, probably owed more to the principal and staff than to the availability of accommodation.

An alternative to the adaptation of older buildings was the provision of premises in conjunction with schools and other institutions. Cambridge continued to build its village colleges, which by the close of 1968 numbered twelve, and in spite of some criticism, obviously met a real need in the rural areas.[1] Other rural counties— Rutland, Leicester, Oxford, Cumberland, Lancashire, and Devon— experimented on similar lines, though only Rutland and Devon adopted the name 'village college'.[2] In many institutions of this kind there was a strong emphasis upon community activities, and the students, with the help of the principal or a tutor-organiser, were encouraged to take the management of the programme as much as possible into their own hands.

In other areas the Ministry permitted a limited amount of additional building to allow dual use of premises, and some authorities were able, for example, to add to new schools a room for an evening institute principal, storage space, a common room, and refreshment facilities for adult students.[3] But there were still far too few full-time principals, far too many dark, cold, cheerless and uncomfortable buildings. The problem of accommodation for adult education was still far from being solved.

The adult education centre at Richmond upon Thames, one of the larger centres in terms of student enrolments, illustrates the kind of difficulties under which L.E.A. work developed at this period. The headquarters of this centre are in a building which was designed as a mechanics' institute and served successively as a grammar school and a technical institute before becoming an institute of further education. In this last capacity it was at first mainly an engineering

---

[1] For the argument for and against see the series of articles and letters in *Adult Education*, Vols. XXXVIII–XL (1965–68), *passim*.

[2] Cf. J. A. Nettleton and D. J. Moore, *School and Community: Adult Centres in Cumberland Schools* (1967). Leicestershire has used the name 'community college'. For Oxfordshire see E. T. Dyke, 'Evening Centres in Rural Communities,' in *Adult Education*, Vol. XXXII (1959–60), pp. 18–22.

[3] H. J. Edwards, *The Evening Institute* (1961), pp. 140–1.

college, but it also gathered to itself a considerable body of adult classes, and from 1962 onwards the engineering and other technical course were gradually transferred elsewhere and the Institute became the centre for adult education for the district. Quickly outgrowing the available accommodation it took over an annexe which had been in turn a tram depot, a pickle factory, an ambulance station, and a fire station.

By 1967–8 the Institute had a total programme of 361 classes, with nearly 6,900 students and nearly 11,000 class-enrolments. There was the usual wide range of subjects and levels. Art, music, languages, and domestic subjects figured prominently. English for foreigners was a special feature, and G.C.E. subjects and shorthand and type-writing continued to form a significant part of the programme. There were courses at university level at one end of the scale and classes for non-readers at the other. In 1966–7 a Students' Association was started to promote student activities and administer a special develop-ment fund. All this lively and diverse development, however, was hampered by all kinds of physical problems. In the annual report for 1966–7 the Principal put the matter as follows:

We have a main building and three annexes in use by day, and use up to twenty outside centres in various parts of the borough ... Some dispersal of the work will always be essential if we are to serve the locality as we should, but much of it is undesirable. It is time consuming and hard to organize. What is more, we operate under considerable difficulty. We teach Drama and Mime without a threatre, Music without music room or concert hall, and physical education without a gymnasium. We have no lecture theatre, and the Institute has no main hall, unless two dressmaking rooms and the canteen are thrown into one. We hold exhibitions without a gallery. There is no library or common room.[1]

One result of all these developments on the L.E.A. side was a considerable influx of new members into the E.C.A. By 1967–8 it had more than forty non-residential member centres, sponsoring a total of over 5,000 classes of which five-sixths were provided by L.E.A.s.[2]

Far and away the largest of the E.C.A. members was the City Literary Institute in London, which after some falling off in enrol-ments in the mid-1950s achieved a remarkable expansion in the decade 1958–68. The number of students, which had been 7,300 in 1957–8, rose to nearly 11,000 in 1967–8, and the number of class

---

[1] For information about the Richmond Institute, and permission to use this quotation, I am indebted to the Principal, Mrs P. M. Leslie.
[2] E.C.A., *Annual Report, 1967–68.*

enrolments showed an even larger increase, from 11,500 to nearly 26,000. Classrooms were occupied almost continuously, morning, afternoon, and evening, and accommodation was so much in demand that some courses had to be transferred to other buildings. A fourth term during the summer, introduced partly to relieve the pressure, uncovered a new group of students unable to attend during the normal terms.

The range and variety of the courses offered by the Institute has been sufficiently indicated above.[1] A special effort was made during this period to develop progressive and advanced work, and to grade the students into reasonably homogeneous groups. The work was departmentalized, with full-time heads of departments for general studies, languages, drama and speech, art, music, musicianship, and education for the deaf; and from 1960 onwards a service of student counselling was introduced which proved invaluable in placing students, maintaining a high level of attendance, and strengthening the corporate life of the Institute. The appointment of a full-time adviser to students three years later was the first of its kind in the country in connection with non-vocational education.[2]

In concluding this section a word should be said about village halls and community centres, which had their beginnings, as we have seen, in the inter-war years and multiplied rapidly when the war was over. These institutions are on the borderline where education meets welfare and recreation, and when Carnegie building grants terminated in 1948 the Ministry of Education took over responsibility for assisting. Its assistance was somewhat intermittent, but voluntary enthusiasm often compensated for the lack of government support, and one way or another the building of halls and centres went ahead. How many of them were providing adult educational facilities it is impossible to say. Certainly a great many community centres called on the help of the L.E.A.s and Responsible Bodies for occasional classes, but only a small number provided any substantial programme. The emphasis tended to be strongly on informal activities, often tremendously interesting and valuable, but not really classifiable as adult education. As a National Institute of Adult Education report put it:

Although not sharply opposed, there are marked differences of emphasis between educational centres in a community setting provided in conjunc-

---

[1] See above, p. 290.
[2] For information concerning the recent history of the Institute I am indebted to the former Principal, Professor H. A. Jones, who has kindly made available to me a set of unpublished annual reports.

tion with Universities and 'Responsible Bodies', and community centres and village halls moving towards educational service from a starting-point of sociability and recreation.[1]

Residential Colleges

The early history of the various long-term residential colleges for adult education has already been described. Those existing in 1939 were, in order of date of foundation: Ruskin College, devoted especially to the education of the industrial worker; Woodbrooke and Fircroft, with their strong Quaker associations; the Co-operative College; Hillcroft, the first women's college; the Catholic Workers' College; Avoncroft, dedicated especially to the education of the rural worker; Coleg Harlech; and Newbattle Abbey. During the war most of these colleges either closed down or operated on a very much re-duced scale: in many cases the building was taken over for other purposes. All of them, however, took up their work once more when the war ended, and the Co-operative movement celebrated the centenary of the Rochdale Pioneers in 1944 by the purchase in the following year of Stamford Hall, Loughborough, which at last pro-vided adequate residential accommodation for the Co-operative College.

The post-war years brought no new long-term college; indeed one of the colleges listed, Avoncroft, had to close. It ceased to function as an agricultural college in 1952, finding that the work it had been doing was being catered for increasingly by farm institutes. It later became a short-term college, closely associated with Birmingham Corporation.

Most of the other colleges, in spite of initial difficulties about fin-ance, accommodation, staffing, and the recruitment of suitable students, became as time went on increasingly prosperous, thanks to more generous grants from the Ministry of Education (and its suc-cessor from 1964 the Department of Education and Science), and a greater willingness on the part of L.E.A.s to grant-aid students. The Robbins Report helped by recommending, in 1963, government grants in aid of building costs, and increased subsistence allowances to students.[1] As a direct consequence Ruskin, Fircroft, Hillcroft and Coleg Harlech were all able to embark upon long-needed extensions to their premises.[2] Only Woodbrooke, because its concern was

---

[1] N.I.A.E., *Social Aspects of Further Education: A Survey of Local Authority Action*(1962), p. 19.
[2] Committee on Higher Education, *Report* (1963), pp. 168–9.
[3] Department of Education and Science, *Education and Science in 1967*, pp. 71–2.

primarily religious, declined to apply for Ministry grant, and continued to have some difficulty in making ends meet.[1]

Ruskin, with assistance from the trade unions as well as public funds, was now particularly well placed: following the £240,000 development completed in ·1966 it was able to provide residential accommodation for 140 students, to whom it offered a choice of subjects in literature or social studies, besides the opportunity of attending lectures in the University of Oxford. Many students stayed for two years to take the University Special Diploma in Social Studies.

The Co-operative College, though not assisted by the Ministry of Education, had outside support from the co-operative societies through the Co-operative Union. By 1968-9 it had developed a variety of courses on such subjects as co-operative management and co-operative economics, and was catering for about 120 students. A small number of students each year took a more general course leading to the Diploma in Political, Economic and Social Studies of the University of Nottingham.[2]

In all the colleges during these years there was an increasing trend for students, on completion of their courses, to go on to further education, usually for teaching or one of the social services. This was particularly evident at Fircroft, Hillcroft, and the Catholic Workers' College, which had a strong social service orientation. At Hillcroft, out of 785 women who entered in the fifteen years immediately following the war, 355 afterwards took up teaching, social work, or some kind of management. Woodbrooke, of course, continued to prepare men and women for religious and social service.

Similar trends were observable at Coleg Harlech and Newbattle Abbey. Coleg Harlech introduced in 1968-9 a two-year course leading to the Diploma in General Studies of the University of Wales, and Newbattle Abbey was at this time considering a similar arrangement. Coleg Harlech, though in common with most of the long-term colleges it now included a proportion of students from abroad, still retained its predominantly Welsh character, and the destruction of its Great Hall by fire on 6th May, 1968, was felt as a national loss. Newbattle Abbey did not succeed in identifying itself— perhaps did not seek to identify itself—quite in the same way with the national tradition, but it was well supported both by the Scottish Education Department and by the L.E.A.s, and after a period of doubt and difficulty at length managed to establish itself on a firm footing.

---

[1] R. Davies, *Woodbrooke 1903–1953* (1953), pp. 87–8.

[2] The Department of Education and Science undertook to pay grant in respect of these students from 1969–70.

The great feature of the post-war period, however, was the development of short-term residential colleges. It has been mentioned above that the first college of this kind was the Lamb Guildhouse at Bowdon, near Manchester. It was the creation of R. D. Waller and derived from his experience of W.E.A. summer schools and undergraduate reading parties. Waller later tried to persuade Manchester University to acquire permanent premises for a residential college somewhere in the Cheshire countryside, but this project fell through, and it was ultimately decided, in 1948, to use for this purpose a large Victorian house named Holly Royde in a Manchester suburb. This had been given to the University in 1944 and had served for four years as a residential centre for work with H.M. Forces. With later additions (the most recent in 1968) it was able to provide accommodation for sixty students, and its proximity to the University proved an immense advantage when it came to securing lecturers.[1]

Here we see, then, three lines of descent of the short term college—summer schools, student reading parties, and Forces Education. The impact of the Forces work is clearly brought out by Professor Peers:

Army Formation Colleges proved a valuable means of rehabilitation and the opportunity of attendance at other residential courses was welcomed by the Services. The universities gladly collaborated in this work. Manchester University with Holly Royde and Nottingham with Lenton Hurst ran continuous courses for members of the Forces in the immediate post-war period and were amply repaid by the experience which they gained of the great possibilities of this form of adult education. They found that much more was gained in a residential course of a week or a fortnight than was possible in longer periods of part-time evening study; and the gain was not limited to the students, since those responsible for teaching found the closer and more continuous contact with their students a more satisfying and fruitful experience than the weekly visit to an outlying class.[2]

The latest study of this subject[3] distinguishes two other lines of descent—one from the Quaker guest-houses referred to above,[4]

---

[1] For the history see R. D. Waller, *Residential College* (Manchester 1954). There were, of course, other early institutions providing short-term courses, e.g. the Bonar Law College, founded by the Conservative party in 1929, and the institutions mentioned by Professor A. J. Allaway, *The Educational Centres Movement* (1961), p. 36, in connection with the rehabilitation of the unemployed in the 'thirties, but these do not seem to belong to the same tradition. Cf. above, p. 282.

[2] R. Peers, *Adult Education: a Comparative Study* (1958), p. 131. After the war Lenton Hurst was used as a residential centre for Nottingham extra-mural courses until 1955, when it became a university hall of residence.

[3] D. Garside, 'Short-Term Residential Colleges: their Origins and Value,' in *Studies in Adult Education*, Vol. I, No. 1 (1969).

[4] P. 265 n.

and the other, much more important, from the Danish Folk High schools. This latter influence came in two ways: first, through the influence of Woodbrooke, Fircroft, and Avoncroft;[1] and later, through the writings and speeches of Sir Richard Livingstone, and especially through his influential little book, *The Future in Education* (1941). Livingstone here made the point that certain subjects, such as literature, history and above all philosophy, 'need experience of life for full and fruitful study'.[2] Hence he argued the vital need for continuing education, and he specially commended the example of the Danish folk high school, where young men attended for continued education during the winter months, and young women during the summer. Economic conditions after the war, he argued, would provide an exceptionally good opportunity for such a development:

> There will be no need to build colleges. All over the country great houses will be vacant, calling for occupation, purchasable for a song. Why should not each Local Education Authority start its own House of Education? It need not follow the exact lines of the P.H.S., if that is found impracticable. It might be used for week-ends, or for weeks, of study, for educational or other conferences. Out of small beginnings great developments might grow.[3]

From all these influences there arose, in the expansive years immediately following the war, a general movement towards the establishment of residential colleges. By 1948 there were already more than a dozen, by 1950 more than a score. All over England stately country houses were being bought up and brought into use. Not infrequently they turned out to be suffering from dry rot, and the task of conversion was always expensive, but in the end these great houses with their gracious rooms and large gardens did offer something that could not have been matched in a purpose-built college—something that was in itself a contribution to adult education.

By 1968 there were about thirty colleges available for short-term residential adult education, besides others which functioned partly as adult education centres and partly as general conference centres. Oddly enough, there was not a single college in Wales or Scotland.

These colleges developed under varying auspices. In 1968 only three—Holly Royde, Albert Mansbridge College, Leeds (1963) and Rewley House, Oxford (1965)—were under university auspices, all

---

[1] See above, pp. 261–3, 281.
[2] R. Livingstone, *The Future in Education* (1941), p. 19.
[3] *Op. cit.*, p. 65. Livingstone uses the initials P.H.S. for 'People's High School'.

of them being associated with the respective extra-mural departments.[1] Of the rest, some were under private auspices—Pendley Manor, Hertfordshire, for example, was the property of its Director Dorian Williams; others were under the auspices of trusts—for example Westham House, Warwickshire; and others again were founded by organisations such as the Y.M.C.A. (the Y.M.C.A. College, Broadstairs, Kent) and the Women's Institutes (Denman College, Berkshire); but the great majority were created and financed by the local education authorities, acting either singly or in groups. The largest colleges, in terms of available student accommodation, were Attingham Park in Shropshire, Burton Manor in Wirral, Grantley Hall in Yorkshire, Holly Royde in Manchester, and Lambton Castle in County Durham.

The great problem facing these colleges was to find students able to attend during the week. The week-end was easy: in an increasingly affluent society many people were eager and willing to attend week-end courses. But in an urban, industrial society the release of workers at other times was much more difficult to arrange. Livingstone had seen this problem but had passed over it too lightly.[2] The early college wardens found themselves face to face with it and had to find a solution. One or two colleges, e.g. Missenden Abbey in Buckinghamshire, operated at first on a week-end basis only; others, e.g. Belstead House in Suffolk, filled in the week-days with courses and conferences for teachers and other employees of the education authority; others again, e.g. Attingham Park, encouraged short mid-week events, such as day-time visits by women's organisations.

In general, however, the colleges came to rely for these mid-week periods on courses of a vocational or semi-vocational character— on such subjects as industrial relations, foremanship, management problems, social administration—for which students could secure release from the employers. The larger colleges, such as Burton Manor and Grantley Hall, ran courses of one or two weeks for groups of this kind, while bringing in other students, for non-vocational studies, at the week-ends. Smaller colleges had to be content with some kind of compromise between the vocational courses needed to keep the institution going and the week-end non-vocational courses which they felt to be their main *raison d'etre*. The interesting thing is that this enforced combination of studies and students of different types proved in the end to be an advantage, helping to break down

---

[1] Madingley Hall, Cambridge, was made available to the extra-mural department from 1950 onwards, but for vacation use only.
[2] *The Future in Education*, pp. 60–2.

the false but long-standing dichotomy between 'liberal' and 'vocational' studies.[1]

On the whole it will be seen that this fourfold partnership of the central government, the local education authorities, the universities, and the voluntary organisations, lumbering and creaking as it has sometimes been, has produced a system of adult education that is varied, comprehensive, and infinitely responsive to individual needs. It might well be possible to produce a more rational and orderly system, but it has to be remembered that adult education is in the main a voluntary and spontaneous activity, which could wither and die if hedged round with too many restrictions. It is more important that it should be alive than that it should be tidy.

[1] On all these problems see G. Hunter, *Residential Colleges: Some New Developments in British Adult Education* (Ford Trust for Adult Education, Pasadena [1952]), and a later essay by the same author in S. G. Raybould (ed.), *Trends in English Adult Education* (1959), Ch. v.

INDEX